D0395992

CENSORED

"[*Censored*] should be affixed to the bulletin boards in every newsroom in America. And, perhaps read aloud to a few publishers and television executives."—Ralph Nader

"[*Censored*] offers devastating evidence of the dumbing-down of mainstream news in America....Required reading for broadcasters, journalists and well-informed citizens."—*Los Angeles Times*

"A distant early warning system for society's problems."
—*American Journalism Review*

"One of the most significant media research projects in the country."
—I.F. Stone

"A terrific resource, especially for its directory of alternative media and organizations....Recommended for media collections."—*Library Journal*

"Project Censored shines a spotlight on news that an informed public must have...a vital contribution to our democratic process."
—Rhoda H. Karpatkin, President, Consumer's Union

"Buy it, read it, act on it. Our future depends on the knowledge this collection of suppressed stories allows us."—*San Diego Review*

"This volume chronicles 25 news stories about events that could affect all of us, but which we most likely did not hear or read about in the popular news media."—*Bloomsbury Review*

"*Censored* serves as a reminder that there is certainly more to the news than is easily available or willingly disclosed. To those of us who work in the newsrooms, it's an inspiration, an indictment, and an admonition to look deeper, ask more questions, then search for the truth in the answers we get."—*Creative Loafings*

"This invaluable resource deserves to be more widely known."
—*Wilson Library Bulletin*

"Once again Project Censored has produced an invaluable guide to the sociopolitical landscape of the United States and the world.... A vital yearly addition to your library."—*Outposts*

CENSORED 1997

The News that Didn't Make the News—

The Year's Top 25 Censored News Stories

PETER PHILLIPS & PROJECT CENSORED

INTRODUCTION BY JIM HIGHTOWER
CARTOONS BY TOM TOMORROW

SEVEN STORIES PRESS
New York

Censored 1997: The News that Didn't Make the News—
The Year's Top 25 Censored News Stories
ISSN 1074-5998

10 9 8 7 6 5 4 3 2 1

Seven Stories Press
632 Broadway, 7th Floor, New York, NY 10012

In the U.K.:
Turnaround Publisher Services Ltd., Unit 3, Olympia Trading Estate, Coburg Road,
Wood Green, London N22 6TZ U.K.

In Canada:
Hushion House, 36 Northline Road, Toronto, Ontario M4B 3E2, Canada

Designed by LaBreacht Design

TO MARIO E. SAVIO

Teacher, Free Speech Activist, Community Organizer
Progressive and Heart Pure Friend
December 8, 1942 to November 6, 1996

"As individuals and as an organization, we choose an end to the disgrace of a massive 'underclass' in a land of such phenomenal wealth and promise: we want a population that is healthy, well-educated, and gainfully employed: we envision a country where race and gender no longer keep people apart. These goals will be achieved neither quickly nor effortlessly, but will require creative struggle, sophisticated organization, and personal commitment. If you share our goals, we welcome you to join us."

—Mario Savio, California at the Crossroads,
Campus Coalitions for Human Rights and Social Justice,
Sonoma State University, 1995

Table of Contents

Preface

CENSORED 1997: The News That Didn't Make the News is Project Censored's twenty-first annual effort to list the most important censored or under-published stories. Project Censored was started in 1976 by Dr. Carl Jensen. For two decades, Carl shepherded the development of a student media research project into an internationally recognized annual review of the systemic limiting of access to important news by the mainstream media.

Actual overt censorship in American media is limited, but corporate-owned media outlets tend to ignore or dismiss stories that run counter to corporate interests. We firmly believe in citizen access to and freedom of the press, and want this freedom to be fully maintained in the United States. To this end, Project Censored functions as a media industry ombudsman, alerting the public to important socio-political issues and occurrences that are not well covered by the mainstream press. We annually select and publish the most important under-covered news stories from hundreds of nominations. In today's corporate merger/takeover climate, our activities are essential to the continued vitality of the First Amendment.

This year, staff, faculty, and students reviewed over 400 stories sent from sources all over the world. These news stories were forwarded to us from hundreds of individuals and groups, who gleaned and nominated important articles mostly from limited circulation or alternative publications. We also worked closely with the Data Center in Oakland, California, whose 500 alternative news magazines were reviewed monthly for potential stories. Our sources supplied material across a broad political spectrum, and many special areas of concern including public policy, the environment, health, consumer rights, and science.

Nominated stories were reviewed and rated using a standardized format by one of our fifty-five faculty or community experts. Stories were ranked in importance, and reviewed for credibility and clarity. Top ranked stories were then submitted to student researchers in the Media Censorship seminar offered at Sonoma State University each year. In this joint Sociology-Communications Studies seminar, upper-division students, previously trained in library research methods, reviewed each story for levels of media coverage in the United States. In November, faculty and student researchers held a joint assessment evening to select the top twenty-five most important under-published stories for the year. Finally, these top twenty-five stories were submitted to our national judges for ranking and selection of the Top Twenty-five *Censored* News Stories of 1996.

Readers will find short synopses of each of the 1996 top twenty-five stories with comments from the original authors in Chapter One. In Appendix E we have reprinted the actual articles covering each of the top five *Censored* stories.

Why does a particular story not receive the coverage it deserves in the national news media? In some cases the mainstream press simply doesn't know about the issue. In other cases, mainstream news editors deliberately choose not to cover the story. While a variety of reasons may be at cause, foremost among them this year seems to have been conflict of interest issues involving the financial concerns of major media advertisers.

Many of us at Project Censored believe that, collectively, journalists are strong believers in freedom of the press and the First Amendment. However, individual journalists receive their assignments from decision makers closely linked to the upper management of major media outlets. A manager's primary concern is to protect the profit margin of the corporation, and offending a major advertiser can have serious financial consequences.

Additionally, ideological perceptions of decision makers in mainstream media set parameters of acceptability regarding controversial issues. Stories that run counter to dominant socio-political perceptions are often seen as too "far out" for the mainstream press. As much as journalists try, complete objectivity is rarely achievable; decisions about what to cover, whom to quote, and how to frame a story all reflect the biases and personal perspectives of the writer. Editors who delegate news assignments are no less personally affected by bias and personal perspectives.

Finally, a significant reason these top *Censored* stories were not covered has to do with the conglomeration of the mainstream press. This has resulted in fewer media outlets, increased pressure on news divisions to produce higher ratings and profits, and in some cases, vast debt burdens for the new and larger corporations. Mergers and buyouts abound, and in an era of corporate downsizing, media organizations and publishers simply are not putting the necessary resources into investigative reporting, which is expensive. Instead, media corporations, practicing 'press-release' journalism, have become dependent on established sources of information available through government and corporate channels. These channels sanitize and spin the news to reflect their special interests, and downsized news organizations do not expend resources to do the in-depth investigative news gathering necessary to counter these packaged versions of the news. Therefore, stories that run counter to major corporate or governmental messages tend to be ignored or discounted.

We at Project Censored believe the only way to insure a completely neutral story assignment process is to have systems of checks and balances within news organizations. Citizen review boards, independent investigative reporters, and ombudsman offices are all ways of protecting objectivity and fairness. Unfortunately, these processes are not broadly used in the privately owned media organizations in the United States. Fewer then 1 percent of the 1,800 daily newspapers in the U.S. employ an ombudsman, an independent columnist whose job it is to reflect the point of view of readers. Fully independent investigative reporters in the mainstream press are equally as rare.

Readers of *Censored 1997* will find some new chapters and expanded coverage of media censorship issues in others. Our Alternative Writer's Market and resource sections have been expanded, and we have added an on-line resource guide. Our new research and book review chapters feature reviews and analysis of recent top media-related books, and an update on current research in the field of media and communications studies. These chapters are designed to alert readers to the latest publications and research that address issues and concerns regarding our mainstream media.

We also have new chapters that feature current writings in the area of First Amendment issues and media monopoly. These chapters present selected guest writers contributing work of major importance to our First Amendment rights.

We are very pleased to be able to include in *Censored 1997* the American Library Association's 1996 "Less Access to Less Information By and About the U.S. Government." This important document is an annual chronology of the federal government's continued pattern of restricting government publications and dissemination and is included in this book for the first time.

Internet connected readers are encouraged to visit our World Wide Web site at http://censored.sonoma.edu/ProjectCensored/ for updated listings of important under-published news stories in the United States. We are hopeful that posting monthly under-published listings on our Web site will help stimulate public demand for expanded news coverage in the United States media.

Continued consolidation of the media may be inevitable given the current political climate and the expanding need for capital to find avenues of profitable returns. Additionally, the ideological value of corporate-controlled information systems is becoming more critical to the higher circles of power as the contradictions of wealth and inequality expand in our society. Top-down solutions do not seem politically possible in the immediate future. However, bottom-up solutions, stimulated by an informed citizenry, can have results at the local level that can reawaken First Amendment fervor in the U.S. Locally organized people can demand and come to expect unbiased quality news coverage. Citizen review boards, editorial pages of community-based publications, ombudsmen, and independent reporters could be a systemic part of any local news organization.

We must all work together to protect our media from serving its own interests instead of the public's. Mega-media corporations, despite being restrained by the structural tyranny of their profit requirements, remain the essential distributors of news and information in our society. We must do everything possible to help them live up to their First Amendment responsibilities.

Peter Phillips, Ph.D.
Sonoma State University
Rohnert Park, California

Acknowledgments

Sonoma State University in Rohnert Park, California, is the host institution for Project Censored. The Project is managed through the Department of Sociology in the School of Social Sciences. We are an applied sociological research project dedicated to freedom of information throughout the United States.

Over 125 people were directly involved in the production of this year's *Censored 1997: The News That Didn't Make the News.* University and program staff, students, faculty and community evaluators, research interns, funders, and our distinguished national judges, all contributed time, energy and money to make this year's book an important resource for the promotion of freedom of information in the United States.

A special thanks goes to Carl Jensen, founder of Project Censored, and director for 20 years. His vision and dedication has made Project Censored an internationally known research project. It was a difficult process for him to retire from the Project this year. He was most professional and supportive during the transition of directorship. He gave me the opportunity to make my own decisions and mistakes, and for that independence I thank him very much. Carl continues to be a close friend to the Project and is now serving as a national judge.

A huge thanks needs to go to the people at Seven Stories Press, who, every year, create a book out of a manuscript in a record two weeks (the time between manuscript delivery and submittal to the printer): publisher Dan Simon; editors Jon Gilbert, Moyra Davey, and Mikola De Roo; book designer

Cindy LaBreacht, and to the wonderful go-getters at Publishers Group West, who see to it that every independent bookstore, chain store, and wholesaler in the U.S. are aware of *Censored* every year. Thanks to our new distributors in Canada, Hushion House, for their support up north, and to Brian Donoghue, David Levine, and Greg Ruggiero at the Learning Alliance, who help organize the annual Censored Awards Ceremony in New York.

Thanks also to the authors of the most censored stories of 1996, for without their often unsupported efforts as investigative news reporters and writers the stories presented in *Censored 1997* would not be possible.

We are also extremely pleased to have Jim Hightower write our introduction. His personal experience having his national radio talk show canceled after a corporate takeover makes him an excellent person to introduce this work, and provide a reality check on censorship in the United States.

This year's book again features the cartoons of Tom Tomorrow. "This Modern World" appears in over 90 newspapers across the country. We are extremely pleased to use Tom Tomorrow's wit and humor throughout the book.

Our national judges, some involved with the Project for 21 years, are among the top people in the country concerned with First Amendment freedoms and major social issues. We are honored to have them as the final voice in ranking the top 25 *Censored* stories.

An important thanks goes to our major donors and Foundation funders including: Anita Roddick, The Body Shop International; C.S. Fund; Stern Family Fund; Office of the President, Sonoma State University; Office of the Vice-President for Academic Affairs, Sonoma State University; School of Social Sciences, Sonoma State University; Warsh-Mott Foundation; and the Playboy Foundation. Without their core support Project Censored simply could not continue. Our overhead costs, beyond Sonoma State University support, exceed $80,000 per year. This money can only come from sources dedicated to freedom of information that have significant financial resources.

Another special thanks goes to Mark Lowenthal, Associate Director of the Project. Mark has been with Project Censored for eight years and his dedication to freedom of information in the United States is evident in his everyday work. Mark handles media relations and most of the national radio and television talk show bookings for the Project. This is a difficult and time-consuming task that gives us exposure throughout the United States. His experience and expertise is greatly valued.

Amy S. Cohen, Administrative Associate, compiled and updated the Media Resource Guide and Alternative Writer's Market. She also fields hundreds of letters and phone calls for the Project and serves as our main in-house editor. Thank you Amy for a job well done.

Jeffrey Fillmore compiled and edited the Guide to On-line Resources and assisted with other sections of the yearbook. He also served as our technical support this year and is responsible for our World Wide Web site development and electronic outreach.

Brian Wilson, formerly of the Sonoma State University Computer and Information Science Department, volunteered his time and expertise, providing additional technical support for Project Censored's electronic outreach programs.

Recognition needs to be given also to Ivan Harsløf, graduate student from the University of Aalborg in Denmark. With support from The American-Scandinavian Foundation, Ivan was able to spend a full semester at Sonoma State University, working daily on the Project. His efforts on the resource guide and the chapter on current media research is greatly appreciated.

The Organization of News Ombudsmen deserves a thank you for its continuing support in assisting with identifying the most superfluous stories published during the past year in our Junk Food News chapter.

Thank you also to Nancy Kranich, who serves on the American Library Association (ALA) Board of Directors, and ALA Associate Director, Anne Heanue, for their assistance coordinating the inclusion of the document "Less Access To Less Information By and About The U.S. Government" in Appendix A.

This year we added 55 faculty/community evaluators to our story assessment process. These expert volunteers read and rated the nominated stories for national importance, accuracy, and credibility. In November, they participated with the students in selecting the final top 25 stories for 1996.

Most of all, we need to recognize the Sonoma State University students in the Media Censorship, Sociology 435, class who worked long hours in the library conducting coverage reports on over 125 under-published stories. Each has become an expert in library research and information retrieval. Student education is one of the most important aspects of the Project, and we could not do this work without their dedication and effort.

Lastly, I want to thank our readers, individual donors, and supporters from all over the United States and the world. Hundreds of you gave contributions from $5 to $500 that went to meet our research and overhead costs, and hundreds more nominated stories for consideration as the most censored news story of the year. Thank you very much!

PROJECT CENSORED STAFF AND RESEARCH INTERNS 1996

Peter Phillips, Ph.D.	Director
Mark Lowenthal	Associate Director
Amy S. Cohen	Administrative Associate
Jeffrey Fillmore	Computer Systems
Dana Alavarez	Intern/Financial Resources
Lori Goldstein	Intern/Library Research
Richard Mellott	Graduate Student Intern/
	Junk Food News Research
Martha Wright	Graduate Student Intern/Grants
Vicky Spann	Intern/Accounting
Brooke Hale	Intern/Research Assistant
Griselda Covarrubias	Office Assistant
Stacey Merrick	Office Assistant
Ivan Harsløf	Graduate Student Intern
	Univeristy of Aalborg/Research

PROJECT CENSORED 1996 NATIONAL JUDGES

* Indicates having been a Project Censored Judge since its founding in 1976

DR. DONNA ALLEN, president of the Women's Institute for Freedom of the Press, founding editor of *Media Report to Women*, Co-editor: *Women Transforming Communications: Global Perspectives* (1996)

BEN BAGDIKIAN,* professor emeritus and former dean, Graduate School of Journalism, UC-Berkeley; former editor at the *Washington Post*, author of *Media Monopoly*, and five other books and numerous articles

RICHARD BARNET, author of 15 books and numerous articles for *The New York Times Magazine, The Nation,* and the *Progressive*

SUSAN FALUDI, Pulitzer Prize winning journalist; author of *Backlash: The Undeclared War Against American Women*

DR. GEORGE GERBNER, dean emeritus, Annenberg School of Communications, University of Pennsylvania; founder of the Cultural Environment Movement; author, *Invisible Crises: What Conglomerate Media Control Means for America and the World,* and *Triumph and the Image: The Media's War in the Persian Gulf*

DR. CARL JENSEN, founder and former director of Project Censored; author, *Censored! The News That Didn't Make the News and Why, 1990 to 1996*, and *20 Years of Censored News* (Fall 1997)

SUT JHALLY, professor of communications, and executive director, The Media Education Foundation, University of Massachusetts

NICHOLAS JOHNSON,* professor, College of Law, University of Iowa; former FCC Commissioner (1966-1973); author of *How To Talk Back To Your Television Set*

RHODA H. KARPATKIN, president, Consumers Union, non-profit publisher of *Consumer Reports*

CHARLES L. KLOTZER, editor and publisher emeritus, *St. Louis Journalism Review*

JUDITH KRUG, director, Office for Intellectual Freedom, American Library Association; editor, *Newsletter on Intellectual Freedom, Freedom to Read Foundation News*, and the *Intellectual Freedom Action News*

FRANCES MOORE LAPPÉ, co-founder and co-director, Center for Living Democracy

WILLIAM LUTZ, professor, English, Rutgers University; former editor of *The Quarterly Review of Doublespeak*; author, *The New Doublespeak: Why No One Knows What Anyone's Saying Anymore* (1996)

JULIANNE MALVEAUX, PH.D., economist and columnist, King Features and Pacifica radio talk show host

JACK L. NELSON,* professor, Graduate School of Education, Rutgers University; author of 16 books, including *Critical Issues in Education* (1996), and over 150 articles

MICHAEL PARENTI, political analyst, lecturer, and author of several books including *Inventing Reality, The Politics of News Media, Make Believe Media, The Politics of Entertainment*, and numerous other works

HERBERT I. SCHILLER, professor emeritus of communication, University of California, San Diego; author of several books including *Culture, Inc.* and *Information Inequality* (1996)

BARBARA SEAMAN, author, *The Doctors' Case Against the Pill, Free and Female, Women and the Crisis in Sex Hormones,* and others; co-founder of the National Women's Health Network, and lecturer

HOLLY SKLAR, author, *Chaos or Community, Seeking Solutions Not Scapegoats for Bad Economics, Trilaterialism,* and many others

SHEILA RABB WEIDENFELD,* president, D.C. Productions, Ltd.; former press secretary for Betty Ford

1996 STUDENT RESEARCHERS IN SOCIOLOGY 435 MEDIA CENSORSHIP

Latrice Babers	Sociology
Tina Barni	Sociology
Robert Browne	Communications Studies
Aaron Butler	Sociology
Kevin Coyne	Communications Studies
Aldo Della-Maggiora	Sociology
Carly Dolieslager	Sociology
Diane Ferré	Communications Studies
Jeffrey Fillmore	Sociology
Brooke Hale	Communications Studies
Doug Hecker	Sociology
Richard Henderson	Communication Studies
Brant Herman	Sociology
James Hoback Jr.	Communications Studies
Jody Howard	Sociology
Amber Knight	Communications Studies
Jeremy Lewis	Communications Studies
Linda McCabe	Sociology
Stacey Merrick	Communications Studies
Anne Shea	Sociology
Kevin Stickler	Sociology
Anne Stalder-Karner	Sociology
Meiko Takechi	Sociology
Deborah Udall	Sociology
Eric Woodward	Communications Studies
Lisa Zwirner	Sociology

PROJECT CENSORED FACULTY, STAFF, AND COMMUNITY EVALUATORS OF 1996

Les Adler, Ph.D., Provost, Hutchins School — History

Ruben Armiñana, Ph.D., President, Sonoma State University — Political Science

Bryan Baker, Ph.D. — Geography

Paul V. Benko, Ph.D. — Biochemistry

Sterling Bennett, Ph.D. — Global Studies

Barbara Butler, MLIS, MBA — Information Research

Edward Castillo, Ph.D. — North American Indians

Ray Castro, Ph.D. — Social Policy

James L. Christmann, Ph.D. — Biology

T.K. Clarke, Ph.D. — Business

Lynn Cominsky, Ph.D. — Physics, Astronomy

Bill Crowley, Ph.D. — Geography

Diana Divecha, Ph.D. — Psychology

Dorothy (Dolly) Friedel, Ph.D. — Geography

Victor Garlin, Ph.D., J.D. — Economics

Robert Girling, Ph.D. — Business, Economics

Mary Gomes, Ph.D. — Psychology

Paula Hammett, MLIS — Information Resources in Social Sciences

The Project Censored crew (SSU faculty, students, and PC staff), November 6, 1996.

Laurel Holmstrom, M.A.	Women's Studies
Pat Jackson, Ph.D.	Criminal Justice Administration
Thomas Jacobson, J.D.	Environmental Studies and Planning
Brian Jersky, Ph.D.	Economics
John Kramer, Ph.D.	Political Science
Ellen Krebs	Library
Wingham Liddell, Ph.D.	Business, Economics
Linda Lipps, M.A.	Human Resources
Donna Luna, M.A.	Education, Testing
Rick Luttmann, Ph.D., CFP	Economics, Budgets
Perry Marker, Ph.D.	Education, Political Science
Doug Martin, Ph.D.	Physical Chemistry
Elizabeth Coonrod Martinez, Ph.D.	Foreign Languages
Jeffrey McIllwain, Ph.D.	Criminal Justice Administration
Robert McNamara, Ph.D.	Political Science
Andy Merrifield, Ph.D.	Public Administration
Debra Moody, Ph.D.	Business, Economics
Catherine Nelson, Ph.D.	Political Science
Jorge E. Porras, Ph.D.	Sociolinguistics
Arthur Ramirez, Ph.D.	Mexican American Studies
R. Thomas Rosin, Ph.D.	Anthropology
Joel Rudinow, Ph.D.	Philosophy
Gardner Rust, Ph.D.	Music
JoAnne Salstrom, M.A.	Testing, Counseling
Larry Hatime Shinagawa, Ph.D.	Sociology
Cindy Stearns, Ph.D.	Women's Studies
Elaine Sundberg, M.A.	Education
Bob Tellander, M.A.	Sociology
Laxmi G. Tewari, Ph.D.	Ethnomusicology
Carol Tremmel	U.S. Immigration Policy
David Van Nuys, Ph.D.	Psychology
Francisco H. Vazquez, Ph.D.	Liberal Studies
Albert Wahrhaftig, Ph.D.	Anthropology
Sandra Walton, MLIS	Archival Management
D. Anthony White, Ph.D.	History
R. Richard Williams, J.D.	Business, Law
Richard Zimmer, Ph.D.	History

SONOMA STATE UNIVERSITY
SUPPORTING STAFF AND OFFICES

Ruben Armiñana: President and Staff in the Office of the President
Don Farish: Vice-President for Academic Affairs and Staff
Jim Myers: Vice-President for Development and Staff
Larry Furukawa-Schlereth: Vice-President for Administration and Finance
Mark Resmer: Associate Vice-President for Information Technology and Staff
Robert Karlsrud: Dean of School of Social Sciences and Staff
William Babula: Dean of School of Arts and Humanities
Carol Cinquini: Manager of School of Social Sciences
Nancy Ramsey: Development Officer, School of Social Sciences and Staff
Susan Harris and the SSU Library Staff
Brian Wilson: Computer and Information Science Department
Paula Hammett: Social Sciences Library Resources
Steve Wilson and the Staff at the SSU Academic Foundation
Katie Pierce and Abby Barker in Sponsored Programs
Alan Murray and Staff at SSU Bookstore
Melinda Barnard and Faculty in Communications Studies
Susan Kashack and Staff in SSU Public Relations Office
Colleagues in the Sociology Department: Noel Byrne, Kathy Charmaz, Susan
    Garfin, Dan Haytin, Robert Tellander, David Walls, and Department Sec-
    retary Laurel Holmstrom

THIS MODERN WORLD
by TOM TOMORROW

LET ME READ YOU SOMETHING, BIFF: "A NEWSPAPER MUST AT ALL TIMES ANTAGONIZE THE SELFISH INTERESTS OF THAT VERY CLASS WHICH FURNISHES THE LARGER PART OF A NEWSPAPER'S INCOME..."

"THE PRESS IN THIS COUNTRY IS...SO THOROUGHLY DOMINATED BY THE WEALTHY FEW...THAT IT CANNOT BE DEPENDED UPON TO GIVE THE GREAT MASS OF THE PEOPLE THAT CORRECT INFORMATION CONCERNING POLITICAL, ECONOMICAL AND SOCIAL SUBJECTS--"

"--WHICH IT IS NECESSARY THAT THE MASS OF PEOPLE SHALL HAVE IN ORDER THAT THEY VOTE...IN THE BEST WAY TO PROTECT THEMSELVES FROM THE BRUTAL FORCE AND CHICANERY OF THE RULING AND EMPLOYING CLASSES."

WHO ARE YOU QUOTING, SPARKY? SOME LEFT-WING WACKO?

ACTUALLY, BIFF, THAT WAS WRITTEN AT THE TURN OF THE CENTURY BY E.W. SCRIPPS, FOUNDER OF THE FIRST MODERN NEWSPAPER CHAIN.

WELL, HE WOULDN'T GET VERY FAR IN JOURNALISM TODAY WITH AN ATTITUDE LIKE THAT.

NO, I SUPPOSE HE WOULDN'T...

web: http://www.well.com/user/tomorrow ... web: http://www.well.com ... Email: tomorrow@well.com

™ TOM TOMORROW©1-10-96

Introduction by Jim Hightower

In the spirit of full disclosure, I must tell you right here at the top that I come to you by way of a meandering journalistic path, having both covered the news and been a coveree. In 1979, having served as editor of *The Texas Observer*, I made the only downward career move one can make from journalism: I entered politics.

So I have seen the media from both sides, and from either view the picture is the same: a national media that not only is corporate in structure, but also in attitude and coverage.

There was a time, not so long ago, when reporters wore rumpled suits, pounded a beat, ate lunch at diners, drank at joints called "Shorty's," drew a modest paycheck, and identified with working stiffs. Today, though, most of our "news" is just another consumer product of conglomerates, delivered to us by an upscale caste of well-manicured media managers (star reporters, assignment editors, anchors, general managers, publishers, and pundits) who drink at private clubs called "The Uptown" and have zero identity with the shot-and-beer crowd at Shorty's.

As a result, the mass-market media machines put out a daily news feed that is neither *of, by,* nor *for* the masses, those 75-80 percent of Americans who do not have a college degree, who are paid less than $50,000 a year, who do not own stocks and bonds, who do not have a pension plan or mutual fund, who are not enjoying any of the "prosperity" that the politicians and the media keep talking about, who consistently tell pollsters that America is being run for the elites and not for ordinary folks like them, and who either are voting against the system or not voting at all.

The true media bias is not to the left, as Loudspeaker Newt Gingrich and his gang keep claiming, nor is it to the right. Rather it is to the top, a class bias that leaves out the real-world experiences of the great majority of citizens.

This media short-change is becoming worse as the conglomeration of our country's media outlets runs out of control, spurred-on by the authorization in 1996 of the new Telecommunications Act. This law is an absolute wet dream for Disney, GE, Murdoch, Westinghouse, and the other Corporate Media Lords who lobbied for it and are now gobbling-up stations, networks, cable systems, on-line services, newspapers, and magazines faster than a herd of hogs eats supper.

That is the bad news.

The good news is that there *is* good news available: reliable, informative, unconstrained media sources that actually tell citizens who is doing what to whom...and why. The 25 stories highlighted in this 1997 edition of Project Censored's yearbook are on subjects that "THE MEDIA" buried, belittled, or ignored altogether, but here the stories are, nonetheless, produced by a scrappy, sassy, scrambling assortment of magazines, Internet writers, community-radio broadcasters, alternative papers, video makers, newsletters, and others that simply will not shut up or let the truth be shut out.

Yes, it would have been better if Koppel had run these 25 on *Nightline* or if the editors of *The New York Times* had squeezed them into "All the News That's Fit to Print," but that will happen on the happy day when Project Censored and the alternative media are no longer necessary. Meanwhile, thank all the gods for the gumption of these alternative outlets, which are recreating a *public* media in our land, a media both responsive and responsible to the workaday majority, not merely to the economic elites.

Periodically in our country, the concentrations of economic, political and media power become so great that democracy itself is undermined, and in such times it is the "alternative" media, the outsiders, the rebels and mutts of communication, that move to the front, connecting people up, clarifying issues, providing perspective, focusing folks on action, speaking truth to power and *making the difference.*

The pamphleteers of the 1770s and '80s were the alternative media of their time. Likewise, in the 1870s and '80s, the populist movement of tenant farmers and urban laborers found its way around the Robber Barons and the baronial press of that age by communicating through an alternative media that included creation of their own local and regional newspapers, a crusading national magazine and a speaker's bureau of 41,000 "lecturers"—41,000 trained speakers who on any given night could spread out across the countryside and bring home the true news of the day.

So here we are another hundred and twenty years down the road, facing economic, political, and media concentration greater than ever, but as these 25 stories make clear, we are no less ready or capable than those who went before us to use the technology of our time, to employ the street savvy and grass-roots gumption it takes to hack new paths of communication around, over, under, and through today's conglomerate media blockages.

My momma, up in my hometown of Denison, Texas, taught me long ago that two wrongs don't make a right, but I soon figured out that three left turns do. It is the three-left-turn ingenuity of today's alternative media that we salute here...and that we count on to deliver our democracy to a higher level.

THIS MODERN WORLD

by TOM TOMORROW

THIS WEEK--A LOOK AT SOME OF AMERICA'S BIG-GEST *WELFARE BUMS*--SUCH AS *ED RENSI*, PRESIDENT AND CEO OF *McDONALDS*, WHICH RECEIVED $466,000 FROM THE U.S. GOVERNMENT IN 1992 TO PROMOTE *CHICKEN McNUGGETS* OVERSEAS...

THINK OF IT AS A CULTURAL EXPORT!

OR *JOHN F. SMITH, JR.*, PRESIDENT AND CEO OF *GENERAL MOTORS*, A COMPANY WHICH RE-CEIVED MORE THAN $110.6 MILLION IN FEDERAL TECHNOLOGY SUBSIDIES AS PART OF A PROGRAM TO CREATE JOBS FROM 1990-1994--DURING WHICH TIME THEY *SLASHED* 104,000 JOBS...

HEY--WHAT'S GOOD FOR *GENERAL MOTORS* IS GOOD FOR--

--WELL, FOR *MY STOCK OP-TIONS*, ACTUALLY...

AND THEN THERE'S *MICHAEL EISNER*, CEO OF THE *DISNEY CO.*, WHOSE RESEARCH INTO *BRIGHTER FIREWORKS* IS BEING SUBSIDIZED BY TAXPAYERS TO THE TUNE OF $300,000 THRU THE DEPARTMENT OF ENERGY "COOPERATIVE RESEARCH AND DEVELOPMENT" PROGRAM...

WHAT'S THE *MATTER?* YOU DON'T LIKE *FIRE-WORKS?* OR *MICKEY MOUSE?*

WHAT ARE YOU, SOME KINDA COMMUNIST?

FINALLY, WE CAN'T OVERLOOK WELL-KNOWN WELFARE RECIPIENT *SAM DONALDSON*, WHO COLLECTS $97,000 ANNUALLY FROM THE U.S. GOVERNMENT IN THE FORM OF SUBSIDIES FOR HIS *SHEEP RANCH* IN NEW MEXICO...

ER--WOULDN'T YOU REALLY RATHER HEAR ABOUT ALL THOSE WEL-FARE MOTH-ERS RECEIV-ING $67 A MONTH...?

HEH, HEH...

BAAA

A COMPLETE SET OF CORPORATE WELFARE POSTER BOYS IS AVAILABLE FROM WOMEN'S INT'L LEAGUE FOR PEACE & FREEDOM, 215-563-7110

CHAPTER 1

The Top 25 Censored News Stories of 1996

By Peter Phillips and Project Censored, with Mark Lowenthal,
Amy S. Cohen, and Jeffrey Fillmore

The mass media in the United States today are owned by about twenty economically powerful corporations. These corporations not only make decisions that affect us all, but also control how policies are portrayed in the mainstream press. The Top Twenty-five *Censored* News Stories of 1996 show how the decisions of the most powerful segments of society can have an impact on the rest of us.

While The Top 25 *Censored* News Stories of 1996 were selected as the most important under-reported stories during 1996, most represent issues that have been ongoing and of increasing concern after the end of the calendar year.

Many of the Top *Censored* News Stories of 1996 reflect the consequences of economic inequality, which is expanding—not only in the United States, but in other countries and between nations as well. In the United States, this trend has particularly significant implications for women, people of color, and immigrants, who have become the targets of scapegoating by the powerful.

Additionally, several of the Top *Censored* News Stories of 1996 disclose negative environmental repercussions of economic and political decisions made by both government and corporations that threaten the health and welfare of the earth and its inhabitants.

In this chapter we provide a detailed analysis of each of The Top 25 *Censored* News Stories of 1996. In each case we start with publication source and author of the original article (or articles). A brief synopsis by Sonoma State University *Censored* researchers of the nominated article follows. We conclude with comments about the article by the original author. Readers can also contact source publications and/or organizations by referring to The *Censored* Resource Guide, Appendix B, for information. A dagger (†) after an article title indicates it is reprinted in Appendix E, "Top 5 Censored Reprints." Following the top 25 stories are comments about this year's nominations by some of our *Censored* judges.

1 CENSORED

Risking the World: Nuclear Proliferation in Space

Sources:
COVERTACTION QUARTERLY
Date: Summer 1996
Title: "Risking the World:
    Nuclear Proliferation in Space"†
Author: Karl Grossman

PROGRESSIVE MEDIA PROJECT
Date: May 1996
Title: "Don't Send Plutonium into
    Space"
Author: Karl Grossman

There has been little press coverage through the years on the use of nuclear power in space and 1996 was no exception—despite the fact that in 1997, the U.S. intends to launch a space probe carrying the most plutonium ever used on a space device.

In October, NASA plans to launch the Cassini probe with 72.3 pounds of plutonium. The probe is to be sent up on a Lockheed Martin-built Titan IV rocket despite there having been a number of accidents involving Titan rockets, including a 1993 explosion soon after launch which destroyed a $1 billion spy satellite system and sent its fragments falling into the Pacific Ocean.

Further, the Cassini does not have the propulsion power to get directly to its final destination, Saturn, so NASA plans a "slingshot maneuver" in which the probe will circle Venus twice and then hurtle back at Earth. It will then buzz the Earth in August 1999 at 42,300 miles per hour just 312 miles above the surface. After whipping around the Earth and using its gravity, Cassini will have the velocity to reach Saturn.

The problem occurs if the probe enters the Earth's atmosphere during the "flyby." If Cassini comes in too close, it could burn up in the atmosphere and disperse deadly plutonium across the planet. According to NASA's *Final Environmental Impact Statement for the Cassini Mission,* if in the "flyby," an "inadvertent reentry occurred, approximately 5 billion of the estimated world population at the time...could receive 99 percent or more of the radiation exposure."

According to author Karl Grossman, the plutonium is not a necessity for the Cassini mission to succeed. The plutonium is to be used to generate 745 watts of electricity to run instruments—a task that could be accomplished with solar energy. Indeed, an official of the European Space Agency (ESA) has said that her agency could have high-efficiency solar cells it has newly developed ready in five years to power a mission to Saturn. But still, NASA, the Department of Energy's national nuclear laboratories, and the corporations which have been involved in producing nuclear hardware for space missions insist on sticking with the nuclear energy on the Cassini.

Grossman's reporting in earlier space missions in which nuclear power was used—Galileo with 49.25 pounds of plutonium and Ulysses with 25 pounds of plutonium in 1990—made the Project Censored list of under-reported stories in 1986, 1987, and 1989.

SSU Censored Researchers:
Brant Herman
Eric Woodward

COMMENTS: The lack of media attention given to the use of nuclear power in space "appears chronic," says writer Karl Grossman. "The cover-up continues in the 1990s while even bigger and yet more dangerous nuclear space shots are planned."

The issue, Grossman stresses, is one of the peoples' right to know—and then the decision on whether to put life on Earth at such an enormous risk could be made collectively. "If the information was out there, an informed decision could be made by those who might be impacted—which is all of us—as to whether to go ahead with this program," says Grossman.

"People should be aware," he says, "that the planned launch of the Cassini space probe uses a rocket with a history of exploding on launch. They should be aware that it will have onboard more plutonium than ever used on a space device. They should know that by NASA's own admission, an accident during the 'flyby' return towards Earth could expose billions of people to radiation. They should know that the history of nuclear power in space has been fraught with accidents—that some 15 percent of U.S. and Soviet missions have undergone mishaps—including the fall back to Earth of the SNAP-9A nuclear satellite system in 1994 that broke up in the atmosphere dispersing 2.1 pounds of plutonium widely over the planet, an accident that has been linked to an increased level of lung cancer on Earth. They should be aware that a solar photovoltaic energy system could substitute for a nuclear system on the Cassini mission—that, indeed, the SNAP-9A accident was a spur to NASA to pioneer solar photovoltaic energy for satellites. They should understand," says Grossman, "that the Cassini mission is one among many space projects involving nuclear space power now being planned. They should know that the use of nuclear power in space connects to a desire by the U.S. military to attain what one recent Air Force report describes as 'the ultimate high ground'—space—and using in the process nuclear power for propulsion and as a power source for weaponry."

Grossman believes that the limited media coverage benefits NASA and the Pentagon, as well as the string of U.S. Department of Energy national nuclear laboratories and companies like Lockheed Martin, which are involved in the design, development, and manufacture of nuclear space hardware.

A professor of journalism at State University of New York/College at Old Westbury, Grossman became a journalist as a result of an internship at *The Cleveland Press* as a college student in 1960. He remarks, "The story might be corny, but over the entrance of *The Cleveland Press* was the motto of the Scripps-Howard newspapers: 'Give light and the people will find their way.' The continuing cover-up of the use of nuclear power in space is a classic example of people not being given the light—so they won't be able to find their own way. Apparently, we are supposed to leave these life-and-death decisions in the hands of an elite band of 'experts.'

"You don't have to be a rocket scientist to know that what goes up sometimes comes down—and sometimes on peoples' heads. Moreover, the situation is not one of 'if,'" stresses Grossman. The fiery November 16, 1996 crash to Earth of the Russian Mars 96 space probe with almost a half-pound of plutonium on board was, he says, "another example of how these accidents happen. Interestingly enough, there was a brief period of media attention when it looked like the probe was to fall near Australia; President Clinton called Australian Prime Minister Howard offering U.S. 'assets' to try to deal with any radioactive contamination. But virtually all the media instantly left the story when it turned out that, in fact, the probe and its plutonium came down as a fireball *on* Chile and Bolivia. Here was a case in which, as the headline of an upcoming article I wrote for *Extra! Update*, a publication of the organization Fairness & Accuracy in Reporting, states: 'Racism Meets Spacism.'"

2 CENSORED

Shell's Oil, Africa's Blood

Sources:
SAN FRANCISCO BAY
    GUARDIAN
Date: February 7, 1996
Title: "Shell Game"†
Author: Vince Bielski

TEXAS OBSERVER
Date: January 12, 1996
Title: "Shell's Oil, Africa's Blood"†
Authors: Ron Nixon and
    Michael King

EDITOR & PUBLISHER
Date: March 23, 1996
Title: "Rejected Ad Flap"
Author: M.L. Stein

WORLD WATCH
Date: May/June 1996
Title: "Dying for Oil"
Author: Aaron Sachs

WORLD WATCH
Date: July/August 1996
Title: "Eco-Justice in Nigeria"
Author: Chris Bright

BANK CHECK
Date: February 1996
Title: "IFC Pulls Out of Shell Deal
    in Nigeria"
Author: Andrea Durbin

In the wake of Nigeria's execution of nine environmental activists, including Nobel Prize winner and leader of the Movement for the Survival of Ogoni People (MOSOP), Ken Saro-Wiwa, evidence has indicated that Shell has fomented civil unrest in Nigeria, contributed to unfair trials, and failed to use its leverage to prevent the unjustified executions. The executed activists were involved in massive protests against Royal Dutch/Shell Group because of the environmental devastation it has caused—particularly in Southern Nigeria's Ogoniland.

Since the executions, Shell has also managed to keep the United States media from informing the public of its actions.

Nigeria's government, under the dictatorship of General Sani Abacha, derives 90 percent of its foreign revenue from oil exports. The United States, home of Royal Dutch's subsidiary Shell Oil Company, located in Houston, Texas, imports almost 50 percent of Nigeria's annual oil production.

In October 1990, Nigerian villagers occupied part of a Shell facility demanding compensation for the farm lands which had been destroyed by Shell. A division manager at Shell

Petroleum Development Company called the Nigerian military for help. The military forces then fired on the villagers, killing some 80 people and destroying or badly damaging 495 homes. A Nigerian judicial inquiry later concluded that the protest had been peaceful. The MOSOP was formed after the massacre to continue protests against Shell. And while Shell has denied having anything to do with the recent executions, Dr. Owens Wiwa, Ken Saro-Wiwa's brother, reported that on three occasions Brian Anderson, the managing director of Shell Petroleum Development Co. in Nigeria, offered to make a deal with Wiwa: Shell would try to prevent the executions if the activists would call off their protests. Wiwa refused, and Shell did not intervene.

After international pleas for Shell's intervention, Shell claimed that it was not—and would not—become involved in Nigeria's political affairs. Internal documents uncovered by journalists and human rights groups contradict this claim.

According to a report by Andy Rowell in the *Village Voice* (November 21, 1995), there is evidence that Shell has been bankrolling Nigerian military action against protesters and that two key prosecution witnesses admitted in sworn affidavits that they were offered bribes by Shell to unjustly incriminate Saro-Wiwa in his trial.

In response to these allegations, Shell has mounted an international media campaign to combat negative publicity. Amnesty International USA said the *Houston Chronicle* refused to run an ad which questioned Shell's stance on human rights violations in Nigeria and that three billboard companies, including Gannett Outdoor Co. Inc., also declined to sell space to the human rights organization.

SSU Censored Researchers:
James Hoback
Anne Stalder

COMMENTS: Vince Bielski, author of the *San Francisco Bay Guardian* arti-

THIS VERBOSE WORLD　　by TOM TOMORROW

THE INFAMOUS TEXACO TAPES WERE APPARENTLY JUST THE TIP OF THE ICEBERG... FOR INSTANCE, A PREGNANT AFRICAN-AMERICAN SECRETARY THERE ONCE RECEIVED THIS CHARMING BIRTHDAY CAKE FROM HER BOSS...*

Happy Birthday Sheryl
It must have been those watermelon seeds

* THIS IS TRUE.

NONETHELESS, PROFESSIONAL APOLOGIST-FOR-BIGOTRY *DINESH D'SOUZA* RECENTLY TRIED TO PUT THE TAPES IN *PERSPECTIVE*--

"...WHAT THEY DO REFLECT IS THE KIND OF FRAGMENTS ABOUT RACIAL DISCUSSION THAT HAVE DISAPPEARED IN THIS COUNTRY IN *PUBLIC* DISCUSSION--

--SO WHAT YOU HAVE IS A DISGRUNTLED FORMER EMPLOYEE IN A SENSE EAVESDROPPING ON A PRIVATE CONVERSATION AND IN A SENSE MAKING THAT PUBLIC IN A *DIFFERENT* CONTEXT!"

--AND WHAT COULD POSSIBLY BE MORE *CLEAR?*

cle, says, "While the execution of the environmental activists in Nigeria was widely reported, most of the media ignored what was the thrust of my story—the links between Shell Oil, the Nigerian military, and human rights abuses. Under pressure, Shell recently admitted it had *paid* the military to protect its facilities—further implicating the oil giant in the human rights abuses.

"Few Americans understand how a multinational corporation could be responsible for the repressive acts of a dictatorship. A better informed public would help pressure Shell into acting more responsibly."

According to Michael King and Ron Nixon, co-authors of the *Texas Observer* article, "Although the Saro-Wiwa execution received extensive coverage, the larger Nigerian story has gone largely unnoticed—and in the months since the execution, there has been little subsequent coverage.

"The most obvious benefits of wider coverage of the Nigeria story would be greater public pressure for an end to Nigeria's military dictatorship, an end to U.S. government favoritism to the Nigerian regime, and an end to the stranglehold that the multinationals hold on the economies of underdeveloped nations, particularly in Africa.

"The Ogoni people have been heroically fighting the Nigerian regime and the Shell corporations virtually on their own; international support makes it more difficult for that struggle to be isolated and defeated.

"In this country, the conventional African story is one of starvation and misery; Americans would do well to know more about the organized opposition to tyranny in Africa and elsewhere. Moreover, it would begin to undermine the millions of dollars expended by Shell and other multinationals in self-serving and intentionally misleading 'public relations' efforts."

Michael King, associate editor of the *Texas Observer*, also mentions the boycott launched against Shell in the wake of Saro-Wiwa's execution,

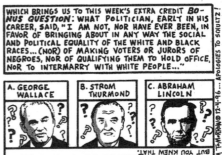

"although its overall effect is unclear (yet another consequence of minimal news coverage)," and notes, "The Nigerian regime has continued to cultivate friends in Congress and the White House." King hopes the wake of the recent Texaco racism scandal will encourage renewed interest in the Shell/Nigeria situation—and says, "The attention of Project Censored to this story could be an important catalyst to additional coverage."

Aaron Sachs, author of the *World Watch* article, "Dying for Oil," believes the mass media picked up the story of the struggle of the Ogoni people only for a few moments, right around the execution of Saro-Wiwa and the eight other activists. Yet coverage was limited and described the hangings "as an outrage and a blip in the Abacha regime's 'transition' to democracy," he says.

"The consumer ought to know—indeed, has a right and a responsibility to know—the consequences of his or her actions and decisions...you might want to know if some of the profits from the gas you regularly buy for your car are going into the pockets of an unelected dictator who is committing environmental genocide within his own country.

"Both the U.S. government and Shell—as well as a few other major oil companies—benefit from the lack of (media) attention. The car/oil lobby is the largest and richest interest group in Washington, and Clinton has refused to impose sanctions on Nigeria largely out of fear that he would alienate Shell and Friends and that gasoline prices might rise a few cents," says Sachs.

M.L. Stein, author of "Rejected Ad Flap," says, "To my knowledge, the story (of Amnesty International USA's inability to purchase media space) did not receive any exposure in the mass media. I believe it was a legitimate story that should have run for its news value alone. I believe that at least a segment of the public is interested in the fact that mainstream newspapers reject some ads and the reasons for it." Stein believes it is important that "the public was deprived of learning about a subject that is of interest to them."

Andrea Durbin, author of "IFC Pulls Out of Shell Deal in Nigeria," discusses another largely unknown aspect of the story: "The fact that Shell was just about to receive a loan from the World Bank to expand its operations was hardly mentioned in coverage." Durbin believes the public would benefit from media exposure "by knowing what their taxpayer dollars, contributed to the World Bank, are used for. Without the campaign to stop the loan, the World Bank would have doled out a $100 million loan to Shell."

Durbin adds, "We are raising the issues, the fact that the World Bank makes loans to corporations, many of them the most profitable companies. We want the public to know what their money is being used for and exactly what kind of 'development' is being promoted. The progress is slow, however, because the media is unwilling to cover the issues."

3 CENSORED

Big Perks for the Wealthy Hidden in Minimum Wage Bill

Source:
THE NEW REPUBLIC
Date: October 28, 1996
Title: "Bare Minimum: Goodies for the Rich Hidden in Wage Bill"†
Author: John Judis
(Reprinted in *Santa Rosa Press Democrat*, October 13, 1996)

On August 20, 1996, President Clinton signed into law the Small Business Job Protection Act of 1996, ostensibly geared to aid small business owners and their employees. The publicized intent of the bill was to raise the minimum wage from $4.25 to $5.15 an hour. However, according to John Judis, senior editor of *The New Republic*, the minimum wage bill included at least ten other significant provisions aimed at neither small business owners nor their employees. Indeed, Judis charges, these unpublicized provisions may negate whatever good the bill may do.

Among the lowlights:
• The bill reinstates tax incentives which encourage leveraged buyouts (LBOs): In a moment of temporary sanity, Congress put into the 1986 tax reform bill a measure preventing firms that engage in LBOs from claiming a tax deduction for the exorbitant fees they pay investment banks and advisors. However, this year's minimum wage bill once again makes these fees deductible and does so retroactively, creating a billion-dollar boon for companies that contested the 1986 ruling.

And in the case of employee LBOs, generally thought to be favorable, Congress slipped into the minimum wage bill a provision that would eliminate a special incentive that allowed banks to exclude half of the interest payments they received on loans for employee buyouts, discouraging employee LBOs of otherwise doomed companies.

• Incentives for multinational corporations: The new minimum wage bill has successfully protected American multinationals from paying taxes on unrepatriated foreign income, a long-standing tax loophole for overseas corporations. In Clinton's 1992 Presidential campaign, he vowed to do away with these tax incentives; however, in 1993 his Administration backed down, merely requiring overseas firms to reinvest their unrepatriated profits in foreign plants and equipment rather than banking them. Under the new minimum wage bill, however, this year's Congress rescinded even that.

• Weakened retirement and pension protection: The bill does away with a requirement that companies must offer the same benefits to lower-wage employees as they do to higher-wage employees, and effectively reverses the Employee Retirement Income Security Act of 1974 (ERISA), which states that if an insurance company takes too much in fees or invests in risky ventures they can be sued.

Additionally, the bill does away with a surtax on luxury car purchases and diesel fuel for yachts, ends a surtax on one-year pension withdrawals over $150,000 (a boon for the ultra-rich), and allows newspaper publishers to treat their distributors and carriers as independent contractors rather than employees in order to avoid paying their Social Security and unemployment compensation.

SSU Censored Researchers:
Brooke Hale
Mark Lowenthal

COMMENTS: John B. Judis, author of the *New Republic* article, says, "I wrote the article because the coverage of the subject had been extremely superficial. The only general publication to deal at all with the fine print was *Business Week*.

"If the public had a better idea what was in the bill Congress passed, they'd be even less enthusiastic about the institution. I've had members of Congress tell me they didn't know what was in it, and were shocked by my article," says Judis.

Judis believes the limited media coverage of the hidden perks of the minimum wage bill serves the interests of "all the various lobbyists, and the politicians that they cajole into doing their business."

4 CENSORED

Deforming Consent: The PR Industry's Secret War on Activists

Sources:
COVERTACTION QUARTERLY
Date: Winter 1995-1996
Title: "The Public Relations
   Industry's Secret War on
   Activists"†
Authors: John Stauber and
   Sheldon Rampton

EARTH ISLAND JOURNAL
Date: Winter 1995-1996
Title: "Public Relations,
   Private Interests"
Authors: John Stauber and
   Sheldon Rampton

Multi-million dollar clients of major public relations firms are behind the creation of false non-profit organizations, which target activists and lobby against legislation that threatens big business. Most of these organizations focus on environmental, consumer, and labor issues. The strategies of these powerful media manipulators include the defamation of activists, their ideas, and the deception of American citizens.

Through the PR industry and the enormous financial resources of their corporate clients, these organizations mobilize private detectives, lawyers, and undercover spies; influence editorial and news decisions; launch phony "grass-roots" campaigns; and use high-tech information systems to influence and manipulate public opinion and policy. With its array of sophisticated persuasive weaponry, the PR industry can out-maneuver, overpower, and outlast citizen reformers.

In one recent—and high-profile—example, the Health Insurance Association of America (HIAA) created the Coalition for Health Insurance Choices (CHIC) to defeat the Clinton Administration's attempt at health care reform. They utilized public opinion polling and lobbying strength to execute its campaign against mandatory health alliances.

"Greenwashing" is the term now commonly used to describe the ways that polluters employ deceptive PR to cultivate an environmentally responsible public image while covering up their abuse of the biosphere and public health. "Astroturf lobbying," a

term coined by Lloyd Bentsen, is another new concept which Bentsen describes as the "synthetic grass-roots movements that now can be manufactured for a fee." *Campaigns & Elections* magazine defines "Astroturf" as a "grass-roots program that involves the instant manufacturing of public support for a point of view in which either uninformed activists are recruited or means of deception are used to recruit them."

These anti-public-interest campaigns generate the false impression of public support in the name of "citizen activism" to promote the goals of corporate clients. Consequently, dissenting voices have been muffled, scientifically proven unhealthy chemicals and practices have been legalized, and public opinion has been profoundly, yet quietly influenced.

SSU Censored Researchers:
Diane Ferré
James Hoback

COMMENTS: According to John Stauber and Sheldon Rampton, co-authors of both articles, "There was virtually no mention or analysis of public relations' role in protecting the status quo and dividing and attacking social change activists," and "the anti-environmental campaign organized by business received almost no in-depth coverage by mainstream media." Wider media exposure of this subject would allow the public to understand "the extent to which 'news' is the creation of PR experts, and the extent to which corporations spy upon and attack citizen activists." The public would also understand "that 'green' claims by business often mask anti-environmental policies."

Stauber and Rampton believe the limited media coverage of this issue serves the interests of "the companies that pollute, which typically pump hundreds of millions of advertising dollars into mainstream media." Media's interests are served as well, "in covering up the extent to which it is complicit in passing on public relations as journalism, and its corporate interest in preserving the status quo." For more on this issue, see the book, *Toxic Sludge Is Good For You: Lies, Damn Lies and the Public Relations Industry* (Common Courage Press, 1995), also by John Stauber and Sheldon Rampton.

5 CENSORED

White-Collar Crime: Whitewash at the Justice Department

Source:
COVERTACTION QUARTERLY
Date: Summer 1996

Title: "White-Collar Crime: Whitewash at the Justice Department"†
Author: David Burnham

While white-collar crime costs America 10 to 50 times more money than street crime, the Justice Department continues to show little interest in taking the problem seriously.

And while the statistics persistently underscore this contradiction, business organizations such as the U.S. Chamber of Commerce and the National Association of Manufacturers continue to claim the federal government restricts business with unnecessary and heavy-handed regulations—and implore Congress to scale back environmental, health, and safety laws.

Based on the centralized records maintained by the Department of Justice (DOJ), the data shows that when it comes to white-collar crime, the federal government almost never brings criminal charges against businesses. Of the more than 51,000 federal criminal indictments in 1994, only 250—less than one-half of one percent—involved criminal violations of the nation's environmental, occupational health and safety, and consumer product-safety laws. Given the huge number of corporations, the private admissions by business lawyers that their organizations often break the law, and a well-documented record of repeated violations, the minuscule number of federal criminal allegations hardly squares with the corporate view of business as the victim of a federal government run amok.

The small number of individuals charged with criminal violations is only one indication of the pro-business bias revealed in the DOJ's own data. Even though Congress passed the Occupational Safety and Health Act (OSHA) in 1970, the actual impact of the law was greatly reduced by the insertion of hard-to-enforce regulations and insufficient funds to provide an effective force of well-trained and well-managed investigators. And in spite of the law, the DOJ has almost always protected businesses from criminal charges—even those with corporate executives who have knowingly exposed workers to conditions that resulted in death. In 1987 alone, 50-70,000 workers died prematurely from on-the-job exposure to toxins—roughly three times the 21,500 people murdered in the same year. In the years between 1970 (when OSHA was created) and 1992, 200,000 Americans died at work, a significant number from known negligence by the employer. Nonetheless, in those 22 years, OSHA has referred only 88 criminal cases to the DOJ, which prosecuted 25 and sent one executive to jail. He served 45 days.

According to Barry Hartman, who was first deputy and then acting assistant attorney general for the DOJ's environmental and natural resources division, "Environmental crimes are not like organized crimes or drugs... There you have bad people doing bad things. With environmental crimes you have decent people doing bad things. You have to look at it this way."

SSU Censored Researchers:
Brooke Hale
Deborah Udall

COMMENTS: According to author David Burnham, "The subject of my article—what the Justice Department *does not do*—is almost never covered by news organizations. This is partly because reporters are spoon fed so much canned information by the department's sophisticated public relations operation about usually meaningless drug busts, etc., that they almost never even think about investigating when the department *fails to act*. This is a serious long term failing of Washington news coverage.

"Because the Justice Department exercises vast discretion in what laws it chooses to enforce, concrete information about its enforcement priorities can sometimes actually result in their change. A politically ambitious U.S. Attorney in Vermont or California, for example, almost certainly would respond to a well-documented article proving she had ignored the environment by refusing to prosecute such cases when sent to her by the EPA.

"The business community has long benefited by the failure of the media to examine the Justice Department's priorities. Because of this failure, the business community has been able to convince the public that it is the poor victim of 'over-regulation.' In addition, a long line of attorneys general have been able to make outlandish claims about their efforts to fight white-collar crime. Both reactions have provided fuel for Congress' anti-enforcement projects."

Burnham says his article was taken from his 1996 book, *Above The Law: Secret Deals, Political Fixes and Other Misadventures of the U.S. Justice Department*, which was formed from data analysis done by an organization he formed called TRAC—the Transactional Records Access Clearinghouse. "TRAC is specifically dedicated to providing news organizations, public interest groups, and others with comprehensive data about federal agencies." In connection with this effort, says Burnham, TRAC also has a series of sites on the World Wide Web, which have been used by hundreds of news organizations looking for information about aspects of the Justice Department that were previously not covered. TRAC can be reached at 202/544-8722.

6 CENSORED

New Mega-merged Banking Behemoths = Big Risk

Source:
MULTINATIONAL MONITOR
Date: June 1996
Title: "The Making of the Banking Behemoths"
Author: Jake Lewis

Nineteen ninety-five was a record year of bank mergers. Chase Manhattan and Chemical bank combined to create the nation's largest bank, with $300 billion in assets—while on the West coast, the merger of First Interstate and Wells Fargo created a new giant with over $100 billion in assets. The massive consolidation of the nation's banking resources has resulted in 71.5 percent of U.S. banking assets being controlled by the 100 largest banking organizations, representing *less than 1 percent* of the total banks in the nation.

Under the Bank Merger and Bank Holdings Company Act, the Federal Reserve is required, before approving any application of a merger, to test how well the convenience and needs of the public are being met by the merger. Critics charge that the Federal Reserve Board is doing a disservice to the American public by not applying this "public convenience and needs" test to the wave of banking mergers—as required by the Bank Merger and Bank Holding Company Acts. In light of this, analysts are concerned that the growing giants of the banking industry will "shift insurance risks to taxpayers, cost jobs, lead to increased rates for bank customer service, make it harder to get loans, and lessen community access to bank branches."

The trend toward bigger banks is creating a system whereby giant banking institutions are taking on "too big to fail" status. Indeed, a failure of any one of these new giants would have a devastating effect on the nation's financial health. And with the Federal Reserve capping the amount that financial institutions have to pay into the government's bank insurance fund at $25 billion, just 1.25 percent of deposits are now insured. Consequently, any bailout of one of these new megabanks would come directly from the pockets of taxpayers.

Studies have also found that banks in concentrated markets tend to charge higher rates for certain types of loans, and tend to offer lower interest rates on certain types of deposits than do banks in less concentrated markets. A 1995 study by the U.S. Public Interest Research Group and the Center for Study of Responsive Law showed that fees on checking and savings accounts increased at twice the rate of inflation from 1993 to 1995 as bank mergers moved forward.

Finally, the trend toward megabanks is closing out community access and making it harder to get loans. In 1995, the Justice Department ordered Wells Fargo to divest itself of 61 branches it acquired through its merger with First Interstate to preserve competition for certain types of lending. But the 61 branches that Wells Fargo divested itself of are being sold to Home Savings and Loan of Los Angeles, which recently decided not to continue its affordable housing lending. In a community where affordable housing is vital to its stability, the decision of Home Savings and Loan is very disturbing.

SSU Censored Researchers:
Latrice Babers
Jeffrey Fillmore

COMMENTS: According to Jake Lewis, who wrote the article for the *Multinational Monitor*, "Most (media) coverage was at the time of the merger announcements. (There was) virtually no tracking of the mergers and their effect on communities after the initial announcement stories.

"Clearly, the massive consolidation of financial resources will have an impact on availability of credit and banking services and fees. The public sees only the flashy PR claims of merger partners—they need more information on what this means in the neighborhoods," says Lewis.

"Banks want their claims of benefits to be the guiding news concerning mergers—they don't want the public to be stirred by in-depth analysis of how the changes affect consumers, jobs, local economies, and banking prices.

"Bank consolidation and economic concentration is continuing—ultimately changing the economic and political landscape of the nation. It ought to be covered now—not as a historical tome to be put together after the fact—and after it is too late to erect safeguards and limit the ill-effects of economic concentration," argues Lewis.

7 CENSORED

Cashing in on Poverty

Sources:
THE NATION*
Date: May 20, 1996
Title: "Cashing in on Poverty"
Author: Michael Hudson

THE HOUSTON CHRONICLE*
Date: July 15, 1996
Title: "Bordering on Scandal
    What Some Pay for Credit"
Author: Michael Hudson

*Excerpted from the book, *Merchants of Misery: How Corporate America Profits from Poverty*, Edited by Michael Hudson (Common Courage Press, 1996).

Corporate America is in the poverty business and making huge profits from the destitute in the United States. Sixty million poor people without bank accounts or access to competitive-rate loans must instead use pawn shops, check-cashing outlets, rent-to-own stores, finance companies, and high-interest mortgage lenders. These businesses generate yearly revenues of $200 to $300 billion and are increasingly owned or subsidized by Wall Street giants such as American Express, Bank America, Citibank, Ford, NationsBank, and Western Union.

While affluent credit card holders can pay as little as six to eight percent annual interest, low-income people are paying as much as 240 percent for a loan from a pawnbroker, 300 percent for a finance company loan, and even an amazing 2,000 percent for a fast "payday" loan from a check-cashing outlet. Large corporations use sophisticated marketing strategies to lure in new customers and increase their business. The overall number of check-cashing outlets in this country has nearly tripled to 5,500 since the late 1980s, and rent-to-own stores have skyrocketed from 2,000 to 7,500 in the same period. With a typical loan rate of 200 percent, Cash America's chain of pawn shops has quickly grown to 325 in the United States and expanded abroad with thirty-four outlets in the United Kingdom and ten in Sweden. The main investor in America's $4.5 billion rent-to-own market is Thorn EMI PLC, a British conglomerate. American Express finances ACE Cash Express, a national chain of 630 check-cashing outlets. Charges average three to six percent of each check's value. Cash America, the country's largest chain of pawnshops, is bankrolled by NationsBank and traded on the New York Stock Exchange.

Even though many of us think of Ford Motor Company in terms of its automobile sales, their Fortune 500 status has actually been achieved through financial services holdings. In 1993, three-fifths of Ford's earnings came from car loans, mortgages, and consumer loans. Associates Corporation of North America is a Ford subsidiary targeting low-income, blue-collar, and minority consumers. In 1994, it financed $18.5 billion in mortgages and consumer loans and earned just under $1 billion in pre-tax profits. Stock analysts estimate that used-car loans for people with shaky credit now top $60 billion a year. Non-bank finance companies like Ford and defense contractor Textron make small loans at rates as high as 300 percent in some states.

Along with astronomically high charges, many low-income con-sumers are also victimized by additional hidden fees, forged loan documents, and harassing collection tactics. And unless there is increased government protection for the destitute or a growth in alternative non-profit financial institutions, big business will continue to expand these practices.

SSU Censored Researchers:
Jody Howard
Anne Shea

COMMENTS: Michael Hudson co-authored and edited the book, *Merchants of Misery: How Corporate America Profits from Poverty* (Common Courage Press, 1996), from which both of these articles were excerpted. According to Hudson, this issue has received very little media attention. "I know of no significant network TV stories on the 'poverty industry' in 1996. (The most recent network TV story was a 1993 *60 Minutes* piece on a single company, Fleet Financial Group, that was accused of fleecing minority borrowers. Since then, a number of companies have moved, without much fanfare, to fill the void left by Fleet's departure from the high-rate mortgage market.) Several magazines and newspapers have done stories on the extraordinary growth of the 'downscale' lending market, but almost none of them have looked in depth at the price gouging and predatory practices that are widespread in this 'poverty industry'...but these articles typically fail to report the vast number of lawsuits and law enforcement investigations that have raised questions of fraud, usury, and other illegal practices in the industry. These allegations have involved some of the biggest players in the downscale market, such as subsidiaries of Ford Motor Co. and NationsBank."

Hudson believes media exposure of this subject "would inform the American public about a nationwide scandal that directly affects as many as 60 million consumers. Widespread attention would help warn potential victims of credit gouging, fraudulent practices, and collection harassment—giving them the information they need to avoid predatory credit deals in the first place, or at least informing them of their rights to fight back after they realize they've been mistreated. Further, if the full extent of the problem were known, it's likely the public and policy makers would take steps to improve consumer protection and fair-lending laws and create alternatives to high-rate predatory financial services. Exposure might also help fuel broader political reforms by exposing the influence that the finance industry wields with lawmakers sympathetic to its profit margins and unsympathetic to consumers. Greater exposure of this story would also encourage more questions in general about corporate conduct and corporate responsibility in America.

"Given the wide array of abuses against low-income and minority consumers, it's impossible for this story to be completely ignored," says Hudson. He says a growing number of local newspapers—such as the *Boston Globe, Atlanta Journal-Constitution*, and *Richmond Times-Dispatch*—have dug into the subject in recent years. An op-ed piece that accompanied release of the book, *Merchants of Misery*, was picked up by 15 newspapers, including the *Houston Chronicle*, but mainly smaller papers.

"In the end," says Hudson, "the story will just keep getting bigger and bigger. More and more Wall Street companies are getting into the market as word spreads about the potential for profits. As *Time* noted, the industry's wild growth 'has sparked some 25 initial public stock offerings, many in the last year. [The value of] shares in a number of the newly public mortgage and auto-finance companies [is] up astronomically: Southern Pacific Funding is up 82 percent, Cityscape Financial has risen 288 percent, and RAC Financial Group Inc. has appreciated 300 percent...Another shot in the arm has come from Wall Street underwriters including Lehman Bros., Alex Brown & Sons, and Merrill Lynch, which bundle sub-prime loans, selling them off to investors as asset-backed (mobile homes, for example) securities.' In fact, the nation's highest paid chief executive is Larry Coss, CEO of

Green Tree Financial of St. Paul, Minnesota, a company that makes higher-interest mobile-home loans to people with weak credit histories. He earned $65.6 million in salary and bonuses in 1995, and was projected to earn $100 million in 1996," says Hudson.

8 CENSORED

Big Brother Goes High-Tech

Sources:
COVERTACTION QUARTERLY
Date: Spring 1996
Title: "Big Brother Goes High-Tech"
Author: David Banisar

INSIGHT
Date: August 19, 1996
Title: "Access, Privacy and Power"
Authors: Michael Rust and
    Susan Crabtree

INSIGHT
Date: September 9, 1996
Title: "New Surveillance Camera
    Cheers Police, Worries ACLU"
Author: Joyce Price
*Reprint from *Washington Times*

George Orwell's prediction concerning government surveillance in his science fiction novel *1984* is rapidly becoming reality in the "free world." Information on individuals in the developed world can now be obtained by governments and corporations using new surveillance, identification, and networking technologies. These new technologies are rapidly facilitating the mass and routine surveillance of large segments of the population—without the need for warrants and formal investigations.

In Britain, nearly all public areas are monitored by over 150,000 closed-circuit television cameras (CCTV). Equipped with a powerful zoom lens, each camera can read the wording on a cigarette packet at 100 yards. These cameras can track individuals wherever they go—even into buildings. In the U.S., Baltimore announced plans to put 200 cameras in the city center. The FBI has also developed miniaturized CCTV units it can put in a "lamp, clock, radio, duffel bag, purse, picture frame, utility pole, coin telephone, and other [objects]" and then control remotely to "pan, tilt, zoom, and focus."

Another type of surveillance camera currently in development boasts the equivalent of X-ray vision, and can penetrate clothing to "see" concealed weapons, plastic explosives, or drugs. Known as the passive millimeter wave imager, it can also see through walls and detect activity. And while neither is expected to be available until later in 1997, the manufacturer has been flooded with calls from law enforcement agencies around the globe. The camera has also prompted suggestions that it is in violation of the Fourth Amendment, which guarantees the right to be secure against unreasonable search and seizure.

Additionally, new biometric technologies which use sophisticated computer-scanning to measure personal characteristics—including fingerprints, retinal patterns, and the geometry of the hand—are already being tested by U.S. immigration authorities at JFK, Newark, and Vancouver airports in place of passports.

Other emerging fields of surveillance include Intelligent Transportation Systems (ITS) which track the movements of all people using public or private transportation. Such systems are linked to ordinary bank accounts and can generate records that show a driver's name and address, and the exact time and place where tolls have been charged. Nine states in the U.S. already use similar systems to track over 250,000 vehicles every day, and 12 more states will soon put their own systems on-line.

While technologically dazzling, such advances threaten to render privacy vulnerable on a scale never seen before—without providing accountability to protect us from those who may misuse it.

SSU Censored Researchers:
Richard Henderson
Stacey Merrick

COMMENTS: Michael Rust, co-author of *Insight*'s article, "Access, Privacy, and Power," says, "Cyberporn received far more attention than questions of who has access to someone else's private information. *Time* and *The Economist* ran articles on [the privacy issue]; the *Washington Post* coverage dealt mainly with pending legislation. From what I could tell, *The New York Times* and network coverage was spotty.

"Because of income disparity, many people lack computer access; the cyber-revolution has left them bystanders," says Rust. "As a result, many news consumers are somewhat glassy-eyed at computer coverage—even when it directly affects them."

Rust believes limited media coverage of the privacy issue serves "Elements within the federal government who would like to hold a 'master key' to the personal files of citizens."

Continued coverage of issues such as cyberporn, Rust says, "will lead to a more wide-ranging examination of privacy issues, but it's a confusing subject, and press, lawmakers, and the public all share in the confusion."

9 CENSORED

U.S. Troops Exposed to Depleted Uranium During Gulf War

Sources:
MILITARY TOXICS PROJECT'S
DEPLETED URANIUM CITI-
ZENS' NETWORK
Date: January 16, 1996
(release of report)
Title: "Radioactive Battlefields of
the 1990s: The United States
Army's Use of Depleted Uranium
and its Consequences for Human
Health and the Environment"
Authors: Pat Broudy, Grace
Bukowski, Leonard Dietz,
Dan Fahey, John Paul Hasko,
Cathy Hinds, Damaica Lopez,
Dolly Lymburner, Arjun Makhi-
jani, Richard Ochs, Laura Olah,
Coy Overstreet, Charles Sheehan
Miles, Judy Scotnicki, and Nikki
F. Bas
Edited by Rebecca Solnit

MULTINATIONAL MONITOR
Date: January/February 1996
Title: "Radioactive Ammo Lays
Them to Waste"
Author: Gary Cohen

SWORDS TO PLOWSHARES
Date: November 7, 1995
(presentation)
Title: "Depleted Uranium: Objec-
tive Research and Analysis
Required"
Author: Dan Fahey

THE VVA VETERAN
Date: March 1996
Title: "Depleted Uranium: One
Man's Weapon, Another Man's
Poison"
Author: Bill Triplett

NATIONAL CATHOLIC
REPORTER
Date: January 19, 1996
Title: "Depleted Uranium, First
Used In Iraq, Deployed in
Bosnia"
Author: Kathryn Casa

Depleted uranium (DU) weapons
were used for the first time in a war
situation in the Persian Gulf in 1991
and were hailed as a new and incred-
ibly effective weapon by the Department of Defense. Since the
Manhattan Project of World War II,
numerous government studies have
indicated that while DU weapons are
highly effective, they are still
extremely toxic and need to be han-
dled with special precautionary tools
and protective gear.

Although army training manuals
were written in the 1980s to warn
tank crews and commanders of the
dangers associated with DU rounds,

the Pentagon failed to warn Gulf War troops of the dangers. The Defense Department did circulate a memo to Gulf War commanders that contained three key points: any vehicle or system struck by a DU penetrator can be assumed to be contaminated; personnel should avoid entering contaminated areas; and, if troops must enter contaminated areas, they should wear protective clothing. Unfortunately, this memo was written on March 7, 1991, eight days after the firing of weapons ceased in the Persian Gulf.

Without this knowledge, and without the necessary protective clothing, the 144th Army National Guard Service and Supply Company was allowed to perform DU battlefield cleanup for three weeks in Kuwait and southern Iraq, where the U.S. Army fired at least 14,000 rounds (or 40 tons) of DU ammunition.

The Department of Energy possesses over 500,000 tons of DU that has been accumulating since the Manhattan Project. Billions of dollars have been spent by the U.S. government to find a final dumpsite for the radioactive waste, but other nations, as well as communities in Maine and New Mexico have resisted the efforts to dump the DU waste in their areas. The use of this weaponry in the Persian Gulf, then, served two purposes. It eliminated enemy troops and weapons and disposed of tens or even hundreds of tons of the radioactive DU on the Persian Gulf battlefields.

The effects of depleted uranium exposure, however, are just beginning to be known. DU has now been linked to many illnesses, including the mysterious "Gulf War Syndrome." Despite widespread concern among Gulf War vets and in U.S. communities about the dangers of DU weapons, the Pentagon, the Department of Energy, and military defense contractors are all excited about the sales potential of DU weapons as well as the transfer of DU to allies for their own weapons production. According to Nuclear Regulatory Commission shipment records, steady transfers— amounting to several million pounds of DU—have been flowing to U.S. allies over the past decade, with Britain, France, and Canada being the largest recipients.

SSU Censored Researchers:
Aaron Butler
Deborah Udall

COMMENTS: Dan Fahey is an activist who works with Swords to Plowshares, a veterans' rights organization. He contributed to the report, *Radioactive Battlefields of the 1990s: The United States Army's Use of Depleted Uranium and its Consequences for Human Health and the Environment*, which was released by the Maine-based Military Toxics Project's Depleted Uranium Citizens' Network in January 1996 as a response to the Army's unreleased report on depleted uranium weaponry. According to Fahey, "The issue of depleted uranium (DU) munitions received virtually no coverage during the past year on network TV, in newsweeklies, and in major daily newspapers. In fact, the focus on exposure to chemical warfare agents during the Gulf War has virtually eliminated the mention of other Gulf War exposures, including DU. Even when the Depleted Uranium Citizens' Network of the Military Toxics Project publicly released a leaked Army report (which contained damaging admissions about the dangers of DU weapons) in January 1996, the story was virtually ignored by mainstream media.

"The issue of DU weapons received more attention in the United Kingdom during 1996 than it did in the U.S., partially because a secret British Atomic Energy Authority report warned that 500,000 people could potentially die from the DU contamination left on the Gulf War's battlefields," says Fahey.

"The Army's desire to avoid public awareness of DU is expressed in the following quote from the leaked Army report on DU: *'When DU is indicted as a causative agent for Desert Storm illness, the Army must have sufficient data to separate fiction from reality. Without forethought and data, the financial implications of long-term disability payments and health care costs could be excessive.'*

"Citizens and soldiers from other countries, as well as those in the U.S., would probably also do well to ponder the following quote [also] from the leaked Army report: *'Since DU weapons are openly available on the world arms market, DU weapons will be used in future conflicts....The number of DU patients on future battlefields probably will be significantly higher because other countries will use systems containing DU.'* Greater public awareness of DU will enable objective decisions to be made about its use in weaponry.

"The health and environmental effects of the 300 tons of DU shot in the Gulf is just a glimpse of the dangers that our society, and the world, will be forced to deal with if and when DU weapons are used in future conflicts. Because DU has a half-life of 4.5 billion years, and because it is extremely difficult and costly to clean up after it has been shot on a testing range or battlefield, DU threatens to pollute future battlefields and poison and kill people for thousands of generations," says Fahey. "...The citizens of Iraq and Kuwait are already suffering the effects of the 300 tons of DU which remain in battlefield areas. Six years after the war, there are still no plans to clean up the contamination.

"During 1995 and 1996, ten members of the DU Citizens' Network presented written or oral testimony about DU to the Presidential Advisory Committee on Persian Gulf War Veterans' Illnesses (PAC). Our work with the PAC included providing them with a copy of the leaked Army report on DU, which even the presidential committee was unable to obtain despite repeated requests over the course of at least six months. Unfortunately, the staff assigned to investigating DU for the PAC discredited the work of the DU Citizens' Network in a phone conversation to me, choosing instead to rely upon Pentagon assertions downplaying both the dangers of DU and the numbers of troops exposed to DU on the battlefield.

"Recent developments include the passage of resolutions on DU by the Veterans of Foreign Wars and American Legion, and two documentaries on DU in progress by film makers from New York and Japan." Fahey says he is currently working with the American Legion to have congressional hearings on DU in the next congressional session and he says the DU Citizens' Network is also currently drafting language for a UN resolution calling for an international ban on DU weapons.

Rebecca Solnit, who edited the report, *Radioactive Battlefields of the 1990s*, added this comment: "Depleted uranium armaments represent nothing less than an intentional effort to spread nuclear waste around the world for a dubious military advantage....DU contamination also exists in military sites across the U.S., and like nuclear testing and weapons manufacture it takes a toll on the very people who are supposed to be protected by U.S. military efforts."

According to Bill Triplett, author of the *VVA Veteran* article, "The mainstream press has pursued the subject of DU, but only as it might relate to what has become known as 'Gulf War Syndrome,' i.e., a possible cause of it.

"I believe the media's hunt for an answer to Gulf War Syndrome (GWS) has blinded them to newsworthy issues that are or may be related to GWS, but that are not causally linked. Put another way, if it doesn't seem to be causing GWS, then we're not really interested in it. DU—like other suspects in the GWS story—has not been identified as a *primary*, suspected cause. But does this mean it is not something worth our attention; especially in light of the Army's own apprehensiveness about its potential health risks independent of its relationship to GWS?" asks Triplett.

Gary Cohen, who wrote the *Multinational Monitor* article, agrees that media silence on the issue benefits the Pentagon: "Armor-piercing DU weapons are powerful new weapons in the Pentagon's arsenal and an important new weapon for sale in the global arms market; and weapons manufacturers like Aerojet and Nuclear Metals, as well as foreign arms merchants" benefit, as well.

Cohen adds, "The U.S. Government's cover-up is similar to its cover-up around Agent Orange exposure and above-ground nuclear testing in the 1950s. The issue highlights the reality that innocent Americans, as well as enlisted men and women, are expendable cannon fodder in the U.S. Government's military adventures, and that it is more important to defend a military company or a weapons system than defend American citizens or the country's environment."

According to Kathryn Casa, who wrote the *National Catholic Reporter* article with a Bosnia angle, there has not been "any coverage in the United States media of how exposure to depleted uranium has affected the Iraqi and perhaps Saudi populations, the only foreign civilians known to have been exposed to DU weapons.

"As my article pointed out, even the U.S. government has admitted that soldiers in the Gulf were inadequately trained to handle weapons containing depleted uranium, and many did not know that they were dealing with DU at all," says Casa.

Casa adds, "With the exception of one *60 Minutes* segment by Leslie Stahl, there has been very little effort to cover the situation in Iraq, where more than half a million children are believed to have died as a result of the war's fallout, including DU contamination and the UN sanctions."

It should be noted that *The Nation* published an important investigative report on the subject of DU weapons in its October 21, 1996 issue. The cover story, "The Pentagon's

Radioactive Bullet," by Bill Mesler, describes how hundreds, perhaps thousands, of veterans were unknowingly exposed to DU in the Persian Gulf.

10 CENSORED

Facing Food Scarcity

Sources:
WORLD WATCH
Dates: May/June 1996
Titles: "Facing Food Scarcity" and
    "Japanese Government Breaks
    With World Bank Food Forecast"
Author: Lester R. Brown

The Japanese Ministry of Agriculture released projections in late December 1995 which show a doubling of world grain prices by 2010. The world prices for wheat and rice will exceed 2 times that of the base year of 1992. Around the same time, *World Watch* published an article, "Facing Food Scarcity," which supports the Japanese Ministry of Agriculture's claim, and according to the World Agricultural Outlook Board, the world's stock of rice, wheat, corn, and other grains have fallen to their lowest level in two decades. These projections differ sharply from that of the World Bank, which has stuck with its projection of continuously declining grain prices over the same period. The Japanese analysis, along with the *World Watch* article take into account past experience with biological growth in finite environments (examples include soil erosion, increased population, and land dehydration), while the economists who are responsible for projecting supply and demand of agriculture commodities for the World Bank and at the UN Food and Agriculture Organization (FAO) do not.

As the world population continues to grow, more and more water must be diverted from crop irrigation to cities for direct consumption. This, along with the loss of agricultural land to housing, creates a drastic imbalance between the number of people and the food production necessary to feed them. The economically integrated world of the late nineties is moving into uncharted territory, facing a set of problems quite different in nature from those faced in the past.

The food shortage will become even more acute in light of the conclusions of the recent World Food Summit in November 1996. Convened by the FAO, the first summit in 22 years forecast that poor countries will be increasingly responsible for feeding their own people, without the aid of wealthier nations. While population is soaring, especially in poor nations, food aid to poor countries is dropping by about half, and the number of hungry people will continue to grow (*San Francisco*

Chronicle, November 18, 1996).

With the World Bank and FAO continuing to project surplus capacity and declining real prices, it is difficult to mobilize support for continued investment in agriculture or for the kinds of social services such as family planning that could help stabilize population growth.

SSU Censored Researchers:
Amy S. Cohen
Jeremy Lewis
Stacey Merrick

COMMENTS: Lester Brown, president of the World Watch Institute and author of "Facing Food Scarcity," says the subject received some coverage in weekly news magazines and major papers around the world because *World Watch* released the story at an international press briefing. "However," he says, "considering the global implications of food scarcity, this subject could stand to have a great deal more media attention, especially in-depth coverage by network TV."

When the Japanese government's food forecast broke with that of the World Bank, Brown wrote an alert in *World Watch* as "one of several 'wake-up call' stories regarding the imbalance between the limits on food production and the demands of an ever-expanding population." He thinks wider media exposure of this "would lay the groundwork for a broader understanding of the food security issue. It might also force the World Bank and the U.N. Food and Agriculture Organization (FAO) to redo their projections using not just economists, but hydrologists, biologists, climatologists, botanists, etc.— scientists who understand the finite laws of biology and the effects on food production of higher temperatures, declining freshwater supplies, and cropland loss."

World Watch Institute seeks to effect change by providing information: to alert the general public to the issue of food scarcity, and to the long-term consequences of ignoring the available information.

"The issue of food scarcity is an opportunity to press for many of the changes in environmental and population policies that are needed not only to ensure food security, but to also build an environmentally sustainable global economy," says Brown. "We see media coverage on the food situation as a way to increase the investment in family planning and associated social needs, such as the education of young females in the developing world; of accelerating the effort to restructure the world energy economy, moving away from a fossil fuels-based economy toward a solar/wind/hydrogen-based economy; of focusing public attention on water scarcity and the steps to deal with it; and of expanding investment in soil conservation, reducing erosion losses to a sustainable level. It is also an opportunity to help people under-

stand that food scarcity, and the environmental and population trends leading to it, may now pose a greater threat to future political stability than military aggression."

Brown believes no one benefits from the lack of media coverage in the long run. "In the short run, the World Bank, the FAO, and policy makers in general are served by the limited coverage, as are multinationals. The World Bank and FAO because...they need not change their way of looking at global issues, in this case, food projections looked at through the micro-lens of economics. Policy makers are served because they do not have to make difficult decisions regarding changes in economic policies that would promote a sustainable global economy rather than the short-term interests of business....Failing to see the full scope of the food issue, they underinvest in family planning and agricultural research. Limited or lack of coverage maintains the status quo, thus change does not happen, and the public is lulled into a false sense of security that their lifestyles, eating and consumption habits, and family planning choices need not change.

"The changes required to reverse the environmental degradation of the planet (using food scarcity as the engine to drive this change) are tremendous. Governments would need to change the way they do business..."

World Watch Institute released a book in September 1996 entitled

Tough Choices: Facing the Challenge of Food Scarcity as a follow-up on this subject. Coverage in major papers followed an international press briefing, yet network TV continues to ignore this issue, according to Brown. "We also convened a briefing for the international press in Rome the day before the World Food Summit opened in mid-November in Rome. This briefing attracted over 80 press individuals and 7 television crews (NHK of Japan, Central Television of China, the BBC, and national networks from Germany, Denmark, Norway, and Sweden). Twenty-six English language wire stories were generated from this briefing. The World Food Summit, relying on the overly optimistic scenarios of food projections of the FAO and World Bank, failed to generate a sense of urgency regarding future food scarcity. Thus, countries will fail to take appropriate action to halt population growth and will continue to underinvest in agricultural research, meanwhile maintaining business as usual."

11 CENSORED

GDP is Meaningless Economic Measuring Stick

Source:
THE ATLANTIC MONTHLY
Date: October 1995
Title: "If the GDP Is Up, Why Is America Down?"
Authors: Clifford Cobb, Ted Halstead, and Jonathan Rowe

If measured by growth in the Gross Domestic Product (GDP), the economy is booming. Productivity and employment are up, and inflation is under control. Yet 70 percent of Americans feel gloomy about the future. The root of this formidable disconnection, this *Atlantic Monthly* article suggests, may be found at the base of the aforementioned GDP. Indeed, the authors theorize, the

THIS MODERN WORLD　　by TOM TOMORROW

A PANEL OF MAINSTREAM ECONOMISTS HAS RECENTLY DECLARED THAT THE CONSUMER PRICE INDEX HAS BEEN *OVERSTATING INFLATION*--

--BY FAILING TO NOTE SUCH EVOLVING "QUALITY OF LIFE" INDICATORS AS *TEEVEES* WITH *50 CHANNELS, VCR'S* WITH *IMPROVED FEATURES,* AND *PERSONAL COMPUTERS* WITH *MORE MEMORY.*

WE *WISH* THIS WERE A JOKE, BUT IT IS NOT.

NOW, SOCIAL SECURITY AND OTHER ENTITLEMENT PAYMENTS RISE WITH THE COST OF LIVING...SO IF THESE SPECIOUS ARGUMENTS ARE ACCEPTED AS *FACT* AND INFLATION ESTIMATES ARE REVISED *DOWNWARD,* ONE PRACTICAL REAL-WORLD EFFECT WILL BE THE *CUTTING* OF BENEFITS TO THE ELDERLY...

WELL MARTHA, THE BAD NEWS IS WE CAN'T AFFORD TO HEAT THE *HOUSE* THIS WINTER--

--BUT BY GOD, IF WE EVER SCRAPE UP ENOUGH FOR A COM-*PUTER,* IT'LL HAVE MORE PROCESSING POWER THAN YOU EVER DREAMED *POSSIBLE!*

whole basis for assessing the status of the economy is absurd, outdated, and insufficient—and that ultimately, we need to re-think our definition of prosperity itself.

The GDP, formerly the Gross National Product (GNP), is a measure of market activity. This means nothing more than the exchange of money between businesses or persons, with no distinction between costs and gain. By the curious standard of the GDP, the happiest event is an earthquake or a hurricane. The most desirable habitat is a multi-billion dollar Superfund site. All of these are a plus according to the GDP, because money is changing hands. The GDP "does not distinguish between costs and benefits, between productive and destructive activities, or between sustainable and unsustainable ones." The more companies deplete natural resources, the more the GDP increases. "This violates basic accounting principles, in that it portrays the depletion of capital as current income."

In light of this seemingly illogical and outdated theory, an alternative system of economic measurement has arisen, called the "genuine progress indicator" (GPI), which—rather than eliminating the GDP—would transform it into a more accurate reflection of the nation's total economic status.

Some of the new factors that would be included:

• *Crime.* Money spent on deterring crime or repairing damages from the effects of social decline, including hospital bills, are factored in.

• *Other defensive expenditures.* They figure in the cost of repairs from accidents, or what people will have to pay for water filters, or air purification systems, or any kind of cost due to an environmental hazard.

• *Resource depletion and degradation of the habitat.* As companies use up the nation's minerals and resources, so will it be noted that a loss in capital is occurring. Damage to health, and environmental consequences will count as a negative

since the money spent is not on growth, but restoration of what was damaged.

• *Loss of leisure.* If people have to work two jobs or longer hours just to stay even, then they aren't really staying even. They are falling behind, losing time to spend with their families, to further their education, etc. The GDP assumes that such time is worth nothing.

In the final analysis, if the nation's indicators of economic progress are obsolete, then they consign us to continually resorting to policies that cannot succeed because they aren't addressing the right problems.

SSU Censored Researchers:
Jeffrey Fillmore
Amber Knight

COMMENTS: Jonathan Rowe, Clifford Cobb, and Ted Halstead, co-authors of the article, work with the group Redefining Progress. Rowe, speaking on behalf of the group, says the subject of their piece did get some coverage, "but the result was typical of the mainstream media. We were raising basic questions about the way the media and policy establishments measure economic progress and well-being—specifically the Gross Domestic Product or GDP. We showed that in a multitude of ways, what the GDP counts as up, Americans experience as down, from family and community breakdown to crime, disease, and environmental

decay; and that this phony accounting has a corrosive effect on public policy. A few major outlets covered the story, mainly because we had devised an alternative to the GDP which provided a concrete number and therefore 'news.' But they quickly reverted to their old ways. The GDP continues to be a totem of economic reportage, cited with reverential awe. Politicians promise to boost the GDP, and nobody thinks to ask what exactly this boost is going to consist of and how it will affect us.

"There is a large and increasing gap between 'the economy' that the media reports on and the one people actually experience. We were trying to get reporters to ask the simple and obvious question that would begin to bridge that gap—a question reporters used to learn on the police beat. If the local police chief announced that 'activity' on the city streets was up 10 percent over the previous year, reporters would demand to know what exactly he or she was talking about: muggings or tree plantings, car thefts or acts of neighborliness and kindness, whatever. Unless you know what the 10 percent increase consists of, the gross statistic says nothing at all.

"The GDP is much the same. It is simply a gross statistical summation of monetary transactions in the economy. It says absolutely nothing about whether life is getting better or worse.

"That the media refuses to see this comes in part from changes in the sociology of the newsroom. Reporters used to work their way up from the police beat; they had a degree of skepticism regarding official statistics and academic experts. Today, by contrast, economic reporters increasingly come not with local reporting experience, but with academic credentials and degrees. Management seeks such people out. Yet they often are so immersed in the language and conceptual apparatus of conventional economic thinking—they so identify with the experts that they continually quote—that they become incapable of asking the simple and obvious questions that most need to be asked.

"If reporters asked these questions—i.e., exactly what is growing, who is benefiting and who isn't, and what is the effect of that growth upon ourselves, our kids, and grandkids—it would open up whole new arenas of economic debate that currently are stifled because of the implicit media blackout on any skeptical thinking regarding the GDP and the assumptions on which it is based.

"Beyond that, of course, major business and financial interests (the latter in particular) might be inconvenienced by greater skepticism regarding the GDP. Such skepticism would lead to greater scrutiny of what actually is expanding in the economy; the awe that surrounds the GDP casts a halo upon everything that goes into it—gambling, cigarette sales, the depletion of natural resources, whatever. A few business leaders have

come to realize that false national accounting will ultimately lead their companies and the entire economy into a big dead end, but such people are still a minority."

12 CENSORED

Milking the Public

Source:
CHICAGO LIFE MAGAZINE
Date: October 1995
Title: "Milking the Public"
Author: Hilary Varner

New research suggests that our milk supply may be increasingly more dangerous. With the increased use of hormones and antibiotics in milk-producing cows comes an increase in the levels of the naturally occurring growth hormone regulator known as "insulin-like growth factor-I" (IGF-I), which has been linked to major health problems. It has been suggested that drinking milk with high levels of IGF-I may lead to an increase in breast or colon cancer.

When the bovine growth hormone Posilac (rBGH), manufactured by Monsanto, was approved by the Food and Drug Administration (FDA) in 1993, many felt the debate on its safety was a moot point. But since the FDA approval, health experts claim new findings concerning the bovine growth hormone are cause for alarm.

The growth hormone regulator IGF-I is present in both cows and humans. IGF-I controls milk production and growth, but the Consumer Policy Institute's Jean Halloran asserts that it is also known to be a "tumor growth promoter." This means that while IGF-I helps us to grow, it also accelerates the multiplication of cancer cells. Studies done on rBGH-injected cows show that IGF-I levels are increased anywhere from 25 to 700 percent.

Dr. Samual S. Epstein, professor of occupational and environmental medicine at the University of Illinois School of Public Health and chairman of the Cancer Prevention Coalition states that "IGF-I is a growth factor for human breast cancer cells, maintaining their malignancy, progression, and evasiveness. IGF-I has been similarly associated with colon cancer."

The main concern by many is simply that IGF-I is very potent and no one is sure of much about how it works. Keith Ashdown of the Cancer Prevention Coalition in Chicago says about IGF-I, "It was never really looked at carefully."

While there are many controversial issues surrounding the use of rBGH, this is one that has direct implications that can dramatically affect us all. However, since the FDA does not mandate labeling of rBGH milk (rather, it prevents the labeling) it is nearly impossible to tell what milk is safe to drink.

Further clouding the issue is the disturbing fact that three former Monsanto employees now work for the FDA—including the executive assistant to the FDA commissioner, Michael Taylor—who signed both the FDA's approval of rBGH and the decision that stores could not label dairy products as "rBGH-free."

In short, Dr. Epstein charges that the FDA has "allowed for uncontrolled, unlabeled sales of treated milk to unwitting customers," and believes that the FDA should revoke its restrictions on the labeling of milk and consider banning the use of the hormones.

SSU Censored Researchers:
Richard Henderson
Lisa Zwirner

COMMENTS: Hilary Varner, an intern at *Chicago Life Magazine* when she wrote her article on rBGH, says most of the related articles she uncovered during the course of her research were found in magazines such as *Mother Earth* or *Parents*, which she says, "definitely struck me as not reaching the general population, especially since almost all of the articles seemed to be simply publishing Monsanto's point of view, a biased source of information, to say the least." Varner believes the public would benefit from mass media exposure of rBGH "by having a chance to choose not to use products from cows that were injected with the hormone; to me it was horrific that such knowledge was deemed not only unimportant, but also as unfair advertising. In addition, however, there remains the possibility that products produced by cows injected with rBGH might cause those who ingest them serious damage, so the public would benefit from more information about rBGH by maybe saving themselves from unnecessary bodily harm.

"The chemical companies, of course, benefit from the lack of media coverage, because as long as the dairy world is satisfied with the results of the hormone and the public continues to buy rBGH-produced products, the dairy world will go on buying rBGH. Those who utilize the hormone benefit from its lack of coverage as well, because they are ensured that they will continue to sell their products to a public who would have something to say if they knew what they might be ingesting."

Varner says she is not aware of any recent developments, and she believes media coverage of rBGH has been insufficient. Since publication of the article, a Monsanto representative wrote a letter to *Chicago Life* stating the article was badly researched and one-sided. The magazine published the letter, along with Varner's sources of information and proof of her conclusions.

13 CENSORED

Gag Me with a Food Disparagement Law

Sources:
UTNE READER
Date: January 2, 1996
Title: "Watch Your Mouth"
Author: Helen Cordes

WASHINGTON FREE PRESS
Date: April 5, 1996
Title: "Lettuce Libel"
Author: Eric Nelson

COLUMBIA JOURNALISM REVIEW
Date: September/October 1996
Title: "The Alar 'Scare' Was For Real"
Author: Elliott Negin

USA TODAY
Date: March 27, 1996
Title: "Warning: You can be sued for insulting vegetables: Industry turns to laws on 'food disparagement'"
Author: Ann Oldenburg

Agribusiness groups including the American Farm Bureau Federation have been, and still are, lobbying for legislation which would make it illegal for anyone to make a claim that a food is unsafe for human consumption without having "sound" scientific evidence to back it up. These gag laws are referred to as "banana bills" or "agricultural disparagement" laws and would enable companies producing perishable goods, such as meat, produce, medicine, and tobacco, to sue anyone who makes a claim that their product—or anything used to process or preserve their product—is unsafe. But who determines what is "sound science?" Thalidomide and DDT were once endorsed by the "sound" scientific community, but later, after links to birth defects and cancers were established, they were banned.

The birth of disparagement laws occurred in 1989 when the legendary CBS news magazine show *60 Minutes* publicized a Natural Resources Defense Council report charging that the chemical Alar, which enhances the appearance of apples, caused cancer. Apples, apple juice, and applesauce were immediately removed from grocery store shelves, resulting in a loss of $130 million to Washington apple growers. In response, the Washington growers sued the television show for $250 million—insisting that their product had been falsely disparaged. Supporters of the agricultural disparagement laws aim to make products easier to market as well as to avoid significant financial losses.

These laws are a direct threat to the free speech rights granted under the First Amendment. Under such food disparagement laws, mass media and individual citizens would lose their right to inform—and to be informed. If you're sued for disparagement and you lose, the punishment in Idaho is typical: you have to pay the plaintiff for recovery of all and any financial loss. In Colorado, you could also go to prison for a year. Perversely, such laws cannot be challenged until someone is charged with violating it. "It's terrifying," says David Bederman, an Emory University law professor who tried unsuccessfully to challenge Georgia's disparagement law. The judge ruled that he couldn't dispute the law until he had a real dispute. But a real dispute could have far-reaching implications.

Currently, there are twelve states that have passed these laws and thirteen that have legislation pending. Critics charge that scientists might not study the effects of pesticides on foods—and that journalists and activists might not report on or discuss such concerns—thus leaving consumers in the dark.

SSU Censored Researchers:
Carli Dolieslager
Amber Knight

COMMENTS: Helen Cordes, author of the article, "Watch Your Mouth," says the topic had received little attention when she began tracking it in late 1994. When she pitched it to *Utne Reader* in early 1995, she had found only "a few obscure references" buried in the back of Texas daily newspapers. "By the time *Utne Reader* gave me the go-ahead," Cordes notes, "I had heard nothing about it on network TV, and clips came only from environmental publications and one journalism magazine.

"Food safety is clearly an issue that affects everyone who eats, which is a pretty inclusive grouping. While I think that some people are generally aware that their food is grown using pesticides, preservatives, and genetically-altered genes, I don't think most realize how dependent the food production system has become on these methods. If people realized (by reading/hearing about it) how 'bad news' about unsafe food is squelched, they would perhaps be moved to make different food choices, such as buying organic foods.

"The big food companies, which spend a lot of money advertising in mainstream media, want to keep this story quiet, along with agribusiness groups. Media outlets which profit from food ads don't want to alienate those accounts.

"I believe there is good news and bad news on the topic of bringing people's attention to food safety issues. First, the bad news—I think there's a trend among many journalists/editors to downplay food safety concerns, as witnessed by the back-lash against the 'food police' who critique the high fat in Americans' diets à la movie popcorn and fast food. I fear that food, raised with topical pesticides, preservatives, or genetically altered methods will get the same 'what's the big deal?' treatment." [Cordes is referring to the Washington D.C.-based Center for Science in the Public Interest.]

The good news, says Cordes, is that "more people are voting with their feet by walking to the organic food section. More food producers will follow the money, and perhaps ultimately the same companies now decrying any criticism of conventional food will be singing the praises of organic food."

Eric Nelson, award-winning writer with the *Washington Free Press* and author of the article, "Lettuce Libel," says he saw no TV coverage of food disparagement laws, nor is he aware of coverage by any newsweeklies. "National papers, including *USA Today* and *Washington Post* did some coverage, but mainstream newspaper stories about state agricultural disparagement laws were relegated to the 'Style' or 'Home' sections. Most stories (mine included) attempted to exploit the humorous angle of 'fruit slander' or some other stupid pun.

Nelson believes "the general public needs to know that the food supply is not safe because of contamination and pesticides. Watchdog organizations such as the Pure Food Campaign and the Environmental

Working Group are doing their best to raise this issue in the public and in the media. However, the threat of lawsuits against these organizations—even if based on unconstitutional disparagement laws—is an attempt to squelch public debate about the safety of what we eat. The mere threat of a lawsuit for speaking the truth will chill public debate about food safety, will diminish our First Amendment rights, and could endanger the survival of public interest groups if they are sued under these laws.

"The public needs to know that the vast majority of these laws would not pass constitutional muster because they effectively shift the burden of proof from the plaintiff to the defendant. Thus, an organization sued under many of these laws faces the presumption that its statements are false and 'not based on reliable scientific data.' Plus, the plaintiff in these actions need not show actual damages resulting from the statement, as is the case with most libel actions. In fact, the Pure Food Campaign notes that industry organizations have advised their members *not* to sue public interest groups under these laws, lest the laws themselves be found unconstitutional. Thus, the laws are meant to sit on the books and chill public speech by their mere existence.

"The public needs to know what industry organizations are sponsoring these food disparagement laws: the Produce Marketing Association is one such group. Another is the Animal Industry Foundation (AIF), a front group composed of meat producers, including the American Farm Bureau Federation, American Feed Industry Association, American Sheep Industry, American Society of Animal Science, American Veal Association, National Broiler Council, National Cattlemen's Association, National Milk Producers Federation, National Pork Producers Council, National Turkey Federation, Southeastern Poultry & Egg Association, and United Egg Producers. These groups have even drafted a 'model disparagement bill' that states can use to draft their own laws."

Elliott Negin, author of the *Columbia Journalism Review* article, "The Alar 'Scare' Was For Real," says there are several aspects of this story the national media missed. "Although the news media made much of a lawsuit filed by Washington state apple growers against CBS' *60 Minutes* for a critical story the show did on Alar, there was next to no follow-up when the courts vindicated *60 Minutes*. Nor have the national media paid attention to the 'agricultural disparagement' laws that have been passed in 12 states. These laws will have a chilling effect on journalists who write about food safety.

"Over the last seven years the news media have been citing the so-called Alar 'scare' as an example of misguided government environmental regulation. This adds to the false perception that the government is too zealous in protecting the environment and is stifling the corporate sector by burdening it with regulations.

"The food processing and chemical industries have made the Alar controversy their Alamo. Since Alar was taken off the market, the two industries, working with high-priced public relations firms, have mounted disinformation campaigns against legitimate studies on the effect of pesticide-treated food on children. If these industries were forced to cut back their use of dangerous pesticides to better protect the public, I assume they fear their profits would suffer. Meanwhile farm workers and the public will continue to be exposed."

Negin feels that since his piece appeared in *Columbia Journalism Review*, his "fellow journalists should now have a better understanding of how they've blown this story." According to Negin, *The New Republic* and *The Nation* rejected query letters for the article before it appeared in *CJR*. He says Environmental Media Services, a non-profit public relations firm, has mailed the article to hundreds of journalists nationwide.

14 CENSORED

Anti-Abortion and Militia Movements Converge

Sources:
ON THE ISSUES
Date: Fall 1996
Title: "The Anti-Abortion Stealth Campaign"
Author: Jennifer Gonnerman

FRONT LINES RESEARCH
Date: October 1996
Title: "Storming Wombs and Waco: How the Anti-abortion and Militia Movements Converge"
Author: Sandi DuBowski

At this point in the turbulent history of the debate over abortion, it seems that opponents can be separated into two groups: non-violent opponents and militants who will use intimidation and violence. While "standard" harassment of patients and clinic personnel through "sidewalk counseling" is fairly commonplace, violent actions are becoming increasingly common. These newer, confrontative practices have included attacks on clinics using butyric acid (a chemical that smells of rancid butter), death and bomb threats, kidnapping, arson, bombings, and murder. The National

Abortion Federation has kept statistics on clinic violence since 1977 and the most recent data (current as of August 1, 1996) showed a cumulative total of 1,894 violent attacks reported on American clinics—including 157 in 1995.

According to researcher and journalist Sandi DuBowski, there is a well-documented connection between both the violent anti-abortion movement and so-called "militia" groups. This includes links between followers of the Christian Identity movement, the followers of the "Freemen" (and their anti-government ideology), the Ku Klux Klan, organized militias, the Gun Owners of America, the U.S. Taxpayers Party, militant anti-abortion groups such as Operation Rescue and the Missionaries to the Pre-born. One recent example is the conviction in July 1996 of three members of the Oklahoma Constitutional Militia (which included a Christian Identity "prophet" and his followers) for conspiring to blow up abortion clinics, along with the Southern Poverty Law Center, and other civil rights targets.

One particularly aggressive and high-profile group is Human Life International (HLI), which systematically exports American-styled anti-abortion tactics to other countries in attempts to remove access to safe, legal abortions for women worldwide. According to HLI, it has 68 branches in 56 countries on five continents. It conducts worldwide seminars and symposiums on abortion and morality-related topics.

According to the World Health Organization, unsafe abortions are one of the leading causes of the more than 500,000 maternal deaths occurring each year. Globally, more than 13 percent of pregnancy-related deaths are associated with unsafe abortions. This figure climbs to 50 percent in countries with restrictive abortion laws such as Latin American nations. Currently in the U.S., 84 percent of all counties lack access to surgical abortion—so even where abortion is legal it may not be easily accessible. Researchers who track these extremist groups caution that if such militant conspiracies spread on a global scale, there will undoubtedly be more women put into the desperate position of risking their lives or health in order to determine whether or when they bear children.

Additional source information: Human Life International, International Planned Parenthood Federation, National Abortion Federation, National Abortion and Reproductive Rights Action League, National Organization for Women, and the World Health Organization

SSU Censored Researchers:
Latrice Babers
Linda McCabe

COMMENTS: According to Jennifer Gonnerman, author of "The Anti-

Abortion Stealth Campaign," Human Life International received virtually no exposure in the American mass media last year or in prior years. It is interesting to note, however, that this group has attracted some press attention in Canada, where pro-choice activists are outraged by the fact that this U.S.-funded group is crossing borders to recruit members.

"Wider [media] exposure of Human Life International would inform the public about the true nature of the battle over reproductive rights. Few people realize that the abortion battle is not just between Democrats and Republicans, but that it is raging well beyond America's borders. Moreover, I think the public would be fascinated to find out how extensive the Catholic Church's involvement is in HLI.

"The entire anti-choice movement benefits from this lack of media coverage because it keeps the public ignorant about how well-funded and strategically advanced they [HLI] are. Ignorant about the activities of Human Life International, many pro-choice people mistakenly believe the fight for reproductive rights is almost won.

"An example of how widespread (but unnoticed) HLI's influence is popped up at this year's Republican convention in San Diego. Flip Benham and other Operation Rescue leaders attracted the attention of 40 television cameras when they started waving gruesome, six-foot high pic-tures of fetuses. But while cameras focused on the fetuses, they missed the posters' fine print, which showed that they had been manufactured by Human Life International. HLI's ability to produce the anti-choice movement's propaganda—buttons, books, bumper stickers, videotapes, plastic fetuses—without enduring scrutiny by the mainstream media allows it to flourish," says Gonnerman.

Since her article was published, Human Life International moved into its new national headquarters in Virginia and increased its staff size, according to Gonnerman. "Meanwhile, the only exposure my story received after publication was some angry remarks on HLI's Web site."

15 CENSORED

Teen Drug "Crisis" is a Myth

Sources:
EXTRA!
Date: September/October 1996
Title: "High On Lies"
Author: Mike Males

THE PROGRESSIVE
Date: May 1996
Title: "The Return of Reefer Madness"

Authors: Mike Males and Faye Docuyanan

In what is slowly becoming a campaign tradition, Bob Dole spent a formidable amount of the 1996 election cycle vowing to end the rampant use of drugs by American teens. In the end, his promises were not enough to win the election, but his call to address the teenage drug crisis certainly garnered copius media attention. According to researcher and journalist Mike Males, however, the U.S. media were taken in by "a politically manufactured hoax." In short, claims Males, "ill-motivated authorities are waging open war against youths and minorities—and the compliant media are leading the cheers."

Consider some of these statistics:

• In June 1994, the Federal Drug Abuse and Warning Network (DAWN) released its annual survey of coroners in four dozen major cities. It found a record-high 8,500 deaths from drug overdoses, drug suicides, and drug-related accidents in 1993. But teenagers made up just *2 percent* of these deaths.

• Of the 1,100 Los Angeles County deaths in 1994 considered drug-related—accidental overdoses, suicides, car wrecks, and other fatal mishaps in which drugs were found—only six involved teens.

• In the same county, teenagers made up only 3 percent of 36,000 emergency room treatments during 1993 for drug-related injuries.

• DAWN's companion survey of hospitals and emergency departments found that teens comprised just 3 percent of the 200,000 admissions involving heroin, cocaine, or marijuana.

• People under age 21 comprised only one in ten admissions to drug-abuse treatments in 1993, down sharply from one in six in 1987.

Each year, the University of Michigan releases a report called "Monitoring the Future," a survey of 50,000 junior and senior high school students that seems to prove the teenage use of drugs is increasing. Males notes, however, that "the unreported findings of the Michigan Survey were far less inflammatory." Two in three high school seniors, and seven in eight eighth-graders had not smoked pot in the year preceding the survey. Only 2 percent of the seniors had ever used crystal methamphetamine, 4 percent had used cocaine, and fewer than one percent had used heroin in the past twelve months.

While these statistics do not seem to support the theory of a teen drug "crisis," they do, however, support the claim that a drug problem exists—but among the parents of teenagers, rather than the teenagers themselves.

According to Males, "Drug death rates are now so high among middle-aged men that they dwarf all the other classes. Middle-agers are now twenty times more likely to die from drugs than are teenagers."

SSU Censored Researchers:
Kevin Coyne
Jody Howard

COMMENTS: Mike Males and Faye Docuyanan, co-authors of the article in *The Progressive*, believe the subject has not been well-covered. "Though this could be said about a number of issues, the media's coverage of the drug war is the worst example of capitulation to official interest since the early days of Vietnam. Worse, even, because while Vietnam reporters had few sources of information other than official briefings, today's press has failed to scrutinize readily available public documents that clearly refute the official line. I [Mike] have yet to meet a single mainstream reporter who has [actually] read the National Household Survey on Drug Abuse, or the Drug Abuse Warning Network surveys, that they breathlessly report. All they do is report what officials and drug war interests say these reports say.

"If we wish to formulate drug policies that truly improve the public health of our society, then these policies must be grounded in knowledge of the facts (regardless of their popularity) rather than unfounded fears and moral panic. Today's drug panic ensues from a 5-percentage-point rise, from 3 percent in 1992 to 8 percent today, in the number of teenagers who use marijuana at least once a month. This is the age group, drug, and drug use style least likely to cause problems, now or in the future. Meanwhile, the drug war is ignoring exploding rates of heroin, cocaine, pharmaceutical, and alcohol abuse among middle-agers that are now causing record hundreds of thousands of emergency hospitalizations and treatments, and thousands of deaths.

"Drug war interests (policy makers, health care professionals, lawyers, grant-funded academics, entrepreneurs, and law enforcement officials) benefit from diversion of public attention away from the massive failures of drug-war strategy: (a) the government's refusal to deal with the drugs dispensed by large corporations (pharmaceutical companies and alcohol marketers), (b) official dereliction in stemming a rising 20-year pattern of heroin and drug abuse among Vietnam veterans, (c) the disastrous strategy of pursuing punitive, prison-interdiction-oriented measures instead of treatment expansion, and (d) the inevitable, skyrocketing rates of addicts and drug abusers with intractable habits. Instead of focusing on a very real, long-term drug crisis mainly among over-30 groups, drug war interests have done what they always have: demonized a powerless, unpopular scapegoat—adolescents. Hence the concoction of a 'teenage drug crisis' surrounding the 5-point rise in marijuana use and last summer's complete manufacture of a 'heroin epidemic' among the young."

Males says he has received calls

from mainstream reporters and op-ed editors (i.e., *L.A. Times, Washington Post, Newsday*) on this issue in the last month, including publication of several stories and opinion pieces, "so perhaps the media is tiring of its role as drug war lapdog. Certainly the histrionics of drug czar McCaffrey over the passage of the California and Arizona medical-pot initiatives, and his arrogance in assuming the media will help him pillory the two states, may be a wake-up call," says Males.

"As a society, we must be able to discern the difference between casual substance use and serious and life-threatening substance abuse. Serious drug abuse does occur among some teenagers, but vital statistics indicate that hard-core drug use is primarily a middle-aged adult problem. For many addicts, drugs are a way to temporarily numb misery and escape from desperation, and any effective treatment involves an understanding and amelioration of the root causes of drug addiction. Waging 'war,' inflicting harsh punishments, and hurling empty political rhetoric are the futile, ineffective, and often harmful strategies we currently employ to solve our nation's drug abuse problems," argues Males.

16 CENSORED

Derivatives: Risky Business

Source:
THE NATION
Date: December 25, 1995
Title: "Golden Fleece"
Author: Arthur E. Rowse

According to a General Accounting Office (GAO) report last year, the face value of worldwide trades involving derivatives—a high-risk type of financial contract whose value is derived from the performance of an underlying asset or market indicator (such as a price or interest rate)—was estimated to be $34.5 *trillion*. Due to both the amounts involved and the global reach of corporate investors, the economic systems of the world could be severely impaired should these financial entities fail. And an economic failure related to the scope and fragility of derivatives could result in a federal bailout reminiscent of the savings and loan fiasco.

Derivatives are limited to large financial players due to several reasons. First, only those with large sums of money can become involved. Second, due to the leveraged nature of these packages, the financial rewards can be huge when successful, but dangerous if not. Furthermore (and again, due to the leveraged nature), losses in the marketplace can be covered by future investments—creating a house of cards which could tumble at any time. The bankruptcy of Orange County, California a few years ago was directly related to their losses in the derivative market.

The danger in derivatives also stems from the fact that they are leveraged in both directions, up and down. They amount to huge bets stacked against the bettor, often with both buyer and seller inclined to cover losses with even bigger bets.

Yet despite the obvious risk derivatives pose, they are still widely used by corporations, mutual funds, and others wanting to hedge their interest and currency bets. Those who traditionally lose the most in the event of a derivatives failure are small investors, wage earners, pensioners, and taxpayers—people who are not even privy to the derivative market.

The GAO is indeed quite worried about the fragility of derivative investments, especially since the concentration of derivatives is in the hands of only fifteen U.S. companies intricately linked to foreign markets. "The sudden failure or abrupt withdrawal from trading of any of these large dealers," warned the watchdog agency, "could cause liquidity problems in the markets and could also pose risks to the others, including federally insured banks and the financial system as a whole."

Furthermore, a year after the GAO issued a warning to bankers and investors regarding the danger of derivatives, little has been done. One key reason is the $100 million legislators have received in recent election cycles from banks, investment firms, and insurance companies—aimed, in part, at protecting derivatives.

Derivatives pose a serious threat to the economic health of the world since they lack a solid financial foundation and are limited in use to the largest players in the world economy. Moreover, the unwillingness of policy makers to recognize the threat these types of investments pose to the global financial market leaves the citizens of the world vulnerable to an annihilation of financial stability brought upon them by investors beyond their realm.

SSU Censored Researchers:
Brant Herman
Mark Lowenthal

COMMENTS: According to Arthur E. Rowse, author of "Golden Fleece," the subject of risky derivatives "was almost completely ignored by the mass media, and when covered at all, it was relegated to the business pages. It continues to be ignored even though almost nothing has been done by regulatory agencies to prevent some of the disasters that have already occurred. The story of derivatives seems to be a lot like the savings and loan scandal. It's far too complex and local for all the business press and a few large newspapers and magazines to handle in a timely and competent manner. Some reporters such as Brett Fromson of the *Washington Post* and Carol Loomis of *Fortune*, have done competent work, but TV news has been out to lunch. The only major report was done by *60 Minutes* a few years ago.

"Some nine months before the Orange County disaster occurred, the story was dumped in the laps of the *Los Angeles Times* and *Orange County Register*. They booted it. (See *American Journalism Review*, March 1995: 22-29.) When the feds fined Bankers Trust $10 million in December 1994, it got only a few lines in major newspaper business sections. When the shocking internal tapes from Bankers Trust became public, *Business Week* made it a cover story, but it didn't get far in the mainstream media even though the material was sensational and had an indirect bearing on all who deal with Bankers Trust (a new oxymoron)." Rowse did not check general newsweeklies for coverage.

"With more media exposure, legislators would have more incentive to either pass reforms or pressure business to institute more meaningful reforms of its own to protect the general public from catastrophic financial losses. It would also strengthen the backbone of the key agencies, the SEC and CFTC. Greater public exposure would also alert the general public, especially those now unaware of their involvement in derivatives through pension plans, mutual funds, brokerage accounts, banks, and other connections.

"The biggest dealers in derivatives, a small number of big banks such as Bankers Trust, benefit from the limited [media] coverage. Proof is the fact that BT is still prospering despite its extremely shabby treatment of its big derivative customers. Ordinary depositors are probably unaware of the extra risk they have taken and may continue to take by dealing with a bank so deeply involved in such shaky financial transactions."

Rowse says he hasn't followed the subject closely since he wrote the piece, which was a shortened version of an article submitted to *The Nation* six months earlier. "I am not aware of any large derivative scandals since then," he says. "Under some pressure by regulators, large dealers have instituted what they say are closer controls over such business in order to be able to react more quickly to danger signals. But the overall situation appears to have changed little, and the forebodings of the GAO continue to twist in the wind awaiting the next disaster, which everyone hopes will not become a worldwide meltdown."

17 CENSORED

Union Do's: Smart Solidarity

Source:
THE NATION
Date: April 8, 1996
Title "Union Do's: Smart Solidarity"
Author: Eyal Press

Fifteen years after Ronald Reagan fired the air traffic controllers, strikes in America have dipped to a fifty-year low, a mere one-eighth the level of two decades ago. In response to this decline, labor has been fighting back through a strategy known as a "corporate campaign."

The concept behind the "corporation campaign" involves "partnering" with other activist groups (environmental, consumer, etc.) and hitting powerful and highly diversified companies on all fronts. Such a coalition works by investigating the company being struck (or perhaps its parent company and/or its other subsidiaries), scrutinizing environmental and investment records, organizing consumer boycotts, submitting shareholder resolutions, complaining to regulatory agencies—and generally doing whatever it takes to pressure management into a fair settlement. As a result of some successes through the "corporate campaign" strategy,

business is striking back by suing labor unions under the Racketeer Influence and Corrupt Organization (RICO) Act —a statute originally created to fight organized crime.

In one representative case, the United Steelworkers local 9121 began a "corporate campaign" against Bayou Steel and RSR. This "corporate campaign" began due to Bayou Steel's proposed contract that gave no pay raise and allowed any union job to be contracted out. The Steelworkers union, with the help of environmental consultants and community groups, documented numerous environmental and worker safety violations at both RSR and Bayou— in fact, generating information that has been useful to activists seeking to block RSR from opening new factories. As a result, the Steelworkers are being sued by both RSR and Bayou under RICO.

Additionally, business leaders are now lobbying Congress to legally ban such "corporate campaign" strategies. In response, workers claim that management is simply trying to ban their most successful recent innovation—simply because it's proven to be occasionally successful. Indeed, they counter, the strategy is based on the First Amendment and the free flow of truthful information.

And with laws already on the books allowing temporary and permanent replacement workers, and with threats of downsizing and corporate flight further casting shadows over labor, business leaders are now working with Congress to alter the rules.

SSU Censored Researchers:
Aldo Della-Maggiora
Stacey Merrick

COMMENTS: Writer Eyal Press says he heard that his article, "Union Do's: Smart Solidarity," was picked up by an NPR stringer, but he has not heard the program. To the best of his knowledge, the issue received no coverage in the mass media. "As far as newsweeklies and major papers, the closest thing I saw was a one-page article in *Business Week* on the general subject of corporate campaigns," says Press. "But the story of the Steel-workers battle against Bayou Steel and the RSR corporation was not told in any detail."

Press believes media exposure of this story would benefit the general public by educating. "First, I think the story illustrates what can be achieved when labor unions work together with environmentalists and community activists (and vice-versa). The stereotype of the labor movement, which is in part justified, is that it is narrowly focused and single-issue-oriented ('we look out for ours...'). This story challenges that stereotype. The workers involved in this struggle learned a lot about environmental issues (such as the dangers of lead), and also discovered that it can be in their interest to think

about how industry affects communities, school children, etc. On the flip side, I think the story illustrates to ordinary citizens how they can work with unions to protect their communities from environmentally destructive and/or irresponsible companies. Finally, I think the story shed light on an important tool—corporate campaigns—which big business is quietly hoping to eliminate.

"The clear beneficiaries [of the lack of media coverage] are the corporations who wish to ban corporate campaigns for exactly the reasons outlined in the article. Corporate campaigns, like recent consumer campaigns waged against The Gap and Nike, can be a big headache for companies. So they're trying to impose all kinds of restrictions on them, which in effect amount to an effort to restrict the free speech rights of labor unions.

"The gratifying feedback I did receive on the article came from labor and environmental activists who want to build bridges between these movements," says Press. "Richard Yeselson of the AFL-CIO's Industrial Union Department says that friends and allies of his discussed the article and passed it around."

With regard to an update on the story, Press says, "Yeselson and others expect that Republicans in Congress will renew their efforts to ban corporate campaigns this year. Meanwhile, Bayou Steel and the union reached a settlement, but the company (and also RSR) maintains its lawsuit against the union."

18 CENSORED

PCBs: Importing Poison

Sources:
THE TEXAS OBSERVER
Dates: March 8, 1996; April 19, 1996
Titles: "Choose Your Poison"; and "Poisoned Welcome"
Author: Michael King

SAN FRANCISCO BAY GUARDIAN
Date: April 24, 1996
Title: "Importing Toxic Waste"
Author: Jim Hightower

In March 1996, the United States Environmental Protection Agency (EPA) repealed a 16-year-old ban on the importation of polychlorinated biphenyls (PCBs), once used as lubricants for electrical transformers. Production and use of PCBs ended in the U.S. after it was learned that they are highly toxic carcinogens.

U.S. industries have disposed of most domestic PCBs. The preferred disposal method to date is burning. Five sites in the U.S. are approved for incineration of PCBs. Meanwhile, our neighbors, Canada and Mexico, have continued to collect old transformers and PCBs, and have stockpiled them, having no safe method of disposal. The ban on importation ideally would compel these other countries to develop their own safe methods of disposal. That hasn't happened. Mexico, for example, still exports this toxic waste to Europe to be destroyed, and as of March had stockpiled about 8,000 tons of liquid PCBs.

Importation of Mexico's and Canada's PCBs is not a response to our neighbors' looming environmental difficulties so much as it is a response to U.S. waste companies' desire to establish lucrative new disposal contracts. Congressional representatives from Ohio, where one waste incineration site is located, reportedly lobbied, at the request of the local waste disposal firm, for the EPA to lift the ban. The firm, S.D. Meyers, would earn an estimated $100 million dollars from new contracts to dispose of Canadian toxic waste. Some experts doubt that U.S. disposal firms would be more efficient than Canadian firms, but they are certainly cheaper, sometimes running about one-quarter of the cost.

Scientists also believe the burning of toxic waste is inherently unsafe, with PCB incineration releasing such hazardous chemicals as dioxins, even PCBs themselves, into the air and water, and eventually the food chain. One chemist said that stored PCBs, even in such mass quantities, are not nearly as harmful as burned PCBs. For example, neighbors of an Arkansas disposal site reported black smoke and noxious fumes coming from that plant. Cancer cases and neurological disorders in the nearby town increased dramatically as well.

Moreover, predictions of the effects of PCB incineration are based on how emissions would affect theoretically clean air. But sites that would incinerate PCBs also burn a variety of other hazardous chemicals; add these emissions to air that is already polluted by other sources. PCB incineration does not, therefore, create a problem that may or may not be significant; it makes an existing problem even worse.

SSU Censored Researchers:
Bob Browne
Jeffrey Fillmore

COMMENTS: According to Michael King, associate editor of *The Texas Observer*, "mainstream coverage of this story was confined to an AP dispatch or two, with no attention paid to the larger issues of PCB manufacture and the question of safe disposal (i.e., without incineration). There may have been a couple of stories at the time the ban was technically lifted; I have seen no coverage at all of the subsequent status of re-importation."

King believes the obvious benefit of additional media coverage "would be public education of the ongoing risks involved in PCB incineration specifically, and toxic waste incineration generally." King describes the "massive public risk" in Texas, where there are two hazardous waste incinerators as well as other sources, such as cement kilns, which have even less regulation, "and the prevailing winds certainly do not stop in Texas," he says. "Great Lakes pollution has been traced to Texas and the Southeast—the continuing inattention to the dangers of waste incineration constitute a largely unacknowledged public health threat nationally and internationally.

"The obvious beneficiary of limited coverage is the hazardous waste industry (producers and incinerators). They have succeeded in maintaining the fiction that incineration destroys hazardous waste, when science and experience demonstrate that incineration simply disperses poisons (in the case of PCBs, the products of incineration are worse than the PCBs themselves) into the air and the food chain.

"As I write, the Mexican border remains open to re-importation, and the Canadian border is expected to be opened early next year; I do not know if Mexican PCBs are currently being re-imported under the new EPA regulations. An effort by Congressman Ken Bentsen to re-instate the ban failed for a lack of Senatorial sponsorship, and the Sierra Club reports that Bentsen's original amendment would not have been effective in any case. The Sierra Club, however, in conjunction with Greenpeace, filed a lawsuit contesting the new EPA regulations; the suit remains pending in federal court and a decision is expected in December.

"I would hope that the new attention brought by Project Censored to this story might result in public pressure against the incineration of PCBs (here or abroad), and more generally at the whole issue of the incineration of toxic waste."

19 CENSORED

Corporate America Spends Big $$ on Pro-China PR

Sources:
COUNTERPUNCH
Date: April 1-14, 1996
Title: "The New China Lobby"
Authors: Ken Silverstein and
    Alexander Cockburn

MULTINATIONAL MONITOR
Date: April 1996
Title: "China's Hired Guns"
Author: Ken Silverstein

SAN FRANCISCO BAY
    GUARDIAN
Date: May 29, 1996
Title: "China Huggers"
Author: Jim Hightower

In its annual battle to preserve "most favored nation" (MFN) trade status, the Chinese government received a big boost from a powerful dose of U.S. corporate money—funnelled through the public relations firm of Hill & Knowlton. The PR firm's lobbying effort, dubbed the "China Normalization Initiative," was paid for by such Fortune 500 companies as Boeing, AT&T, General Motors, Allied Signal, General Electric, and the Ford Motor Company.

The campaign, which paid off in June 1996 with the Congressional renewal of China's MFN status, was necessary due to China's reputation for human rights violations, child labor, and prison-camp abuses. The alleged torture of dissidents were also criticisms that Hill & Knowlton was paid to refute and/or minimize.

American companies involved in the pro-China PR blitz spent over $1 million on the campaign which was supposed to convince the public that the Chinese leadership is deserving of greater sympathy. Critics argue that 11,000 Chinese were executed last year by their government—some for minor crimes—and that an even greater number of abuses go unreported. The wretched conditions of Shanghai's orphanages are also an ongoing human rights violation that is largely absent from the annual debate over the renewal of China's MFN status.

The exploitation of China's economic potential by American corporations is big business. Bilateral trade between the two countries rose to $55 billion last year and U.S. direct investment in China has gone from $358 million in 1990 to $5.4 *billion* in 1995. Corporations budgeting their money toward the pro-China PR campaign include:

• Boeing, which has racked up sales of $3.9 billion and estimates that China will purchase $100 billion worth of new aircrafts during the next two decades.

• AT&T, which projects earnings of $3 billion from China by the year 2000.

• GM, which in 1995 inked a $2 billion joint venture to manufacture automobiles for China's domestic market.

• Motorola, which has $1.2 billion worth of investments in China—and they plan on constructing a new plant in China to manufacture pocket pagers.

• Ford Motor Company, which purchased a $40 million share in a truck manufacturing plant last November in China's Jianxi province.

Among its many activities, Hill & Knowlton was instrumental in putting corporate representatives in touch with members of Congress, and hiring scholars to draft op-ed articles for major newspapers and to speak at media events. These "third party" advocates, as they are dubbed by industry, are well paid for their labors but seldom reveal their affiliations to the public.

Hill & Knowlton's PR blitz clearly demonstrates how corporate America, aided by the U.S. government, distorts the image of a foreign government whose value as a trading partner conflicts with its disregard for international standards of conduct.

SSU Censored Researchers:
Tina Barni
Doug Hecker

COMMENTS: According to Ken Silverstein, editor of *CounterPunch,* "The topic of the covert business lobby for China is barely touched upon in the mainstream press. And keep in mind

THIS MODERN WORLD   by TOM TOMORROW

ANOTHER PRESIDENTIAL CAMPAIGN IS UNDERWAY, AND AMERICANS ARE BEING *INNUNDATED* WITH INFORMATION...OF COURSE, MOST OF IT IS *WRONG...*

GOSH--I DIDN'T KNOW THAT BOB DOLE WAS A VETERAN OF THE *CIVIL WAR!*

THAT'S *NOTHING!* I READ THAT BILL CLINTON IS ACTUALLY THE *UNABOMBER!*

AT THE LOWER LEVELS OF THE DEBATE, THERE ARE THOSE WHO RELY ON *RUSH LIMBAUGH* FOR THEIR NEWS AND ANALYSIS...

--AND WHO, ACCORDING TO A NINE MONTH STUDY CONDUCTED BY THE ANNENBERG SCHOOL OF COMMUNICATIONS, CONSIDER THEMSELVES TO BE THE BEST INFORMED OF VOTERS--BUT ARE, IN ACTUAL FACT, THE *LEAST* WELL-INFORMED...

SOMEHOW THIS IS NOT AN EXTRAORDINARY SURPRISE.

that the area I addressed—Fortune 500 firms hiring a PR firm to manipulate news coverage—is but one aspect of a vast corporate campaign, budgeted in the tens and millions of dollars, to help China win friends and influence people (especially members of Congress). The ultimate goal of the campaign is to gain *permanent* most favored nation trade status for Beijing, in place of the current annual presidential review. None of this merits more than a glance from the press.

"The public would benefit from [media] exposure to this subject in several ways. First, people should know that a fair amount of what they read in their daily newspapers has been placed, directly or indirectly, by public relations firms (an example being the case covered by my article). A 1991 survey by Jericho Promotions, a PR firm in New York City, found that 38 percent of 2,432 journalists surveyed said they got half of their stories from public relations flacks and an additional 17 percent said they used their PR people for

every story. Second, people should know that the foreign policy debate doesn't take place in a vacuum and is greatly influenced by corporate money and private interests.

Silverstein did not seek to obtain wider exposure for this story but noted that *CounterPunch* is sent to many journalists, although none inquired about this particular issue. "I've learned from past experience that an 'alternative' publication really has to have a 'blockbuster' (i.e., pictures of a political figure in bed with a prostitute) in order to whet the interest of the mainstream press. In this case— a story about big business hiring a PR firm to manipulate public opinion—I felt it was a waste of time to even bother. After all, that's just business as usual inside the beltway. Most reporters in Washington don't even blink an eye at this sort of routine, everyday corruption (perhaps because so many of their friends and associates work in PR and other subsidiary sectors of the political-industrial complex). Thank god they're so lazy," says

Silverstein. "Otherwise, there'd be no need for the alternative press."

According to Jim Hightower, author of "China Huggers," "The slight coverage our country's China policy receives is mostly relegated to the business sections, where it is mired in the arcane language of corporate economists or wrapped in the silly sloganeering of free-trade boosterism.

"America's China policy is begging for a full media exposé and a serious public discussion about what is at stake for ordinary folks—i.e., shipping more of our manufacturing jobs to China's low-wage hellholes, giving America's technological know-how to a competitor who will soon be using it against us, and selling out our people's democratic values and fundamental belief in human rights. It is a corrupt policy that is being bought by the campaign contributions and lobbying fees of the U.S. corporate chieftains who will profit enormously at the expense of us and the Chinese people—a classic example of why the New Global Economy amounts to Globaloney.

"The top executives of conglomerates moving massive amounts of U.S. capital to China" are who benefit from the lack of media coverage given this issue, according to Hightower, "along with the politicians who take money from these conglomerates, and the dictatorial and murderous rulers of China. I might add that Disney Inc. (which owns ABC), General Electric (which owns NBC) and Westinghouse (which owns CBS) all have massive investments in China and have a huge direct financial stake in maintaining the Clinton policy.

"President Clinton has officially de-linked any human rights issue from considerations of trade with China, and he is aggressively pursuing a new strengthening of the Asian Pacific Economic Cooperation Forum (which met in Manila this month, including a Clinton audience with the Chinese president in, of all places, the 'green room' of the Bank of Manila) to forge a new 'NAFTA' that will include China."

20 CENSORED

U.S. Alone in Blocking Export Ban of Toxic Waste to Third World

Source:
COUNTERPUNCH
Date: March 15, 1996
Title: "The Poison Trade"
Authors: Ken Silverstein and
    Alexander Cockburn

Last September, representatives from 84 countries gathered in Geneva for the Basel Convention. Their purpose was to pass an international ban which would put an end to the exporting of toxic wastes into poorer countries by the twenty-four wealthy nations in the Organization for Economic Cooperation and Development (OECD). These rich nations generate 98 percent of the 400 million tons of toxic waste produced each year, most of which comes from European and American corporations that eagerly ship their hazardous by-products to Africa, Asia, Latin America, and the Caribbean. The United States is the only OECD country that refuses to support such a ban.

In 1994, President Clinton supported a ban on hazardous waste exports, but at last year's Basel convention his Administration sent representatives to lobby *against* the ban. Rafe Pomerance, U.S. Deputy Assistant Secretary of State felt that such a ban, "would discourage recycling." U.S. industries protested the ban, advancing the argument that Third World countries should be given an 'opportunity' to import, process, and repackage hazardous waste produced by First World corporations. The U.S. Chamber of Commerce has urged the U.S. Government to meet with non-OECD countries to convince them that it would be in their economies' best interest to support free trade in toxins.

The problem with relying on other countries to dispose of or recycle these toxins is that they often do not have adequate facilities to do so in a safe manner. This has already led to negative environmental and health problems. Recently Greenpeace produced a video, "Slow-Motion Bhopal: Toxic Waste Exports to India." Among many disturbing practices the Greenpeace video documents are car batteries and zinc ash which are sent to the Bharat Zinc plant in Bhopal, India where they are melted down and remolded into metal containers and other products that are sold to Indian consumers. Greenpeace also showed dangerous working conditions for the employees, many of whom are children. They wade barefoot without masks or gloves through a toxic dumpyard, inhaling lead at 100 times the level tolerated in the West. Tests of soil near the site disclosed severe lead contamination and poisons leaching into surrounding surface and ground water. Larry Summers of the Treasury Department wrote in a memo that it was quite sensible to locate toxic operations in the Third World, because a lower life expectancy in those countries kills off workers before cancers caused by toxins have time to kick in.

SSU Censored Researchers:
Anne Stalder
Lisa Zwirner

21 CENSORED

Inside INS Detention Centers: Racism, Abuse, and No Accountability

Source:
COVERTACTION QUARTERLY
Date: Summer 1996
Title: "Behind the Razor Wire:
Inside INS Detention Centers"
Author: Mark Dow

With the overpopulation of undocumented immigrants, those in the custody of the Department of Justice's Immigration and Naturalization Service (INS) are now being widely transferred to local jails across the country. This transferring of prisoners has not only become a means of reducing the size of immigrants in the INS's nine service processing centers, but it has also become an abusive and frequently lucrative business.

The immigrants are not only being held in contract facilities operated by such private security firms as Wackenhut Inc. and Corrections Corporation of America, but also in some 900 local jails across the country. INS claims that the transfers are due to overcrowded situations in its detention centers, but detainees claim that transfers are used as a form of intimidation and punishment.

"Detention-for-profit" is also another issue. Some local governments have been paid as much as $2 million to hold the detained. Local jails and corrections companies have been projecting profits from INS contracts. Employment has also been created out of the influx of transfers. Louisiana's Oakdale Detention Center, one of the largest INS detention facilities in the country, was created and widely supported by local officials and citizens to replace jobs when the town's paper mill closed down. Conversely, detainees are also being considered by the Defense Department for use as a form of cheap and controlled labor.

Detainees are frequently subjected to verbal and physical abuse. The abuse is often undocumented and not investigated. In 1995, the INS finally issued a report admitting that it should have had more oversight of its Esmor facility—which was a contract facility that was closed down after an uprising by detainees protesting inhumane conditions, indefinite detention, and guard brutality. And while this self-criticism by the INS was welcomed, it has for years ignored similar complaints of mistreatment in its facilities.

Racism and a lack of accountability are also present, with discrimination extending to whistle-blowing INS officers who try to help. The Krome North Service Processing Center, an isolated INS detention facility at the edge of the Everglades in Miami, has a particularly notorious history of brutality and is the site of hostile activity against Africans.

Watchdog agencies have done little to remedy the situation. The Justice Department's own watchdog agency, the Office of Inspector General (OIG), lacks both the resources and independence according to Human Rights Watch/America. Many of the OIG investigators were either Border Patrol or INS agents. Some 1,300 complaints against INS officers to the Justice Department have yielded only nine prosecutions, six guilty pleas, and one conviction.

SSU Censored Researchers:
Tina Barni
Meiko Takechi

COMMENTS: "Last year, the media did, of course, devote a lot of coverage to the 'issue' of immigration," says author Mark Dow. "But according to the terms of the debate, both 'pro' and 'con' tend to share a view of immigrants as somehow *alien*. Being a notch below humanity, they easily become invisible victims. That's theoretical; on a more practical level, I think it is simply hard for many people—including, in my experience, reporters—to believe that our government effectively sanctions the kinds of abuse I have tried to document. Also, the victims in these cases often fear speaking out, since they remain at the mercy of the system and the individuals who have abused them. Sometimes they have attorneys to speak for them; often they do not. So, in the limited coverage this issue does receive, the spokespeople for the abusive system (in this case the INS) usually get the last word."

Dow believes wider media exposure of this subject would "first of all, help potential victims. The public, if informed, would have the opportunity to respond one way or the other. I believe that if the issue were covered honestly, then public opinion would increase the protection of those in INS custody, however slightly. As Tony Ebibillo, a Nigerian who was beaten and forcibly tranquilized by Miami INS officials, put it several years ago, 'I am quite sure that everybody will agree with me that despite the fact that I was residing here illegally, I still have the right to be treated humanely.'

"In June 1996, the Office of the Inspector General issued a report entitled *Alleged Deception of Congress*. Interestingly, the report was released to Congress, but not to the public. The report details the elaborate efforts of Miami INS officials to deceive a visiting congressional delegation about the Miami INS operations, including the dangerous overcrowding of the Krome detention center (see my 'Deception, Dehumanization and the INS,' *Haiti Progrés*, July 24-August 7, 1996).

"This deception received national media attention. In its aftermath, officials seem determined to make cosmetic changes to the local detention center. Reporters and activists have been allowed into Krome—a sure sign that the INS has something to sell. Time will tell how substantive the changes are. If Krome is indeed made more efficient, living conditions may improve for detainees—a welcome change. But one should not lose sight of the bigger picture: more and more immigrants are being detained and the privatization of detention continues to grow. Streamlining the INS detention machine—what a Pennsylvania attorney has termed a gulag—means the likelihood of even less (if that's possible) meaningful oversight of what goes on inside the INS detention centers.

"In October and November 1996, a group of Indian Sikhs seeking political asylum went on a month-long hunger strike, beginning in a county jail in the Florida panhandle, and ending at the Krome detention center in Miami. INS officials met with the strikers and apparently convinced them that their cases would be fairly reviewed. The 'detainees,' as usual, have little recourse, particularly given the new, increasingly repressive immigration laws signed by President Clinton. They can only hope for the best," says Dow.

According to Dow, his article in *CovertAction Quarterly* was used by attorneys in Pennsylvania to help raise money for a pro bono legal project for representing detained Chinese refugees, and the Amnesty International Refugee Office in San Francisco has used it as an educational tool.

22 CENSORED

The Refrigerator Revolution and Repairing the Ozone Layer

Source:
WORLD WATCH
Date: September/October 1996
Title: "The Refrigerator Revolution"
Authors: Ed Ayres and Hilary French

WORLD WATCH
Date: January/February 1996
Title: "Ozone Repair"
Author: Chris Bright

While other countries have been using other environmentally safe chemicals as alternatives to ozone-depleting chlorofluorocarbons (CFCs), the United States is using chemicals that are still threatening the ozone.

The global refrigerator business and the chemical industry that supplies it have grown to be multi-billion-dollar manufacturing industries in the United States, and it is largely because they are investing money in hydrochlorofluorocarbons (HCFCs) and hydrofluorocarbons (HFCs) as alternatives to CFCs.

CFC gases that are commonly used in refrigerators and air-conditioners are set to be banned because they damage the ozone. Since the ratification of the Montreal Protocol, the international agreement signed in 1987 to phase out the production of CFCs, the use of CFCs has fallen more than 75 percent from its 1988 peak of 1,260,000 tons to 295 tons in 1994. In Europe, chemical compounds known as hydrocarbons (HCs) are being extensively marketed and used as a replacement for CFCs. The advantages of HCs are that they are both ozone-friendly and have minimal impact on greenhouse gases (they are made from propane and butane and are unpatentable). There are over 5 million HC refrigerators now in use all over the globe.

In the United States, however, chemical manufacturers have invested their money in HCFCs and HFCs as alternatives to CFCs. They are ozone-friendlier than CFCs, but are also notorious greenhouse gases, which means they contribute to the pressing global threat of climate change. Perhaps most significantly, however, these combinations are *patentable* and companies like Dupont expect to make huge profits from them. Additionally, HCFCs and HFCs break down more rapidly and

are about as harmful as CFCs over the short term. Because of their poor environmental impact, HFCs and HCFCs are poor substitutes for CFCs and are due to be discontinued in 10 years, which will render all the new HFC refrigerators now being made in the United States obsolete.

In their recent book, *Mending the Ozone Hole* (Massachusetts Institute of Technology Press), authors Arjun Makhijani and Kevin Gurney argue that it is technically possible to heal the ozone layer in about 35 years. However, because of HCFC and HFC production in the United States, unnecessary additional stress is being placed upon the ozone layer, and reliance on these chemicals are delaying ozone repair.

SSU Censored Researchers:
Aaron Butler
Meiko Takechi
Deborah Udall

COMMENTS: Ed Ayres and Hilary French of the World Watch Institute co-authored "The Refrigerator Revolution." As far as they know, the issue of ozone-friendly replacement chemicals "has received virtually no attention from the mass media. That may be partly due to a kind of mental compartmentalization: the people who were mobilizing to cope with ozone depletion—the widening of the ozone hole—were so focused on reducing the huge quantities of CFCs being released into the atmosphere that they ignored the dangers of chemicals being prepared to replace them." When new ozone-friendly hydrocarbon technology came along, "the media were thrown off by a disinformation campaign in which the conventional refrigerator manufacturers used scare tactics to try to kill off the new market."

Ayres and French believe the general public could create a demand for the new technology just as the Europeans have, if it was aware that "the new 'CFC-free' refrigerators and air conditioners still contain other ozone-destroying chemicals and highly potent greenhouse gases, *but* that a newer technology being used in Europe is completely benign. The new market could make an important reduction *both* in the [environmental] damage being done to the Earth's radiation shield and in the accumulation of greenhouse gases that may be causing climate change."

When asked whose interests are served by the lack of media attention given to ozone-friendly replacements, the authors replied: "Refrigerator and air-conditioner manufacturers and chemical companies that bet on the wrong horse when it was time to replace CFCs now want to make sure their horse is the only one in the race....The chemical companies especially benefit by making HFC and HCFC replacements for CFCs that are patentable. We believe that these companies don't want the new, cleaner technology to prevail

because it uses a process that is in the public domain, and that they therefore can't make as much profit from it."

Chris Bright, senior editor of *World Watch*, believes the issue covered in his piece, "Ozone Repair," has not received sufficient attention by mainstream (particularly U.S. broadcast) media, due to "the difficulty that television news especially has in covering complex and long-term environmental issues, like ozone depletion. Television news likes its stories simple, short, and generally close to home," says Bright, "but I think the greatest issues of our day—issues like the loss of biodiversity or the failure to achieve environmental justice in much of the world—tend to be messy, chronic, and very diffuse."

23 CENSORED

Trouble in Mind: Chemicals and the Brain

Source:
RACHEL'S ENVIRONMENT & HEALTH WEEKLY
Date: June 20, 1996; July 4, 1996
Title: "Chemicals and the Brain, Parts I and II"
Author: Peter Montague

Scientists are discovering that chemicals in our environment are impacting our hormones and permanently changing how we live and who we are. Everyone is exposed throughout their lives to large numbers of man-made chemicals.

In a statement issued by a group of international scientists and physicians who attended a workshop in Erice, Italy, great concern was expressed regarding the effects of hormone-disrupting chemicals on the brain and the central nervous system.

Hormones are chemical messengers that travel in the bloodstream, turning on and off critical bodily functions to maintain health and well-being. Hormones control growth, development, and behavior in birds, fish, reptiles, amphibians, and mammals, including humans. Disruption of these hormones in the wombs of humans or in the eggs of wildlife may reduce intellectual capacity and social adaptability. This loss has the ability to change the character of human societies or destabilize wildlife populations.

Industrial hormone-disrupting chemicals are found in native populations from the Arctic to the tropics; and, because of their persistence in the body, can be passed from generation to generation. These synthetic chemicals are found in pesticides, plastics, shampoos, detergents, cosmetics, and other products we use in our everyday lives.

Thyroid hormones are essential for normal brain functions throughout life. Interference with thyroid hormone function during development leads to abnormalities in brain and behavioral development. Similarly, exposure to man-made chemicals during early development can result in malformations.

Because certain PCBs and dioxins are known to impair normal thyroid function, it is suspected that they contribute to learning disabilities, including hyperactivity, attention deficit disorder, and perhaps other neurological abnormalities.

According to Dr. Theo Colborn, one of the participants at the workshop, and author of a book on the subject, most research funds used for testing new chemicals concentrate on cancer and ignore other risks, like hormone disruption.

"This preoccupation with cancer," she points out in her book entitled *Our Stolen Future* (Colborn, Dr. Theo, Dianne Dumanoski, and John Peterson Myers, Dutton, 1996), "has blinded us to evidence signaling other dangers. It has thwarted investigation of other risks that may prove equally important, not only to the health of individuals, but also to the well-being of society."

The statement ended by suggesting that a concerted effort should be undertaken to deliver this message to the public, key decision makers, and the media.

SSU Censored Researchers:
Jeffrey Fillmore
Anne Shea

COMMENTS: Peter Montague, author of "Chemicals and the Brain, Parts I and II," and editor of *Rachel's Environment & Health Weekly,* says, "As I noted in my articles, so far as I can tell, only the *Los Angeles Times* and the *Sacramento Bee* covered any part of this story. Every other media outlet seems to have ignored it.

"For the past five years, the public has been given bits of information about industrial chemicals mimicking (or otherwise obstructing) the hormone system in wildlife and humans," says Montague. "Much coverage has been devoted to the hypothesis that human sperm counts have been dropping for 50 years, presumably because male children developing in the womb are exposed to hormone-disrupting chemicals (pesticides, and so forth).

"The point of my story was that these same chemicals may be interfering with the intellectual development of children as well. I believe parents would be more concerned to learn that the IQs of their children were being diminished by chemicals than they would to learn that their sons' sperm counts might eventually be found deficient.

"It seems clear to me that the chemical manufacturers (and, in some cases, major chemical users) benefit by having this story sup-

pressed or ignored. The chemical manufacturers alone earn $170 billion per year," says Montague.

"This story will continue to develop next year. The substance for my articles was a statement issued by a group of scientists, stating their conclusion that common industrial and household chemicals may damage the brain by disrupting the hormone system. In early 1997, this same group of scientists will publish a series of peer-reviewed papers supporting what they summarized in their initial statement. At that point, it will become clear that there is considerable evidence underlying their conclusions.

"This subject raises a most fundamental issue about the way our society treats chemicals. Presently the burden of proof for the safety of chemicals lies with the general public. Chemical companies can introduce new products at will. If a company conducts a health study of a new chemical, it must supply a copy of the study to the EPA at the time it announces its plans for marketing the new chemical—but the law does not require any health studies, so few are done. About 1,000 new chemicals come into commercial use each year, and no one has to demonstrate safety prior to marketing a new chemical. The public is then exposed to the new chemical and, if the public can prove that it is being harmed, then a regulatory control process may be initiated. (In the case of pharmaceuticals, the burden of proof is reversed; the manufacturer of a new drug must demonstrate its safety and efficacy to a reasonable degree prior to marketing.) I believe the evidence that some common chemicals can interfere with our hormones will generate a national debate over the 'burden of proof' and where it should lie."

24 CENSORED

Dark Alliance: Tuna, Free Trade, and Cocaine

Source:
EARTH ISLAND JOURNAL*
Date: Summer 1996
Title: "Tuna, Free Trade, and Cocaine"
Authors: Ken Silverstein and Alexander Cockburn
*Reprint from a longer version of the same article in *Counter-Punch*.

If recent history is any guide at all, one can only conclude that President Clinton's free trade policies have been immensely valuable to drug-smuggling cartels based in Italy, Colombia, Venezuela, and Mexico. The ongoing dolphin-safe tuna debate sharply illustrates U.S. indifference to the problem of international drug trafficking. According to the Administration's own Drug Enforcement Agency (DEA), approximately 90 percent of the worldwide flow of cocaine and heroin is transported and maintained by fishing fleets—with Mexico as one of the most successful traffickers.

By the late 1980s, the Mexican fleet, with 70 big boats, dominated smuggling operations. The country's boats and canneries were privatized—with tuna industry shares divided up between prominent Mexicans in the ruling PRI party.

In the early 1990s, legislation for dolphin-safe standards on tuna fishing closed the lucrative U.S. and western European tuna markets to Mexican, Venezuelan, and Colombian fleets that continued to use the outlawed "purse-seine net" technique. As a result, the Mexican fleet began to shrink, thus limiting their overall smuggling capacity. In the fall of 1995, Mexican President Ernesto Zedillo came to Washington for talks with President Clinton. During these talks, Zedillo raised the specter of a World Trade Organization complaint about the Mexican tuna ban. President Clinton assured him that U.S. domestic legislation would solve the problem more prudently.

On May 8, 1996, the Clinton Administration's legislative reversal of the ban cleared the House Resource Committee. With this passing, the Mexican tuna fleet, owned by narcotraffickers and high-ranking Mexican officials, is expected, once again, to expand.

As critics of the Clinton Administration's policy have noted, Mexico has become so dependent on the hard currency it receives from drug trafficking that any significant crackdown on its narcotics cartels would jeopardize economic recovery, and further deterioration of Mexico's economy would hurt NAFTA, destabilize Mexican politics, and increase immigration.

Today, with the help of NAFTA and tuna boat drug smuggling, Mexico has become one of the most important countries of legal trade—and illegal drug trafficking—across the U.S. border. And the free trade agreements will continue to be a boon for the world's drug smuggling cartels because of the relaxed inspection of commercial cross-border traffic between Mexico and the U.S. In addition, liberalized international banking rules have made it easier to launder billions in drug revenues.

SSU Censored Researchers:
Diane Ferré
Doug Hecker
Kevin Stickler
Lisa Zwirner

25 CENSORED

The Truth About "Inert" Chemicals

Sources:
RACHEL'S ENVIRONMENT AND
  HEALTH WEEKLY
Date: November 23, 1995
Title: "Many Pesticides, Little
  Knowledge"
Author: Peter Montague

EARTH ISLAND JOURNAL
Date: Fall 1996
Title: "The Truth About Inerts"
Author: Charmaine Oakley

The *American Heritage Dictionary* defines "inert" as "Not readily reactive with other elements." This does not necessarily describe chemicals such as sulfuric acid or kerosene. However, a 1972 law allows household pesticide manufacturers to include these chemicals as "inert" ingredients in their products without revealing their presence to consumers.

There are over 20,000 different household pesticide products. These pesticides contain over 300 active ingredients and up to 2,300 inert ingredients. However, in accordance with the Federal Insecticide, Fungicide, and Rodenticide Act (FIFRA) which prohibits disclosure of "secret" pesticide formulas, inert ingredients are not listed on product labels—ostensibly, to protect manufacturing secrets. While up to 99 percent of a household pesticide may be considered "inert" only the active ingredients are listed on the product label and regulated by law. In actual practice, pesticide manufacturers decide what to call inert and what to designate as an active ingredient subject to Environmental Protection Agency (EPA) regulation. This has produced a situation where ingredients in some pesticide products are considered active and regulated by the EPA, but in other pesticide products are unregulated, inert ingredients missing from the label.

The truth is: Most "inerts" are not inert. They are biologically, chemically, and toxicologically active. Many inerts are in fact more toxic than the active ingredients. A 1991 EPA report lists over 1,400 of the inert ingredients used in housed pesticides as either potentially toxic, toxic, or of unknown toxicity. These "inert" ingredients of unknown toxicity include chemicals and compounds such as epoxy resin, malathion, kerosene, and sulfuric acid. One category of solvents known as xylenes, an "inert" ingredient in as many as 2,000 pesticides, is linked to increased frequency of leukemia in workers and may cause memory and hearing loss, liver and kidney damage, eye irritation, inflamed lungs, low birth weight, and even fetal death.

Evaluating the toxicity of inert ingredients has low priority at the EPA, receiving less than 1 percent of the pesticide program's budget, and has no specific procedure or time frames for review.

While the reason given for withholding information on inerts of pesticides is supposedly to protect manufacturing secrets, Louise Mehler, Program Director of the California EPA's Worker Pesticide Illness Surveillance Program, states, "The chemists here say that since the invention of the mass spectrometer, anybody who wants [to find out the ingredients] can really find out."

The secrecy surrounding so-called inerts highlights the duplicity of a pesticide policy that claims to protect public health, while actually safeguarding private economic interests.

SSU Censored Researcher: Jeffrey Fillmore

COMMENTS: Peter Montague, author of "Many Pesticides, Little Knowledge," and editor of *Rachel's Environment & Health Weekly*, wrote his article about the lack of knowledge surrounding "inert" ingredients in pesticides. "So far as I know," he says, "this story received no coverage in the mass media. Even when a federal court in the District of Columbia ruled in October 1996, that the EPA had improperly denied information to the public about 'inert' pesticide ingredients, the story was ignored.

"If the truth about 'inerts' were told in the mass media, people might organize to force full disclosure of inerts. The resulting knowledge might fuel greater concern for the danger of pesticides."

According to Montague, the pesticide industry benefits from the lack of media attention given to the existence of "inert" chemicals. The food industry benefits secondarily, he says. "It is principally the pesticide industry that benefits because the food industry would adjust if the use of pesticidal chemicals diminished substantially. The pesticide industry is a $29 billion per year enterprise, dominated by six chemical giants," he notes.

"If the general public knew that the safety of multiple pesticides in food couldn't be established scientifically by governments, many members of the public might think twice about accepting pesticide-laden food as the norm. They might even make an extra effort to seek out minimally-contaminated food, such as 'organically grown' produce and meat."

As for recent developments concerning disclosure of "inert" substances, Montague points to the implications of the federal court's decision. "After the federal court ruling on October 11, 1996, the American Crop Protection Association (a trade group for the pesticide industry) asked the judge to review the deci-

sion, which the judge did. The decision was sustained. However, this was not a sweeping decision, as some environmentalists have claimed. The decision said that the EPA cannot make a blanket policy against the disclosure of inerts, but must treat each pesticide on a case-by-case basis. Former EPA official James Chem told *Pesticide and Toxic Chemical News* (November 6, 1996), 'The...case has placed a crack in the wall of confidentiality surrounding confidential statements of formula.' Nevertheless, the wall of confidentiality remains," says Montague.

According to Charmaine Oakley, author of "The Truth About Inerts," "The mainstream media is skittish about pesticide issues in general— and out-and-out criticisms of the pesticide industry in particular. The idea that pesticide labels do not adequately inform consumers of a product's ingredients or associated risks cuts against the whole mainstream mentality that nothing *really* harmful is on the market. To report that, yes, big business values money over health and, no, the EPA doesn't test a majority of pesticide ingredients would open a big can of worms.

"The public needs to know that chemicals designed for household use are poisons and are not indisputably safe...pesticide labels do not tell the whole story...that, in fact, they are lying by omission. More consumer skepticism about pesticides could save lives. Alternatives are available, and health concerns can motivate the public to action—exactly what the chemical industry doesn't want.

"After *Earth Island Journal* published my story, the NCAP/EPA trial came to a close. The court ruled that inerts are not exempt from Freedom of Information Act requests. When someone asks what a pesticide's ingredients are, the EPA is required to list them. This historic ruling significantly expands the public's right-to-know (if the public finds out about the ruling). I haven't seen any mass media exposure of the trial's favorable conclusion," says Oakley.

COMMENTS BY PROJECT CENSORED JUDGES

CARL JENSEN founded Project Censored in 1976 in an effort to determine whether certain issues were systematically omitted by the nation's news media. With the help of students in a small media censorship seminar, he sought to explore and publicize such under-reported news stories in an effort to stimulate journalists and editors to provide more coverage of important issues, and to encourage the public to seek out alternative sources of information. After twenty years as director, Jensen retired in 1996, but he currently serves as a Project Censored judge. He had this to say about this year's selection of "censored" stories:

"It's hard to believe that as Project Censored starts its third decade there are still so many critical issues not reaching the public. In fact, even some of the issues originally raised in 1976—including selling banned pesticides, and drugs to Third World countries, inadequate nuclear reactor safeguards, and dangerous non-prescription drugs—continue to be overlooked to this day.

"The censored nominations of 1996 reveal corporate imperialism by Shell Oil, environmental degradation of the ozone, threats to our economy by mega-bank mergers, dangers to our health by 'inert' chemicals and milk additives, and continued subservience to the plutocracy with bigger and better tax loopholes for the wealthy.

"If even a modicum of the media coverage given to the third year of the O.J. phenomenon were devoted to any of these issues, we would see an outraged public forcing an embarrassed Congress to take steps to correct the problem.

"As newspaper circulation figures and network news ratings continue to decline one has to wonder when the media will recognize the public wants more hard news and less junk food news," said Jensen.

BEN BAGDIKIAN, author and former dean of the Graduate School of Journalism, University of California, Berkeley, has served as a Project Censored judge since 1976 (though he refrained from voting during years when his own work was under consideration for the "Top *Censored* News Stories" list). Regarding this year's selections, he said, "I think that the panel's nominating a large portion of underplayed stories about anti-social corporate activity is a wise choice. The uninhibited free market attitude in governmental, corporate, and media emphasis, is creating large-scale public health problems and jeopardizing the financial security of ordinary workers.

"That is the basic reason I chose the failure of the Department of Justice to prosecute white-collar crime at a time when TV news and Page One headlines stress all other crimes. Many of the other ills identified in the 25 nominations this year flow out of the failure to hold corporate media accountable for its anti-social and illegal activity," said Bagdikian.

JACK NELSON, Rutgers University professor and Censored judge since 1976, said, "This year I was more impressed (depressed) with censored stories within the U.S. than by global stories. It may be the recent media emphasis on serious problems in Bosnia, Middle East, Africa, etc., and the resulting lack of coverage of significant U.S. issues. The choice for numbers 1, 2, and 3 are always difficult because the stories are so significant and so little known."

SHEILA RABB WEIDENFELD, president of D.C. Productions Ltd., and Censored judge since 1976, said, "Once again, Project Censored shines a light in the dark corners of journalistic complacency. The media establishment runs after the same stories while great reporting is consigned to outlets most of us never see.

"Take the Gulf War Syndrome. We know the government knew more than it admitted about the continuing health problems of Gulf War veterans. Evidence of other disregard for the health of our soldiers is found in the story on the use of depleted uranium during the Gulf War.

"Another example of significant, but unknown, investigative journalism is the *CounterPunch* report on the unholy combination of tuna fishing, free trade, and cocaine. This insight into the relationship between the availability of drugs and NAFTA deserves the attention that often accompanies recognition by Project Censored.

"In this era where pack journalists are employed by media conglomerates, alternative media fills the vital need for true investigative reporting. By definition, alternative journals don't receive much attention from the major outlets, and their important stories would be lost without organizations like Project Censored."

RHODA H. KARPATKIN, president of Consumers Union of the U.S., non-profit publisher of *Consumer Reports*, said, "Several of this year's nominated stories highlight efforts to silence activists and public interest groups. In effect, this represents a form of double censorship. Alternative points of view are discouraged and suppressed at their source, greatly diminishing the possibility that these perspectives can appear in news stories. We see this trend in efforts to silence environmental activists in developing countries, and in the sophisticated public relations campaigns to discredit public interest organizations in the U.S.

"Another example of this trend are the so-called 'food disparagement' laws. Growers associations, pesticide manufacturers, and conservative activists have rallied to create 'food slander' laws in a dozen states. From a consumer point of view, these laws are very troubling. Most of them contain provisions that seem clearly designed to intimidate scientists and public interest groups from highlighting current and potential threats to the food supply, and to punish them if they do so.

"It's essential for consumers that the media report a variety of views on issues such as the environment and food and product safety, so these issues can be openly discussed, and all points of view heard and considered," said Karpatkin.

SUSAN FALUDI, journalist, said, "It's stunning how many stories of literally catastrophic and global consequence are being ignored—nuclear proliferation in space, a worldwide food-supply crisis looming, worldwide financial trades with devastating potential. And how *many* important stories go uncovered; it was difficult to choose from the selection of censored stories this year. They were *all* important. Perhaps this expansion in *un*-coverage is related to that other uncovered story which made it to the *Censored* list twice this year: the ever-rising power and sophistication of public relations institutions to conceal criminal behavior and launder the dirtiest corporate and governmental secrets."

FRANCES MOORE LAPPÉ, co-director of the Center for Living Democracy, said, "I am struck especially by revelations about maneuvers that limit citizens' right to speak out—and therefore fundamentally undercut our democracy. I also found particularly alarming the number of actions these stories expose that fundamentally threaten our health and planet's integrity. I hope that this year's *Censored* stories get significant exposure as a result of your efforts.

"I am continually dismayed by the smaller and smaller slice of reality that mainstream news chooses to cover, all the while claiming that they don't make choices at all but only 'report the news'!"

WILLIAM LUTZ, professor of English at Rutgers University, said, "More and more, the news delivered to us by the major news media is not the news. As news becomes more like entertainment, the more it loses to other forms of entertainment. Perhaps newspaper readership is down because people don't find the news in newspapers anymore. Perhaps people realize that what newspapers offer is not relevant to their lives. As these stories demonstrate, there is plenty of news that is relevant to our lives, but it is ignored by the news media. If the news media would stop trying to entertain and start informing, perhaps people would see newspapers and all the news media as important to their lives, and to the health and well-being of society as a whole.

"Thomas Jefferson did not advocate a free press that would entertain but a free press that would inform. Project Censored each year tries to remind the press and the news media of that simple but powerful fact."

HERBERT SCHILLER, professor emeritus of communication, University of California, San Diego, said, "I am surprised that there were no entries that commented on the void in substantive issues in the 1996 presidential campaign. Neither candidate mentioned, much less criticized the transnational corporate order which is imposing the harshest measures on working people in countries around the world.

"Relatedly, the issue of the 'balanced budget'—a favorite of the transnational corporate order—is a recipe for further starving the social sector. Didn't anyone mention this looming disaster?" asked Schiller.

JULIANNE MALVEAUX, an economist and syndicated columnist, commented on this year's nominations: "There are a set of new events that rivet our attention, and a set of subtle forces that, in buttressing the status quo, affect the quality of our lives. It is easier for editors to feature that which is riveting than that which is substantive, and as a result, we have missed that slice of news that speaks of economic relations, hidden aspects of legislation, international oppression, and the secret war on activists.

"Too many people are tempted to say 'nonsense' when they read that the CIA may be responsible for the proliferation of crack cocaine in African-American communities. But the nominations for the best censored stories of 1996 reveal that those who conspire to keep wealth in just a few hands don't have to hold mentions with minutes and motions. All they have to do is to appeal to sympathetic legislators (it's called 'follow the money') to make protections for multinationals the price of a minimum wage increase. All they have to do is manufacture a teen drug crisis to divert attention from more pressing issues. All they have to do is make fact seem so fantastic that it is generally dismissed.

"So while Shell Oil has its fingerprints on the massacre of Ken Saro-Wiwa and the Ogoni Nine, and while pawn shops, finance companies, and check-cashing outlets profit from poverty, some of our major news outlets routinely headline the toe-sucking shenanigans of political operatives. That is why the work of Project Censored is so important, and why 'the news that didn't make the news' makes a real difference in our lives."

DONNA ALLEN, founding editor of *Media Report to Women*, said, "I judge by this year's nominations that what the mass media are not writing about the most, is that the nation is facing, without adequate information, two major threats: to our *physical* health and our *economic* health; 1) dangerous pollution in many forms from nuclear waste and uranium to chemicals, and even in our milk; and 2) dangerous economic trends that are shifting income upward, through bank mergers and derivatives, robbing the poor when needing to cash their meager checks, even to loading the minimum wage bill with big perks for the already wealthy.

"But we need more attention on the media themselves and their monopoly power to not report these threats—and especially with the increasing concentration in the new electronic media. And worse, these behemoths are now increasingly moving into content and programming as well as control of the technology."

MICHAEL PARENTI, author and lecturer, said, "Once more the mainstream corporate-owned media have stuck to their two basic operating principals:

1. No puffery is too trivial as to be denied lavish and fulsome treatment.

2. No vital issue is too momentous not to be ignored and suppressed, especially if it discomforts those who wield politico-economic power.

"As in previous years, the Project Censored selections for 1996 are weighted toward environmental and consumer interests, the abuses of individual corporations, and the delinquency and complicity of particular government agencies and departments—all important realities. However, along with *specific stories* that are suppressed, Project Censored might want to consider *whole subject areas* that are ignored or grossly misrepresented.

THE TOP 25 CENSORED NEWS STORIES OF 1996 **95**

"Thus, there are many stories in the media about NAFTA and GATT, but hardly a mention of how such international agreements undermine the democratic sovereignty of all signatory nations and hand over supernational power to an unaccountable international corporate oligarchy...

"Another example: For decades the mainstream (i.e., corporate-owned) media have suppressed any discussion about the goals and interests of U.S. foreign policy and the U.S. national security state. Why does the United States support so many suppressive right-wing governments that engage in death squads and mass killings? Why does the U.S. government seem not much concerned about human rights in those countries? Why does it show perpetual concern for human rights only in Cuba and a few remaining Marxist countries? Why has the U.S. national security state actively waged wars to overthrow democratically-elected governments as in Chile (1973), Guatemala (1956), Greece (1967), and a score of other countries.

"Another example: CIA involvement with the international drug trade has been going on for a half-century: Corsica, Sicily, Indochina, Afghanistan, Central and South America. It has been a matter of public record for over twenty years, a focus of investigation by *three* congressional investigations (the Church committee, the Pike committee, and the Kerry committee). Yet the story was ridiculed and the evidence supporting it was suppressed by the media. *Newsweek* called Senator Kerry 'a randy conspiracy buff.' But recently, when the story could no longer be ignored, when Gary Webb's *San Jose Mercury News* series got out across the world on the Internet, then the major media launched an all-out disinformation war against the investigation. There should be a way that Project Censored could bring a panel judgment upon this kind of concerted media disinformation campaign.

"To change the subject: One of the censored stories I selected as among the most important was entitled 'White-Collar Crime: Whitewash at the Justice Department.' I think we should drop the term 'white-collar crime,' for it conjures up an image of a white-collar worker embezzling funds. Instead, it should be called what it is: 'corporate crime,'" said Parenti.

HOLLY SKLAR, author and new Project Censored judge, said, "This year's nominations tell us about significant threats to health, safety, and privacy, and warn us about efforts to further curtail consumer protection, labor organizing, and civil liberties. They expose corporate crime and propose a new way to measure our economy.

"Project Censored not only spotlights the stories we need to know about, it challenges us to work every angle we can to get stories out in a timely fashion and democratize the media over the long run. So much more can be done to create a rippling effect among all forms of alternative media (print, broadcast, electronic) and between alternative and mainstream media. For example, journalists who write primarily for alternative media should try, and try again, to also place articles in mainstream media, including through the op-ed pages (the Progressive Media Project, for example, has had great success in distributing op-eds). Those with mainstream access should do as much as possible to cover important stories and highlight good sources. We need more people to call in to talk shows, write letters to the editor (praising pieces you like, as well as critiquing what you don't); do reviews; suggest library, newsstand, and bookstore selections; and join discussions and publicize stories and resources on the Internet.

"Many stories are buried because of media bias. Many other stories that might have had much wider circulation are never seriously promoted. Social change organizations must make media and public relations work a priority. Right-wing organizations like the Heritage Foundation systematically pitch their stories and spokespeople every day to reporters, editors, and talk show bookers, and promote them widely through the Internet. They respond promptly to requests for information and interviews. We must make sure we are never censoring ourselves with unreasonably low expectations, narrow strategies, poor media practices, and unnecessarily limited media resources. The more doors we open today, the more doors we will be able to open tomorrow," said Sklar.

BARBARA SEAMAN, author and lecturer, and a new Project Censored judge, said, "I am delighted to have 'discovered' *CovertAction Quarterly*, a publication of which, I am ashamed to say, I had not really been aware. Of its several outstanding nominations, I vote for 'The Public Relations Industry's Secret War on Activists' as a resounding first-place choice—magnificently documented—the term in it that haunts me is 'controlling the debate...' This is exactly what I have experienced in my own efforts to speak out on the downside of bovine growth hormones, new contraceptives such as Norplant, hormonal menopausal treatment. (Indeed, I wrote about this in 1994, in my foreword to a book called *The Menopause Industry* by Sandra Coney.) It's also very sad that in the women's health movement, some of the most respected grass-roots consumer groups have recently gone 'astro turf.' That is, they took large sums of money from industry and changed their agenda, just as described in the Stauber/Rampton article. This is apparent with OWL (Older Women's League), which is now a PR arm of Merck, pushing its new osteoporosis drug, and Y-Me, a breast cancer organization, taking money from Dow and defending its breast implants. Many of the other issues described in nominated articles have been minimized, distorted, or concealed through exactly the kinds of activities described in 'Secret War,' so I perceive this article as the 'fountainhead' among this year's candidates," said Seaman.

CHAPTER 2

Censoring the Telecoms Debate

By Mark Lowenthal

In reverential terms mirrored by most of the nation's major news outlets, the *San Francisco Chronicle* described the Telecommunications Act of 1996, or Telecoms bill, as "the most significant accomplishment of a Congress that for more than a year has wrestled over budget issues with little concrete result" (February 2, 1996). Indeed, *The New York Times* flatly proclaimed it "sound telecommunications policy" (February 9, 1996). Most news accounts also included understated quotes from politicians like Republican Congressman Billy Tauzin ("This is a grand celebration of the free-market system") and executives like Pacific Telesis CEO Paul Quigley ("This is the most important legislation, I believe, in the history of this country").

Virtually ignored in mainstream news coverage, however, were the provisions that posed the greatest threat to the public interest.

The bipartisan "reform" bill extended the current duration of broadcast licenses granted to local stations from five to ten years (later reduced to eight), making the current license renewal process even easier for broadcasters. This provision makes it far more difficult for civic groups or individuals to challenge the licenses of even the most irresponsible broadcasters—the only legal means by which citizens can ensure broadcaster accountability over the *public* airwaves.

The bill also removed all numerical limits on television and radio station ownership, meaning that one individual or company can own an *unlimited* number of television and radio stations—including up to eight radio stations in the same market. For the first time in history, one company can now own radio, and network and cable television stations—*all in the same market.*

Perhaps most disturbingly, the Telecoms bill raised the national "audience cap" to 35 percent, meaning that all news media in the entire country could be controlled by a handful of companies or individuals.

Most citizens knew nothing of these provisions.

Instead, the press emphasized the bill's supposed benefits—new jobs, lower prices, and increased competition.

"We've got economic studies, conducted by the best, that show that nationally this legislation is going to account for 3 million new jobs," boasted Pacific Telesis CEO Quigley (*San Francisco Chronicle*, February 2, 1996). But within just a few months came the news of communications giant AT&T *slashing* 40,000 jobs and Pacific Bell cutting another 10,000. And in the wake of subsequent mergers announced since the Telecoms bill's signing, such as that of Bell Atlantic and NYNEX, the two companies have already announced plans to eliminate 3,000 jobs—not counting the 5,000 jobs scheduled to be cut as the last phase of NYNEX's preexisting two-year-old program to cut 17,000 positions. And in another test of the post-Telecoms bill "job creation" thesis, industry analysts are estimating that 1,200 jobs will disappear due to the pending Time Warner-Turner Broadcasting merger (*The Commercial Appeal*, October 11, 1996).

Perhaps the most tangible gain to consumers that was anticipated from the Telecoms bill was that of cable and phone rate reduction. And yet there was no such provision anywhere in the bill. The rate reductions promised by proponents of the bill were *expected* rate reductions which, the logic went, would result from increased competition. Ironically, prior to passage of the bill the public enjoyed legally enforced price reduction and cost control as mandated by the Cable Rate Reduction Act of 1992. But the Telecommunications Act of 1996 eliminated the Cable Rate Reduction Act.

As for increased competition, while it is true that the Telecoms bill will create intense competition, it will do so only between the very few giants at the top—while the overwhelming majority of other players are put at risk and rendered unable to compete. Wiping out 90 percent of the marketplace—including most *independent* voices—while leaving a literal handful of corporate behemoths, can hardly be called enhanced competition.

Quite predictably, the passage of the Telecommunications Act set off a mind-boggling wave of media company mergers and acquisitions. Yet the frenetic pace of the feeding frenzy—and particularly the enormity of the transactions—seemed to take everyone except Wall Street stock analysts by surprise.

In roughly chronological order, here's how it went:

Jumping out of the blocks two days *before* President Clinton officially signed the landmark Telecoms bill into law, Jacor Communications Inc. announced that it was acquiring the Noble Broadcast Group Inc. for $152 million. The acquisition boosted Jacor to be the fifth-largest radio company in the U.S.—a position the restless company held for all of eight days before buying Citicasters Inc. in a deal worth $770 million.

The acquisition of Citicasters added 19 stations, which gave Jacor a total of 54—making it the largest owner of radio stations in the country. And thanks to the freshly signed Telecoms bill, Jacor's radio properties include six stations in Cincinnati and eight in Denver—which means that Jacor now controls what is estimated to be *over half* of the total advertising dollars spent on radio in both cities (*The New York Times*, February 14, 1996).

Also wasting little time was baby bell US West, which less than three weeks after the enactment of the landmark deregulation bill, swallowed up the country's third-largest cable television company, Continental Cablevision, Inc. for a cool $5.3 billion.

The next major merger occurred on the perhaps fittingly perverse date of April 1 when SBS Communications Inc. spent $16.7 billion to acquire the California-based Pacific Telesis Group (PacTel), creating a new company with $21 billion in combined annual revenues and more than 100,000 employees (though analysts say subsequent layoffs are inevitable).

The splashy SBS/PacTel merger was upstaged a mere 21 days later, when Bell Atlantic Corporation announced that it was taking over the NYNEX Corporation in a deal worth $22 billion—the second-largest takeover in U.S. history. The newly combined company became the country's second-largest phone company, accounting for a third of the nation's long-distance volume.

On June 21, things began heating up on the radio and television front, when radio giant Westinghouse Electric (number one, nationally, in radio revenue) acquired radio giant Infinity Broadcasting (number two in radio revenue) for $4.23 billion.

In terms of radio, the newly-formed colossus is now three times larger than its closest competitor, commanding nearly a third of all U.S. radio advertising revenue (based on 1995 expenditures). With its acquisition, Westinghouse now owns more than 80 stations with combined annual revenues of about $1 billion, including 10 in both Chicago and Dallas, eight in San Francisco, seven in New York, and six each in Los Angeles, Philadelphia, Boston, Houston, and Detroit.

Aside from now being the nation's largest radio broadcaster, Westinghouse, with 16 television stations reaching one third of the national audience, is also the country's largest television broadcaster...well, *was* the country's largest television broadcaster.

A mere month later, the Tribune company (owners of the *Chicago Tribune*) paid $1.13 billion for Renaissance Communications Corp., adding six TV stations to vault over Westinghouse as the top owner of television stations in the U.S., reaching more than a third of all households (*American Journalism Review*, October 1996). Once primarily a newspaper company, Tribune now derives more than half of operating income from its television properties. But just weeks after Tribune had settled on its throne...

Rupert Murdoch dropped $2.48 billion to acquire New World Communications Group (and its 10 TV stations)—thus making Murdoch's News Corp. Ltd. the biggest owner and operator of television stations in the U.S. The purchase of New World now gives Murdoch, through his News Corp., a grand total of 22 TV stations (the most ever in U.S. history) including stations in 11 of the top 12 U.S. markets, reaching some 40 percent of all homes (*American Journalism Review*, October 1996).

Getting dizzy? Take a deep breath.

As July came to a close, the Federal Trade Commission (FTC) drove a stake through the heart of consumer and public interest advocates by approving—without a court battle—the pending $7.5 billion merger of Time Warner and Turner Broadcasting System, thus creating Time Warner-Turner, the world's largest media conglomerate with more than $20 billion in annual revenues.

Indeed, the newly-merged company is enormous. Aside from its massive publishing empire and formidable holdings in movies, recorded music, the Internet, and theme parks, Time Warner is the country's second-largest cable operator. This latter component is significant because Telecommunications International (TCI), the nation's largest cable operator, acquired a 9 percent stake in Time Warner (through its part ownership of Turner)—thus joining the country's two biggest cable operators and three of the largest owners of cable programming services.

In light of this, Federal Trade Commission staffers made an impassioned case to block the merger and were prepared to take their case to the courts.

According to the industry newsletter *Media Daily*, FTC staffers spent the better part of June "piling up more and more evidence against [Time Warner and Turner] and fine tuning their case to sway commission members" (*Media Daily*, June 27, 1996).

According to *Media Daily*, however, "Allegedly, in a series of unusual meetings, the companies [took] their case directly to a few senior officials—with no staff investigators present—to tell their side of the story."

Three weeks later, the FTC gave the merger the green light.

August saw American Radio Systems (ARS), Inc. jumping into the fray to purchase EZ Communications in August for half a billion dollars—tripling its size and ending up with a grand total of 96 stations in 20 markets across the U.S. Notably, although the transaction elevated ARS into broadcasting's upper echelon as one of the "big three" radio companies, it did not even rate a major story in the *Wall Street Journal* (*American Journalism Review*, December 1996).

In September, WorldCom Inc. devoured fellow telecoms company MFS Communications Co. Inc. in a $13.4 billion takeover; and Hughes Electronics purchased the PanAmSat Corp. for a measly $3 billion.

These acquisitions set the stage for the last blockbuster deal of the year, in which British Telecommunications (BT) surprised many by snapping up U.S. phone giant MCI in a deal worth $20.3 billion. The new company, to be called Concert, is projected to be the most profitable communications company in the world with a workforce of 183,000 and revenues (based on 1995 earnings) of $37.9 billion and projected 1996 earnings of $4.7 billion.

The sideshow to the year's mind-numbing wave of takeovers and mergers was the spectacle of media barons and huge corporate behemoths crying "antitrust!" as their competitors engaged in the same type of predatory behavior that made the whining giants...well, the whining giants that they are.

Media mogul Ted Turner attacked Westinghouse's ownership of CBS and General Electric's of NBC as "a frightening thing," (*Santa Rosa Press Democrat*, June 7, 1996). The day after the British Telecommunications-MCI merger was announced, AT&T shot off a press release calling on the Federal Communications Commission to give the merger "the scrutiny it deserves" (*USA Today*, June 21, 1996). And Rupert Murdoch filed an anti-trust suit against Time Warner after the company declined to carry Murdoch's Fox News Channel (FNC) on its New York cable system—instead opting for FNC competitor MSNBC. In its complaint, Murdoch's News Corp. called the Time Warner-Turner merger "a blueprint for the monopolization of cable television by two cable television giants" (*Communications Daily*, October 10, 1996).

So at the end of the first year of the new deregulated, post-Telecommunications Act age, where do we find ourselves?

Far from the world of an expanding media marketplace, with greater consumer choice, lower costs to consumers, and a rapidly growing job market—what we see before us is a wholly inverted snapshot of the much-hyped promised land.

At the end of the first year of the post-Telecoms act era, we see that well over $100 billion was spent on mergers and acquisitions—more than double what was spent during 1995. We can see that there are 127 fewer companies operating commercial radio stations in the United States than in 1995. And we see that in the top 50 U.S. markets an average of six companies now control 92 percent of the radio advertising revenues (*Chicago Tribune*, August 9, 1996). Welcome to the new world order.

Why is all this consolidation business so important?

Aside from undermining the traditional principal of maintaining a vibrant marketplace of ideas, a larger problem can be found in the uniform nature of the new class of media owners. As large corporations, the management teams that run them tend to think like...well, large corporations. Principles like "journalistic independence," "the public interest," and "ethnic and class diversity" tend to fade from the collective consciousness of the individual media outlets and are quickly replaced by buzzwords and concepts like "market share," "demographics," and "operating margin."

In that context, press freedoms—and the ability to gather news—are coming under increased attack. After a 1995 incident in which CBS General Counsel Ellen Oran Kaden intervened, on the basis of "tortious interference," to prevent *60 Minutes* from airing a segment in which a former Brown & Williamson employee blew the whistle on the tobacco industry, a wave of so-called "trash-torts" has surged forth—lawsuits that focus not on whether the facts of a news story are true, but rather on how the facts were gathered. A subsequent 1996 example of one such "trash-tort" involved an ABC *Prime Time Live* exposé of Food Lion (a grocery chain with more than 1,100 stores) in which a hidden-camera showed unsanitary conditions, including rat-gnawed cheese, and spoiled chicken that had been washed in bleach to mask the smell. Rather than sue for libel, a case which Food Lion most certainly would have lost, the supermarket chain instead sued ABC for fraud, trespass, and "breach of employee loyalty." In late December 1996, a federal jury ruled in favor of Food Lion.

According to journalist Alicia Shepard, some industry observers have asserted that CBS's original decision to cave in to Brown & Williamson "reflects a rise in power and a change in emphasis for media lawyers, whose role traditionally has been to help the newsroom find ways to get information printed or aired. Some say news executives appear to be relying more on their attorneys to do a cost-benefit analysis before they decide whether to run a story" (*American Journalism Review*, January/February 1996).

In the world of bookselling, consolidation by the largest chain stores also can have a chilling effect, as in-store advertising policies increasingly favor megaselling titles at the expense of independent voices. Patently anti-competitive, this system is based, in essence, on large corporate bookstore chains colluding with large corporate publishing houses to artificially manipulate the very free-trade marketplace that corporate owners so fervently champion. The net effect of such schemes clearly bodes ill for both independent book publishers and booksellers—it will (and is) driving them out of business. And it is bad for the book-buying public which will have less and less access to authors and ideas that corporate executives deem less salable or ideologically undesirable.

Corporate influence over popular culture also extends to the music industry in a frighteningly heavy-handed manner, as the rules concerning what is "acceptable" art is increasingly being defined by...once again, corporate America.

As Wal-Mart director of corporate relations Dale Ingram explained to *The New York Times* (November 13, 1996), "Producers of music know up front that Wal-Mart is not going to carry anything with a parental advisory on it, and that's something they're going to have to factor in when they produce the product." According to the *Times*, "Due to Wal-Mart's clout, record labels and bands now design new covers, drop songs, electronically mask objectionable lyrics, and even change lyrics to gain a place on Wal-Mart's shelves." Video rental chains such as Blockbuster, "whose 4,500 outlets account for 25 to 30 percent of video rentals nationwide," have similar policies, leading to the increasingly common practice (by film studios) of recutting movies for video release, often without the director's consent.

While the mainstream press touted the virtues of the Telecoms bill, several studies surfaced that contradicted those claims, including one in 1995 by *Business Week* and Mercer Management Consulting which found that half of the companies that underwent major mergers in the '90s underperformed their peers. And researchers John Ying at the University of Delaware and Richard Shin at the Federal Trade Commission, analyzing the performance of local phone companies like San Francisco-based Pacific Bell, found that many were already too big and breaking them apart "would likely produce considerable cost savings to society" (*San Francisco Chronicle*, November 11, 1996).

Perhaps the great irony of this chapter in U.S. history is that while pro-business, anti-regulatory, and free-market enthusiasts have long railed against "big government" and the inherent threat that it poses to freedom and democracy, these same voices have neglected to mention that unrestrained private power can present an equally formidable threat. Indeed, the threat posed by such private power might be even greater than that posed by "big government," for unlike our three-branch system of government, there are few mechanisms that ensure accountability over private power—*except the press*—which the rapidly consolidating private power in question now owns.

So in the end it seems that while George Orwell was right about "Big Brother," he may have had the lineage wrong. Instead of a State-controlled ministry of information, the coming "Big Brother" will represent a privatized (read: corporate) ministry of information—"Big Brother, Inc."—with guess whose interests in mind.

CHAPTER 3

Censored Déjà Vu: What Happened to Last Year's Most Censored Stories

By Peter Phillips, with research assistance by Lori Goldstein

Project Censored continually monitors mainstream media for coverage on our most censored stories from previous years. This year we have conducted a systematic review of coverage on the top ten stories of 1995 and a select group from previous years.

Project Censored's list of censored news stories seldom generates mainstream press coverage. Corporate-owned media have a vested interest in maintaining the illusion that they cover all the news that is important for U.S. citizens to know. However, we know from conversations with journalists working in mainstream media that our annual press release and this book regularly circulate in newsrooms nationwide.

While we cannot claim one hundred percent success in inspiring additional coverage on all of these important stories, we have certainly contributed to the increased awareness of these issues among the American public. Over 35 alternative press weeklies carried our list of *Censored* Stories of 1995, covering most major metropolitan areas in the U.S.; thousands of copies of *Censored 1996* were distributed in libraries and bookstores in every state, city, and town, and Project Censored staff were interviewed on over 135 radio talk shows during this past year. Numerous newspapers and national magazines also covered our stories including the *Los Angeles Times, Utne Reader, Mother Jones*, and American Library Association's *Newsletter of Intellectual Freedom.*

We have provided a brief synopsis of previous years' stories and then an update on the coverage or developments that occurred in 1996.

1995 # 1 CENSORED STORY
TELECOMMUNICATIONS DEREGULATION: CLOSING UP AMERICA'S "MARKETPLACE OF IDEAS"

The Telecommunications Deregulation Bill eliminates virtually all regulation of the United States communication industry. Pushed through Congress under the guise of 'greater competition,' the bill would in reality have the opposite effect of creating huge new concentrations of media power by dismantling current anti-trust regulations and limits on media ownership.

The legislation dismantled regulations which limit the number of radio stations that can be owned by a single company. Previously, no one single company could own more than 40 stations. The new legislation would remove the limits completely —allowing one company to own every AM and FM radio station in the United States. It also would lift the current FCC ban on joint ownership of a broadcast radio or TV license and a newspaper in the same market— allowing a single company to have 100 percent control over the three primary sources of news in a community.

THIS MODERN WORLD by TOM TOMORROW

Consumer advocate Ralph Nader warned, "Congress is moving the law in the wrong direction, toward greater concentration and fewer choices for consumers." Nader also said the predictable result of placing even greater power in the hands of fewer giant media moguls will be less diversity, more pre-packaged programming, and fewer checks on political power.

SOURCE: *Consumer Project on Technology*, July 14, 1995, "Federal Telecommunications Legislation: Impact on Media Concentration," by Ralph Nader, James Love, and Andrew Saindon; an Internet newsletter.

COVERAGE 1996: Certainly 1996 was a banner year for mega-mergers in the communications industry. The Telecommunications Act of 1996 paved the way for massive takeovers, buy-outs, and mergers. Capping the 1996 corporate monopolization of media was the Time Warner purchase of Turner Broadcasting System, which created a $20 billion dollar revenue-generating giant. Westinghouse Electric paid $3.9 billion for Infinity Broadcasting, making it the owner of the nation's largest group of radio stations. Congressperson Pat Schroeder had warned during the debate on the bill in October 1995 that "supermegadragon" companies would be created as a result of media concentration and...that the bill "should empower the consumer rather than enslave him" (*Television Digest*, October 30, 1995).

Bigger is better seemed to be the general consensus represented by mainstream media's coverage of their own increased consolidation. Associated Press business writer Scott Williams wrote, "...Does the merger of No. 1 Westinghouse with No. 2 Infinity put too much wattage in too few hands? Not necessarily. On the contrary, broadcasting executives and others say that Westinghouse-Infinity could help stimulate creativity and diversity on the airwaves" (*Press Democrat*, Santa Rosa, CA,

July 5, 1996). A few voices of concern were heard by mainstream journalists. In an editorial published in *The New York Times* on May 18, 1996, Frank Rich discusses how mega-media corporations are promoting their own corporate interests. Rich states, "In the era of mega-media conglomerates, journalism is merely another tool in what mongols call synergy—the dedication of an entire, far-flung multi-media empire to selling its products with every means at its disposal." Mark Landler (*The New York Times*, August 8, 1996), discussed some critics' concerns about how mega-mergers limit the number of news voices in the system. However, he says the "jury's still out on whether feverish consolidation of the media business corrupts the news system in any systematic way."

The alternative press in the United States has taken a much stronger position with regard to media consolidation. Jim Naureckas, editor of the magazine *Extra!*, wrote an article in the March issue of *In These Times* entitled "Info-Bandits: Media Conglomerates Hijacked Telecommunications Policy With Millions in PAC Money." Naureckas strongly reinforced the importance of Project Censored's number one story of 1995 and explained how the "public-interest point of view was lost in the debate over the Telecommunications Act." *The Nation* magazine devoted the entire June 3, 1996 issue to exposing what their cover story called "The National Entertainment State." Twenty-three writers and media analysts covered the full range of media consolidation issues. Mark Crispin Miller's article, "Free the Media," was the lead story, and Miller's media ownership chart was featured as a centerfold. Project Censored considered this article so important that we have reprinted it in Chapter Seven.

1995 # 2 CENSORED STORY

THE BUDGET DOES NOT HAVE TO BE BALANCED ON THE BACKS OF THE POOR

Congress could go a long way toward balancing the budget by 2002 without slashing Medicare, Medicaid, education, and social welfare. In fact, the Washington-based Center for Study of Responsive Law has identified 153 federal programs that benefit wealthy corporations but cost taxpayers $167.2 billion annually. For comparative purposes, federal support for food stamps, housing aid, and child nutrition costs $50 billion a year.

An analysis by *Public Citizen* reveals how Congress could balance the budget by cutting "aid to dependent corporations": The federal budget and tax codes are rife with huge subsidies to business—the sums involved make traditional "pork barrel" spending look like chicken feed.

Public Citizen President Joan Claybrook said the budget ax misses the subsidies for the wealthiest and most powerful U.S. corporations. "The proposed $250 billion, or 15 percent cut in Medicare, demands serious sacrifice from the more than 80 percent of seniors with incomes below $25,000—yet big corporations on the public dole are not asked to sacrifice at all."

SOURCE: *Public Citizen*, July/August 1995, "Cut Corporate Welfare: Not Medicare," by John Canham-Clyne, pp. 1, 9-11.

COVERAGE 1996: Major media in the United States still refuses to link government spending deficits and corporate welfare. Instead, the major legislative reduction of spending in 1996 was the Welfare Reform bill, which will withdraw approximately $60 billion from low-income communities over the next five years. The only mainstream coverage on corporate welfare in 1996 was a *Wall Street Journal* article, "Bold Talk on Corporate Welfare Cuts Fades as Political Campaigns Heat Up" (March 20, 1996). In the article Jackie Calmes aptly writes, "...Ending corporate welfare had been a rallying cry for budget cutters on both sides of the political aisle. But both the White House and Congress have backed away from that campaign, in part because they apparently found it difficult to cut subsidies, credit programs, and tax breaks for business interests at the same time they were

seeking campaign contributions from many of those same interests." Even Robert Reich, the "most outspoken liberal in the Clinton Administration," has called for good "corporate citizenship," meaning that corporations should be more concerned with the general welfare of their workers and communities (*Los Angeles Times*, March 10, 1996). Apparently Reich's proposal is a recommendation for voluntary change, which seems unlikely in a profit-driven multinational corporate system. If Congress insists on balancing the budget without increasing taxes on the rich or cutting subsidies to corporations, then the only alternative is continued withdrawal of benefit programs to low-income and working people in the country.

1995 # 3 CENSORED STORY

CHILD LABOR IN THE U.S. IS WORSE TODAY THAN DURING THE 1930s

Every day, children across America are working in environments detrimental to their social and educational development, their health, and even their lives.

In 1992, a National Institute of Occupational Safety and Health (NIOSH) report found that 670 youths ages 16 to 17 were killed on the job from 1980 to 1989. A second NIOSH report found that more than 64,100 children went to the emergency room for work-related injuries in 1992. Seventy percent of these deaths and injuries involved violations of state labor laws and the Fair Labor Standards Act (FLSA), the federal law which prohibits youths under 18 from working in hazardous occupations.

"Child labor today is at a point where violations are greater than at any point during the 1930s," said Jeffrey Newman of the National Child Labor Committee, an advocacy group founded in 1904.

Businesses aren't worried about the child-labor violations that they commit because the laws are rarely enforced. One report found that the average business could expect to be inspected once every 50 years or so. Inspectors spend only about five percent of their time looking into child-labor problems.

SOURCE: *Southern Exposure*, Fall/ Winter 1995, "Working in Harm's Way," by Ron Nixon, pp. 16-26.

COVERAGE 1996: Ron Nixon seems to be the primary journalist concerned with massive child-labor abuse in the United States. In a follow-up article to his Top *Censored* Story of 1995, Nixon tells how the House of Representatives passed a bill allowing youths under 18 to load paper compactors, even though a report by the National Institute for Occupational Health Science found numerous injuries resulting from the operation of these balers. Nixon explains, "The Food Marketing

Institute, the lead trade organization behind the baler appeal, gave $173,369 to legislators from 1991 to 1994." Other opponents of child-labor laws and regulations have joined an anti-regulation task force called Project Relief, which gave $10.5 million to legislators, mostly Republicans, during the 1994 elections.

The Associated Press released a story regarding child-labor abuse throughout the third world in November 1996, but no mention of child-labor violations in the U.S. was discussed. (*Press Democrat,* Santa Rosa, CA, November 12, 1996). The most recent coverage of child-labor abuse in the U.S. was the mainstream press' reportage of Calvin Klein's advertisements that "eroticize" children (*Washington Post,* September 9, 1995). It seems that major media is open to critical reviews of child-labor abuse in other countries, but doesn't seem to support investigating child-labor abuse in the United States.

1995 # 4 CENSORED STORY
THE PRIVATIZATION OF THE INTERNET

The Internet was essentially sold last year. The federal government has been gradually transferring the backbone of the U.S. portion of the global computer network to companies such as IBM and MCI as part of a larger plan to privatize cyberspace.

There are already warning signs about efforts to limit free expression and on-line debate. In 1990, the Prodigy on-line service started something of a revolt among some of its members when it decided to raise rates for those sending large volumes of e-mail. When some subscribers protested, Prodigy not only read and censored their messages, but it summarily dismissed the dissenting members from the service.

If cyberspace is deprived of true public forums, we'll get a lot of what we're already used to: endless home shopping, mindless entertainment, and dissent-free talk. If people can avoid the unpalatable issues that might arise in these forums, going on-line will become just another way for elites to escape the very nonvirtual realities of injustice in our world. As the "wired" life grows exponentially in the coming years, we'll all be better off if we can find that classic free speech street corner in cyberspace.

As the Supreme Court said in *Turner Broadcasting v. FCC (1994)*, "Assuring that the public has access to a multiplicity of information sources is a governmental purpose of the highest order, for it promotes values central to the First Amendment."

SOURCE: *The Nation*, July 3, 1995, "Keeping On-Line Speech Free: Street Corners in Cyberspace," by Andrew L. Shapiro, pp. 10-14.

COVERAGE 1996: While the privatization of the Internet continues unabated, several issues concerning free speech have arisen as court cases this year. The U.S. Government's Communications Decency Act, which was design to ban indecency on-line, was challenged in court by 22 plaintiffs, including the American Booksellers Association, the American Society of Newspaper Editors, the American Library Association, and the Association of American Publishers. Project Censored national judge, Judith Krug, of the American Library Association (ALA), stated in February, "We are talking about the future of communications. If librarians have to limit what we make available [on-line] to what's appropriate for a five or a seven-year-old, we're going to have to close up shop" (*USA Today*, February 2, 1996). Sections of the law were ruled unconstitutional in June by a Philadelphia federal court. On December 6, 1996, the Supreme Court agreed to review the ruling and a decision is expected by July of 1997. The case was described by Marc Rotenberg of the Electronic Privacy Information Center in Washington D.C. as "the most important First Amendment case...in thirty years" (*Press Democrat*, Santa Rosa, CA, December 7, 1996).

Complicating the issue has been the proposed introduction of on-line gambling by a Las Vegas casino (*Kansas City Star*, October 5, 1996). Will people located in states where gambling is illegal be allowed to place bets on-line? The *Electronic Engineering Times* reported, "The

Internet...is challenging the very notions of sovereignty and statehood, who can make laws and enforce them" (October 14, 1996). David Post of the Georgetown University Law Center is quoted as saying, "The radically decentralized, boundary disregarding characteristics of the global network will force us to confront truly profound questions about the nature of law making power and the nature of law itself" (*Electronic Engineering Times,* October 14, 1996).

If states lose the power to regulate information flow on the Internet and private firms assume full management responsibilies, then the assumption would be that freedom of information will be for only those who can afford it, or even worse, those who use the Internet to critically challenge private power may find themselves denied access completely. It seems that with Internet privatization, some state regulation will be necessary to protect our First Amendment rights. Content regulation and/or censorship must be challenged, be it public or private.

1995 # 5 CENSORED STORY
U.S. PUSHES NUCLEAR PACT BUT SPENDS BILLIONS TO ADD BANG TO NUKES

The U.S. Department of Energy is planning a multibillion-dollar project to resume production of tritium—a radioactive gas used to enhance the explosive power of nuclear warheads.

The choice is between investing billions of dollars in a huge particle accelerator, using theoretically workable but untested technology, or contracting with privately-owned nuclear reactors. The choice could mean the ordering of the first reactor in the U.S. since the 1979 Three Mile Island nuclear accident. Either choice involves immense political, financial, environmental, and national security risks, yet the American public is little aware of the enormity of the decision to be made.

THIS MODERN WORLD by TOM TOMORROW

Energy Secretary Hazel O'Leary has been under intense congressional pressure to choose the reactor option and to build it at the Energy Department's Savannah River, South Carolina, weapons plant where all of the tritium for the nation's nuclear arsenal has been produced.

In late May, the *Washington Post* reported that the House committee had approved legislation requiring the Energy Department to begin development next year of a nuclear reactor that would produce tritium for the nation's nuclear warheads, generate electricity, and burn plutonium as fuel. Meanwhile, the National Security Committee tacked the provision onto the defense authorization bill.

The public should be made aware that there is a third option: *not* to produce the tritium needed to add more bang to America's nuclear warheads.

SOURCES: *Washington Post*, May 5, 1995, "U.S. Seeks Arms Ingredient As It Pushes Nuclear Pact," p. A1, and May 28, 1995, "House Bill Would Order Nuclear Reactor As New Source of Tritium," p. A20, both by Thomas W. Lippman.

COVERAGE 1996: Mainstream press coverage continues to present the need for tritium nuclear weapons production as necessary for our national defense. The *Federal News Service* reported a speech by the Deputy Secretary of Energy, Charles Curtis, to the Senate Arms Services Sub-Committee on March 13, 1996: "Tritium gas is a critical element in the operation of nuclear weapons....Because tritium...decays at the rate of about five percent per year, it must be replenished on a periodic basis. Since 1988, the U.S. has had no capability to produce this essential gas." Despite the U.S. agreement under the START II treaty to reduce our stockpiles of nuclear warheads to 3,500 by the year 2003, President Clinton had approved a new nuclear weapons stockpile memorandum that would

*SEE SAN JOSE MERCURY NEWS, AUG. 18-20, 1996 -- ONLINE AT www.sjmercury.com/drugs/...

allow the U.S. to maintain "warhead reserves" that would enable them to rebuild quickly to a larger arsenal if necessary (*Defense News,* April 12, 1996).

The added need for a reserve stockpile of nuclear weapons and the "critical" need for tritium, prompted the Department of Energy to issue a request for proposals to nuclear power plants. This started a competitive mini-nuke rush by regional nuclear power plants to be chosen as the producer of tritium for the Department of Energy. Cash-starved public utilities throughout the U.S. including Niagara Mohawk Power Company, Wisconsin Energy Company, Duke Power, and Virginia Power, all lined up to compete for the tritium production contract. This bidding competition was only covered in local or regional newspapers, where local citizens waged vigorous resistance to the safety and ethical issues of civilian power plants making nuclear bomb materials.

On September 24, the U.S. Department of Energy announced it had awarded a $3 billion contract to Burns and Roe Enterprises, Inc. to design and construct a proton accelerator to produce tritium gas at the government's Savannah River site in South Carolina (*Bergen Record Corporation,* September 24, 1996).

Undebated in the national press is the possibility of not producing tritium gas at all, nor has there been any questioning of the policy of continuing nuclear weapons production into the 21st century.

1995 # 6 CENSORED STORY
RADICAL PLAN FROM NEWT GINGRICH'S THINK TANK TO GUT FDA

Newt Gingrich's Progress and Freedom Foundation has a radical plan to privatize much of the FDA supervision of drugs and medical devices. If enacted, the Progress and Freedom Foundation's plan will place responsibility for drug development, testing, and review in the hands of private firms hired by the drug companies themselves, while retaining a weakened FDA to rubber-stamp their recommendations. Additionally, the plan limits the liability of drug companies that sell dangerous drugs to the public.

The Progress and Freedom Foundation plan also limits the drug company's liability should a patient be injured or killed by a dangerous drug or medical device. According to the plan, a victim could not sue for punitive damages if the manufacturer of the product could show it met regulatory standards (no matter how weakened they were) during development and testing.

The foundation has financial backing from some of the biggest names in the pharmaceutical industry, including Bristol-Myers Squibb Co., Eli Lilly & Co., and Marion Merell Dow. Another drug manufacturer, Glaxo, has given an undisclosed amount to the foundation. The pharmaceutical industry also contributed over $1.6 million to the Republican party in the 1993-94 election cycle.

SOURCE: *Mother Jones*, September/October 1995, "Agency Under Attack," by Leslie Weiss, p. 28.

COVERAGE 1996: The Progress and Freedom Foundation continued its active campaign to reform the Food and Drug Administration (FDA). Foundation President Jeff Eisenach, quoted on ABC's *Nightline*, said, "We simply think the process [drug approvals] should be decentralized, that much of the work should be moved out of the hands of government bureaucracies into efficient private sector agencies" (Progress and Freedom Foundation Web Site). The Progress and Freedom Foundation has ties to the most conservative foundations and think tanks in the U.S., including Heritage Foundation, Hudson Institute, and the American Enterprise Institute. Their board of directors includes two former Reagan Administration officials and conservative public commentator Arianna Huffington.

Direct links with Newt Gingrich and ongoing pharmaceutical industry funds have given the Foundation significant clout in the Washington, D.C. arena. Gingrich has led the attack on the FDA in Congress (*Washington Post*, October 28, 1996). One Republican called the FDA "the Family Destruction Agency," for not quickly approving a home drug testing kit for parents to monitor possible drug use by their children (*UPI*, September 26, 1996).

The FDA has succumbed to industry and congressional pressure and revamped their procedures for biotechnology oversight in June 1996 making the regulations "less cumbersome" (*Bioworld*, June 13, 1996), and is continually on the defensive in Congress. For additional information, see Ron Nixon's analysis of the "Corporate Assault on the FDA," in *CovertAction Quarterly*, Winter 1995-96.

1995 # 7 CENSORED STORY
RUSSIA INJECTS EARTH WITH NUKE WASTE

For more than three decades, the Soviet Union and now Russia have secretly pumped billions of gallons of atomic waste directly into the earth and, according to Russian scientists, the practice continues today. The three widely dispersed sites are all near major rivers. The wastes at one site already have leaked beyond the expected range and "spread a great distance," the Russians said.

The amount of radioactivity injected by the Russians is up to three billion curies. By comparison, the accident at the Chernobyl nuclear power plant released about 50 million curies of radiation, mostly in short-lived isotopes that decayed in a few months. The accident at Three Mile Island discharged about 50 curies. The injected wastes include cesium-137, with a half-life of 30 years, and strontium-90, with a half-life of 28 years and a bad reputation because it binds readily with human bones.

The Russians are now working with the U.S. Department of Energy to try to better predict how far and fast the radioactive waste is likely to spread through aquifers. It might leak to the surface and produce regional calamities in Russia and areas downstream along the rivers. If the radioactivity spreads through the world's oceans, experts say, it might prompt a global rise in birth defects and cancer deaths.

SOURCE: *The New York Times*, November 21, 1994, "Poison in the Earth: A Special Report; Nuclear Roulette for Russia: Burying Uncontained Waste," by William J. Broad, p. A1.

COVERAGE 1996: There was no follow-up coverage of this short-lived story by any major media outlets in the United States. Perhaps the story was too close to the United States Department of Energy's practice of injecting nuclear waste into the ground, which was not suspended until 1985 (*UPI*, November 1, 1985). However, Russia's involvement in the nuclear waste disposal business is far from

over. Although little U.S. press coverage on this sensitive topic has been forthcoming, it is clear that U.S. firms are interested in the possibility of shipping our nuclear waste to the former Soviet Union. Westinghouse developed a proposal to ship low-level nuclear waste to Russia on air flights from Bangor International Airport in Maine. The plan was dropped when local citizen groups organized in opposition (*Bangor Daily News*, February 6, 1996).

A CNN report on March 5, 1996, said that Russian authorities have about 70,000 containers of nuclear waste from submarines they wanted to dispose of safely. The traditional practice had been dumping at sea (a practice also done by the United States), but Norway and Russian environmentalists had been objecting. The *Los Angeles Times* reported (February 29, 1996) that: "Radioactivity from dumped Russian nuclear waste could be carried in icebergs to the Atlantic, where it could poison fish and pose risks to humans."

A trilateral cleanup program by Norway, the United States, and Russia was initiated on September 30, 1996. Two million dollars was committed to begin nuclear clean-up in Europe's arctic region (*Times Journal*, September 30, 1996).

In the Pacific region, a joint Japanese-Russian venture contracted with U.S. firm Babcock & Wilcox Government Group, an operating group of McDermott International, Inc., to build a $25 million liquid radioactive waste treatment plant near the eastern port of Vladivostok. Russian environmentalists were worried that Russia was trying to get into the lucrative nuclear waste disposal business (*Inter Press Service*, December 6, 1995). Their concerns seem to be warranted: Taiwan disclosed in July of 1996 it will send 5,000 barrels of nuclear waste to Russia for disposal in late 1996 or early 1997 (The American Political Network Inc., September 25, 1996).

There is a tendency in the U.S. media to address this issue in the way *The Commercial Appeal* did on October 12, 1996: "The United States has a nuclear waste problem of its own but thankfully nowhere near the magnitude of the Soviet Union." Apparently, our nuclear waste is not as serious or lethal as Russian waste. Given this general attitude, it is unsurprising that the coverage of nuclear waste disposal remains a murky, disjointed topic in the U.S. press. At best, the public is getting only a small part of the story.

1995 # 8 CENSORED STORY
MEDICAL FRAUD COSTS THE NATION $100 BILLION ANNUALLY—OR MORE

The United States' $1 trillion annual health bill is 14 percent of the gross domestic product, making the medical industry the largest business in the land. Of this sum, a staggering amount is stolen. According to the National Health Care Anti-Fraud Association, the yearly swag totals between $31-$53 billion; according to the authoritative General Accounting Office, the annual take is $100 billion; according to other investigators, the amount is as high as $250 billion.

Health-care providers have developed a whole series of scam techniques including the following:

Upcoding: a doctor performs one medical procedure and charges the insurer for another (more profitable) one; *Unbundling*: the whole is sometimes worth less than the sum of its parts. A wheelchair broken down into its components—a wheel here, a seat there—with a separate bill for each, can mean bigger profits; *Pharmacy Fraud*: a corrupt pharmacist, often abetted by a physician and a patient, dispenses a generic drug rather than a brand-name drug and pockets the difference; *Psychiatric Schemes*: in the 1980s, the nation experienced an "epidemic" of clinical depression, as hospital chains filled their beds with teenagers, the overweight, and substance abusers; *Home Health Care*: this includes overbilling, billing for services not rendered, kickbacks, the use of untrained (i.e. inexpensive) personnel, and the delivery of unnecessary equipment; *Ghost Patients*: there are doctors who continue to treat patients after they're dead and doctors who work more than 24 hours a day.

SOURCE: *Mother Jones*, March/April 1995, "Medscam," by L.J. Davis, pp. 26-29, 71, 74.

COVERAGE 1996: CNN did a special on June 29, 1996, that showed how the insurance industry was cracking down on fraudulent claims. Citing the $100 billion per year fraud figure, CNN featured stories on several arrests and convictions of medical fraud perpetrators.

In California, *Business Wire* reported (July 12, 1996) how Delta Dental Plan uncovered a dental scheme of billing for services not rendered by Russell F. Moon, D.D.S. Over several years Dr. Moon billed tens of thousands of dollars for services when in fact patients received far less treatment. The U.S. Attorney handling the case stated, "Ten percent of our nation's total healthcare bill is lost to fraud."

The *Orlando Sentinel* covered the crackdown by Florida's Insurance Commissioner on insurance Fraud (September 17, 1996). Sixty-three doctors, insurance agents, policyholders, and employees were arrested for false medical claims and fake claims for workers' compensation. Insurance Commissioner Bill Nelson was quoted as saying, "Fraud is estimated to cost $100 billion nationwide and inflates the cost of insurance by up to 30 percent."

Laboratory Corp. of America, based in Burlington, North Carolina, agreed to pay a $182 million penalty for millions of tests not needed for diagnosis or treatment (*Los Angeles Times*, November 22, 1996).

Medical fraud has been getting some attention in the mainstream press. With better public awareness, chances of fraud and deception could diminish in the United States. The danger is that prosecutors and investigative reporters will see the high-profile cases as solving the problem and will fail to conduct ongoing in-depth systemic investigations.

1995 # 9 CENSORED STORY
U.S. CHEMICAL INDUSTRY FIGHTS FOR TOXIC OZONE-KILLING PESTICIDE

In 1994, the UN listed elimination of methyl bromide (MB) as the most significant remaining approach (after phase-out of CFCs and halons) to reducing ozone depletion. UN scientists conclude that eliminating MB emissions from agricultural, structural, and industrial activities by the year 2001 would achieve a 13 percent reduction in ozone-depleting chemicals reaching the atmosphere over the next 50 years.

In 1991, the U.S. accounted for nearly 40 percent of the pesticide's use worldwide. For 60 years, MB has been used to kill pests in soils and buildings, as well as on agricultural products. Soil fumigation to sterilize soil before planting crops is by far the largest use of MB in the U.S. Worldwide, most MB is used for luxury and export crops, like tomatoes, straw-berries, peppers, tobacco, and nursery crops.

The Methyl Bromide Global Coalition (MBGC)—a group of eight international MB users and producers—has launched a multimillion-dollar lobbying campaign to keep the product on the market. A leaked document from the Methyl Bromide Working Group, which includes Ethyl Corp. and Great Lakes Chemical Corp., the country's major MB producers, ignores reports of record ozone depletion, and states, "If we continue to work together, we stand an increasingly good chance of being able to use methyl bromide well beyond the year 2001."

SOURCE: *Earth Island Journal,* Summer 1995, "Campaign Against Methyl Bromide: Ozone-Killing Pesticide Opposed," by Anne Schonfield, p. 19.

COVERAGE 1996: Growers still face a ban on methyl bromide by 2001 in the United States, but numerous forces are calling for a longer period of time for phasing out the chemical. Methyl bromide, while one of the major destroyers of the ozone layer and a dangerous poison to farmworkers, also increases farm yields and profits (*San Francisco Chronicle,* February 2, 1996). The pressure on farmers is that they may lose sales to other nations who are taking a longer time period to phase out methyl bro-

mide than proposed in the United States. "New controls on HCFCs will not affect the European Union. The phase-out date is now 2020..." (*Chemistry and Industry,* December 18, 1995).

An early battle for continued use was played out in California in 1996. While farm workers rallied in protest, Governor Pete Wilson called a special session of the legislature to extend the date of a California ban on methyl bromide two years (*Fresno Bee,* December 24, 1996; *Lafayette Business Digest,* December 22, 1996). Wilson signed the bill extending use in California on March 12, 1996 saying, "We cannot afford to put California's trade and agricultural economies at a disadvantage" (*Press Democrat,* Santa Rosa, CA, March 13, 1996). Translated, Wilson's message is that that chemical company and agri-business profits take precedence over farm workers and environmental concerns.

Meanwhile, a *World Meteorological* report stated, "Ozone levels plummeted to record lows over Britain and Scandinavia this winter exposing inhabitants to some to the worst levels of ultraviolet radiation recorded in densely populated areas" (*Press Democrat,* Santa Rosa, CA, March 13, 1996). New analysis techniques using NASA satellite data showed that ultraviolet radiation is increasing 9 percent per decade in the middle and higher latitudes where most of the people live in the world (*Press Democrat*, Santa Rosa, CA, August 8, 1996).

1995 # 10 CENSORED STORY
THE BROKEN PROMISES OF NAFTA

The USA-NAFTA coalition promised that the North American Free Trade Agreement (NAFTA) would improve the environment, reduce illegal immigration by raising Mexican wages, deter international drug trafficking, and most importantly, create a net increase in high-paying U.S. jobs.

Now, some two years after the agreement became law, an analysis by the Institute for Policy Studies revealed that in Mexico the standard of living may be better for the wealthy, but there's been a 30 percent increase in the number of Mexicans emigrating to the U.S.; the peso devaluation of December 1994 cut the value of their wages by as much as 40 percent (making them far less able to buy U.S. goods today than they were before NAFTA); interest rates on credit cards climbed above 100 percent; retail sales in Mexico's three largest cities have dropped by nearly 25 percent. This continuing economic crisis in Mexico is expected to cause the loss of two million jobs in 1995.

NAFTA's promises to U.S. workers also have been broken: the Department of Labor's NAFTA Transitional Adjustment Assistance program reported that 35,000 U.S. workers qualified for retraining between Jan-uary 1, 1994, and July 10, 1995, because of jobs lost to NAFTA. A University of Maryland study estimates that more than 150,000 U.S. jobs were cut in 1994 as a result of increased consumer imports from Mexico. And since the peso devaluation in December 1994, the U.S. trade surplus with Mexico has turned into a deficit expanding from $885 million in May 1994 to $6.9 billion a year later, wiping out any basis for claiming that NAFTA is a net job creator for U.S. workers.

SOURCES: *CovertAction Quarterly*, Fall 1995, "NAFTA's Corporate Con Artists," by Sarah Anderson and Kristyne Peter, pp. 32-36. *Mother Jones*, January/February 1995, "A Giant Spraying Sound," by Esther Schrader, pp. 33-37, 72-73.

COVERAGE 1996: NAFTA continues but media criticism has also been increasing. Ralph Nader's group Public Citizen released a report in the fall of 1995 showing massive negative impacts on U.S. jobs caused by NAFTA. Numerous mainstream news organizations covered the story during the late fall and early winter of 1995-96, including: the *Toronto Sun, National Public Radio, Los Angeles Business Journal,* Reuters, *Arizona Republic, Star Tribune, Chattanooga Free Press, Hearst Inter Press, Wisconsin State Journal, San Diego Union-Tribune, Des Moines Register,* and the *Christian Science Monitor*.

Some election year coverage on NAFTA continued throughout the spring with Pat Buchanan taking an anti-NAFTA stance in his presidential campaign. Discussion of NAFTA's negative impacts on the U.S. economy was also part of Ross Perot's failed presidential bid.

Twin bills called the NAFTA Accountability Act were introduced in the House and Senate in September 1996 with 108 co-sponsors. These bills, if passed, would require the Administration to certify that the goals of NAFTA are being met, or the U.S. must renegotiate or withdraw from NAFTA (*Los Angeles Times*, September 25, 1996).

The North American Integration Development Center at the University of California in Los Angeles issued a report on NAFTA in December 1996. The study showed that the net gain of jobs to the United States due to NAFTA since 1994 has been only 2,990 jobs (*San Francisco Chronicle*, December 20, 1996). This figure does not take into account the continued exporting of jobs by U.S firms to Mexico at a rate of more than 10,000 jobs per year. Adding these job losses to post-NAFTA calculations means that the U.S. has lost over 30,000 jobs to Mexico since 1994.

OTHER PROJECT CENSORED STORIES IN THE NEWS

1989 #7 CENSORED STORY
CONTRAGATE: OLIVER NORTH, A CIA OFFICIAL, AND OTHERS BANNED FROM COSTA RICA FOR CONNECTIONS TO DRUG SMUGGLING

In July of 1989, Oliver North, a former CIA station chief, and other major Contragate figures were barred from Costa Rica. The order was issued by none other than Oscar Arias Sanchez, president of Costa Rica and winner of the 1987 Nobel Prize for Peace. President Arias was acting on recommendations from a Costa Rican congressional commission investigating drug trafficking. The Commission concluded that the Contra re-supply network in Costa Rica, which North coordinated from the White House, doubled as a drug smuggling operation.

The commission's probe of the Contra network centered around the northern Costa Rican ranch of U.S. expatriate John Hull because of the quantity and frequency of drug shipments in the area. According to *Extra!*, North's personal notebook mentioned the "necessity of giving Mr. Hull protection." North's notebooks also contain dozens of references to Contra-related drug trafficking, including one entry dated July 12, 1985: "14 million to finance came from drugs."

Barred from Costa Rica was Oliver North, former National Security Advisor John Poindexter, former U.S.

Ambassador Lewis Lamb, Major General Richard Secord, and former CIA station chief Joseph Fernandez.

The reaction of the U.S. press to this story in 1989 was one of complete indifference. The Associated Press completed a lengthy wire report on July 22, 1989, which carried the story into almost every newsroom in the United States. The mainstream media, however, either ignored the story completely, or, like the *Washington Post* and the *Miami Herald*, relegated it to "In Brief" sections. *The New York Times* and all three major television networks failed to mention the story at all.

SOURCE: *Extra!*, October/November 1989, "Censored News: Oliver North & Co. Banned from Costa Rica," pp. 1, 5.

COVERAGE 1996: Stories about CIA-Contra drug smuggling have been around for over a decade. A congressional inquiry in 1986-88 by a Senate subcommittee headed by Senator John Kerry found that the CIA may have chosen to overlook evidence that some Contra groups were dealing in drugs. The subcommittee's report was barely covered by the mainstream press and caused little stir at the time (*Press Democrat*, Santa Rosa, CA, October 31, 1996). However, a three part article written by Gary Webb published in the *San Jose Mercury News* reopened the CIA-Contra drug issue to national debate (August 18, 19, and 20, 1996). Webb's exposé claimed that not only did the CIA know about Contra drug shipments, but that these shipments were some of the first inexpensive cocaine to be distributed to mostly low income black neighborhoods in Los Angeles, and aided the explosion of crack use in the inner city. Coverage of Webb's account came out in quite a few newspapers throughout the United States during the following weeks, although often the accounts were presented along with a strong CIA denial statement. *NBC Nightly News*, *Newsweek*, and *ABC News* all gave perfunctory accounts of the story in September 1996.

On September 12, 1996, an outraged Congressional Black Caucus, before an audience of 1,500, called for an investigation of the connections between the CIA and California-based Contra drug rings (*San Jose Mercury News*, September 13, 1996). A week later Barry McCaffrey, Clinton's national drug control policy director, stated, "...Until the American public is fully satisfied, there must be a full and thorough investigation" (*Press Democrat*, Santa Rosa, CA, September 16, 1996). The following month the National Bar Association called on Clinton to name a special prosecutor to conduct an investigation into the charges (*Press Democrat*, Santa Rosa, CA, October 26, 1996). The controversy brought new attention to the claim of Celerino Castillo III, a former DEA agent, that he had sent reports to the DEA headquarters in 1985 and 1986 stating that the Contras were smuggling drugs through Ilopango, a U.S. airbase in El Salvador that the CIA used for logistical support. Castillo also reported that he was told by U.S. Ambassador to El Salvador, Edwin G. Corr, "My hands are tied because these are Contra operations being run by the White House" (*San Francisco Chronicle*, September 24, 1996).

During the next few months *The New York Times, Washington Post* and the *L. A. Times* all ran articles or editorials that questioned or attempted to debunk the *San Jose Mercury* story. While technical issues have been debated and matters of interpretation questioned, the *Mercury*'s article has essentially stood up to the challenge. The U.S. Senate Intelligence Committee has been holding hearings on the issue since November, which have primarily been, so far, mostly a platform for further denials by former Contras and various government officials.

Norman Solomon reported on December 31, 1996 (*Creators Syndicate*) that a London-based daily newspaper, *The Independent*, disclosed details of an interview with a former Nicaraguan Air Force pilot, who had ferried drugs for the Contras. The pilot, Carlos Cabeza, claimed that in the 1980s he flew cocaine to the San Francisco Bay area and that he delivered the proceeds to Contra leaders in Miami and Costa Rica. According to Solomon,

The Independent also stated that Cabeza said he met in Costa Rica with CIA agent Ivan Gomez, who was the person responsible for coordinating the transfer of drug profits to the Contras.

Many questions still need to be clarified and perhaps more revelations are to follow. Clarence Lusane writes in *CovertAction Quarterly* (December 3, 1996): "Have the CIA and other U.S. intelligence agencies, through covert operations and other activities, facilitated a flow of drugs into the United States...? The answer is an unqualified yes."

1995 #11 CENSORED STORY

GIANT OIL COMPANIES OWE U.S. MORE THAN 1.5 BILLION DOLLARS

Seven of the largest oil companies in the United States—Texaco, Shell, Mobil, ARCO, Chevron, Exxon, and Unocal—owe the federal government more than 1.5 billion dollars in uncollected royalties, interest, and penalties, according to a well-documented report by the Project on Government Oversight (POGO). POGO is a nonpartisan, non-profit organization that investigates conflicts of interest and abuse in government.

The Department of Interior (DOI), the agency responsible for collecting these royalties, is a willing partner of the oil companies in this extraordinary corporate welfare program. In addition to the forthcoming Inspector General report, DOI has ignored: U.S. Department of Commerce comments about the problem; a DOI Office of Policy Analysis that calls for the Department to determine the amount of royalties due, including interest and criminal penalties, if any, and to initiate collection procedures; and the DOI Minerals Management Service conclusion that "we should pursue potential Federal royalty underpayments."

To date, the Department of Interior has failed to collect these funds and the nation's press has taken scant notice of this classic example of corporate welfare.

SOURCE: *Project on Government Oversight Reports*, April 1995, "Department of Interior Looks the Other Way: The Government's Slick Deal for the Oil Industry," by the Project On Government Oversight, pp. 1-19.

COVERAGE 1996: Alexander Cockburn wrote in *CounterPunch* (July 16, 1996) that this debt was still outstanding and that the desperately underfinanced California schools system was being shorted $375 million dollars that should have been their share of the royalties. The U.S. Minerals Management Service billed the oil companies for their past due royalties from 1983 to 1988 (*Oil and Gas Journal*, October 28, 1996). However, election year politics were in full bloom, and the oil companies lobbied for changes in the law that would retroactively release them from their past due debts. In late July, Congress passed the Federal Oil and Gas Royalty Simplification and Fairness Act—a clear example of congressional misnomers—that released the oil companies from having to pay royalty debts older than seven years (*Washington Post*, August 6, 1996). President Clinton used his pre-convention vacation time in Wyoming to host oil company executives in a Yellowstone Park meadow to announce his support of the bill (Cockburn, *The Nation*, September 9, 1996). A gleeful Larry Nichols, chairman of the public lands committee of the Independent Petroleum Association of America, stated, "The reason for a statute of limitations is to make parties resolve disagreements while memories are still fresh and records are still available" (*Washington Post*, August 6, 1996). So, the oil companies got to keep their $1.5 billion dollars, Clinton was re-elected President, and the American public no longer has to worry that oil executives are overburdened with record-keeping requirements.

1995 # 14 CENSORED STORY
THE GULF WAR SYNDROME COVER-UP

While the Pentagon denies that U.S. soldiers were exposed to chemical and biological warfare agents during the Gulf War, its own records contradict the official line. Now, four years after the war's end, tens of thousands of Gulf War personnel have come down with one or more of a number of disabling and life-threatening medical conditions collectively known as Gulf War Syndrome. The syndrome's cause is unclear, but veterans and researchers have focused on the elements of a toxic chemical soup in the war zone that includes insecticides, pesticides, various preventive medicines given experimentally to GIs, and smoke from the burning oil fields of Iraq and Kuwait. There also is reliable evidence that one of its causes is exposure to low levels of chemical and biological warfare (CBW) agents during the war.

Despite Pentagon denials, evidence of CBW exposure during the war is abundant and mounting. In response to a Freedom of Information Act request by the Gulf War Veterans of Georgia, in January, the Pentagon released 11 pages of previously classified Nuclear, Biological, and Chemical Incident (NBC) logs. The NBC log excerpts, which cover only seven days of the war, document dozens of chemical incidents. They also reveal chemical injuries to U.S. GIs, discoveries of Iraqi chemical munitions dumps, fallout from allied bombing of Iraqi chemical supply dumps, and chemical attacks on Saudi Arabia.

And there always is the military bureaucracy's natural instinct to cover itself in the face of any problem or scandal. Finally, the cover-up is being compounded by evidence that the military has harassed and mistreated Gulf veterans who have reported ill-effects.

SOURCE: *CovertAction Quarterly*, Summer 1995, "Gulf War Syndrome Covered Up: Chemical and Biological Agents Exposed," by Dennis Bernstein, pp. 6-12, 55.

COVERAGE 1996: On April 3, 1996, the Pentagon released a survey that "found no evidence of Persian Gulf War syndrome and said 36 percent of the patients suffered from psychological or ill-defined ailments" (*Press Democrat*, Santa Rosa, CA, April 3, 1996). This survey was conducted over a two-year period at a cost of $80 million and claimed to have been based on "thorough medical examinations" of the 20,000 Gulf War veterans registered with the Pentagon's Comprehensive Clinical Evaluation Program. Then, on June 22, in front page headlines across the nation, the Pentagon was forced to admit that U.S. troops "may" have been exposed to nerve gas when Army units blew up an Iraqi ammunition dump a few days after the war ended (*Press Democrat*, Santa Rosa, CA, June 22, 1996). Terry Allen writes in *Covert Briefs:* "It turns out, government officials had known it all along: A November 12, 1991 military action report, not released to the public but obtained by [Dennis] Bernstein, confirmed that when U.S. troops exploded Iraqi bunkers in Kamisiyah, chemical weapons agents were released" (*Covert Briefs*, September 21, 1996, Alternative News Service, http://www.global.com/TAO/ainfos.html).

The Pentagon's disclosure of possible exposures opened the floodgates of media coverage on the Gulf War Syndrome. The Pentagon acknowledged in a report in August that "chemical weapons were detected as many as seven times in the first week of the 1991 Persian Gulf War" (*Press Democrat*, Santa Rosa, CA, August 22, 1996). In September, under congressional pressure, the Pentagon acknowledged that more than 5,000 U.S. troops may have been exposed to chemical weapons (*Press Democrat*, Santa Rosa, CA, September 9, 1996). By October this 5,000 figure had risen to 15,000 (*Press Democrat*, Santa Rosa, CA, October 2, 1996). By the end of October the Pentagon agreed to notify 20,000 Gulf War veterans that they may have been exposed to nerve gas *(USA Today*, October 23, 1996). The CIA, on the other hand, confirmed in a September 28, 1996, *Newsday* report that up to 130,000 U.S. troops may have been exposed to chemical warfare agents (*The Atlanta Journal*, November 1, 1996). A study from the Centers for Disease Control found that "troops deployed in the Gulf were more than three times as likely as troops elsewhere to suffer from chronic diarrhea, joint pain, skin rashes, fatigue, depression, and memory loss" (*Press Democrat*, Santa Rosa, CA, November 26, 1996). Key military logs, which chronicled the period of chemical weapons exposures in the Gulf War, turned up missing at military records storage facilities run by the National Archives last year. A search by the Pentagon has failed to find the missing pages (*San Francisco Chronicle*, December 5, 1996).

There seems to be little doubt that the Pentagon engaged in a cover-up of chemical weapons exposures of U.S. troops during the Gulf War. The whole story may never be told, but the public is getting glimpses of how the Pentagon operates and it is clear that we have been misled over the past five years. For a related issue, see Project Censored's number nine story this year on the depleted uranium weapons exposures during the Gulf War in Chapter One.

1995 # 15 CENSORED STORY
THE REBIRTH OF SLAVERY IN THE DARK HEART OF SUDAN

In the last several years, pure chattel slavery—the use of people as property—has quietly re-emerged as a social institution in Sudan. And as a participant in this slave trade, Sudan's government has good reason to make sure it remains a secret. While the number of slaves in Sudan is easily in the thousands, a more precise figure is difficult to calculate. A UN special investigator reported in 1994 that in the past several years, tens of thousands of black Christians and animists were abducted from southern Sudan and the Nuba Mountains and brought to the north.

Slaves in southern Sudan are sometimes sold openly in "cattle markets," a term that illustrates the value Arab traders place on the humans exchanged there. Women and children are sold for as little as 200 to 300 Sudanese pounds in the Nuba Mountains area.

Unfortunately, slave labor is not limited to the Sudan, nor even Africa. The Anti-Slavery Society of Australia charged that between 104 million and 146 million children—some as young as four—are forced to work in appalling conditions to make consumer products for Western nations (Associated Press, September 19, 1995).

SOURCE: *The Boston Phoenix*, June 30, 1995, "Africa's Invisible Slaves: Human Bondage Resurfaces in the Dark Heart of Sudan," by Tim Sandler, pp. 16-20.

COVERAGE 1996: It took a long time for U.S. media to give more than superficial coverage to the slave trade in Sudan. Almost ten years ago, Hamza Hendawi wrote about two Khartoum University lecturers who published a book in 1987 documenting that hundreds of children in southern Sudan were being kidnapped and sold as slaves (Reuters, September 1, 1987). Since then there has been intermittent coverage on this issue: *Los Angeles Times*, July 6, 1991; *Houston Chron-icle*, September 22, 1991; *Dallas Morning News*, December 19, 1992; *Cleveland Plain Dealer*, May 13, 1993; *The Arizona Republic*, April 10, 1994; *The New York Times*, July 13, 1994 and July 30, 1994; *Baltimore Sun*, July 14, 1994; *Christian Science Monitor*, August 4, 1994; *The Detroit News*, April 16, 1995; *San Francisco Examiner*, April 16, 1995; and Project Censored's number 15 story for 1995 by *The Boston Phoenix*.

In early 1996, Louis Farrakhan, head of the nation of Islam, questioned the accuracy of the reports on Sudan slavery asking, "Where is the proof?"(*Press Democrat*, Santa Rosa, CA, March 24, 1996). This challenge prompted the *Baltimore Sun* to send two reporters, Gilbert Lewthwaite and Gregory Kane, to Sudan for validation of the slavery story. In a lengthy three part series published in June of 1996, Lewthwaite and Kane reported on the ongoing slave trade in Sudan and actually purchased two young boys and returned them to their father.

One has to wonder if proving Farrakhan wrong was more of a motivation for in-depth investigative reporting on the Sudan slavery issue than the slavery issue itself. Given the media's historically limited and intermittent coverage of the Sudan slavery issue, it may be valid to question the motivation behind the expenditures for an overseas investigative reporting assignment nine years after the story was initially disclosed.

THIS MODERN WORLD

by TOM TOMORROW

Panel 1:

AND NOW FOR SOME EXPERT ANALYSIS, WE TURN TO OUR REGULAR COMMENTATOR, *SPARKY* THE *WONDER PENGUIN!* SPARKY, WOULDN'T YOU AGREE THAT THIS ELECTION IS *ALREADY* OVER?

ABSOLUTELY, BIFF! IT'S *YESTERDAY'S NEWS! SERIOUS* PUNDITS ARE ALREADY LOOKING AHEAD TO THE GORE/KEMP CONTEST IN THE YEAR 2000!

Panel 2:

OF COURSE, *THAT* ONE'S PRETTY MUCH CONSIDERED A ROUT AT THIS POINT -- BUT THE *2008* BATTLE BETWEEN *RALPH REED* AND *COURTNEY LOVE* MIGHT PROVE INTERESTING...

Panel 3:

AND THEN THERE'S THE PROBABLE 2012 MATCHUP BETWEEN *RUSH LIMBAUGH* AND *CRACKERS THE CORPORATE CRIME-FIGHTING CHICKEN!* BUT WHAT PUNDITS REALLY WANT TO KNOW IS, WILL *AGE* BE AN ISSUE IN THE PRESIDENTIAL RACE OF 2024 -- WHEN *MACAULAY CULKIN* IS EXPECTED TO GO HEAD-TO-HEAD WITH *SIGFREID & ROY!*

Panel 4:

PERSONALLY, *I'M* LOOKING FORWARD TO THE 2072 CAMPAIGN BETWEEN DAN QUAYLE'S *CRYOGENICALLY PRESERVED BRAIN* AND THE *CHANNELLED SPIRIT* OF *ELVIS!* THAT ONE'S GOING TO RAISE SOME INTERESTING ISSUES, DON'T YOU AGREE?

YOU'RE TRYING TO MAKE SOME KIND OF *POINT* HERE, AREN'T YOU?

TOM TOMORROW © 10-30-96

CHAPTER 4

The Junk Food News Stories of 1996: What Media Uses to Fill Space and Entertain Us to Death

By Peter Phillips and Richard Mellott

Each year Project Censored surveys the members of the Organization of News Ombudsmen to determine the least important well-covered news stories in the mainstream press. Carl Jensen, founder of Project Censored, coined the name for these stories as "Junk Food News."

Our number one most censored story on the potential dangers of the upcoming Cassini space probe has received little attention from the mainstream press. Why we need to rocket 72 pounds of deadly plutonium-238 into space, and then slingshot it around the earth, has yet to be seriously debated in national media. Do we trust technology so much that that we are willing to risk an environmental disaster, or are there safer, more reasonable technologies that could be developed over time? Is the public really aware of the dangerous risks being taken in the name of science? How do other nations feel about the risk of 72 pounds of plutonium spilling out into our global environment.

In contrast, the mainstream press is spending vast resources to report on 'news stories' that may have little or no socio-environmental consequences nor any value other than pure titillation. Superficial news entertainment keeps the public stimulated and ill-informed. This combination of diminishing public debate on important issues and the abdication of democratic power to public/private bureaucrats and 'experts' is telling.

On Monday, October 21, 1996, at about 3:30 a.m., Madonna felt the first labor pain. Shortly thereafter she was taken to Good Samaritan Hospital in Los Angeles. Then the media began to arrive, setting up camp outside the hospital, awaiting any and all developments.

The tabloids and "people" columns in newspapers and magazines all over the world jumped on the story, and eight and a half hours later, at 4:01 p.m., Madonna gave birth to a 6-pound, 9-ounce girl. Name: Lourdes Maria Ciccone Leon.

People, the Time Inc. weekly magazine that's turned "junk food news" into a multi-million dollar empire, went on to report the following about Madonna and her newborn in its October 28, 1996 issue:

• The pediatrician: Paul Fleiss, father of Hollywood madam Heidi.

• When and where she was when she learned she was pregnant: March in Buenos Aires, filming the musical, *Evita*.

• First cravings: poached eggs (fourth month).

• Morning sickness: no.

• What Madonna did two weeks prior to giving birth that one relative said she hadn't seen her do in years: the dishes.

• Madonna's first recorded words after eight and half hours of labor: "Ugh. I just want some french fries from McDonald's."

• What a heavily-sedated Madonna said on the way to the delivery room: "Goodbye, everyone. I'm going to get my nose job now."

• What Madonna said after giving birth: "This is the greatest miracle of my life."

Madonna's may have been the most celebrated pregnancy, but it wasn't the only one that was touted by media around the world. Toss in the pregnancies, deliveries, and postnatal news about celebrities Melanie Griffith, Christie Brinkley, Rosie O'Donnell, and Jane Seymour, among other lesser known stars, and what you get is the number one Junk Food News (JFN) story of the year.

That's what the National Organization of News Ombudsmen concluded in Project Censored's annual survey of the most over-covered, insignificant news stories.

1996 TOP 10 JUNK FOOD NEWS STORIES

#1. CELEBRITY PREGNANCIES
#2. THE BRITISH ROYALS
#3. THE MACARENA
#4. THE KENNEDYS' AUCTION AND WEDDING
#5. DENNIS RODMAN
#6. LISA MARIE DUMPS MICHAEL JACKSON
#7. O. J. SIMPSON (Part III)
#8. ELLEN COMES OUT
#9. PRIMARY COLORS
#10. DICK MORRIS

Celebrity pregnancies edged out the British Royals, The Macarena, and the Kennedy family. These were the stories that finally toppled O.J. Simpson, who faded to fifth place after two years as the number one story. Simpson, though, was still the most dominant junk food news nominee in number of stories and column inches of newsprint. No other person or topic came close.

Of course, the continuing coverage of Simpson, whose wrongful death civil trial was coming to a close at year's end, wasn't confined to supermarket tabloids. This was mainstream media ink—thousands of gallons of it. The *Los Angeles Times* printed approximately 83 column feet of news coverage on O.J. Simpson in 1996. Given the *Los Angeles Times'* average daily circulation of approximately one million papers, this adds up to over 15,720 miles of O.J. news coverage printed last year. *The New York Times* came in a distant second with only 7,800 miles of newsprint distributed covering O.J. Simpson.

As usual, media's obsession with wealth, fame, and sex permeated the top ten. And given the chance to cover all three themes in one fell swoop, they seldom resisted. One prevalent philosophy: when in doubt about how to fill a news hole, you can't go wrong with Michael Jackson. An annual junk food news fixture, Jackson and "the allegations" against him placed sixth in 1993. Then he teamed with Lisa Marie Presley to finish fourth in 1994, and proceeded to place sixth in 1995. And Jackson is already poised for another top ten finish in 1997: He and Debbie, his wife (as of early December), were expecting their first child in February—and the tabloids and gossip columns were already predicting a custody battle two months before the baby was due.

Given the amount of sex that's found annually on the junk food news scene, it was only a matter of time before someone got pregnant. A lot of celebrities did in 1996. The media dug deep into this trend, leaving no case of colic undiagnosed nor breast-feeding secrets of the rich and famous unreported.

The British Royals put up a good fight before bowing to the pregnant celebs. Lady Di, Prince Charles, Fergie, and even Di and Chuck's 14-year-old son, Prince William, provided the media with a steady stream of news remarkably void of any significance.

The Kennedys, America's own version of royalty, also had a busy year. There was the family auction followed by the marriage of J.F.K., Jr., whose first front cover, of his christening, was in *Life* magazine on December 19, 1960.

CHEAP AND EASY NEWS

Most media ombudsmen agree junk food news is easy and inexpensive to produce.

"It's easier to focus on these stories than to make the important stuff— public issues— interesting," says Elissa Papirno, reader representative of the *Hartford Courant*.

There is no digging for facts. You just grab a file photo and come up with a semi-clever phrase for the headline, such as "Mama Madonna" or "Lady Di-Vorce" or "Jacko Facing Custody Battle." The characters are celebrities. Nothing needs to be explained," says Jean Otto of Denver's *Rocky Mountain News*. "These stories allow lots of lip-smacking and nothing more."

Project Censored founder Carl Jensen believes the "growing plethora of junk food news in today's media can best be attributed to the media's increasing concern with their bottom line."

Jensen, who leads his top ten selections with "Lisa Dumps Michael," O.J. Simpson (Part III), and The British Royals, says JFN nominees this year such as pregnant celebrities and Disneyworld's 25th Anniversary are two exam-

THIS MODERN WORLD   by TOM TOMORROW

ples of the corporate sponsor or celebrity press agent doing all the work for the media. "There is rarely any cost involved for travel or research in developing a junk food news story," Jensen says.

Some media representatives say the chatty news they print in their "people" or gossip columns is a matter of supplying their readers with the news they crave. But many admit to the dangers of fanning the flames of frivolity. Considering the important news that goes unreported, one could well charge the media with irresponsibility towards the American public.

Junk food news "sells papers and it's cheap," says Phil Record of the *Fort Worth Star-Telegram*, whose top JFN selections were celebrity pregnancies, Dennis Rodman, Howard Stern, and The Macarena. "We pander to the appetite of the public—it's a *Hard Copy* mentality." Record admits, "You have to sell newspapers, but I think you try to find a good balance. We have to be conscious of what our readers want, and their idea of what's news isn't always our idea. But we try very hard to stay connected to our readers." Record queried the *Star-Telegram* staff for top junk food news stories of 1996, "and The Macarena got the most votes."

Joe Sheibley, reader representative of *The News Sentinel* of Fort Wayne, Indiana, likens the role of an editor to that of a parent sensitive to his kids' nutritional needs. Try to limit the junk food. And make sure they eat their vegetables. "The important news is like spinach," he says. "As a grown-up, you know they need a certain amount of vitamins and minerals for a healthy life. I think we have to play that role."

Lynn Feigenbaum, public editor of the *Virginia-Pilot* of Norfolk, Virginia says, "I'm not a snob. I realize people like a certain amount of junk food news. I think it becomes a matter of where you put it in the paper and finding the right quantity...Life is tragic; elections are boring."

For many dailies, people columns serve as the main junk food news outlet. Miriam Pepper, reader representative of the *Kansas City Star*, says when her paper does provide junk food news, it's done in small dosages. "I don't think our paper really went crazy over most of those stories," she said. After searching her paper's computer files, Pepper said she found eleven references to "Madonna" and "pregnancy" in *Star* stories, and two other references to "Madonna" and "pregnant." Simpson, meanwhile, had 1,676 references in the past two years, according to Pepper.

In several stories that received JFN votes in 1996, the media emerged as the main story, not just as the vehicle to report it. One example is *Primary Colors*, the book by the "anonymous" journalist, Joe Klein. Another was the widespread coverage of Richard Jewell as the prime suspect in the Olympic bombing case. "*Primary Colors* and Richard Jewell showed the media's self-indulgence, though on different sides of the mirror," says Otto. "Klein emerged as a sort of hero; Jewell as the anti-hero." Otto calls the coverage of the Jewell story a disgrace. The British Royals? "Of no relevance," she says. Celebrity pregnancies? "Who cares?" Jerry Garcia's death anniversary? "Let it go!" *Primary Colors*? "Did it matter?"

According to Emerson Stone, freelance journalist, media sensationalize such stories because "they have this wish to compete at the lowest common denominator, rather than the highest. This is also known as a 'death wish,' and it is a leading reason why so many lump journalists and countless others into something called 'the media.'"

Other nominations for stories that did nothing but waste valuable media space include the typical daily Wall Street report that tries too hard for relevance. Says Stone, "One day's statistics say our economy is booming, then we're told on the next day we're starting a long plunge. There's no long range view."

Members of the Organization of News Ombudsmen participating in this year's survey of Junk Food News were:

Lynn Feigenbaum	*Virginia Pilot &Ledger-Star*
Roger Jimenez	*La Vanguardia*, Barcelona, Spain
Arthur Nauman	*Sacramento Bee*
Jean Otto	*Rocky Mountain News*
Elissa Papirno	*The Hartford Courant*
Robert Retzlaff	*Post-Bulletin,* Rochester, MN
Gayle Williams	Gannett Suburban Newspapers
Marcelo Nogueira Leite	*Floha De Paulo*, Sao Paulo, Brazil

Miriam Pepper	*Kansas City Star*
Phil Record	*Ft. Worth Star-Telegram*
Joe Sheibley	*News Sentinel*, Ft. Wayne, IN
Emerson Stone	*Communicator Magazine*, CT
Carl Jensen	Cotati, CA
Jerry Finch	*Richmond Times-Dispatch*, VA

Ombudsmen serve as independent reviewers and public complaint reporters in major newspapers around the world. They are generally empowered by their editors or publishers to critique published articles, and investigate on and report public concerns and complaints regarding the newspaper. In the United States fewer than one percent of 1,800 daily newspapers employ an ombudsman or reader representative. More papers would probably employ ombudsmen if the public came to expect and demand such an outlet for broad public concern.

Our Junk Food News survey is conducted as a counter-point to The Top 25 *Censored* News Stories list. Major media systematically fail to challenge the rich and powerful or to take on important socio-environmental issues that would challenge the status quo of the American corporate-government partnership. Instead, media is filled with vast volumes of superfluous garbage designed, in the words of Neil Postman, to "entertain us to death." Admittedly, many of us are often quick to read the latest update on O.J. Simpson, but front page coverage, media time, space, and resources spent on junk food news represent what economists call "opportunity costs." The resources and staff allocated to junk food news are resources not spent on important investigative reporting or in-depth analysis of critical issues in society. Some entertainment is valid and fun, but major media are essentially moving toward a full entertainment model in place of protecting our right and need to know what important issues we face today.

Maybe it is time for media to move junk news into a special section of the newspaper and into non-prime time news and keep the front pages and prime time for important news. By creating a "people" gossip section in media, those interested in the latest exposé of Madonna can have their junk news food fix, and those of us not interested can ignore it. Clearly, however, it is time to reallocate media resources to critical investigative coverage. Putting some of those resources into ombudsmen, independent investigative reporting, and local community access pages would be a good start in the right direction.

THIS MODERN WORLD

by TOM TOMORROW

LET'S FACE IT, FOLKS--FROM TOBACCO INDUSTRY **DISSEMBLING** TO THE EXPLODING **FORD PINTO,** THERE ARE **COUNTLESS** EXAMPLES OF CORPORATIONS BETRAYING THE PUBLIC TRUST... AFTER ALL, WHY ELSE WOULD THEY SPEND SO MUCH MONEY EACH YEAR ON **IMAGE ADVERTISING?**

DO PEOPLE AT LARGE COMPANIES WHICH ROUTINELY RAVAGE THE ENVIRONMENT REALLY PURCHASE AIR TIME TO BROADCAST PICTURES OF FUZZY LITTLE BUNNIES?

PEOPLE **DO!**

THE UNSANITARY, BOTTOM-LINE PRACTICES OF THE CORPORATE **MEAT INDUSTRY** HAVE LED TO THOUSANDS OF HOSPITALIZATIONS-- AND EVEN DEATHS-- FROM BACTERIAL POISONING.... INCLUDING, MOST FAMOUSLY, THE 700 PEOPLE SICKENED AND FOUR CHILDREN KILLED BY E. COLI-CONTAMINATED **JACK-IN-THE-BOX HAMBURGERS** IN 1993...

REPUBLICANS, OF COURSE, ADDRESSED THIS ISSUE--BY ATTEMPTING TO **REDUCE** INDUSTRY OVERSIGHT...

SUDDENLY I'M NOT SO HUNGRY.

ONE OF THE UGLIEST **HISTORICAL** EXAMPLES OF CORPORATE MALFEASANCE IS PERSONIFIED BY INDUSTRIAL ICON **HENRY FORD...** A VIRULENT ANTI-SEMITE AND LONG-TIME ADMIRER OF ADOLF HITLER, FORD ACTUALLY SUPPLIED VEHICLES TO THE NAZIS **DURING** WORLD WAR II (THROUGH A BRANCH OF HIS COMPANY IN VICHY ALGIERS)...

FORD IS ALSO SAID TO HAVE SENT HITLER 50,000 REICHMARKS EACH YEAR ON HIS **BIRTHDAY...**

"DEAR ADOLF--YOU'RE NOT GETTING OLDER--YOU'RE GETTING **BETTER!**"

THAT HENRY--ALWAYS SO **THOUGHTFUL...**

IN SHORT, THE SANITIZED PUBLIC FACE OF CORPORATE AMERICA HAS OFTEN MASKED SOME PRETTY UNPLEASANT TRUTHS...WHICH IS WHY REVELATIONS THAT TEXACO EXECUTIVES USED RACIAL SLURS IN PRIVATE LEAD **US** TO ASK ONE SIMPLE QUESTION: IS ANYONE ACTUALLY **SURPRISED** BY THIS..?

WHAT? TOP OIL EXECS WERE LESS THAN COMPLETELY ENLIGHTENED, SOCIALLY CONSCIOUS INDIVIDUALS?

GOSH--I ALSO HEAR THERE'S NO **TOOTH FAIRY!**

EXCUSE ME? AND WHO EXACTLY DO YOU THINK USED TO LEAVE THOSE QUARTERS UNDER MY PILLOW, MISTER SMARTY PANTS?

TOM TOMORROW@11-20-96

CHAPTER 5

Censorship Within Modern, Democratic Societies

By Peter Phillips and Ivan Harsløf

Is it possible to understand censorship in a modern society, where the flow of information is rapidly accelerating and communication technology makes it possible to expose almost every corner of political and social life to a wide audience? Is there any value in discussing censorship in democracies, where freedom of expression is ensured in constitutions and amendments?

By reviewing some of the current research within the field of communications, we wish to establish a broad analytical framework for the identification of censorship mechanisms as they may occur in modern democratic societies. Media concentration is rapidly changing the face of censorship and new broader definitions are needed to understand the full dimensions of the issue. We conclude this chapter with a report on our 1996 study of how one of the most informed groups about the media situation—U.S. newspaper editors—perceive media concentration as a threat to First Amendment rights.

Censorship is normally considered a *defensive* phenomenon, in the sense that censorship is a mechanism that deliberately prevents information from reaching the public. It is regarded as a function exercised by authorities—

in public as well as private organizations—to control the content of publications (Fairchild, 1976). Even in modern democratic societies this overt form of censorship continues to occur, as well as its more subtle variations. In fact, legal regulation of freedom of expression continues to be seen as an important part of almost all democratic constitutions (Lipset, ed., 1995), as well as international conventions.

John Keane, in his book *The Media and Democracy* (1991), regards state censorship as a phenomenon which continues in modern democracies. He identifies a tendency toward the creation of mutually-protecting undemocratic processes within and between modern capitalistic societies. This is, according to Keane, one of the main threats to the free flow of information about state activities. Governments use a number of mechanisms to regulate and distort the exchange of information and opinions between their citizens. These can include legal tools, such as secret services declaring 'emergency situations' or initiating pre- or post-censorship of publications for state security reasons, or simply lying to the public about governmental actions or positions.

This kind of information management seems to be the case in the current CIA-drug smuggling affair. The CIA has denied any direct involvement with the Contra drug smuggling operations in the 1980s; however, it has become increasingly clear that at least some elements of the CIA knew the drug smuggling was occurring. Therefore, by omission, it was actually lying to the public (Webb, 1996). Similarly, one of the most recent examples of state censorship has been the U.S. military establishment's control of press coverage during the Gulf War (Haines, 1995). (For more details about state censorship see, "Less Access to Less Information," Appendix A).

The use of such tactics is not, however, limited to government agencies. Likewise, private corporations may overtly censor outgoing information, as in the case of Ford Motor Company and the Pinto's exploding gas tank (Hills, 1987).

Indeed, the defensive application of censorship as a concept seems the most obvious because of its direct links to the traditional images of the zealous censor cutting, banning, burning, and retouching. However, it might be necessary to take into consideration more *offensive* traits of censorship if we want to fully understand the existing patterns of repression within modern societies. The expansion of the concept of censorship to include offensive public relations activities by powerful deep-pocketed corporations establishes the promotion of certain versions of reality in the public as an important mode of censorship.

This year's number 19 censored story provides us with an example of offensive censorship. The story reveals how major corporations have hired the public relations firm Hill & Knowlton to do a pro-China campaign to influence Congress and the American public in order to secure China's trade status as a "most favored nation" (Silverstein, 1996). In their book, *Toxic Sludge is Good for You* (1995) (see review, Chapter 6), Stauber and Rampton give a comprehensive account of the growing *propaganda-for-hire* industry in the U.S. that is increasingly involved in the promotion of special interests in order to influence political debates and public opinion. Offensive censorship is the strategic *structuring of information* released to the public by large powerful corporations or governmental agencies.

Images of the zealous censor or "public relations official" imply that censorship is an intentional act performed on the *manifest* level. But in a modern market economy, other processes of more intangible and *latent* natures should not be ignored. Jansen (1991) and Keane (1991) both put forth the notion of *market censorship* in order to visualize the idea that economic forces strongly determine what information is reaching the public. Thus, market censorship—extending Adam Smith's classic metaphor—is censorship conducted by the invisible hand of the market. For example, editors and owners of news organizations will tend not to pursue certain news stories that might offend major advertisers. Market censorship also includes the notion that news organizations are actually marketing groups that are constantly analyzing readership numbers and viewer percentages. This analysis tends to lead to the selection of news stories for their public-titillating qualities rather than their societal news value or educational attributes.

The way in which this latent mode of censorship operates is analyzed in Herman and Chomsky's book *Manufacturing Consent* (1988; and updated in Herman, 1996). They claim that because the media is firmly imbedded in the market system, it reflects the class values and concerns of its owners and advertisers. According to Herman and Chomsky, the media maintains a corporate class bias through five systemic filters: concentrated private ownership; a strict bottom-line profit orientation; over-reliance on governmental and corporate sources for news; a primary tendency to avoid offending the powerful; and an almost religious worship of the market economy, which strongly opposes alternative beliefs. These filters limit what will become news in society and set parameters on acceptable coverage of daily events.

Chomsky (1989) is careful to point out that the propaganda model is a structural theory that shows how large or significant interests in society influence decision making by simply being powerful in their own right. He does not try to claim that government or corporate media owners directly and systematically dictate news coverage perspectives to editors and producers. However, a number of researchers have given numerous examples of this type of media control (Parenti, 1986; Demac, 1988; Bagdikian, 1992; Mazzocco, 1994; and Stauber and Rampton, 1995). Certainly a limited process of overt influence is operating as well, but in Chomsky's marketplace perspective, overt control is unnecessary, because the system will tend to do it automatically.

Ben Bagdikian's (1992) ongoing concern that monopoly control and continued concentration of media organizations threatens the First Amendment emphasizes the importance of the propaganda model for understanding censorship in modern society. Increasingly concentrated mega-media organizations will only diminish any possibility of news organizations resisting marketplace pressures.

That media ownership has an important impact on what becomes news, and how the news is treated, is well-documented by Wasburn (1995). In a comparative content study of commercial, public, and government broadcast content in the U.S., Wasburn found the newscasts of commercial broadcasting organizations tended to be uniform, rarely critical, and most likely to present news as mere facts, with little, if any, contextual background information. Furthermore, a highly ethnocentric view of the world was frequently offered in the commercial newscast. There was also a clear absence of stories dealing with international events. In contrast, the publicly-owned news organizations in the study were more prone to give an account of the context in which news events were embedded, and to give the public some insight into foreign affairs.

If we come to understand that censorship, in its defensive and offensive modes, operates within a societal structural system dominated by the powerful, we come very close to the Marxist/Gramscian theory of cultural hegemony. This theory implies that values, ideologies, and issues of the powerful are transmitted through societal institutions as socio-cultural mechanisms that cultivate ideas and inform the masses. Mass media is but one institution within a structural framework of domination and control evident in a capitalist society. Some thorough work on how the corporate media distorts the news in favor of upper-class interests and official government positions has already been done. The works of Cohen and Solomon (1995), Croteau and Hoynes (1994), and Haines (1995) all extensively document current corporate media bias in presenting and framing the news.

However, the validity of this perspective has been historically debated. Altheide (1984) pointed out numerous examples of media criticism of elites and governmental policy which he suggested renders the hegemonic or propaganda perspective incomplete. Nevertheless, the fact that Watergate-like exposures of government corruption or corporate malfeasance do occur does not necessarily diminish the overall pressures for news organizations to operate within the parameters of power expectations in society.

Carrage (1993) maintains that this kind of critique depends on what scale one allows for the occurrences of contradictions within the dominant ideology in the application of hegemonic theory. And in fact, by accepting some contradictions and inconsistencies on the manifest level, the system could be said to maintain the illusion of pluralism (shared power) for public consumption while maintaining an ongoing compliance with dominant ideologies and interests.

The two dichotomies of censorship—defensive vs. offensive and manifest vs. latent—which have been presented here, are inserted in the grid below (*Figure 1*) as the horizontal and vertical axis respectively. This construction will enable us to plot the various modes of censorship as they may occur in modern democratic societies.

FIGURE 1: MODES OF CENSORSHIP

MANIFEST

	restraints on expression	strategic public relations structuring information	
DEFENSIVE			OFFENSIVE
	market filters (competition, media concentration)	cultural hegemony/ conforming values	

LATENT

The following are examples of different types of censorship in the four fields of the grid.

Within the *manifest-defensive* field, we find the restraints which are deliberately exercised on the flow of information. The field includes the traditional understanding of censorship as cutting and deleting information before publication or release as well as post-publication restraints. The censorship initiators in this regard can be state authorities, corporations, and organizations, as well as private citizens.

Moving to the *manifest-offensive* field of the grid, we see that strategic public relations efforts by powerful corporations or government agencies to promote certain versions of reality are also a part of censorship in that they are deliberate efforts to modify or change the public's understanding of an issue.

The *latent-defensive* field represents the controlling news filters grounded in society's structurally determined marketplace and amplified by ongoing media concentration.

Finally, the *latent-offensive* field contains the notion of cultural hegemony which promotes dominant class values and beliefs on the public. Cultural hegemony is the formation of frames of understanding that set parameters of acceptable ideas for coverage and discussion in news organizations that are reflective of the most powerful interests in society.

THE HUMAN DIMENSION

In discussing censorship one often tends to forget the role of the media audience—the readers, listeners, and viewers. How does the selective, free media consumer fit into this system of censorship? The relationship between the media and the audience has been subject to thorough examination. Particularly within the last fifteen years, it has been increasingly recognized that the audience is not a defenseless, passive, and cognitively uniform mass, but rather a diverse group of active, interpreting individuals (for an overview of this approach, see e.g. Biltereyst, 1995). Becker and Kosicki (1995) suggest that media effects should be regarded as a transaction between audience members and messages producers, with neither fully dominating.

It is important to make a distinction between collective and individual

THIS MODERN WORLD   by TOM TOMORROW

transactions. The former implies that the audience reacts to the content provided by the media, but that this content to a certain degree is determined by expectations about audience interests. These expectations are based on prior experiences with audience behavior. The content-reaction outcome is thus shaped by a continuous negotiation between the producers and the audience. By refusing to pay attention to certain kinds of media messages, the audience sends a collective signal to media producers to change the content. This is one of the reasons that U.S. Saturday morning television has almost completely eliminated female lead characters in cartoons. Media networks were losing half of their market share by running female leads because little boys refused to watch cartoons with female leads while girls would watch either (Carter, 1991).

The collective signals sent from the audience are not only related to quantitative measures of numbers of readers, listeners, and viewers, but also to the demographic 'quality' of these, assessed within the parameters of market segmentation. Different advertisers demand different audience groups with specific economic profiles and consumption habits. Media producers are to some extent compelled to adjust media content so that they deliver suitable audience groups to advertisers (Stabile, 1995).

The public does have an influence on media content, but this content modification may reflect consumer prejudices and individual socio-emotional desires for entertaining stimulation over reflective or hard-hitting news. News organizations often say they are just giving the public what it wants. However, market share-based consumer viewing reports place media organizations in competition with each other to develop the most entertaining news coverage, but not necessarily the most accurate or important. The question becomes: what does the public really want? Psychological theories of self-

actualization and maturation stress that basic human nature pushes people to seek to understand themselves in terms of their social environment. Does this mean humans really just want entertaining stimulation or do we naturally seek to become more informed and aware of our social environment?

Ben Bagdikian (1992) claims the American public is taking diminishing interest in news events, as reflected in the decline of newspaper readership and newscast viewership, due in part to mass media's lack of a critical qualitative coverage of important news events, and a drifting toward news as entertainment. In 1993, journalist Dan Rather was quoted as saying, "We have all succumbed to the Hollywoodization of news...We trivialize important subjects...and give the best slots to gossip and prurience" (*Sacramento Bee*, October 1, 1993: A-22). Is more entertaining news really a reflection of the public's desire or is the public's lowered interest in news a reflection of the fact that basic human needs for meaning and understanding are not being met? The basic assumption that is in use to address this issue will have an increasingly important influence on concentrated mega-media systems. Does the public drive the media or is the media driving the public to a lower level of expectations? Qualitative aspects of what future societies will look like may well result from how we answer this question.

As it should be clear from the outlining of various modes of censorship mechanisms in Figure 1, media concentration appears to be a major cause of the systemic filtering of public information in a modern society. The impact of media concentration will be subject to further examination in the following section.

AN ALTERNATIVE PERSPECTIVE ON MEDIA CONCENTRATION

In a new film on media censorship, "Fear and Favor in the News Room," University of California, Berkeley Professor Emeritus Ben Bagdikian says the press is like a cathedral and a bank. The cathedral has the responsibility to tell the people the moral truths about themselves, while the bank collects their money. The two roles represent a potential conflict for the press in the United States today. The press is the only industry specifically protected by the Constitution, due to its professional duty to maintain the free flow of information, a responsibility essential to the democratic process. Bagdikian's concern is that the media have evolved into massive corporate entities that are advertiser-driven profit machines, and are rapidly drifting away from their duty to provide the public with vital information.

Ben Bagdikian first published his book, *The Media Monopoly*, in 1983 and has updated four editions with a fifth pending (Spring 1997). His primary thesis is that media corporation mergers and takeovers are diminishing the number of news sources and this threatens freedom of information in our society:

No single corporation controls all the mass media in the United States. But the daily newspapers, magazines, and broadcasting systems, books, motion pictures, and most other mass media are rapidly moving in the direction of tight control by a handful of huge multinational corporations. (Bagdikian, 1992: 3)

Bagdikian (1992) documents how the controlling interests of America's mass media were reduced from 46 to 23 corporations between 1981 and 1992, and he predicts there will be fewer than a dozen by the turn of the century. He is careful to note that journalists and editors still maintain strong ethical standards regarding objectivity, the First Amendment, and public access to information, but claims these standards tend to become structurally suppressed by bottom-line fiscal considerations as media corporations consolidate.

In a country where several daily newspapers have traditionally operated in a single city, we now have reached a point where 98 percent of U.S. cities have only one daily and 80 percent of these are owned by corporate chains. Gannett Inc., the largest newspaper chain in the U.S., currently owns over 80 dailies spread throughout the U.S., with a total readership of over six million (Alger, 1996; Bagdikian, 1992).

In *Culture Inc.* (1989) Herbert Schiller laments the corporate takeover of public expression by larger and larger privately-owned companies. He cautions against the complete privatization of cultural discourse and warns against the internationalization of media conglomeration. He also cites Bagdikian's work as essential to understanding media power formation.

Ever since public media advocates lost the national fight against the privatization of radio in 1934 (for a detailed history, see McChesney, 1991), the Federal Communications Commission (FCC) has set limits on the number of radio and television stations any single corporation could own. These limits were greatly reduced under the federal Telecommunications Act of 1996. This bill was described in the press as a grand celebration of the free market system. However, the nation's major news outlets did not find it the least bit newsworthy that for the first time in history, one individual or company could own an unlimited number of televisions and radio stations. The fact that the bill would allow one company to own radio, network, and cable television stations all in the same market also went unreported. Major news outlets did not find it worthwhile to report that the national "audience cap" had been raised to 35 percent, making it legal for only three companies to eventually own and control our entire news and information system (Lowenthal, 1996). Mass media coverage of the Telecoms bill fits the propaganda model perfectly. Self-interested corporate-owned news outlets did not critically debate the most important communications legislation passed by Congress in the past 60 years. Instead, the media industry contributed over two million dollars in PAC funds to Congress during the first half of 1995 to support pushing through the Telecoms bill (Naureckas, 1996).

Even the alternative press in the United States paid little attention to the monopoly impacts of the Telecoms legislation. Ralph Nader and James Love wrote a letter to the editor of TAP-INFO (an Internet newsletter) in July of 1995 decrying the bill as a closing up of the marketplace of ideas in America. They stressed the dangers of deregulating media ownership and warned of the monopoly impacts of the bill. Nader and Love's letter was eventually named the most censored story of 1995 by Project Censored, but still there was little or no debate on the issue of media concentration before passage of the bill (Jensen, 1996).

Since passage of the Telecoms bill, the issue of media concentration has become a cause célèbre among alternative publications in the United States. In late February 1996, the Institute for Alternative Journalism, managers of the national alternative news service Alternet, hosted a Media and Democracy conference in San Francisco which was attended by over 700 alternative press journalists, editors, and publishers. A central theme for the entire conference and the topic addressed by keynote speaker Ben Bagdikian was the negative impacts of the Telecoms bill and the threat of media monopoly in the United States. *The Nation* ran a special issue last June devoted to "The National Entertainment State" with comments by twenty media critics and a media concentration centerfold map (*The Nation*, June 3, 1996). (A reprint of *The Nation* article is in Chapter 7.) Similarly, The *Monthly Review*'s July 1996 issue was completely devoted to communications issues.

Mega-mergers and buyouts of national media organizations have accelerated rapidly in the past two years. Disney's takeover of ABC, Westinghouse's absorption of CBS and recent merger with Infinity, Microsoft's partnership with GE's NBC, and Time Warner's merger with Turner's CNN have created massive new media entities. In a 1996 update on propaganda theory, Ed Herman said:

The dramatic changes in the economy, communications industries, and politics over the past decade have tended to enhance the applicability of the propaganda model. The first two filters—ownership and advertising—have become ever more important. The decline of public broadcasting, the increase in corporate power and global reach, and the mergers and centralization of the media, have made bottom line considerations more controlling (Herman, 1996: 124).

The key concerns of propaganda theory, as expounded by Chomsky and Herman, and Bagdikian's media concentration, are as follows:

1. Media concentration is threatening freedom of information in the United States and this directly impacts the quality of democratic citizen participation.

2. Corporate media is diminishing the quality of investigative reporting and increasing the level of entertainment-oriented news coverage.

3. The public is taking an increasingly skeptical view of corporate news and is quantitatively limiting viewing and reading activities.

4. Editors tend to assign and approve stories that meet the expectations of their corporate owners and advertisers, and edit or cut stories that might tend to offend them.

5. Journalists within major media corporations will tend to ignore or tone down stories that might offend editors, owners, or advertisers.

6. Major mainstream corporate media outlets will tend to support the foreign affairs policies of the United States Government, and have become increasingly dependent on government sources for news story content.

In 1996, we conducted a study of these issues, by going directly to one of the most informed sources of information on the press—editors of U.S. newspapers. Our research focused on how alternative press and some mainstream editors currently view media concentration and the other issues listed above. A questionnaire was designed and field tested among participants at the Media and Democracy Conference in San Francisco in February 1996. Results from the field test allowed us to modify and clarify the questionnaire for our national survey. We used eighteen opinion statements reflecting both positive and negative aspects of propaganda/Bagdikian theory. Survey participants were given five choices in response to each statement: strongly agree, agree, disagree, strongly disagree, or no opinion. We had three sets of directly paired opposite statements to control for inconsistencies among the respondents. Also included in the statements were five questions of related interest, but not specifically selected to test our selected theories.

We used the mailing list from the Association of Alternative Newsweeklies (AAN) as our target group. Survey instruments were mailed to the editors of all 108 AAN newspapers. Twenty-eight surveys were returned giving us a 26 percent return rate representing an adequate sample for drawing general conclusions about propaganda/Bagdikian theory concerns among alternative newspaper editors in the United States.

In order to compare our alternative editors' survey results to current concerns of mainstream editors, we mailed out 200 surveys to editors of daily newspapers in the United States. This represented a 12.5 percent sample of 1,800 daily editors. We received twenty-five responses, a sample inadequate for drawing general conclusions about the total population, but certainly an interesting basis for comparison to the responses from the alternative press editors.

Overall, our fifty-three survey respondents represented mainstream and alternative newspapers in twenty-six states spread throughout the United States. The respondents were 86 percent male, 96 percent white, 47 percent were under 45 years of age, and 53 percent were over. The surveys were completely anonymous. All surveys were mailed with a cover letter explaining the research and contained self-addressed stamped envelopes for easy return. Of the 308 surveys mailed, we had an overall return rate of 17.2 percent.

For the purposes of this paper we collapsed the occupation categories into mainstream press and alternative press respondents. We then cross-tabulated the survey results for each individual question matching them with either mainstream or alternative editors.

Questions 1, 3, 4, 5, 8, 10, and 13 followed positive statements congruent with propaganda/Bagdikian theory. Questions 2, 6, 7, 11, and 14 followed statements negative to the theory, and questions 9, 12, 15, 16, and 18 were related topical questions not specifically addressed by the theories. Questions that were paired opposites followed statements 10-11, 13-14, and 15-18.

The paired opposites questions show a general consistency in the respondents agreement with propaganda/Bagdikian theory. The most theory-specific statements were 10 and 11, which had to do with media concentration:

STATEMENT 10. Consolidation of newspaper and media ownership into the hands of fewer and fewer corporations is a threat to the freedom of information in the United States.

STATEMENT 11. An increase in the amount of investigative journalism is likely to occur as major newspapers and broadcast stations are merged or consolidated into larger corporations.

Alternative press editors overwhelmingly expressed concern about media concentration. Ninety-two percent of alternative editors agreed with question 10 and 89 percent disagreed with question 11. Particularly interesting were the mainstream editors' responses to these questions. Sixty percent of the mainstream editors surveyed agreed with question 10 and 67 percent disagreed with question 11.

Questions 13 and 14 followed statements that had to do with the quality of news coverage in mainstream daily newspapers in the United States:

STATEMENT 13. Celebrity or entertainment-oriented news stories are becoming a greater part of most major newspapers' daily content.

STATEMENT 14. The quality of serious news stories has been improving at major newspapers and media outlets in the United States.

Again, alternative press editors' opinions were strongly consistent with propaganda/Bagdikian theory. Ninety-two percent of alternative press editors agreed with question 13 and 78 percent disagreed with question 14. Mainstream editors, while not quite as strong in their concerns, also were consistent with the theory, with 66 percent agreeing with question 13 and 64 percent disagreeing with question 14.

The final set of pair opposites were questions 15 and 18. These questions followed statements directed at the influence of right- and left-wing think tanks on U.S. newspaper press coverage. While not directly related to propaganda/Bagdikian theory, editors' perceptions concerning sources of information flow, as they relate to newspaper content, certainly seemed relevant to the issue of corporate influence on the media and the political direction of the national press:

STATEMENT 15. Right-wing political think tanks have had an increasingly greater influence on editorial policies at major newspapers.

STATEMENT 18. Left-leaning or liberal think tanks tend to have a strong influence on major national newspapers' editorial policies.

Alternative press editors are concerned with increasing right-wing influence on the mainstream press. Seventy-five percent of them agreed with question 15, and 71 percent disagreed with question 18. However, among mainstream editor respondents, 56 percent disagreed with question 15, meaning that many mainstream editors do not believe that right-wing think tanks have increased their influence. Yet, 71 percent disagreed with question 18 as well, perhaps meaning that they see neither left- nor right-leaning think tanks as having a strong influence. We found the results on these paired opposites interesting. It is clear that alternative press editors felt the right wing had a stronger influence on the mainstream press in the United States, but only 29 percent of mainstream editors surveyed thought there was such an influence.

Questions 3, 4, and 5 followed statements that had to do with the possibility that editors and journalists might kill or modify stories in order not to offend corporate owners or advertisers:

STATEMENT 3. Editors of major national newspapers occasionally kill news stories that they believe would run counter to the economic or ideological interests of the owners of their papers.

STATEMENT 4. Editors of major national newspapers occasionally kill stories that they believe would run counter to the economic or ideological interests of important advertisers.

STATEMENT 5. Journalists at major national newspapers occasionally tone down or shape news stories in order to conform to perceived expectations of owners or advertisers.

The results for these three questions are as follows:

STATEMENT	ALTERNATIVE EDITORS AGREEING	MAINSTREAM EDITORS AGREEING
3	78 %	42 %
4	78 %	48 %
5	82 %	40 %

The above results show that alternative press editors tend to believe that mainstream editors and journalists modify news stories to fit expectations of advertisers and owners, and that a significant minority of mainstream editors surveyed agreed with them. Nevertheless, this set of questions suggests a distinct difference between alternative and mainstream editors on this issue. The disagreeing mainstream editors were also more likely to strongly disagree on these three questions as well, suggesting that journalistic ethical resistance to owners/advertiser news manipulation is still a strong value among many mainstream editors.

We presented two statements that attempted to explore the issue of quality news reporting in corporate news systems verses independent or alternative newspapers:

STATEMENT 8. Newspapers owned by large multinational corporations tend to have a higher ideological filtering process for news stories than independently-owned newspapers.

STATEMENT 16. Independent 'alternative' newspapers and broadcasters tend to offer a more in-depth analysis of important news stories than major newspapers and national broadcasters.

Alternative press editors tended to agree with both statements, with 66 percent for question 8 and 68 percent for question 16. Mainstream editors took a negative view with 52 percent disagreeing with question 8 and 84 percent disagreeing with question 16. Here again we found differences between our two sets of editors. It seems clear that alternative editors believe in the high quality of independent newspapers, and that mainstream editors may not share this perspective.

A closely-related question to the above followed statement 2:

STATEMENT 2. Alternative newspapers tend to be less thorough in story development than major newspapers.

Mainstream editors surveyed actually split on this statement with 48 percent agreeing and 48 percent disagreeing (4 percent no opinion), whereas 82 percent of alternative editors disagreed with the statement. This seems to indicate that there is probably a good deal of respect by mainstream editors for the work alternative newspapers do, and, as indicated above, alternative editors feel their news work is qualitatively equal to—or better—than major newspapers.

Another closely-related question to independent verses corporate newspapers followed the statement: "Alternative press journalists tend to have greater freedom in reporting controversial stories than major national newspaper journalists" (*Statement 9*). Seventy-eight percent of alternative editors agreed with this statement, whereas only 44 percent of the mainstream editors were positive. Alternative editors firmly believe that their journalists have greater freedom in reporting the news than mainstream newspaper journalists, and a significant minority of mainstream editors may tend to agree with them.

Statements 1 and 17 addressed two specific aspects of propaganda/ Bagdikian theory—that of increasing public skepticism and mainstream media support of U.S. Government foreign policy positions:

STATEMENT 1. The U.S. public is becoming more critical of the information distribution role played by major newspapers and national media outlets.

STATEMENT 17. United States Government foreign policy positions tend to be reflected in major newspaper coverage of important foreign affairs.

STATEMENT	ALTERNATIVE EDITORS AGREEING	MAINSTREAM EDITORS AGREEING
1	68 %	78 %
17	96 %	60 %

In these two areas, concerns expressed by both sets of editors were consistent with propaganda/Bagdikian theory. Mainstream editors may actually agree with question 1 at a slightly higher rate than alternative press editors, meaning that they are in the forefront of mainstream public criticism and perhaps more aware of it. That 96 percent of alternative editors see the mainstream as supporting U.S. foreign policy was not a surprise, but that 60 percent of mainstream editors may agree was something we had not expected. It seems that in this area both alternative and mainstream editors tend to recognize

THIS MODERN WORLD   by TOM TOMORROW

that the mainstream press generally reflects the foreign policy positions of the United States Government.

The last three questions were added to assess if alternative and mainstream editors share or disagree with right-wing issues concerning the supposed liberal bias of the press and public media, and the importance of the free market economy. Each of the statements were designed to positively reflect general right-wing concerns about the media today and an agreement with the statement would indicate sympathy with current right-wing media criticism:

STATEMENT 6. Journalists at major national newspapers tend to have a liberal bias in reporting the news.

STATEMENT	ALTERNATIVE EDITORS DISAGREEING	MAINSTREAM EDITORS DISAGREEING
6	71 %	60 %

STATEMENT 7. Publicly-owned television and radio stations tend to have more bias in news reporting than privately-owned stations.

STATEMENT	ALTERNATIVE EDITORS DISAGREEING	MAINSTREAM EDITORS DISAGREEING
7	85 %	56 %

STATEMENT 12. The hidden hand of the economic marketplace tends to protect freedom of the press in the United States.

STATEMENT	ALTERNATIVE EDITORS DISAGREEING	MAINSTREAM EDITORS DISAGREEING
12	69 %	40 %

Alternative press editors' disagreement with questions 6, 7, and 12 indicates a general lack of sympathy for right-wing media issues, whereas mainstream editors seem less sure and tend to believe that there is a "liberal bias."

Our survey results lead us to believe that alternative press editors in the United States tend to be concerned about the main issues presented in propaganda/Bagdikian theory, and that to a lesser degree, mainstream editors probably share these concerns. Additionally, alternative press editors tend to believe that right-wing think tanks have had an increasingly greater influence on the major press in the U.S., and that left-leaning think tanks are less influential. They tend to reject right-wing perspectives on the liberal bias of media in the U.S. and the importance of free market systems for news services. Alternative press editors also feel that independent news organizations probably have greater editorial and journalistic freedom than mainstream groups, and that independent news organizations are more thorough in their story development than their mainstream counterparts.

Mainstream editors tend to disagree with the non-theory related statements. They view neither left- nor right-wing think tanks as having increased influence. Nor do they agree that alternative media have greater story development than the mainstream. It seems that mainstream editors might be split on the free market issue. This leads us to believe that the Bagdikian perspective, in which editors and journalists are ethical hard working people in a structurally changing system, is possibly correct.

Multi-national conglomeration, mixed media market intrusions, new technologies, and horizontal/vertical corporate expansions/takeovers will likely continue to alarm journalists and First Amendment advocates. The recently passed federal telecommunications legislation will likely accelerate these concerns and increase public dissatisfaction as well as professional journalist alienation.

Chomsky, Herman, and Bagdikian have given us a theoretical framework to measure ongoing hegemony. Their frame is compatible with hegemonic theory to the extent that media systems continue to structurally concentrate their distribution and funding processes. The extent to which professional journalists and editors, the public at large, and the alternative press will resist these structural changes, however, remains to be seen.

This work suggests that expanded survey studies of mainstream and alternative editors would likely help monitor these issues, and provide a deeper grounding of the theories. Freedom of the press is important to the preservation of democracy and a valuable sociological endeavor worthy of broader study.

BIBLIOGRAPHY

Adair, Stephen, "Class Domination and Ideological Hegemony," *Quarterly Journal of Ideology*, vol. 12, no. 3 (1988): 15-35.

Alger, Dean, *The Media and Politics*, 2nd Edition. Wadsworth Publishing Company, 1996.

Altheide, David L., "Media Hegemony: A Failure of Perspective," *Public Opinion Quarterly*, vol 48 (1984): 476-490.

Bagdikian, Ben H. *The Media Monopoly*. Boston: Beacon Press, 1992.

Becker, Lee B. & Gerald M. Kosicki, "Understanding the Messages-Producer/Message-Receiver Transaction," *Research in Political Sociology*, vol. 7 (JAI Press, 1995): 33-62.

Biltereyst, Daniël, "Qualitative Audience Research and Transnational Media Effects," *European Journal of Communication*, vol. 10, no. 2 (London: SAGE, 1992): 245-270.

Carrage, Kevin, "Critical Evaluation of Debates Examining the Media Hegemony Thesis," *Western Journal of Communication*, no. 57 (1993): 330-348.

Carter, Bill, "Children's TV, Where the Boys Are King," *The New York Times*, May 1, 1991.

Chomsky, Noam & Edward Herman, *Manufacturing Consent: The Political Economy of the Mass Media*. Pantheon, 1988.

Chomsky, Noam, *Necessary Illusions: Thought Control In Democratic Society*. Boston: South End Press, 1989.

Cohen, Jeff & Norman Solomon, *Through the Looking Glass: Decoding Bias and Blather in the News*. Common Courage Press, 1995.

Croteau, David & William Hoynes, *By Invitation Only: How the Media Limit Political Debate*. Common Courage Press, 1994.

Demac, Donna, *Liberty Denied: The Current Rise of Censorship in America*. New York: PEN American Center, 1988.

Fairchild, Henry Pratt (ed.) *Dictionary of Sociology And Related Sciences*. Totowa: Littlefield, Adams & Co., 1976.

Haines, Harry W., "Putting Vietnam Behind Us: Hegemony and the Gulf War," *Studies in Communication*, vol. 5 (JAI Press, 1995): 35-67.

Herman, Edward, "The Propaganda Model Revisited," *Monthly Review*, vol. 48, no. 3 (New York: Monthly Review Press, 1996): 115-128.

Hills, Stuart, *Corporate Violence*. Rowman and Littlefield, 1987.

Jansen, Sue Curry, *Censorship: The Knot That Binds Power and Knowledge*. Oxford: Oxford University Press, 1996.

Jensen, Carl, *Censored: The News That Didn't Make The News and Why*. New York: Seven Stories Press, 1996.

Keane, John, *The Media and Democracy*. Cambridge: Polity Press, 1991.

Lewis, Charles, "Making Sense of Common Sense: A Framework for Tracking Hegemony," *Critical Studies In Mass Communications*, vol. 9 (1992): 277-292.

Lipset, Seymour Martin (ed.), *The Encyclopedia of Democracy*, vol. 1., [Donald A. Downs & Samual Nelson: "Censorship"]. Washington: Congressional Quarterly, Inc., 1995: 188-191.

Lowenthal, Mark, "Censoring The Telecoms Debate," *Albion Monitor*, February 18, 1996 (URL-http://www.monitor.net).

Mazzocco, Dennis, *Networks of Power: Corporate TV's Threat To Democracy*. Boston: South End Press, 1994.

McChesney, Robert, "Press-Radio Relations and the Emergence of Network, Commercial Broadcasting in the United States, 1930-1935," *Historical Journal of Film, Radio and Television*, vol. 11, no. 1 (1991): 41-57.

Nader, Ralph & James Love, "Telecommunication Deregulation: Closing Up of America's 'Marketplace of Ideas.'" *TAP-INFO*, July 15, 1995 (listproc@tap.org).

Naureckas, Jim, "Info-Bandits: Media Conglomerates Hijacked Telecommunications Policy with Millions in PAC Contributions," *In These Times*, March 4, 1996: 14-17.

Parenti, Michael, *Inventing Reality*. St. Martin's Press, 1986.

Postman, Neil, *Amusing Ourselves to Death*. New York: Penguin Books, 1985.

Sallach, David, "Class Domination and Ideological Hegemony," *The Sociological Quarterly*, vol. 15 (1974): 38-50.

Schiller, Herbert, *Culture Inc.: The Corporate Take Over of Public Expression*. New York: Oxford University Press, 1989.

Silverstein, Ken, "China's Hired Guns," *Multinational Monitor*, April 1996.

Sproule, J. Michael, "Progressive Propaganda Critics and the Magic Bullet Myth," *Critical Studies in Mass Communication*, Vol. 6 No. 3 (September 1989): 225-246.

Stabile, Carol A., "Resistance, Recuperation, and Reflexivity: The Limits of a Paradigm," *Critical Studies in Mass Communication*, no. 12 (1995): 403-422.

Stauber, John & Sheldon Rampton, *Toxic Sludge is Good for You!: Lies, Damn Lies and the Public Relations Industry*. Monroe: Common Courage Press, 1995.

Wasburn, Philo C., "Democracy and Media Ownership: a Comparison of Commercial, Public and Government Broadcast News," *Media, Culture and Society*, vol. 17 (London, Thousand Oaks, and New Delhi: SAGE, 1995): 647-676.

Webb, Gary, "Dark Alliance," the series, *San Jose Mecury News*, August 18, 19, and 20, 1996.

CHAPTER 6

Reviews of Current Books on Media, Censorship, and the First Amendment

Project Censored staff selected twelve books on media, censorship, and the First Amendment for review by scholars from various disciplines. These works represent both academic and general interest books published in the last two years, and were selected to give our readers an overview of important ongoing issues in the field. For more information visit Project Censored's World Wide Web site at: http://censored.sonoma.edu/ProjectCensored/

INFORMATION INEQUALITY:
The Deepening Social Crisis
in America
Herbert I. Schiller
Routledge, 1996
Reviewed by: Marshall Battani

Those familiar with Herbert Schiller's work have come to expect a deft analysis and critique of the political and economic machinations that drive the corporate takeover of public expression in the United States and abroad. His newest book, *Information Inequality: The Deepening Social Crisis in America*, is no disappointment as Schiller reprises and synthesizes arguments maintained over the course of his career. These arguments critique the rise of the information society as an extension of corporate control over culture and communication and take on new urgency because, "For the first time in almost a century, capitalism exists without powerful, organized opposition." Confronted with both the so-called "failure of socialism" around the world, and a pervasively cynical U.S. society willing to accept the intrusion of market principles into every aspect of life within the United States, Schiller introduces his analysis by posing the vexing question of where resistance to corporate control might come from.

Before directly answering the question of resistance, Schiller takes the reader over familiar territory. In the first three chapters Schiller chronicles the transformation of the institutional infrastructure of the United States made possible by "the deregulation of economic activity, privatization of functions once public, and commercialization of activities once social." According to Schiller, the tempo of this transformation has accelerated in the last fifteen years, and, given the increasing centrality of communication and information to U.S. and global economies, this transformation has had a devastating effect on the democratic character of American society. The irony of our current era is that, despite the impressive capabilities of communication and information technologies, we live in a state of "Data Deprivation" (the title of Chapter Three) in which we produce tremendous amounts of information with little or no social value. The result is both an "invisible" social control—accomplished through the routine processes of "filtering" as the corporate-controlled mass media and other cultural institutions select the stories and images they will transmit—and more blatant assaults on democratic expression stemming from the increasing corporate presence and influence over elections, non-profit organizations, day-to-day government business, and the "public" schools.

This is the sort of analysis readers have come to expect from Schiller and it comes as no surprise when he turns his gaze in Chapters Four through Seven to the global ramifications of these developments. In these chapters Schiller uses his well-developed critique of the global marketing of U.S. popular culture (see his *Communication and Cultural Domination*, 1976) to make sense of the latest showpiece of the corporate communication sector: the Internet. In his earlier work, Schiller demonstrated the destabilizing effects that global marketing of U.S. popular culture has on developing states and here he incorporates the commercialization of the Internet as the latest development of American imperialism. As Schiller describes it, the Internet—first devised for military superiority—is accelerating a less militaristic, but no less imperialistic, drive toward capitalist domination.

Ultimately, claims Schiller, "Private information monopolies are contributing, by their fierce, and to date successful, opposition to social oversight, to the growing global and national crisis of governability" and he finishes by urging the reader to look inside the media giants themselves to find the seeds of resistance.

MARSHALL BATTANI is a Ph.D. candidate in Sociology at University of California at Davis.

SELLING THE AIR:
A Critique of The Policy
of Commercial Broadcasting
in the United States
Thomas Streeter
University of Chicago Press, 1996
Reviewed by: Andy Merrifield

Streeter's book looks at the history of United States governmental policy on the use of radio and television by the private sector, employing an ideological and legalistic structure. The author contends that the system developed to control that part of the airwaves left available to the general public evolved out of a functionalist view of society and the market. Streeter argues that this functionalist view was evolving as part of the evolution of corporate liberalism as the primary structure for the operation and control of the U.S. political-economic system. He further contends that the policies pursued by the national government in the first two decades of the twentieth century played a pivotal role in creating the private industry, disputing the interpretation that the government responded to a burgeoning market with regulation. This reading of the issue reverses the normal perception of how government operates.

In attempting to demonstrate his argument, Streeter relies first on a lengthy discussion of the U.S. political culture of corporate liberalism. According to the author, this form of liberalism relies on the government to protect the ongoing and dominant features of liberalism, most particularly the retention of private property. Regulation therefore saves private ownership, more than it hampers it.

The rest of the book chronicles the legislation and policy implementation of private broadcasting to clarify how this philosophical commitment to corporate liberalism not only supports private property and "free enterprise," but in the process tends to best support larger and wealthier private organizations against the claims of smaller private groups or individuals. In Streeter's interpretation, the corporation wins, not the entrepreneur or the amateur. The most important early legislation passed to deal with private broadcasting—the Radio Acts of 1912 and 1927 and the Communication Act of 1934—all underpin and promote broadcasting as a medium used to sell advertising for national businesses. This was not the inevitable outcome. The nature of the industry did not lead inexorably to the victory of the large corporation; however, the political power of the major corporations and the belief in corporate liberalism by mainstream politicians and opinion leaders did. The legislation that followed for both radio and television tended to endorse and enhance this outcome.

The author's purpose is not only explanatory, but prescriptive. He argues that with the massive changes in communication media—changes like cable, fiber optics, and the "net"—that it is time to revisit the discussion of broadcasting structure and corporate liberalism. He calls for a whole new debate. Rather than a narrow discussion on practical issues like censorship, the discussion should be much more fundamental: "What does ownership mean" and "ownership for whom?"

ANDY MERRIFIELD, PH.D. is an Associate Professor of Political Science at Sonoma State University and a Project Censored evaluator.

NETWORKS OF POWER:
Corporate TV's Threat
to Democracy
Dennis W. Mazzocco
Boston: South End Press, 1994
Reviewed by: Myrna Goodman

Among the more intriguing facts Dennis Mazzocco includes in this study of the growth and eventual merger of ABC and Capital Cities Corporation, is his description of ABC's early connections with Walt Disney Studios. In 1954, ABC entered into an alliance with Disney Studios by purchasing thousands of shares in Disneyland, which was in the planning and design stages. Leonard Goldenson, president of ABC at that time, also used his connections with a Dallas banker to broker a substantial amount of the additional capital Disney needed but had been unable to find to begin the project. "In exchange for this financial help, ABC received all of the profits from Disneyland's food concessions for 10 years..." The early connection between ABC and Disney is made all the more interesting now that Disney has purchased ABC/Capital Cities.[1]

Mazzocco carefully documents how deregulation and the lure of potentially enormous profits in the communications industry have led to an increasingly less diversified media. The continuing consolidation of media outlets into the hands of fewer and fewer owners has also adversely affected the flow of information in the public interest. Changes in ownership rules have allowed large media conglomerates like ABC/Capital Cities to turn to mass marketing strategies and this in turn has homogenized broadcast programming. It should come as no surprise that the insiders at ABC and Capital Cities have also consistently

[1]Mazzocco wrote this book before the Disney/ABC/Capital Cities merger.

molded the content of programming to reflect their conservative political ideologies.

Mazzocco devotes a full chapter (Chapter Four) to an exploration of the intricacies of the Capital Cities/ABC takeover/merger. The negotiations took place in the midst of the Reagan Administration's dismantling of several of the last remaining FCC regulations on broadcast ownership limits. A former Capital Cities vice-president, James Quello, who was also a commissioner on the FCC at the time, strongly supported deregulation. In light of all this, it is unsurprising that the relaxing of FCC rules limiting ownership of broadcast stations eventually enabled ABC/Capital Cities to expand into markets that had previously been closed to them. Expansion of the number of stations under its control provided enormous profits for its investors. The additional outlets allowed a reduction in programming costs because they could be spread over a broader distribution system. This homogenization of programming has had a serious effect on the quality and diversity of the information provided to the general public. Mazzocco's discussion of how these successful deregulation efforts have undermined the quality and diversity of programming is especially cogent and informative.

An important part of this book is the author's analysis of the consistent influence of conservative ideology on the programming content at ABC. One need only turn to Mazzocco's discussion of ABC's dealings with ultra right-wing Republican journalists during the 1940s and 1950s to learn that intrusion into ABC's programming by CIA Director Casey during the 1980s was predated by J. Edgar Hoover several decades earlier. During the postwar and McCarthy eras, a network of Hollywood conservatives who were interconnected by friendship and political ideology found ABC a willing partner in their attempts to influence public opinion. During that time, ABC radio and television stations broadcast the programs of Louella Parsons, Walter Winchell, and George Sokolsky, all of whom were "...virulent anti-communist conservatives."

With their help, J. Edgar Hoover was persuaded to have his series on the FBI broadcast on ABC. Hoover chose ABC because he was assured that the program would be produced by ABC's Hollywood affiliate, "...Warner Brothers, a strong supporter of the 1950s anti-communist purges in Hollywood." ABC productions of programs about the FBI on both radio and television presented Hoover and the FBI as clean-cut, all-American heroes at a time when they were systematically harassing political activists. [2]

[2] It is no small irony that Mazzocco reports that ABC was responsible for bringing Rush Limbaugh to New York City from a station in Sacramento, CA. ABC eventually syndicated and distributed his programs nationally.

Mazzocco's personal experiences as a former television worker for ABC sharpen his insights and analyses. He is also sensitive to the reduction in union influence in the broadcast media and has first-hand experience with the changing working conditions at the TV networks. Although on occasion the narrative moves back and forth in time and strands the reader, this is a vital and important study that brings the reader a richer understanding of what has been lost in the media. Mazzocco's last chapter contains a thoughtful, detailed program of action that he believes can remold the media into an institution that serves the public interest. This book deserves the attention of anyone who believes restoring democracy to the media is vital and important work.

MYRNA GOODMAN is a Ph.D. candidate at the University of California at Davis and lectures in Sociology and Women's Studies at Sonoma State University.

THE MEDIA AND MODERNITY:
Social Theory of the Media
John B. Thompson
Stanford University Press, 1996
Reviewed by: Ivan Harsløf

Whereas the interplay between the communications media and democracy *per se* has been the subject for various studies, the role of the media in the more overall development of modern societies has by and large been left unexplored by social scientists. In *The Media and Modernity: Social Theory of the Media*, it is John B. Thompson's ambition to examine the role of the media in these transformative processes.

According to Thompson, democracy, as a way of rule, is increasingly coming under pressure as a result of a number of processes which together constitute what is called modernity.

Because processes of globalization are leading to international relationships of dependence and interdependence, political decisions taken in the single nation-state may have consequences far beyond its territorial frontiers. In a similar way, decisions taken today may have vital impact on future generations. The free scope left for political decisions is becoming increasingly narrowed by forces external to the control of democracy. Political institutions are gradually losing their legitimacy in the public eye, a trend which is reflected in the declining membership in political parties in a number of countries. Cynicism and disillusionment have to some extent replaced political engagement. And inequalities, created by the market, are challenging the principle that democracy should be a system where all citizens can participate on equal terms.

John B. Thompson analyzes how the development of communications media has been, and is increasingly, interwoven in these coercive processes of modernity. It is his intention to bring the analysis of the media, and its development, into the center of social science. Throughout the book, he puts forward the argument that the development of the media, and its impact on the institutions which are shaping modern societies, should be regarded as one of the main constituting factors for the organization of the world of today.

Thompson outlines a broad concept of communications media as the production, transmission, and reception of symbolic forms mediated by a technical and institutional apparatus. Visibility is a term which Thompson puts forward in order to characterize the impact that the development of media has on political and social life. By increasing the ability to locate phenomenons and make them visible to a broad audience, the media have fundamentally changed the conditions for democracy, as well as for any other political system. The political establishment can no longer fully restrict its self-presentation. The success of politicians and political institutions is, according to Thompson, greatly dependent on how they manage their visibility.

However, there is an aspect of media-created visibility which Thompson unfortunately does not really consider. There is no doubt that the development of media has expanded the pool of information about the political sphere available to the public, thus making the "back regions" of political systems more vis-ible. But a more critical examination of the dominating media today might add another dimension to the notion of visibility: the tendency in the media to focus on the direct visible 'facts' rather than the less visible conditions which form them. In a modern world, the links between cause and effect can be so complex and intangible that they hardly can be visualized given the superficial way in which the most dominating types of media approach the investigative process.

According to Thompson, our sense of the past, present, and future has been changed because of the development of communications media. A "mediated historicity," based on the growing number of symbolic forms produced by the media, has gradually replaced the oral form of handing over experience and tradition from one generation to the next as the most important source of images of the past. Similarly, a "mediated worldliness" has been established by the media. This means that our sense of the present world to a great extent lies beyond the sphere of our personal experience, drawing instead on the images of the world provided by the media. Finally, the accelerating speed of the communications flow has changed the experience of time and thus our sense of the future; as life intensifies, the future becomes less predictable and the prospective span of time which is considered in the present becomes shorter.

Thompson regards the media as a

part of the solution as well as part of the problem confronting the modern world. He assigns a crucial role to the media in the formation of a "deliberative" democracy set up to cope with the processes of modernity. Thus, the media are a potential promoter of awareness of an increasingly common destiny among the inhabitants of the world.

Thompson's theoretical elaboration is accompanied by a thorough and insightful account of the actual development of communications technology and media institutions. Beginning with the Middle Ages in Europe, he tracks the roots of the media industry and shows that its origin is linked to major economic, political, and religious developments. A whole chapter is devoted to the globalization of communication. Here we get an overview of the activities of the transnational media conglomerates, as well as the influence of sophisticated transmission technology. Thompson discusses the unequal placement of media producers among the continents, leading to an asymmetrical flow of information in favor of the industrialized world, and he considers unequal access to the information to be due to the lack of appropriate receiver technology.

Overall, *The Media and Modernity* is a comprehensive and substantial contribution to mapping the ubiquitous media in the landscape of social science. It provides us with a coherent framework of concepts and thus places media analysis in a holistic understanding of the modern world.

IVAN HARSLØF is a graduate student at the University of Aalborg, Denmark.

MEDIA MATTERS: Race and Gender in U.S. Politics
John Fiske
Minneapolis: University of Minnesota Press, 1996.
Reviewed by: Catherine Nelson

In this at times brilliant book, John Fiske analyzes media events that reflect the cultural struggles of Americans as they attempt to come to terms with, and exert influence upon, the social changes in the United States as it moves from a society dominated by a relatively homogeneous, Eurocentric consensus to a diverse, multicultural social order. In particular, Fiske reviews the role the media played in reporting and creating three main events in the early-1990s: the Dan Quayle/Murphy Brown family values debate, Anita Hill's charges against Supreme Court nominee Clarence Thomas, and the Rodney King beating and its aftermath. Fiske argues that in all three cases (and in the O.J. Simpson criminal trial addressed in the Epilogue), the media perpetuated a specifically white discourse that dominates our political order.

Understanding the philosophical approach used in this book is key to understanding its true worth. Fiske is an avowed postmodernist, and throughout the book, clarifies and re-emphasizes his analytical framework. He states repeatedly that in a postmodern age, no truth is absolute or even stable. This is especially significant in an evaluation of the media's role in creating reality. The media does not cover an event as a neutral observer reporting the truth; rather the media provides a representation of the event loaded with meaning, to the extent that we cannot rely upon a clear distinction between the real event, and its mediated representation. Meanings are made and used in particular historical, social, and political conditions, and are employed to extend or defend the interests of a particular community. This process defines postmodern discourse, which Fiske argues is always a terrain of struggle on an unlevel playing field. The danger of the media's involvement is that as it serves to perpetuate the dominant white discourse, it makes others invisible, silencing alternate views against which dominant meanings can be evaluated. Indeed, Fiske's most useful contribution is in his use of postmodernism to show us the discourses of the others against whom whiteness is defined, and upon whose subordination and silencing it depends.

While Fiske's discussion of gender is overshadowed by his attention to race, his comments about the media representation of Anita Hill's charges of sexual harassment against Supreme Court nominee Clarence Thomas are noteworthy. The confirmation hearings protrayed black sexuality, and its historical white meanings, in a way that led some African Americans to view them not in terms of the high-tech lynching of Clarence Thomas, but of the lynching and raping of African Americans in general. In a representation as old as slavery, Clarence Thomas was the black male as sexualized racial threat to the white social order, a threat white supporters of Clarence Thomas had to overcome by focusing not on what Clarence Thomas did, but on what Anita Hill allegedly was: the hypersexualized black female. She then bears the responsibility for the situation, making her the perfect decoy for the white male members of the Senate Judiciary Committee. While white women characterized the hearings as a gender issue and came to Anita Hill's support on that basis, Fiske argues that gender alone cannot explain the significance of the event. Race and gender both are necessary to understand how it perpetuated white attempts to control the threat of black sexuality.

Fiske is at his best in his discussion of the Rodney King beating and its aftermath as a media event. He contrasts the original videotape of the beating made by George Holliday with a home video camera, with the computer enhanced version made for the trial of the white officers accused of using excessive force. Fiske terms the original home video "videolow," characterized by its "...poor and unsteady focus, unplanned camera position and angle, and its subservience to 'real time' (no editing)." The videolow was "...low in clarity but high in authenticity," as it was a reflection of the lowness of the social position from which it spoke, and the true experiences of the disempowered. The "videohigh," on the other hand, was computer-enhanced, and either frozen in individual frames during the trial, or slowed, or reversed. It was used to create a specific reality in which the victim of the beating, Rodney King, was actually the aggressor, threatening the police officers in such a way that they had to use excessive force to subdue him. In the process, Rodney King was transformed into "...an animalized threat to white civilization." As Fiske argues, what is seen is what matters; the distinction between what is unseen, even if "true," and how it is represented by the media, even if recreated, not only makes no difference, but "...is no longer achievable." In this manner, it is possible to make Rodney King responsible for the white police officers' actions, and blacks in general "...in control of their own subordination, through their control over the degree of their submissiveness," all the while erasing "...white power and responsibility from the picture." Fiske's introduction into the discussion of Black Liberation Radio, and other "knowledge gangsters," who provide alternative discourses, provides a means to put that responsibility back into the picture.

While Fiske's thesis about the invisibility of whiteness is not unique (see bell hooks and Ruth Frankenberg, for example), his illumination of postmodernism and white discourse in media events is a powerful contribution to the existing literature. He ultimately concludes that while no truth is absolute because all knowledge is mediated, we are still faced with the task of deciding what to treat as true. Fiske warns that mediated knowledge can be used to keep things invisible, as white discourse strives so mightily to do, or it can be used to reveal things that can challenge the representations of those who have power. Fiske clearly engages in the latter.

CATHERINE NELSON, PH.D. is an Assistant Professor of Political Science at Sonoma State University and a Project Censored evaluator. She specializes in political theory and the politics of gender and race.

POWER OF NEWS
Michael Schudson
Cambridge: Harvard University
    Press, 1995
Reviewed by: Robert McNamara

Michael Schudson's *Power of the News* is not only a valuable critique of those unexamined "myths" concerning the role of the media in a democratic society, but also a worthwhile discussion on the notion of a "democratic process" in American politics today. Rather than simply accepting many of the well-established views of media critics, Schudson goes a step further. Thus, Noam Chomsky and Edward Herman are viewed as holding a "sophomoric, populist vision" which sees "capitalist self-interest at every turn." Of course media owners are driven by markets, the author argues, yet "media owners must also be obedient to market demands or at least their sense of what the market demands." The complexity of the American population and of the media industry itself suggests the equation is much more complex than simply pleasing the powers that be.

It is in this light that Schudson puts forth his thesis: News is a form of culture. Journalism "...is the matrix of institutions and outlooks that produce people who understand their situation in these terms." With this thesis in mind, Schudson embarks upon an interesting and well-documented study which argues that the media are not nearly as important as "popular reflexes" would suggest. Rather, more important influences on the fabric of society come from family, schools, state government, and perhaps even the criminal justice system. Yes, the media are important. Yet they tend to

follow—not lead. What they produce (and reproduce) is not information but, instead, what is generally accepted public knowledge (culture) given certain political structures and traditions.

To support this argument, Schudson goes against the grain of conventional thinking among media critics and questions many of the long-held beliefs (myths) that the media themselves have perpetuated.

Media critics and political consultants regularly cite as conclusive evidence that the eye is more powerful than the ear in American politics. Leslie Stahl's experience reporting on Reagan for CBS or the Kennedy-Nixon televised debate in 1960 are often noted as support of this contention. Yet, do the "eyes" really have it? Schudson challenges this long-held assumption that the public can simply be mesmerized by television images, noting that it does not take into account many other factors. In fact, the American people do have other things on their minds (e.g., paying bills, getting the kids off to school, etc.) which those inside the beltway tend to overlook. In addition, the public does pay attention to polls, economic indicators, and other factors which reflect their own personal situation. Thus, while the media elite tend to overestimate the power of the visual, Schudson argues, at the same time they also "underrate their own power to reinterpret the visual."

Schudson adds to this critique of "telemythology" by challenging another general argument in media politics. It has long been accepted by media critics that television turned the American public against the Vietnam War. In fact, there is very little evidence to support this, Schudson argues. Rather, the anti-war movement was well ahead of the media on this one. Television coverage of the Vietnam War provided very little combat footage in the years during which opposition to the war mounted.

Schudson saves his best example of the power of media myths, however, for an entire chapter on "The Illusion of Ronald Reagan's Popularity." Contrary to some conclusions that Ronald Reagan was a great communicator and his mastery of television led to his mastery of the American public, Schudson contends that the more important factor in Reagan's success as a media star was the Washington establishment's fascination with Reagan. In fact, compared to his elected predecessors, polls indicated that Reagan actually had the lowest average approval rating for the first two years of his Administration—just as his legend of "the Great Communicator" grew the most.

As for other misconceptions on the power of media in American politics, Schudson explores the "myths" surrounding the role of the media during Watergate. Did two young *Washington Post* reporters really bring down the President of the United States as some media elite would have us believe? Of course not. Rather, the press was but one institution among many, with Congress, the courts, and the FBI, among others, all making equally important contributions.

Perhaps the only time Schudson strays from his otherwise thought-provoking analysis is in the section entitled "The News in Historical Perspective." This material is somewhat out of place from the otherwise exciting thesis being explored. Granted, the book is a collection of essays dating as far back as 1982. Yet, perhaps these particular essays (e.g., "A History of the News Interview") would be most appreciated in another collection.

Schudson's conclusions address the question, "Can the news media help create a more democratic society?" Yes, he argues. Not only can they, but they should. Yet, while a classical democracy may be the ideal, the reality is that not all citizens are or ever will be "rational, intelligent, active, and constant participants in the political process." Thus, the role of the media, Schudson argues, is to reflect the virtues of "schizophrenia." That is to say, the role of the news media should be to act as if classical democracy were within reach, yet, also reflect the reality of American political culture which tells us there are many who will never be informed participants in the political process.

Overall, while the reader may not accept all of his critique (some media consultants will certainly take issue with his skepticism of the power of the media as a driving force in primary elections), Schudson, nevertheless, offers much food for thought concerning the otherwise accepted "truisms" in media politics. The book is a refreshing contribution to the discourse on power and the media in American political culture.

ROBERT McNAMARA, PH.D. is an Assistant Professor of Political Science at Sonoma State University and a Project Censored evaluator.

THE MEDIA AND POLITICS, 2nd ed.

Dean E. Alger
Belmont: Wadsworth Publishing
    Company, 1996
Reviewed by: John F. Kramer

The founding fathers considered one business to be so important to the proper functioning of democratic government that they gave that business, in the First Amendment to the Constitution, constitutional protection from government interference. That business wasn't dry cleaning, or even shipbuilding. It was, of course, the press. Now, more than two centuries later, in a continental nation of 260 million citizens, with weakened political parties but powerful interest groups, and an interdependent world of five and a half billion people, the mass media has become virtually the only link between most citizens, their government, and the rest of the world.

Today, as Walter Lippmann observed almost 75 years ago, the media paint the pictures in our minds upon which we act or don't act as citizens of a democracy.

So we should welcome this thoughtful, readable, and comprehensive review of (mostly) American media and politics. The book is intended as a primary text in a college level course on politics and the media, or as a reference for media scholars. But it is so clearly and interestingly written that lay readers with a concern for the role of media in American politics will find it an accessible and thoughtful guide to the subject.

What do scholars know, for example, about Ronald Reagan's or Bill Clinton's effectiveness on television? In what ways do they move their audience? How do the *pictures* change the nature of political discourse?

In two chapters on the nature of communication and persuasion and the characteristics of mass media, Alger introduces recent media research findings on both of these presidents. For Clinton, he analyzes the effectiveness of Clinton's biographical campaign video, "A Place Called Hope." For Reagan, Alger shows how Reagan successfully used his television persona to calm fears about his governmental policies.

The text begins with a brief but effective discussion of the unique importance of the media in a democracy. It turns then to the nature of communication, information processing, political socialization, and public opinion. Here Alger emphasizes the dominant medium of socialization: television. If our images of Washington and Jefferson come primarily from textbooks, certainly our erroneous beliefs about Canadian health care or the likelihood of being mugged come to us via television.

Television is different from other media. It often reaches us when we are passive, and uncritical, with a directness and intimacy which can greatly enhance its believability. Its pictures more easily arouse our emotions which in turn enhances our recall of its messages.

Is the unique power of television justification for caution in its control and use? Alger considers this issue in a discussion of media policy in this most capitalistic of media arenas: the United States. He describes the drive toward conglomeration and monopoly during recent times and the deregulation of the Reagan era which helped facilitate this concentration. He worries about the consequences: the relatively few sources that dominate the media and news, their ability to move profits from one division to another to drive out competition, and the possibility of censorship or conflict of interest. How, for example, will NBC cover the nuclear power issue now that its giant corporate owner, General Electric, is a major producer of nuclear power plants?

Alger's summary of the diminished regulatory environment and increased media concentration of the 1980s and early 1990s ends before the passage of the Telecommunications Reform Act of 1996. The Act and additional mega-mergers which followed have accelerated the trends which Alger describes.

It is through the news that media have the most direct effect on politics, public opinion, and public affairs. For newspapers and news magazines, the news is essential for attracting readers. For broadcasters, until the mid-1970s, a strong news organization was the hallmark of a credible network. It was, in addition, a demonstration of the public service required as a condition of the stations' licenses.

But as the networks and stations were taken over by the conglomerates, they became profit centers. This included the news organizations. So the news became entertaining, in order to attract audiences. Local news also had to draw audiences, lest the networks lose the flow of the audience into prime time. Consultants were hired to change the sets, to promote banter and happy talk. And improvements in technology allowed nearly instantaneous coverage of accidents, crime, and violence. Story priorities became, "If it bleeds, it leads." Newspapers and news magazines began also to change their format and content in the competition for audiences.

In this bottom-line era, Alger's recalling of the evolution of broadcast regulation and the expectation of stewardship on the part of the broadcasters is very important. The FCC's Fairness Doctrine obligated broadcasters not only to be fair in their coverage of news and public affairs, but also "to devote a reasonable amount of time to the coverage of controversial issues of public importance."

Dating back to the 1940s, the Fairness Doctrine was created by the FCC when an owner of several radio stations "ordered his news staff to 'slant, distort, and falsify' news against such 'enemies'...as President Roosevelt...and to place such stories...with those about communists and criminals so that they might seem related." President Reagan's FCC appointees abolished the Fairness Doctrine in 1987. Nowadays, the FCC wouldn't give such broadcaster behavior a second thought.

Alger describes the news-creating process and the organizational and technological factors that effect the process. He then turns to the more difficult assessment of the effect of the news on the public. Here we learn of the earliest surprising research finding of minimal effects and of the more recent findings of subtle but quite consequential effects: agenda-setting, priming, framing, and others. In matters that we care about, the media do not tell us what to *think*, but rather what to think *about*. Moreover, the manner of presentation of stories in the media can influence *how* we think about them. Thus, the most important biases may be both subtle and inadvertent. A news story on poverty featuring interviews in a homeless shelter may lead viewers to see poverty as a matter of personal failure rather than a consequence of governmental and business employment policies. Alger presents these complex recent research findings in a brief but clearly written summary.

Following the general discussion of news and its effects, the text turns to coverage of governmental institutions, of foreign affairs, and elections. Because communications in elections have been much studied, there is much to report. Alger discusses first the methods by which we study elections, then the news coverage of campaigns, and finally the effects intended and unintended on the public. This is a very informative discussion of the major research findings. Readers will quickly recognize the game scenario for election coverage and then be troubled by the findings that the public learns more about candidate issue positions from political advertising than from the evening news.

The text concludes with a brief comparison to politics and the media in Europe and a reprise of some of the issues identified in earlier chapters of the role of the media, especially television, in a democratic society.

The Media and Politics successfully synthesizes much of what we know about the effects of the media on American politics. For each topic, the references are a fine guide to the most important contributions in that area. The book stands as a thoughtful and sometimes troubling contribution to our understanding.

JOHN F. KRAMER, PH.D. is a Professor of Political Science at Sonoma State University and a Project Censored evaluator.

THROUGH THE MEDIA LOOKING GLASS:
Decoding Bias and Blather in the News
Jeff Cohen and Norman Solomon
Monroe, Maine: Common Courage
    Press, 1995
Reviewed by: Rick Luttmann

The authors of *Through the Media Looking Glass*, have written and spoken widely on media matters. Jeff Cohen is the founder and executive director of FAIR, the acronym for the media-watch organization Fairness and Accuracy In Reporting. Cohen and Solomon write a syndicated weekly column called "Media Beat."

This book is a provocative look at the failures of the mainstream press in America to get out the news the American people need in order to make democracy work. The whole philosophy of democratic government depends on people knowing the facts, knowing what their political leaders are doing, knowing what their own interests are, and knowing who will benefit and who will lose from any proposed public policy. The free press is supposed to assure the people's access to this information. Measured against this standard, the U.S. press is a dismal failure.

What's the problem? Probably not evil intent by reporters and journalists, but certainly—in the authors' view—evil intent by greedy and self-serving politicians, capitalists, and publishers. Though the authors never used the word "conspiracy," there is certainly a culture among the elite and powerful classes pulling the strings in our country that works against the people's interests. If the American people really understood what is in this book, there would be another Boston Tea Party!

This book is essentially a compilation of the authors' weekly columns. Most were written in 1993 and 1994, and so deal with events of that period. The essays are neatly divided by subject and include the following topics:
• "Big Media, Big Money": If you believe that "follow the money" is a good idea, it will serve you well in understanding contemporary journalism. News sources don't exactly lie, but there is a distinct bias nonetheless toward the corporate point of view. The owners of media empires are quintessential capitalists; the "pundits," the movers and shakers in the press, are from the elite

classes. The news they select, the "experts" they quote, the opinions they express—it's all from a certain monoculture at the top of our society. The news of interest to the "little guys" is almost never covered in the mainstream press.

• "The Public's Airwaves": a discussion of how the public resource—the frequency spectrum—has been usurped by private corporations for their own self-service.

• "Talk Radio": Limbaugh and his ilk, the Radio Right, White Hate, Extremists, Militias.

• "Violence on Television": It sells. It may not be the most important news, but it sure attracts viewers—and therefore advertisers.

• "Covering (Up) the Environment": It isn't in the corporate state's interest to worry about the abuse of the environment, much less to pay to clean it up or keep it clean.

• "Public Health": The interests of the public in health care matters are not necessarily consonant with those of big corporations, so guess what news you'll hear about.

• "Prejudice and the Media Curve": The ills of society can be so easily blamed on the lower (read "colored") classes by those in a comfortable position who like things pretty much the way they are—and that includes most of the mainstream journalism establishment.

• "Labor in the Margins": You'd never know from the American press that there's a labor movement out there. You'd never know labor has a "side" when there's a strike, and they might be justified in whatever interference they cause with the smooth flow of economic activity. There's a "business section" in most daily papers, but never a "labor section."

• "Clinton Priorities on the Home Front": Clinton, the Wimp President, hasn't just drifted to the right. The media have been pushing him.

• "Human Rights Abroad": We hear about this very selectively. When Saddam gasses his Kurds, it's all over page 1. When Turkey commits cultural genocide against its Kurds, well—Turkey is an ally after all. The press will be all over somebody like Khaddafy or Castro—somebody "we" don't like—but you'll never hear a word about the incredible atrocities committed by "our" guys, like say Jonas Savimbi of Unita in Angola.

• "Behold the Global Marketplace": Free trade gets more concern than free press in the mainstream media. Some of their reporting and "opining" on NAFTA and GATT could have been mistaken for satire, it was so blatantly biased.

• "The Media Beat Goes On": In celebration of George Orwell's 90th birthday, the authors present their current P.U.litzer Prizes for the foulest media performances.

Taken as a whole, it's a pretty sorry story. The problem is, it's getting worse. As control over the media passes into the hands of fewer and fewer people who are becoming richer and richer, the hope for the people to get the news they need from the mainstream press fades.

It must be acknowledged, however, that the authors of this book have a bias themselves. First of all, there are honest, honorable, and reflective journalists working in the mainstream—but you don't hear much about them here. Secondly, there are "good" corporations—companies which respect the environment, treat their workers civilly, etc. And finally, even those corporations that are not particularly honorable: yes, they may be greedy, let's acknowledge that—it's sort of in the nature of corporation—but that doesn't mean they are an unmitigated evil for humanity. They do, after all, perform two important functions for us: they provide us employment, and they create the goods and services we demand. The interests of the corporations aren't always diametrically opposite those of the rest of society, and it is a mistake to assume automatically that whatever is good for General Motors is definitely not good for the country.

RICK LUTTMANN, PH.D. is a Professor of Mathematics at Sonoma State University, a Project Censored evaluator, and is active in the War and Peace studies series.

BOARD OF EDUCATION V. PICO

John C. Gold

New York: Henry Holt and Co., Inc. (Twenty-First Century Books), 1982
Series Title: Supreme Court Decisions, 1994.
Reviewed by: Rosemary Powers

Controversies in education, particularly regarding what children should be allowed to read, are not new. When the movement to establish compulsory and common or "public" schooling began, certain citizens resisted the idea because they felt the schools might take away *their* right to determine what their children should learn. They came to support the concept grudgingly, after being convinced that *other* children (new immigrants and poor children especially) needed to learn things *their* parents would likely disapprove if they were to become "true Americans." School board members—who have assumed the right to determine what information (and thus "whose" information) will be available in schools—have always claimed that their decisions about school texts, resources, and programs reflect the majority values and morals of their community. They have rejected books or program proposals using this same argument. In these cases, they insist that they are making appropriate educational selections, and are not censoring legitimate information.

But what happens when (as is often the case) these decision makers represent only a segment of the community? If certain books are offensive (for political, moral, or religious reasons) to a majority of the board members, should they be able to remove them from a school library? These questions of rights, morals, and values often end up in court—and courts have not been consistent in their rulings on these issues.

In *Board of Education v. Pico* (1982), by John C. Gold, we have a brief but useful review of some of the most important legal cases in recent U.S. history involving conflicts between students' rights (to information and freedom of expression) and public school boards' rights to determine the educational programs and resources that will be available in their schools. Gold traces the history of the landmark 1982 case involving a dispute over nine books removed from a school library by the School Board of the Island Trees Union Free School District No. 26, Long Island, New York. (The banned books were *Slaughterhouse Five, The Fixer, The Naked Ape, Down These Mean Streets, A Hero Ain't Nothing but a Sandwich, Soul on Ice, Laughing Boy, Best Stories by Negro Writers, A Reader for Writers,* and *Black Boy*). Those who opposed the school board's decision, in a six-year battle that reached the U.S. Supreme Court, included students (Steven Pico, senior class president, and four other students), their parents, librarians, the New York ACLU, and several of the authors whose books had been banned.

Board of Education v. Pico is a short book (93 pages) that provides a fascinating glimpse of the process involved in attempting to resolve these deep differences about "freedom to learn" and "appropriate education." As we are presented with the story of the Pico case, we are introduced to many other legal cases dealing with similar questions, and discover that the courts have not been consistent in supporting either the rights of students or of school boards. The claim that First Amendment rights are being violated does not always make it so. At the same time, courts have sometimes determined that a school board's decision regarding what is "educationally appropriate" *has* violated students' rights, and these rulings become the basis for claims in other cases. Although some of the material in the book was surely high drama for those most closely involved, what we see most clearly in this account is the painfully slow process and narrow basis on which these legal decisions are usually made—whether by local courts or by the U.S. Supreme Court. The section describing the argument before the Supreme Court provides a fine introduction to how these judicial reviews are conducted—and will be useful to anyone wanting a quick picture of that process.

This book is very accessible, amply illustrated with pictures of the most active people involved in the case (including the Supreme Court justices), and would be especially appropriate for high school government or literature courses as a resource for student projects dealing with First Amendment rights and/or book censorship. It could also be a useful and sobering introduction for citizen groups who are faced with growing attempts by ultra-conservative individuals and groups to remove specific books or programs from public schools. Attempts by these groups to gain school board majorities have been somewhat successful. Most recently, national far-right organizations like "Focus on the Family" have encouraged members to seek seats on the governing boards of libraries as well as school boards in an attempt to challenge what they call the "ultra-radical" views of the American Library Association—a group which has been consistently in support of the "freedom to read."

From my experience with the 1990-91 California textbook controversy, I know how highly charged these cases can be and how deeply personal relationships can be affected in these local communities. I wish this had come through more strongly in the book. The author's decision to present complicated legal cases in such a brief space results at times in rather one-dimensional portraits of the people involved. We know, by the end of the book, that the books were returned to the library, and we know that the (now former) students and their allies felt victorious while the (still active) school board members remained steadfast in their opposition. What we don't know is how or if this controversy changed the community—other than that people had grown tired of the fight and wanted it to be over.

When the lawyer for the Island Trees School Board argued his case before the Supreme Court, Justice Thurgood Marshall asked repeatedly about the standards the school board had followed when it banned the books. The lawyer replied that standards would be difficult to set because "you are dealing with such imponderables as morals, social values, ethics." *Board of Education v. Pico* reminds us that when people in power assume the right to determine these "imponderables"—and others insist on *their* right to participate in determining what "morals, social values, ethics" will be supported in the community—we are faced with a challenge to our common life that the courts are reluctant to attempt to—and likely cannot—resolve.

ROSEMARY POWERS is a doctoral candidate in Sociology at the University of California at Davis. In 1990-91, she studied the controversy over the *Impressions* textbook series, an elementary school language arts program, as it played out in small rural school districts in the state of California. She is currently studying conflicts over sex education in public secondary schools.

MEDIA, PROCESS, AND THE SOCIAL CONSTRUCTION OF CRIME: Studies in Newsmaking Criminology
Edited by Gregg Barak
New York: Garland Publishing, Inc., 1994, 1995
Reviewed by: Barbara Bloom

The mass media are powerful and complex social agents who shape the social construction of reality and provide a pervasive vehicle of social control in today's society. The media's role is often the subject of widespread debate, particularly when the topic is the coverage of crime. The book, *Media, Process, and the Social Construction of Crime*, is a collection of essays which explore the relationships between the media, newsmaking, and crime. Gregg Barak and the contributors to this volume assert that crime information is devised so that it reinforces certain forms of social control.

While criminologists like myself often criticize the media for its sensationalistic and stereotypic approach to crime, Barak maintains that criminologists themselves have a role in terms of influencing the media and its presentations of crime. The media's social power can be used in a positive, pro-social fashion. Criminologists can and should engage in educating the media and the public about the social reality of crime. As Barak and others argue throughout the book, there is a critical need for the development of a "newsmaking criminology."

The introductory chapter provides an overview of the media's role in the social construction of crime and its primary system for legitimizing values and enforcing norms—the criminal justice system. Here Barak asserts that the examination of the interrelationships between media, society, and criminology is essentially a complex and dynamic enterprise. Barak states that "media images of crime control in the United States are constituted within the core of the social, political, and psychological make-up of American society." In this context, crime news is rudimentary and reduced to covert forms of stereotyping that socially construct criminals and victims alike.

Following the Introduction, the book is divided into two sections: "Constructing Crime News" and "Reconstructing Crime News." The chapters in the second section deal with news coverage in a variety of contexts. Topics such as violence and the media; how crime becomes news; predator criminals as media icons; media, cops, and crime; and an analysis of the national reporting of states' news are covered in depth.

The third and final section deals directly with the issue of newsmaking criminology. In Chapter Nine, "Newsmaking Criminology: Reflections on the Media, Intellectuals, and Crime," Barak indicts the fields of criminology and criminal justice for ignoring the ways in which they could use mass media for the purposes of informing, interpreting, and altering ideologically-constructed images of crime and punishment. Here Barak concludes that "the role of a newsmaking criminologist is possible because journalists' values and practices are not fixed rigidly but are rather fluid. The newsmaking process involves not only the ongoing negotiations and conflicts among newsroom personnel at all levels but also the interaction of newspeople with newsmaking sources, both elite and nonelite."

In Chapter Ten, "Becoming a Media Criminologist: Is Newsmaking Criminology Possible?" Cecil E. Greek tests Barak's proposition that criminologists can use their expertise to better inform and provide empirically-based images of crime and the criminal justice system. Greek concludes that although "it is difficult to communicate the complexities of social scientific research through various media formats, criminologists should seek permanent ongoing relationships with the press."

Finally, in Chapter Eleven, "Newsmaking Criminology as Replacement Discourse," Stuart Henry argues that in order for criminologists and others to transcend their "passive constitution of such socially and publicly consumed crime truths, it is necessary for criminologists to actively intercede in the constitutive process of newsmaking." Stuart asserts that "oppositional discourse" can work to expose biased media images and replace them with demystified images of crime and justice.

The significance of this book is its challenge to criminologists—its thought-provoking queries, several of which I've struggled with both as an academic and an advocate. While I continue to question how we as criminologists can place our own "journalistic spins" on crime and justice issues as Barak and others encourage us to do, I appreciate this volume's perspective and call to action.

This book expands the boundaries of newsmaking criminology considerably and serves as an excellent vehicle for stimulating public debate about the influence of the media on the social construction of crime. To the extent that criminologists can engage journalists and media analysts, the more opportunities will arise to influence public discourse and public policy.

BARBARA BLOOM, PH.D. is a Lecturer in Criminal Justice Administration at Sonoma State University, and she serves as a consultant on criminal justice matters to various states and counties.

BY INVITATION ONLY: How The Media Limit Political Debate
David Croteau and William Hoynes
Common Courage Press, 1994
Reviewed by: Doug Martin

The guests interviewed on television news/public affairs shows like *The News Hour* on PBS or *Nightline* on ABC appear by invitation only. The question addressed by David Croteau and William Hoynes in their book *By Invitation Only* is: Who is invited? Their answer, which will surprise no one who has carefully watched these programs, is that the guest list is greatly dominated by current and former government officials, corporate business leaders, men, whites, academic experts—that is, establishment types. The central idea of *By Invitation Only* is that limiting guests to these groups amounts to anti-progressive political bias. Thus, the subtitle of this book is *How the Media Limit Political Debate*.

Croteau and Hoynes present an impressive array of data concerning the guest lists of *The News Hour*, *Nightline*, and other similar public affairs shows that they regard as representative of public affairs television. Before reviewing that data, however, we should note the theoretical basis which forms the core of the book. The authors raise a question which I am sure has occurred to most readers: How is it that both the political right and left can claim that the media is biased against them? The authors resolve this apparent paradox by claiming that the left and the right attach a different meaning to the word "bias."

When the right refers to the media as "biased," they mean, according to the authors, that "media coverage is not an accurate reflection of the true nature of events." The barometer of accuracy, of course, is the degree to which descriptions of events accords with that of conservatives. Croteau and Hoynes, however, present a deeper criticism of the conservative claim, a criticism which, I am sure, any observer of the post-modern academic wars can see coming. Namely, there is no true nature of events, so the traditional view that the news is a mirror held up to the world is intellectually untenable. In the views of Croteau and Hoynes, understanding of current events revolves around "larger questions about power, interpretation, and the social construction of reality." This view then leads easily to the progressive definition of "bias." Media bias arises from a lack of diversity of perspective in the coverage and analysis of events. Democratic process and the welfare of citizens is best served, in this view, by allowing and encouraging critical discussion of public affairs with representatives of a broad range of ideological viewpoints and social or economic characteristics. Thus, we see that it is not enough for media to claim to deliver objective or truthful newscasts, since "truth" is to some large degree a matter of perspective and situation. Rather, important issues can be best brought to light through a dialectic process of point and counter-point. Croteau and Hoynes claim this is not happening on television public-affairs programming.

So what did they find when they tracked the guests on *The News Hour*, *Nightline, Firing Line,* and others? Much of *By Invitation Only* reports on the conclusions from the analysis of many months of broadcasts on these and other television shows. Many pages of the book are devoted to displaying and discussing the data, but the central idea is simple and clear; the in-depth discussions on these public affairs shows are dominated by a rather narrow group. The great majority of guests are white, male professionals who are employed in government, corporations, universities, or in journalism. Politicians are, of course, heavily represented and there were slightly more Republicans than Democrats, a result of the fact that most of the data was collected during the Bush Administration. A very small fraction of the guests could be described as citizens, activists, workers, or "outsiders" with strong dissenting views.

The findings are clear. Does this, then, constitute a strong argument for media bias? To their credit, Croteau and Hoynes paraphrase some of the media response to their analysis. Jim Lehrer of *The News Hour* replied that his is a news show and the interviews are newsmaker interviews, therefore the limited range of guests is not surprising. Of course, in the theoretical position of Croteau and Hoynes, this is a thin shield since the concept of news is inseparable from diverse and critical discussion. Ted Koppel of *Nightline* replied that journalists can pose questions which are hard-hitting and they should be able to represent the diversity of perspectives encouraged by Croteau and Hoynes. It is worth quoting the authors at length:

Who, except for an environmentalist, will raise pointed questions about corporate culpability for environmental decay? Who, other than a peace activist, will raise fundamental questions

THIS MODERN WORLD by TOM TOMORROW

THE MEDIA ROOM AT THE PRESIDENTIAL DEBATE IN HARTFORD WAS SET UP IN A CONVENTION CENTER BASEMENT SEVERAL BLOCKS FROM THE ACTUAL DEBATE HALL...IN OTHER WORDS, MOST JOURNALISTS TRAVELLED ALL THE WAY TO HARTFORD IN ORDER TO *WATCH THE EVENT ON TV*...

BUT THIS WAY WE CAN SEE THE DEBATE THE WAY THE *AMERICAN PEOPLE* SEE IT!

OF COURSE! WHAT COULD BE MORE LOGICAL?

CATERING FOR THE PRESS WAS PROVIDED BY *PHILIP MORRIS* AND ITS SUBSIDIARIES, PRIMARILY *KRAFT FOODS*...

HEY, HOW ABOUT SOME *KRAFT* BRAND PARMESAN CHEESE TO GO WITH YOUR PASTA?

WANT SOME *KRAFT* BRAND SALAD DRESSING ON THAT SALAD?

UM...SURE...

about the history of U.S. Government intervention in the Third World? More generally, who is going to raise the questions about the underlying assumptions which Nightline and other media share?...The inclusion of critical voices is the surest way of guaranteeing a robust debate.

By Invitation Only successfully points out the elite nature of the groups which constitute the great majority of interviews on typical public affairs broadcasts. However, while Croteau and Hoynes present brief discussions of the news/public affairs dichotomy, objective reporting versus partisan debate, and other fundamental journalistic issues, I came away with the sense that there is more work to be done on these topics before we understand "How the Media Limit Political Debate." In spite of this, By Invitation Only effectively sensitizes us to one powerful way in which the media shapes our sense of the "news."

DOUG MARTIN, PH.D. is a Professor of Chemistry and Science Education at Sonoma State University, a Project Censored evaluator and a worldly philosopher by personal inclination.

TOXIC SLUDGE IS GOOD FOR YOU: Lies, Damn Lies and the Public Relations Insustry

John Stauber and Sheldon Rampton
Common Courage Press, 1995
Reviewed by: Robert Tellander

When a comic book character with an all-white smile holding a green glass of steaming crud offers you a sip and Molly Ivins is quoted just beneath it, "Terrific! Don't miss it," you know that the authors—John Stauber, founder and director of the Center for Media & Democracy, and Sheldon Rampton, who writes and edits with Stauber the quarterly, *PR Watch: Public Interest Reporting on the PR/Public Affairs Industry*—are practicing what they reveal and teaching us about an effective, if absurd, process that has become an

American standard for public disclosure. Because of the massive amount of research, the clothesline of dirty laundry the authors hang out to dry reveals a corporate and governmental life that rationalizes itself in terms of systems and not people, in terms of profits, and not the common good.

Tracing the history of public relations from Ivy Lee and Sigmund Freud's nephew, Edward Bernay, we learn of the development of an information industry molded to serve the American industrial complex, and even less honorably, the power brokers anywhere, and most shockingly, Adolf Hitler himself. *Ad hominum* arguments and guilt by association are themselves techniques of the PR industry and for the casual reader, they can also become the negative assumption of the "evil empire" within the United States. Conflict theory serves the authors well to reveal mounds of evidence containing the ugly consequences of the powerfuls' disregard for the public interest. If you wanted to know about how we got into the nuclear power mess, the cigarette/lung cancer debacle, toxic sludge spread over your backyard, and the chemical pollution of what you eat and drink, read this book. If you want to know how to fight back, read this book. If you want to understand why this process occurs, the analysis comes up short and implies a consistent "devil theory" executed by the power elite. This is a fault of the usefulness of conflict theory: it reveals patterns which you would otherwise not see. To equate the bias of the tool of inquiry with reality, however, makes manifest the reification of a liberal view, not a sociological insight into the nature of the social process. Nevertheless, it is useful and enlightening information which provokes thought and forces us to ask 'Why?'

Sociologically, what the book reveals is how public relations works. Simply put, it surveys the cultural norms and values of a society, conforms whatever attitude a client wants emphasized to that profile, and creates a situation of "implied consent." Remember when President Richard Nixon would argue that "the silent majority supports him?" If you disagreed, you had to become "unsilent" and thus be identified as a radical, trouble-maker, and un-American, or disagree politely and not manifest any contradictory behavior. Public relations works by co-opting consensus by fitting its presentations to "spin" in the direction the social wheel is rolling. Because we base our prime social values on the individual, the "consumer," and not society as a whole, we cannot approach the persuasive power and wealth of corporations who argue in our terms about their interests. In terms of its usefulness, this book serves as the current generation's update of Vance Packard's earlier work on this subject, *The Hidden Persuaders.*

As a whole, the book reveals the specter of large scale organizations, a Weberian landscape of 'rationalized institutions,' which in and of themselves provide an alternative to democracy, not a threat to democracy. The authors' populist solution of letting the "chips-fall-where-they-may" where "not-in-my-backyard" local movements arise to take on the corporate Goliaths seems hopeful more than realistic. The more likely outcome will only heighten frustration among the conscious and serve to polarize us all into a "new class war," where the haves push around the have-nots. The pro-active approach raises the question, "How do you make the rich and powerful—the organized and unaware—accountable to the public good?"

The authors focus the problem well: "As the world moves toward the end of the twentieth century, it seems to have solved many of its image problems, but few of its real ones." However, they do not resolve those and show that we are at a precipice. The authors in the summary cite Alex Carey who grounds the dilemma more solidly on a broader historical and level playing field: "The twentieth century has been characterized by three developments of great political importance: the growth of democracy, the growth of corporate power, and the growth of corporate propaganda as a means of protecting corporate power against democracy." Left with a new consciousness, the book challenges us to infiltrate the system and redefine it for the good of all. Consequently, it is an intellectually provocative book and not a tome of radical complaints. May these corporations come to the same consciousness and legitimize their place in this new social world.

ROBERT TELLANDER is a Professor of Sociology at Sonoma State University. He was the Fall 1996 Department Chair, and is a Project Censored evaluator.

THIS MODERN WORLD   by TOM TOMORROW

Panel 1: ACCORDING TO RECENT POLLS, SUPPORT FOR THE REPUBLICAN "REVOLUTION" IS WANING AND NEWT GINGRICH IS CURRENTLY ONE OF THE LEAST POPULAR POLITICIANS IN HISTORY--OR SO WE ARE *TOLD*... BUT COULD THESE JUST BE *LIES* FROM THE NEFARIOUS *LIBERAL MEDIA*..?

GREAT NEWS, COMRADES! OUR DISINFORMATION CAMPAIGN IS BRINGING US EVER CLOSER TO OUR DREAM OF A *SOCIALIST UTOPIA*--

--AND OUR *ADVERTISING REVENUES* ARE UP *TWENTY PERCENT!*

Panel 2: CONSERVATIVES SEEM TO BELIEVE SO... CONTINUING TO BEHAVE AS IF *NOTHING* COULD BE MORE APPEALING TO THE AMERICAN PUBLIC THAN SMALL-MINDED *VICIOUSNESS* AND IDEOLOGICAL *EXTREMISM*...

I'LL CERTAINLY VOTE FOR ANY POLITICIAN WHO PROMISES TO LET POOR CHILDREN *STARVE SLOWLY TO DEATH!*

I THINK ANYONE WHO MAKES LESS THAN $20,000 A YEAR SHOULD BE *THROWN TO LIONS* ON *LIVE TV!*

Panel 3: CONSIDER, FOR EXAMPLE, CHARGES THAT BOB DOLE IS TOO *LIBERAL*--AND, EVEN MORE BIZARRE, THAT *PAT BUCHANAN* IS ACTUALLY A RAVING *LEFT-WINGER*...

SURE, HE WANTS TO OUTLAW ABORTION AND BUILD A WALL ALONG THE MEXICAN BORDER--BUT HE SHOWS SOME *MODICUM* OF CONCERN FOR THE FUTURE OF THE AMERICAN WORKER!

JEEZ-- WHAT A TREE-HUGGING *WACKO!*

Panel 4: OF COURSE, TERMS LIKE "CONSERVATIVE" AND "LIBERAL" DON'T REALLY BEGIN TO DESCRIBE THE NUANCES OF THE POLITICAL LANDSCAPE THESE DAYS... WHEN MOST REPUBLICAN PRESIDENTIAL HOPEFULS SOUND MORE LIKE TEEN-AGED *ANARCHISTS* THAN MIDDLE-AGED *CAREER POLITICIANS*...

WHO NEEDS THE GOVERNMENT ANYWAY, MAN?

YEAH! LIKE, SMASH THE *STATE*, DUDE!

NEWT   Phil   BIAFRA

TOM TOMORROW © 1-17-96   Email: tomorrow@well.com ... web: http://www.well.com/user/tomorrow

CHAPTER 7

FREE THE MEDIA[1]

by Mark Crispin Miller

The accompanying chart following this chapter offers just a partial guide to our contracting media cosmos. It demonstrates the sway of the four giant corporations that control the major TV news divisions: NBC, ABC, CBS, and— if the Feds allow it—CNN. Two of these four corporations are defense contractors (both involved in nuclear production), while the other two are mammoth manufacturers of fun 'n' games. Thus we are the subjects of a *national entertainment state*, in which the news and much of our amusement come to us directly from the two most powerful industries in the United States. Glance up from the bottom of each quarter of the chart, and see why, say, Tom Brokaw might find it difficult to introduce stories critical of nuclear power. Or why it is unlikely ABC News will ever again do an exposé of Disney's practices (as *Prime Time Live* did in 1990); or, indeed, why CNN—or any of the others— does not touch the biggest story of them all, i.e., the media monopoly itself.

Focused as it is on those colossi that control the TV news, this chart leaves out other giants: Rupert Murdoch's News Corporation, John Malone's Tele-Communications Inc., and Sumner Redstone's Viacom, none of which are (yet) telejournalistic powers. Likewise, the octopus that is S.I. Newhouse has not one tentacle appearing here, since he mainly glides within the world of print,

[1]Adapted from *The Nation*, June 3, 1996.

darkening magazines and publishing concerns instead of newscasts. There are also foreign players, like Sony (Columbia, Tri Star), whose holdings are not charted here.

We therefore need further maps of this contracting universe: more big pictures and also local maps, so that folks everywhere will know who owns their daily paper, TV and radio stations, cable franchise, and city magazine. We need industry-specific maps, to show who owns each culture industry: the newspapers, the magazines, the book business and music business, cable, radio, and the movie studios—as well as the major on-line services that help us get around the Internet.

Such maps will point us toward the only possible escape from the impending blackout. They would suggest the true causes of those enormous ills that now dismay so many Americans: the universal sleaze and "dumbing down," the flood-tide of corporate propaganda, the terminal inanity of U.S. politics. These have arisen not from any grand decline in national character, nor from the plotting of some Hebrew cabal but from the inevitable toxic influence of those few corporations that have monopolized our culture. The only way to solve the problem is to break their hold; and to that end the facts of media ownership must be made known to all. In short, we the people need a few good maps, because, as the man said, there must be some kind of way out of here.

Certainly the domination of our media by corporate profiteers is nothing new. Decades before Mr. Gingrich went to Washington, there were observers already decrying the censorious impact of mass advertising. The purveyors of "patent medicine"—mostly useless, often lethal—went unscathed by reporters through the twenties because that industry spent more than any other on print advertising (just like the tobacco industry a few years later). The electrical power industry attacked the concept of public ownership in an astonishing campaign of lies, half-truths, and redbaiting that went on from 1919 to 1934. That propaganda drive entailed the outright purchase of newspapers (e.g., the Copley chain) and the establishment of the trust-oriented stations of the NBC radio network.

Although the utilities' program was exposed, the corporate drive to eat the media was not halted by the New Deal. Indeed, as Robert McChesney tells us, the Communications Act of 1934 killed the soul of U.S. broadcasting, defining it forever as commercial. Thereafter, with ever fewer exceptions, radio and then TV were subject to the market-driven whims of the sponsor, who by the early sixties and on the whole made pap of both the news and entertainment sold through the electronic media. Some of the brightest talents spoke out memorably against the drift: Edward R. Murrow scorned the trivialization of TV news, and Rod Serling, before his exile to *The Twilight Zone*, publicly condemned the fatal softening of TV drama by the likes of U.S. Steel and BBD&O. Bad as they often were, those earlier manipulations of the media were only a foretaste of what is happening now. Here no longer is a range of disparate industries, with only certain of them dangerously prey to corporate pressure, or to the warlike caprice of some Hearst, Luce, or Northcliffe. What we have now, rather, is a culture gripped in every sector by an ever-tightening convergence of globe-trotting corporations, whose managers believe in nothing but "the market" *über alles*.

This new order started to get obvious in the spring of 1995, when the Federal Communications Commission (FCC) summarily let Rupert Murdoch off the hook for having fudged the actual foreign ownership of his concern (an Australian outfit, which Murdoch had not made clear to the busy regulators). The summer then saw ABC sucked into Disney, CBS sucked into Westinghouse, and Ted Turner's mini-empire slated for ingestion by Time Warner: a grand consolidation that the press, the White House, Congress, and the FCC have failed to question (although the FTC [Federal Trade Commission] is finally stirring).

With the mergers came some hints of how the new proprietors would henceforth use their journalists: Disney's ABC News apologizing to Philip Morris— a major TV advertiser through Kraft Foods—for having told the truth, on a broadcast of *Day One*, about P.M.'s manipulation of nicotine levels in its cigarettes; and CBS's in-house counsel ordering the old newshounds at *60 Minutes* to bury an explosive interview with whistleblower Jeffrey Wigand about the addictive practices of Brown & Williamson.

Such moves portend the death of broadcast journalism, as does the radical cost-cutting now being dictated by the networks' owners. And yet some good seems also to have come out of this *annus horribilis* of big waivers, big mergers, big layoffs, and big lies. Suddenly, the risks of media monopoly are now apparent not just to the usual uptight minority of activists and scholars but, more and more, to everyone. People want to know what's going on, and what to do about it. The time has therefore come to free the media by creating a new, broad-based movement dedicated to this all-important mission: antitrust.

Although it will certainly go to court, this movement must start with a civic project far more arduous than any spate of major lawsuits. In fact, there can be no such legal recourse yet, because there is no organized mass movement that would endow such actions with the proper standing. Since the bully days of Teddy Roosevelt, the drive against monopoly has always been initiated not by solitary lawyers but by an angry public. "The antitrust laws are enforced in one period and not enforced in another, and the reason is pure politics," notes Charles Mueller, editor of the *Antitrust Law & Economics Review*. Such laws can take on the media trust, says Andrew Schwartzman of the Media Access Project, only when "the general public helps convince the prosecutors in the federal government that the future of democracy depends on freedom in the marketplace of ideas."

Thus this movement must start by getting out the word—and there's the rub. Our problem has no precedent, for what's monopolized today is no mere staple such as beef or oil but the very media whereby the problem could be solved. Indeed, the media trust suppresses information and debate on *all* monopolies. "You and I can't get the antitrust laws enforced," says Mueller, "and the reason we can't is that we don't have access to the media." To fight the trust directly, then, would be to resume the epic struggle that gave us our antitrust laws in the first place—one that the robber barons themselves soon halted by buying interests in the magazines that had been attacking them. With reformist monthlies like *McClure's* thus safely "Morganized," the muckrakers formation now threatens to contain us all. Today's antitrust campaign will therefore have to be a thorough grass-roots effort—one that will work *around* the mainstream media so as to free them by and by.

This movement will depend on those idealists who still work within the media: those who would do a good job if they could, but who've been forced to compromise, and those working from the margins—the stalwarts of the alternative press and of groups like Fairness & Accuracy in Reporting. All should henceforth pay attention to developments within the different culture industries. The American Booksellers Association, for instance, filed an antitrust suit against Random House for illegally providing discounts to the national bookstore chains and retailers. Those in other industries should likewise make a fuss. With the help of independents in the film business, the Justice Department ought to take a look—again—at monopolistic practices in Hollywood. Creative Artists Agency, for instance, yearly packages a number of obscenely pricey movies for the studios, in each case demanding that the studio either use the agency's own stars, writer(s) *and* director—*and* pay them the salaries dictated by the agency—or take a hike. Since C.A.A. itself grabs the commissions on those salaries, its way of doing business represents a highly profitable conflict of interest.

That scam has also helped to jack up ticket prices for the rest of us—and the movies are a lot worse for the practice, which pairs up talents not because they might work beautifully together but just because they profit C.A.A. Likewise, the A.B.A.'s showdown with Random House has far broader implications, for the extinction of the independent bookstores could insure as well the disappearance of those titles that are not best sellers, and whose authors will not be up there trading ironies with David Letterman of Westinghouse, or grinning, between commercials, through a segment of GE's *Today Show.*

That the media trust costs everyone is a fact that this new movement must explain to everyone. The public, first of all, should be reminded that it owns the airwaves, and that the trust is therefore ripping everybody off—now more than ever, since those triumphant giants don't even pretend to compensate us with programs "in the public interest." Likewise, we should start discussing taxes on mass advertising. Such a tax, and the tolls on usage of the airwaves, would yield enough annual revenues at least to pay for public broadcasting, whose managers would then no longer have to try to soothe the breasts of savage congressmen, or sell out for the dubious largesse of Mobil, Texaco, and other "underwriters." In 1994, according to *Advertising Age,* corporations spent a staggering $150 billion on national advertising. That year, it cost $1.8 billion just to pay the full tab for PBS *and* NPR.

And yet, to most Americans, the economic arguments against the trust may matter less than its offenses against taste. Grossed out by what they see and hear, a great majority have had their unease exploited by the likes of Pat Buchanan and Bob Dole, and ignored, or mocked, by many on the left. This is a mistake. The antitrust movement should acknowledge and explain the *cultural* consequences of monopoly. While the right keeps scapegoating "Hollywood" (*aka* "the Jews"), this movement must stick to the facts, and point out that the media's trashiness is a predictable result of the dominion of those few huge corporate owners.

Thus our aim is certainly not censorship, which is the tacit goal of rightist demagogues like Ralph Reed and the Rev. Donald Wildmon. The purpose, rather, is a solution wholly constitutional—and, for that matter, sanely capitalistic. We would reintroduce a pleasurable diversity into the corporate monoculture. Some crap there always is, and always will be: It is the overwhelming volume of such stuff that is the danger here inside the magic kingdom. Where just a few huge entities compete, ever more intently, for the same vast blocs of viewers, and where the smaller players are not allowed to vary what we're offered, the items on the screens and shelves will, necessarily, have been concocted to appeal to what is worst in us. It is this process, and not some mysterious upsurge of mass barbarism, that will explain the domination of the mainstream by the likes of Murdoch, Jenny Jones, Rush Limbaugh, Judith Regan, Arnold Schwarzenegger, Howard Stern, Charles Barkley, Gordon Liddy, Butt-head, and Bob Grant.

Although, thus far, the right alone has decried the media's nastiness, when it comes to antitrust, those pseudo-populists would never walk the walk, since they themselves are part of the behemoth: Limbaugh's TV show belongs to Gannet/Multimedia, Pat Robertson's Family Channel is partially owned by TCI, and Bob Dole—despite his mock attack on Time Warner—has done his best to give the giants all they want. Those on the right would not dismantle the monopoly, which they would like to run themselves (and which to some extent they do already). It is therefore the left's responsibility to guide this movement, since on this issue it is actually much closer to the people.

Such an effort will require that the left stop being too hip for its own good, and start to honor the concerns of the appalled majority. "Two-thirds of the public thinks TV shows have a negative impact on the country," notes *U.S. News & World Report* in a major poll released in April, "and huge majorities believe TV contributes to social problems like violence, divorce, teen pregnancy, and the decline of family values." This is no hick prejudice but a sound mass response to the routine experience of all-pervasive titillation. "The greatest anxieties are expressed by women and by those who are religious, but," the pollsters found, "the anger is 'overwhelming and across the board.'"

Of course, there are some deep antipathies between the left and those uneasy "huge majorities"—some out there don't want to be disturbed by *anything*, and the general audience may never go for feminism, and may forever cheer for shows like Desert Storm. Nevertheless, we have the obligation to make common cause with the offended—for what offends both them *and* us has all alike been worsened by the downward pressure of the trust. The ubiquitous soft porn, the gansta manners, the shock jocks, and the now-obligatory shouting of the F-word are all products of the same commercial oligopoly that is also whiting out the news, exploiting women, celebrating gross consumption, glorifying guns, and demonizing all the wretched of the earth.

There are pertinent movements under way. In early March, there was an important and well-attended Media & Democracy Congress in San Francisco, organized by the Institute for Alternative Journalism, whose purpose was to unify the forces of the progressive media to fight the trust before it can rigidify beyond democracy. Soon after, in St. Louis, the first convention of the Cultural Environment Movement was held; founded by George Gerbner, the CEM is committed to the broadest, toughest possible campaign for media reform.

The arousal of mass interest would raise possibilities for major legal action. The FCC could be served with a class-action suit for its neglect of the antitrust laws—as could President Clinton for his failure "to see that [those] laws are faithfully executed." It might be feasible to sue them on First Amendment grounds. Although the giants themselves cannot be nailed for censorship, the movement could, says antitrust attorney Michael Meyerson, sue the U.S. Government for collusion in the corporate move against our First Amendment rights.

While such distant possibilities await broader public support, some current cases show what could be done. Time Warner's acquisition of the Turner Broadcasting System has not yet won the blessing of the FTC, and there have been some strong petitions to deny the agency's approval. Looking further ahead, we must begin undoing what the media trust itself accomplished through the Telecommunications Act of 1996, which was devised to rush us in the wrong direction (and which the media—both mainstream and alternative—largely failed to examine). For a start, we might examine the notion of an eventual move to force the four colossi to divest themselves of their beleaguered news divisions. For public relations purposes, GE (say) could still boast its affiliation with NBC News—a most impressive civic contribution—but the annual budget for the news would come from the same sort of trust fund, based on corporate taxes, that would pay for PBS.

Right now, however, what we need to do is tell the people who owns what. This campaign of public information must involve the whole alternative press, as well as unions, churches, schools, and advocacy groups—and progressives on the Internet, which is still a medium of democratic promise, although that promise is also at risk. Indeed, the same gigantic players that control the elder media are planning shortly to absorb the Internet, which could be transformed from a thriving common wilderness into an immeasurable de facto cyberpark for corporate interests, with all the dissident voices exiled to sites known only to the activists and other cranks (such renovation is, in fact, one major purpose of the recent telecommunications bill). Therefore, to expect the new technology to free us from the trust is to succumb to a utopian delusion.

Which is another way of saying that there is no substitute for actual democracy—which cannot work unless people know what's going on. And so, before we raise the proper legal questions and debate the legislative possibilities, we need simply to teach everyone, ourselves included, that this whole failing culture is an oversold dead end, and that there might be a way out of it.

MARK CRISPIN MILLER is a Professor of Film and Media Studies and chairman of the writing seminar at Johns Hopkins University. He is also the author of *Mad Scientists: A Study of U.S. Propaganda*, forthcoming from Norton in 1997.

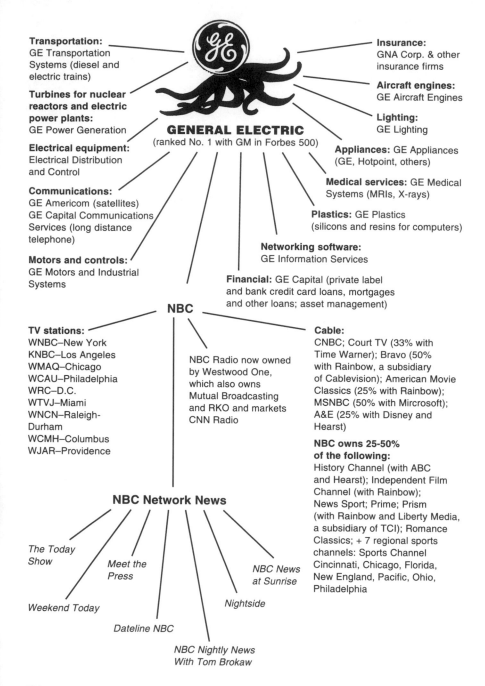

This map appeared in the June 3, 1996 issue of *The Nation* and does not reflect subsequent mergers and acquisitions. Look for updated versions of this map in future editions of *The Nation*.

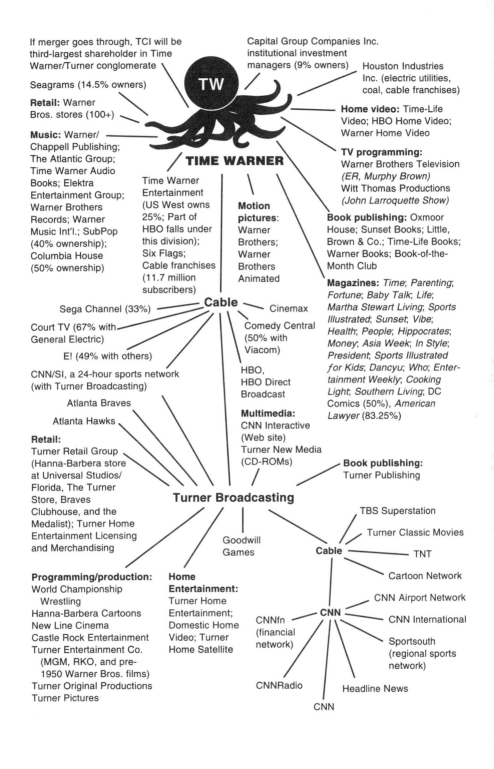

If merger goes through, TCI will be third-largest shareholder in Time Warner/Turner conglomerate

Capital Group Companies Inc. institutional investment managers (9% owners)

Houston Industries Inc. (electric utilities, coal, cable franchises)

Seagrams (14.5% owners)

TW

Retail: Warner Bros. stores (100+)

Home video: Time-Life Video; HBO Home Video; Warner Home Video

Music: Warner/ Chappell Publishing; The Atlantic Group; Time Warner Audio Books; Elektra Entertainment Group; Warner Brothers Records; Warner Music Int'l.; SubPop (40% ownership); Columbia House (50% ownership)

TV programming: Warner Brothers Television *(ER, Murphy Brown)* Witt Thomas Productions *(John Larroquette Show)*

TIME WARNER

Time Warner Entertainment (US West owns 25%; Part of HBO falls under this division); Six Flags; Cable franchises (11.7 million subscribers)

Motion pictures: Warner Brothers; Warner Brothers Animated

Book publishing: Oxmoor House; Sunset Books; Little, Brown & Co.; Time-Life Books; Warner Books; Book-of-the-Month Club

Magazines: *Time; Parenting; Fortune; Baby Talk; Life; Martha Stewart Living; Sports Illustrated; Sunset; Vibe; Health; People; Hippocrates; Money; Asia Week; In Style; President; Sports Illustrated for Kids; Dancyu; Who; Entertainment Weekly; Cooking Light; Southern Living;* DC Comics (50%), *American Lawyer* (83.25%)

Sega Channel (33%)

Cable

Cinemax

Court TV (67% with General Electric)

Comedy Central (50% with Viacom)

E! (49% with others)

CNN/SI, a 24-hour sports network (with Turner Broadcasting)

HBO, HBO Direct Broadcast

Atlanta Braves

Atlanta Hawks

Multimedia: CNN Interactive (Web site) Turner New Media (CD-ROMs)

Retail: Turner Retail Group (Hanna-Barbera store at Universal Studios/ Florida, The Turner Store, Braves Clubhouse, and the Medalist); Turner Home Entertainment Licensing and Merchandising

Book publishing: Turner Publishing

Turner Broadcasting

TBS Superstation

Turner Classic Movies

Goodwill Games

Cable

TNT

Cartoon Network

Programming/production: World Championship Wrestling Hanna-Barbera Cartoons New Line Cinema Castle Rock Entertainment Turner Entertainment Co. (MGM, RKO, and pre-1950 Warner Bros. films) Turner Original Productions Turner Pictures

Home Entertainment: Turner Home Entertainment; Domestic Home Video; Turner Home Satellite

CNN Airport Network

CNNfn (financial network)

CNN

CNN International

Sportsouth (regional sports network)

CNNRadio

Headline News

CNN

Sid R. Bass et al. (crude petroleum and natural gas production, 6.02% owners before merger)*

Berkshire Hathaway Inc. (Insurance; Warren Buffet, C.E.O.; ranked No. 60 in Forbes 500; 12% owners prior to merger with Disney)*

State Farm Insurance (6% owners prior to merger)*

Music: Hollywood Records; Wonderland Music; Walt Disney Records

Multimedia: Disney Interactive; Disney.com; Americast (with some Baby Bell companies, in development); ABC Online (interactive network for America Online)

Mighty Ducks (N.H.L. ice hockey team); California Angels (American League baseball team; 25% ownership and controlling interest, with option to buy remaining shares upon the death of Gene Autry)

Home video: Buena Vista

DISNEY/ CAP CITIES
(ranked No. 48 in Forbes 500)

Book publishing: Hyperion Books; Chilton Publications

Retail: 429 Disney stores; Childcraft Education (mail order toys)

Theme parks/resorts: Disneyland; Walt Disney World Resort; Disneyland Paris (39%); Tokyo Disneyland (royalties and fees only); Disney Vacation Club (Vero Beach, FL; Hilton Head Island, SC; Orlando, FL); WCO Vacationland Resorts (recreational vehicle parks, country general stores); Disney Institute (75-acre fitness resort in Orlando); Celebration (planned community near Orlando—in development); Disney Cruiseline (planned)

Motion pictures: Walt Disney Pictures; Touchstone Pictures; Hollywood Pictures; Miramax Film Corp.; Buena Vista Pictures (distribution arm)

Newspapers:
Fort Worth Star-Telegram; Kansas City Star; St. Louis Daily Record; Narragansett Times; Oakland Press and Reminder (Pontiac, MI); *County Press* (Lapeer, MI); *Times-Leader* (Wilkes-Barre, PA); *Belleville News-Democrat* (IL); *Albany Democrat* (OR); *Daily Tidings* (Ashland, OR); *Sutton Industries* and *Penny Power* (shoppers)

Magazines:
Chilton Publications (trade publications); Fairchild Publications (*W., Women's Wear Daily*); *L.A. Magazine*; *Institutional Investor;* Disney Publishing Inc. (*FamilyFun* and others)

TV and cable: Disney Channel; Disney Television (58 hours/week syndicated programming); Touchstone Television (*Ellen, Home Improvement*); A&E (37% with Hearst and GE); Lifetime Network (50%); ESPN (80%); ESPN 2 (80%); Buena Vista Television (*Home Again*)

ABC Radio (owns 21 stations, largest radio network in U.S., serving 3,400 stations and covering 24% of U.S. households)

ABC

ABC Video

TV stations (covering 24.5% of U.S. households): WABC–New York, WLS–Chicago, KFSN–Fresno, KTRK–Houston, WPVI–Philadelphia, KGO–San Francisco, WTVD–Raleigh-Durham, WJRT–Flint, MI, WTVG–Toledo, KABC–Los Angeles, (KCAL in L.A. for sale by agreement with Justice Dept.); Also owns 14% interest in Young Broadcasting, which owns: WTVO–Rockford, IL; WTEN–Albany, NY; WLNS–Lansing, MI; KLFY–Lafayette, LA; WKRN–Nashville, TN; WATE–Knoxville, TN; WRIC–Richmond, VA; WBAY–Green Bay, WI

ABC Network News

PrimeTime Live

Good Morning America

Good Morning America (Sunday)

World News This Morning

World News Tonight (Saturday and Sunday editions)

20/20

Nightline

This Week With David Brinkley

World News Now

World News Tonight With Peter Jennings

* Ownership percentages are not finalized. Because 82% of stockholders opted for shares and not cash, Disney is still working out with shareholders whether they will be paid in fractional shares or with partial cash payments.

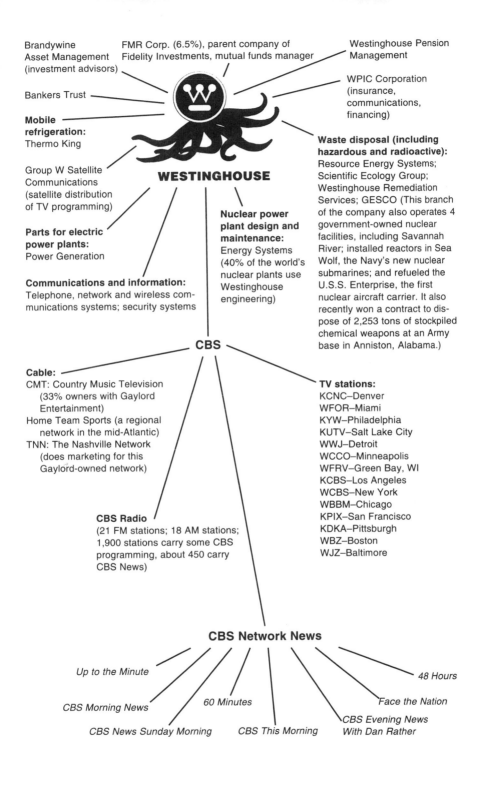

Brandywine Asset Management (investment advisors)

FMR Corp. (6.5%), parent company of Fidelity Investments, mutual funds manager

Westinghouse Pension Management

WPIC Corporation (insurance, communications, financing)

Bankers Trust

Mobile refrigeration: Thermo King

Group W Satellite Communications (satellite distribution of TV programming)

WESTINGHOUSE

Parts for electric power plants: Power Generation

Communications and information: Telephone, network and wireless communications systems; security systems

Nuclear power plant design and maintenance: Energy Systems (40% of the world's nuclear plants use Westinghouse engineering)

Waste disposal (including hazardous and radioactive): Resource Energy Systems; Scientific Ecology Group; Westinghouse Remediation Services; GESCO (This branch of the company also operates 4 government-owned nuclear facilities, including Savannah River; installed reactors in Sea Wolf, the Navy's new nuclear submarines; and refueled the U.S.S. Enterprise, the first nuclear aircraft carrier. It also recently won a contract to dispose of 2,253 tons of stockpiled chemical weapons at an Army base in Anniston, Alabama.)

CBS

Cable: CMT: Country Music Television (33% owners with Gaylord Entertainment) Home Team Sports (a regional network in the mid-Atlantic) TNN: The Nashville Network (does marketing for this Gaylord-owned network)

TV stations: KCNC–Denver WFOR–Miami KYW–Philadelphia KUTV–Salt Lake City WWJ–Detroit WCCO–Minneapolis WFRV–Green Bay, WI KCBS–Los Angeles WCBS–New York WBBM–Chicago KPIX–San Francisco KDKA–Pittsburgh WBZ–Boston WJZ–Baltimore

CBS Radio (21 FM stations; 18 AM stations; 1,900 stations carry some CBS programming, about 450 carry CBS News)

CBS Network News

Up to the Minute

48 Hours

CBS Morning News

60 Minutes

Face the Nation

CBS Evening News With Dan Rather

CBS News Sunday Morning

CBS This Morning

THIS MODERN WORLD

by TOM TOMORROW

MANY AMERICANS BELIEVE THAT THE ANSWER TO SOCIETY'S PROBLEMS IS *SIMPLE*-- WE'VE JUST GOT TO *GET TOUGH ON CRIMINALS*!

> LOCK THEM UP AND THROW AWAY THE KEY!

> I DON'T KNOW WHY WE DIDN'T THINK OF THIS SOONER!

UNFORTUNATELY LIFE TENDS TO BE A LITTLE MORE COMPLICATED THAN THAT (AS THOSE OF YOU OVER THE AGE OF 15 MAY HAVE NOTICED BY NOW)... AND IN REALITY, MANDATORY SENTENCING LAWS HAVE LED TO ASTONISHING INJUSTICES...

> FOR INSTANCE, AS *NEWSWEEK* RECENTLY NOTED, RAPISTS ARE ROUTINELY SET FREE AFTER FOUR YEARS -- BUT A NUMBER OF PRISONERS CONVICTED OF NOTHING MORE SERIOUS THAN SELLING *MARIJUANA* ARE DOING *LIFE WITHOUT PAROLE*...

IN CALIFORNIA, THE PRISON GUARD'S UNION WAS ONE OF THE MAJOR CONTRIBUTORS TO THE "THREE STRIKES" INITIATIVE -- WHICH HAS, OF COURSE, LED TO THE BUILDING OF MORE PRISONS (AND THE HIRING OF MORE GUARDS)... NOW THE HEAD OF THE UNION HAS THE CHUTZPAH TO COMPLAIN THAT PRISONS ARE FILLING UP WITH "HARDCORE CRIMINALS WHO HAVE NO HOPE AND NOTHING TO LOSE..."

> --NECESSITATING, COINCIDENTALLY ENOUGH, STILL *MORE* GUARDS...

> IS IT JUST *ME*, OR IS THE *TAIL* WAGGING THE *DOG* HERE?

ANOTHER POINT TO CONSIDER IS THAT WHEN THE KEY *HAS* BEEN THROWN AWAY, THE PRISONERS STILL NEED TO BE TAKEN CARE OF... AND AT THIS RATE, OUR NATION'S PRISONS ARE GOING TO START TURNING INTO *RETIREMENT HOMES* WITHIN THE NEXT FEW DECADES...

> NURSE...WHAT WAS IT I DID AGAIN?

> OH, YOU WERE *VERY BAD* ...YOU SOLD SOME *MARIJUANA* TO SOMEONE, FORTY OR FIFTY YEARS AGO! -- NOW TAKE YOUR MEDICINE FOR ME, OK?

TOM TOMORROW © 1-24-96

"Crimes of Silence" is based on a talk on crime, prisons, and the media given by Peter Sussman at Sonoma State University, October 7, 1996. An important aspect of understanding how the powerful limit First Amendment rights is to document the diminishing of these rights for the least powerful in society. In Germany, for example, during the 1930s, attacks on the rights of gays, Jews, and gypsies were tolerated by the German people because they were the least accepted groups in their society. Similarly, challenges to the First Amendment rights of convicted felons are often seen by American people as unimportant because felons have been negated by the society at large. However, it is absolutely necessary to protect the rights of the least favored in society if we expect to retain these same rights. Diminishing of freedom for one is the lessening of freedom for us all.

CHAPTER 8

CRIMES OF SILENCE

By Peter Y. Sussman

In no other area of social policy I can think of is public perception—shaped by news media coverage—so much a part of the problem itself as in the area of crime and punishment. Police crackdowns are initiated, judicial sentences are handed down, and laws are passed in an atmosphere of fear, and even hysteria, occasioned by the most recent "crime of note," and we journalists are the ones doing the noting. The news media share deep complicity for the ever-more-apparent failures of our criminal justice system. So do the prison systems that not only wall off prisoners from the outside world but wall off the outside world from prisons, so that the public is unable to shape effective policies to keep people from going to prisons in the first place.

There are three basic phases of the criminal justice process: (1) the crime and its immediate aftermath, (2) the judicial proceedings, and (3) the punishment. News media have police beats to report the crime and its aftermath; that is, the initial day or days of the criminal justice process. Then they have court beats to cover the judicial proceedings; that takes care of the next few months of the process. But the third part of the process, the punishment, specifically prison, can take many years, and there are very few news outlets in this country that cover it at all. With rare exceptions, there is no prison beat.

In August 1986, when I published in the *San Francisco Chronicle* Dannie Martin's first commentary on prison life, the 46-year-old convict had a rap sheet that spanned more than 30 years. He had done about 21 years in reform schools, prison camps, jails, prisons, penitentiaries, even a workhouse chain gang, and he was five years into a 33-year sentence for bank robbery at Lompoc federal penitentiary in central California. He was, as he later wrote, a criminal by any definition I know of. I had done 22 years as an editor at the *Chronicle*, and I could not then imagine a more unlikely writer, let alone colleague, than this burly convict known to his fellow prisoners as Red Hog.

Yet our unusual journalistic collaboration, though that would have seemed far too grandiose a word for what we began doing that summer, has had a widening national impact. In more than 50 essays, the self-educated bank robber has given a human face to his fellow convicts, challenging prevailing American attitudes toward prisons and prisoners during a time when the United States surpassed the former Soviet Union and South Africa to become the nation with the highest percentage of its population behind bars. Dannie has lived in extreme situations and seen others *in extremis*. Perhaps one needs to see people at their worst to also recognize the best that they are capable of. For whatever reason, Dannie was able to write with compassion and honesty about a world that contained little of either. His revealing freelance narratives and engaging writing style soon gained him a large readership, both in northern California and—through wire-service syndication—in newspapers throughout the country.

The response was also enthusiastic among Dannie's fellow convicts; like all prisoners, their deadening isolation had been reinforced by the stereotyped ways they were regarded by the world outside the walls. Countless correspondents from jails and prisons have told us over the years that they never expected to see their perspective portrayed in the news media. In Dannie they found a voice, someone who did much to "help 'jail people' become 'regular people,'" in the words of one convict letter-writer.

In the five-plus years over which these prison essays were written, Dannie and I made few overall assessments of our venture as we shaped each story for publication in the *Chronicle*. Indeed, prison life, like journalism, is notoriously a day-by-day existence, with little room for sweeping evaluations or projections. But in retrospect, ours appears to have become the most sustained attempt in memory to tell the inside story of prison life in a general-circulation newspaper.

Through most of those years, I conferred with Dannie almost daily by phone, living the prison life vicariously (by far the best way to do time). In turn, I was his primary link with the readers and their interests and with the reporters who wanted to tell the world of this compelling writer and the legal stir he had kicked up. In our collaboration is a useful metaphor. As Dannie gained more of a stake in the society whose values he had ignored all his life, we forged a mutual trust. Dannie and I—a junkie who had spent most of his adult life inside prisons and an editor who had seen prisons only from a car window—were passing figurative messages back and forth between our respective worlds. We were opening the way for dialogue about crime and punishment in this culture that has had too much of each.

"The legal stir" I refer to followed a crackdown by federal prison officials in 1988. After two years of writing for the *Chronicle* without official response, Dannie wrote a piece critical of his warden's policies and ended up in "the hole" two days after I published his essay. A week after that, he was transferred hastily out of the federal penitentiary in Lompoc to get him as far from me as possible—and charged with violating a never-before-enforced prison regulation restricting writing by prisoners in the news media.

The regulation Dannie was charged with violating outlawed bylines in the news media and compensation for writing in the news media; and it outlawed "acting as a reporter," a provision whose meaning was never defined. To protect Dannie after an adverse ruling at the district court level, I was compelled to run his reports from prison under the byline: "By a Federal Prisoner." I felt like an editor in apartheid-era South Africa. The federal prison authorities interpret their regulatory authority so broadly that they apparently feel they have a right even to tell newspaper editors on which page of the newspaper they can run stories by federal prisoners.

This "inmate reporter" regulation was drafted originally in the 1970s to control the writings of imprisoned anti-war activists and other "extremely anti-establishment" inmates, to use the words of the man who headed the Federal Bureau of Prisons at the time. In other words, it was a politically-motivated regulation designed to control the content of free-world newspaper articles originating in prisons.

The regulation's intent—its unconstitutional intent—was made explicit during appeals court arguments when the Justice Department attorney said that the Bureau of Prisons "had to draw a line somewhere. They chose to draw it in a way that goes after the news media," which prompted one newspaper attorney to summarize the hearing by saying, "I have only one thing written down on my pad: 'They chose to go after the news media.'"

That federal prison regulation is still in effect, intimidating other prisoners who might recklessly consider writing down their views and submitting them to a newspaper or magazine.

The crackdown on Dannie began a legal battle that generated national interest and taught me a great deal about the dynamics of prison life. I have learned subsequently of a number of other First Amendment battles involving news media access rights to prisoners (I'll get back to one of those later), and I have come to believe that official intransigence has done a lot to isolate prisoners unnecessarily. As I indicated earlier, the result has been that we on the outside do not have the information we need to evaluate public-policy issues involving crime and punishment.

Why should we care what happens in prison? For one thing, a rapidly increasing proportion of our public resources are going to financing prisons, often in competition with education and social programs that might more effectively prevent future criminal behavior.

Furthermore, how people are treated in prison has a lot to do with how they act when they get out, so that much of our crime problem is really another facet of our punishment problem. I cite, as just one small example of the kind of insights we could gain from prisoners, the following words from my co-author Dannie Martin; he is talking about the decades-long determinate sentences being meted out to prisoners, especially those convicted of relatively minor drug offenses:

> *The public is unable to imagine what the added time does to a convict and what it does to his family.*
>
> *Two years is a lot of time. Twenty or 30 years is a Mount Everest of time, and very few can climb it. And what happens to them on the way up makes one not want to be around if and when they return.*
>
> *The first thing a convict feels when he receives an inconceivably long sentence is shock. The shock usually wears off after about two years, when all his appeals have been denied. He then enters a period of self-hatred because of what he's done to himself and his family.*
>
> *If he survives that emotion—and some don't—he begins to swim the rapids of rage, frustration, and alienation. When he passes through the rapids, he finds himself in the calm waters of impotence, futility, and resignation. It's not a life one can look forward to living. The future is totally devoid of hope, and people without any hope are dangerous—either to themselves or others.*

The criminal justice process operates in a vacuum of public understanding. Legislators and penal officials are shaping criminal justice policies based on stereotypes and half-truths, on anger and fear, on political propaganda and crackpot theory. Nevertheless, much of the public appears to be comfortable with its state of ignorance. It is far easier to barricade one's problems and fears behind walls of concrete, rolls of razor wire, and reams of cliché than to deal with the realities of criminal experience in our society.

But the people we have put out of sight and out of mind continue to exist, and they are shaped—or warped—by the conditions to which we have relegated them. Willful public ignorance has never solved any social problem, and I believe it has seriously distorted and aggravated our recent crime problems.

Now the people of California have taken to voting directly on criminal punishments through the initiative process—I'm thinking here of the three-strikes initiative—with no real information on the effects of their vote on the people sentenced. Who is going to prison under the law? Are they the people we intended to put away? And what is the effect of prison on them and on crime patterns?

The news media cannot answer such critical questions without access to prisons and prisoners. They also cannot answer them without independent and clear-eyed scrutiny of the issues. Before returning to the problem of prison access, I'd like to take note of just a few of the structural problems in journalism that I think are driving the distorted coverage of crime and, especially, punishment; they serve to reinforce stereotypical and false images of crime and criminals in ways that I will be discussing later.

With more than a million and a half people in this country's jail and prison cells at any one snapshot moment—and millions more on probation and parole, and still more millions in their families—we can no longer afford the luxury of inattention or the perils of distortion.

The people who work in the news media generally reflect the concerns and interests of the population they come from. Many news stories come from tips; those tips come from the friends, associates, and contacts of the people who work in our newsrooms. They are largely white, middle-class or upper-middle class, often uneasily protective of their position on the social ladder, and many of them are simply unable to imagine ways of looking at things that are not of their own class or ethnic experience. Yet, increasingly, prison is becoming a matter of race and class.

In addition, as the "news business" turns into a branch of just-plain business—partly through corporate mergers—the news media play to the marketplace, to the demographics, to disposable income. Too many TV stations, for instance, have allowed Nielsen ratings to guide their news judgment. Newspapers, often prompted by hired editorial consultants, run long service features on how to lose weight and which CDs to buy. In journalism, these are called "service" stories, but they provide a service to individual consumers— individual consumers with disposable income—and not necessarily to society itself. Although I do not share the view of some critics that most daily coverage decisions in the newsroom are nothing more than covert business decisions, they are nevertheless influenced heavily by the corporate cultural soup of which they are an ingredient.

The solutions to these structural problems are obvious: We journalists must rediscover our traditional responsibility to our community and not just our demographics or markets. And we must hire for our newsrooms the people who can give us a broader perspective on this crime beat, as on all others. Only a diverse news staff can understand and eliminate the misrepresentation that characterizes much of our coverage of crime and punishment.

Whatever the origins of the news media's blind spots, there will be always be institutions working overtime to make sure the media's blinders remain in place. Few institutions are more secretive than the nations' prison systems. It's disheartening how normally skeptical journalists and citizens buy into prison officials' censorship at all levels.

Here's another case history of prison censorship at work:

Right now in California, state corrections officials have imposed a ban on face-to-face news media interviews with prisoners. Several other states have imposed or are considering similar bans. California's new regulations were in effect for many months before an enterprising journalist disclosed the restrictions. For those first months, the regulations were not announced; no hearings were held; there was no public regulatory process; the rules were not published for either the public or prisoners. Attorneys and journalists tried unsuccessfully to obtain copies of the secret regulations. Yet we journalists were being kept from interviews—and at least one convict was being punished—based on those apparently nonexistent rules. It was an abuse of power, and it was illegal.

When the regulations were finally announced formally, at 4 p.m. on a Friday afternoon, they were put into effect within days under emergency procedures that were not occasioned by any emergency. The five-day public comment period began on a Saturday morning, so the comment period was half over before even the most dedicated observer of the corrections archipelago knew it had begun. The way those regulations were announced was designed to keep them secret for as long as possible and to deter public comment until they were in effect.

The prison system in California has been found by federal judges to be engaging in unconstitutionally cruel treatment of high-security and mentally ill convicts. But prison officials have cut off direct, face-to-face media access to the people who brought those court suits. In other words, public officials have effectively muzzled their accusers.

More recent revelations detail, in the words of a *Los Angeles Times* news story—"torture, killing, and cover-up" committed by guards at Corcoran State Prison. The unimaginable atrocities at Corcoran included staged "cockfights" between prisoners known to be antagonistic. Guards and other officials are said to have invited guests to these so-called "gladiator days." Bets were placed on the combatants. And when on occasion prisoners didn't stop fighting on command, they were shot. In the eight years of the prison's existence, seven inmates have been shot dead by guards and more than 50 others wounded by gunfire.

Especially troubling is that the highest-level officials at Corcoran condoned the brutality, and appeals for relief to department brass in Sacramento were routinely rejected. Representatives of the department even tried to stop whistle-blowing guards at Corcoran from taking their information to the FBI, which is now, finally, investigating the savagery committed there.

But, again, the very bureaucracy that is accused of wrongdoing is restricting media access to the people who are suffering from inhuman abuses at its hands.

One California prisoner is being punished for suggesting in a letter to a freelance journalist ways of trying to set up an interview to comply with the Department of Corrections' then-secret, unpublished regulations. Boston Woodard is a trusty who has used his long prison sentence to initiate and further a number of important social projects like literacy training, racial cooperation through integration of prison rock bands, and fund-raising for local agencies that deal with abused children. (The group Prisoners Against Child Abuse has raised more than $80,000 for the agencies over the past five years. Many of its members, of course, were themselves abused children.)

The harmless information Boston Woodard passed along to a journalist in a letter had come from a prison official, but Woodard was punished nonetheless. He was removed from his treasured job as editor of the last remaining prisoner newspaper in California (where he had recently published an editorial critical of the media interview restrictions), he was confined to quarters, and he lost valuable "good time" toward his release. His prison record has been permanently sullied for a made-up offense called "circumventing policies"—policies that didn't exist in any rule book, and even if they had, his actions would not have been in violation of them. It was Woodard's first serious infraction in the 15 years he had been incarcerated.

Can you imagine the outcry in the press and among the public if comparable abuses were discovered in another government agency and the news media were forbidden *by the accused agency* to investigate them effectively?

The California regulation appears to be directed less at managing the prisons than managing what we on the outside can read, see, and hear from inside the joint. It is a classic violation of the First Amendment, a principle that was devised to assure our ability to learn about and talk freely about public officials and institutions. The Department of Corrections chooses instead to characterize news media interviews as "a public forum in which [prisoners] can espouse their often sociopathic philosophies." Do they really not understand our constitutional right to hear and evaluate for ourselves even what they choose to characterize as sociopathic philosophies?

Prison officials also cite in defense of the new interview ban that citizens are running around in Charles Manson T-shirts, giving young people a bad example, and encouraging them to engage in a life of crime. Blame for those dangerous T-shirts is laid at the feet of the news media that have interviewed Manson. The department tells us, too, that the prisons have responsibility for public safety, that that includes not just physical safety as generally assumed but *emotional* safety, and that therefore the prisons may control what you and I see on television to protect our emotional safety.

As Supreme Court Justice John Paul Stevens wrote in an unrelated case recently:

The First Amendment directs us to be especially skeptical of regulations that seek to keep people in the dark for what the government perceives to be their own good.

Nonetheless, not only have many journalists passively accepted institutional restrictions, but they have compromised crime-and-punishment coverage by capitulating to public, political, and commercial demands.

Crime sells. Or more precisely, the fear of crime sells. And because crime sells, certain high-profile crimes are used in the same way that sex is used by some ad firm associates to promote all kinds of unrelated products. A slinky woman sprawled languorously across the hood of an automobile is used to sell the car whose hood she caresses lovingly. Similarly, the ominously cadenced recitation of some criminal act is employed to sell everything from California Governor Pete Wilson's personal political fortunes to legislation, such as the three-strikes law, that will determine the shape of our society for generations to come.

What we journalists say about prisons also tends to reflect what the public wants to hear about prisoners and other criminals. Without knowledge or understanding of the people involved, the public does what it always does: substitutes generally accepted stereotypes for unavailable factual information. Journalists uncritically accept distorted public attitudes and self-serving political agendas, and in the process they further distort public perceptions. It's an endless loop of misinformation and misunderstanding.

Accurate coverage is impeded, too, by the portrayal of prisons and crime for the purposes of entertainment. With the corporate and programming convergence of entertainment media and news media into one amorphous thing called "the media," entertainment values are supplanting news values in many newspapers and on the airwaves.

It has been widely observed over the years how times of social or economic change or uncertainty increase a sense of generalized unease and promote simplistic solutions. Mass entertainment is a covert way of simultaneously expressing and sublimating our social fears through stereotypes.

In print and on the airwaves, entertainment is currently blending with and subsuming the news. We have even invented ugly new hybrid words for this hybrid phenomenon, words like infotainment and docudrama, advertorial and infomercial, which are nothing more than ways of describing the dilution of news and opinion with entertainment, which is in turn often commercially motivated. Fictional TV cop shows merge into fact-based stories like *America's Most Wanted*. Tabloid magazine shows blur the lines of conventional genres. Ideologues like Rush Limbaugh entertain with fanciful social notions while purporting to convey factual information. So-called news shows feature embarrassingly silly banter and shock photos and many other such noninformational entertainment devices.

And presiding over the entire process are news corporations that are increasingly the subsidiaries of entertainment conglomerates.

Entertainment values are inherently non-journalistic. In entertainment, what we read or hear or see becomes important for the *feelings* with which it leaves us and not for its accuracy or importance. And nothing satisfies more readily than the easily understandable, the simple emotional reaction based on familiarity. In other words, stereotyping—that convenient shorthand by which we falsify experience—substitutes for news judgment. Crime reporting is overwhelmingly stereotype-based. It is our new mythology, and we journalists become unwitting mythologists, telling the stories that people choose to guide their lives by rather than the stories of more representative miscreants.

It's the Christians and the lions, the good guys and the bad guys, the white hats and the black hats, the 49ers and the Dallas Cowboys, and, of course, those celluloid cowboys and Indians. It's Polly Klaas and Richard Allen Davis. Stories. Myths.

A girl with the all-American name of Polly is murdered after being abducted from her own home during a slumber party in a white, middle-class suburb of San Francisco. It was an all too typical setting but a most atypical crime. Nevertheless, that crime was transmuted into a mythological event with the connivance of the news media and at the specific instigation of politicians, several of whom dominated the girl's funeral with their showy presence. The case became a gargantuan media feeding frenzy, with no sense of balance or proportion.

In effect, Polly Klaas' murder became a modern morality play. The trouble with morality plays is that they are based on simplistic allegories that by definition purport to stand for something other than what they actually represent. They are inherently non-journalistic. They are used for entertainment and moral guidance, not factual enlightenment.

Journalism works by anecdote. It is the reporting of matters of social import through specific examples, or anecdotes. We journalists tell stories. How representative our stories are is a critical issue; indeed, it is a more important element in achieving objectivity than the conventional, artificial balancing of two contrasting views.

California journalists chose to tell—to overtell—the story of Polly Klaas with the implication that it was somehow a representative crime. But it was not a representative crime at all. Coverage that was factual on its face became a serious form of media distortion because the emphasis itself was misplaced.

When Polly Klaas was murdered, the attention we journalists gave to this one murder out of many was based on more than stereotyping and myth-making. It was also based on the personal agendas of politicians who were running for office and needed a myth to synthesize and exploit public fears. The attention focused on Polly Klaas' accused killer, Richard Allen Davis, was used to win passage of California's harsh new three-strikes legislation and to assure the re-election of Governor Wilson. But, again, the Richard Allen Davis to whom we have been exposed on the airwaves and in print is a media anecdote. In some senses, he is not as representative of the prison population as, say, Duane Silva.

Who is Duane Silva, and why do we know nothing about him? We know nothing about him partly because he is so typical, so ordinary, so boring. His is not a story that plays to subterranean fears; it is not a story of use to politicians; it is not a story with an easy solution. In short, it lacks entertainment value.

Duane is a 23-year-old who has been mentally ill all his life with something the doctors call schizo-affective disorder. He has an IQ of 70, which is characterized as borderline retarded. As a result of his problems, this gentle young man spent most of his school years in special-ed classes. Duane had two felonies on his record when the three-strikes legislation was enacted in 1994. His felony convictions were the result of a plea bargain intended by judge and attorneys to keep the mentally ill man out of prison, where they agreed he didn't belong. The offenses were arson, but what he actually had done was set fires in trash cans...in the delusional belief that he was helping local police by burning illegal drugs.

Duane's third strike was the theft of some coins and a VCR from a longtime friend's house, just days after the three-strikes law went into effect. He sold the VCR for pinball money and then dialed 911 and told police where he had seen a VCR just like the one taken from his friend's house. Of course, the VCR was immediately traced back to Duane, and this vulnerable, mentally ill man is now doing 30 years to life on the mainline of Folsom prison, where he is at great risk of rape and death because of his confusion and his meek and credulous personality.

Sometimes, entertaining stereotypes derive from the very attempt to write well, to tug at the readers' emotions with vivid imagery. Take, for example, the story of a girl's disappearance that ran on March 4, 1996, in the *San Francisco Chronicle*, datelined Hanford, Kings County. The story began:

This is one of those small towns where nothing really bad is ever supposed to happen.

Remember that. That's the beginning of the story on a girl who disappeared. So far, nothing about the missing girl. The story continues:

Shady parks and playgrounds are easy to find. Schools and churches stand quietly around every other corner. Lemoore Naval Air Station, where pilots fly F-18 jet fighters a few miles west of here, seems to provide a sense of security and order.

OK, we're two paragraphs into it, and still no mention of that missing girl. It's all atmospherics so far—a rural, safe world, protected from the dangers posed by unstable outsiders. Then, in the third paragraph, the reporter writes:

So when another girl disappears off the face of the earth—the third in the last two years from this area...

Finally, the specific occasion for this rural portrait is revealed. Later in the story, the reporter writes:

This community in the central San Joaquin Valley between Highways 5 and 99 is a prosperous town, surrounded by endless farms where cotton, alfalfa, grapes, and dairy cows are raised. The snow-capped Sierra is clearly visible 50 miles to the east after the morning fog burns off.

But residents clearly are aware that it is also surrounded by a world where life is sometimes cheap. There are four prisons nearby, including Corcoran State Prison 17 miles south, where Charles Manson, mass murderer Juan Corona and Bobby Kennedy's assassin, Sirhan Sirhan, are housed.

You see how the entertainment values, the mythological subtext, dominate this story of a girl's disappearance? The *Chronicle* chose to travel to a distant "rural paradise" to report this presumed crime, though murders occur regularly within easy walking distance of the *Chronicle*'s offices in downtown San Francisco. Why did they choose to emphasize this particular case? Because the girl's disappearance gave itself so easily to myth, to stereotype, to entertainment. Its mythological subtext—evocative, even if unrepresentative—is the stated reason for the coverage. It starts right there in the first paragraph: "This is one of those small towns where nothing really bad is ever supposed to happen."

Needless to say, Charles Manson, Juan Corona, and Sirhan Sirhan remain safely incarcerated and had nothing whatever to do with the girl's disappearance. Nor did the prison itself, which is 17 miles from the town where the girl vanished. Those notorious criminals are evoked to provide a kind of lurid frame for a story that is totally unrelated to them. In short, the story titillates rather than educates. It panders to and reinforces widespread public fears instead of informing with a valid sense of context.

In fact, the remote farm area where the disappearance occurred is no Eden. In some circles, it is as well known for its rural methamphetamine factories as for its cotton, alfalfa, grapes, and cows. But that fact might have ruined a good yarn.

The suspect finally arrested in the case was a resident of this pure town—the father of the victim's 12-year-old playmate—and not an evil outsider preying on all-American rural innocents.

Still another dangerous practice distorting our news coverage is news by icon. Since news is increasingly a subset of entertainment, graphics play a bigger role in news presentation, both in newspapers and on the airwaves. Graphics and graphic design are the pretty packages in which news stories are served up. Graphic elements rely on immediately identifiable, common, and accessible features for their impact. Nothing is more immediately identifiable, more common, or more accessible than a stereotype. Examples are the logos that loom from the screen over a television newscaster's shoulders, summarizing a complex story with a simplistic icon like a gun or a hypodermic needle or the profile of a menacing black face or a single male alcoholic slumped by a shopping cart. Those images often carry more weight than the words read by the newscaster.

We're all familiar with the prison stereotypes: prisons as dens of angry, violent, brutish subhumans. But the bulk of the prisoners are more like Duane Silva. More than three-quarters of the people imprisoned in California for three-strike offenses are nonviolent. Many of them were put away for life for trivial crimes and addictions, and many of them are mentally ill and/or retarded. We journalists are not telling that story effectively, and prison officials are conspiring to keep us from telling it.

It is well past time for journalists to correct the distortions they have brought to public perception of crime and prisons. We journalists must begin by covering prisons and the people in them, as real people and not ciphers. We cannot allow our coverage to be dominated by simplistic morality, by entertainment values and devices, or by self-promoting politicians. And we must, as a matter of professional imperative, aggressively challenge the many regulations and other barriers erected by authoritarian public officials between us and these important news stories.

If we were talking about the real people who largely inhabit our prisons, we would be conveying a very different story, and one that might help us to overcome our crime problems rather than wallow in them.

We would be learning, for example, that enforced dependence may not be the best way to teach drug-dependent people to function independently in society. In general, dependence does nothing to foster self-reliance and other social survival skills. We would also be learning that telling people daily in a hundred different ways that they are scum may not be the best way to teach them self-esteem, which is another critical social survival skill. And we would be learning that disposing of the handicapped behind electrified wire does nothing to wipe out either disability or crime.

I'd like to close with quotes from a current and a former prisoner. First, from Boston Woodard, who is at this writing languishing in the hole at the California Men's Colony in San Luis Obispo, in central California; the quote is from a letter to me soon after he was fired from his prison editor's job and punished for reaching out to the news media despite secret state prison interview restrictions:

> *This is the first time in my prison life I haven't felt like there was no hope regarding something these* [Department of Corrections] *bastards have fabricated. What you folks* [several journalists calling attention to his plight] *are doing means more than you know. There's no doubt that the attention I've been receiving regarding my being canned helped quash the many reprisals I would have received from prison officials. If they weren't censoring this letter I would give you specifics.*
>
> *I have heard it through the prison grapevine that other news folk have been inquiring about my situation because of an article that was picked up by the Associated Press. I don't know what the hell we're going to do when people like you are completely blocked out from us.*

And finally, a letter my co-author Dannie Martin wrote me in connection with a forum on his own punishment for writing openly in the news media:

> *The real issues, I believe, are: (1) Does a convict have a First Amendment right to publicly define himself and his surroundings? And (2) does the public have a First Amendment right to hear a prisoner's viewpoint....*
>
> *Any permanent harm that comes to us all won't be because of what we talk about. It will come from what was passed over in silence.*

PETER Y. SUSSMAN spent 29 years as an editor at the *San Francisco Chronicle*. Today he is an independent author and editor and the president of the Northern California chapter of the Society of Professional Journalists.

APPENDIX A

Less Access to Less Information By and About the U.S. Government

XXVI, A 1996 Chronology: January-June (revised)
and XXVII, A 1996 Chronology: June-December
By the American Library Association (ALA) Washington Office

For the past 15 years, this ongoing chronology has documented efforts to restrict and privatize government information. It is distributed as a supplement to the ALA Washington Office Newsletter and as an electronic publication at http://www.ala.org/washoff/lessaccess.html. While government information is more accessible through computer networks and the Freedom of Information Act, there are still barriers to public access. The latest damaging disclosures facing the Clinton Administration involve allegations of concealing information and claiming executive privilege. Continuing revelations of Cold War secrecy show how government information has been concealed, resulting in a lack of public accountability and cost to taxpayers.

Another development, with major implications for public access, is the growing tendency of federal agencies to use computer and telecommunication technologies for data collection, storage, retrieval, and dissemination. This trend has resulted in the increased emergence of contractual arrangements with commercial firms to disseminate information collected at taxpayer expense, higher user charges for government information, and the proliferation of government information available in electronic format only. This trend toward electronic dissemination is occurring in all three branches of government. While automation clearly offers promises of savings, will public access to government information be further restricted for people who cannot afford computers or pay for computer time?

On the other hand, the Government Printing Office (GPO) Access system and the Library of Congress THOMAS system have enhanced public access by providing free on-line access to government databases. A study prepared in July 1996 by GPO for Congress recommends a five- to seven-year transition to a more electronic depository program instead of the rapid two-year transition proposed in 1995 by the House of Representatives.

ALA has reaffirmed its long-standing conviction that open government is vital to a democracy. A January 1984 resolution passed by ALA's Council stated that "there should be equal and ready access to data collected, compiled, produced, and published in any format by the government of the United States."

In 1986, ALA initiated a Coalition on Government Information. The Coalition's objectives are to focus national attention on all efforts that limit access to government information, and to develop support for improvements in access to government information.

With access to information as a major ALA priority, library advocates should be concerned about barriers to public access to government information. Previous chronologies were compiled in two ALA Washington Office indexed publications, *Less Access to Less Information By and About the U.S. Government: A 1981-1987 Chronology*, and *Less Access to Less Information By and About the U.S. Government: A 1988-1991 Chronology*. The following selected chronology continues the tradition of a semi-annual update.

CHRONOLOGY

Postal Service Withholds Customer Service Survey Data

According to the General Accounting Office, the Postal Service is spending $11.9 million to survey businesses on how well it delivers their mail, but is keeping the results secret. In 1993 when the Postal Service hired the Gallup Organization to survey its business customers, many businesses expected the results to be made public. But according to GAO, after the Postal Service got the first results in April 1994, the agency decided against making them public, apparently fearing the information would help its competitors.

Additionally, six weeks ago postal officials said they will no longer publicize a key consumer satisfaction rating that the postal service developed to evaluate what residential customers around the country think of their mail service. The GAO suggested in its report to Representative John McHugh (R-NY), chair of the House Postal Service Subcommittee, that the agency should make greater public use of the ratings, not less. (McAllister, Bill, "Postal Service Won't Reveal Data from Customer Survey," *Washington Post*, January 3, 1996: C1)

Citizen Oversight Needed

The New York Times editorialized: "Too little has been made of a landmark victory for open government. Hundreds of millions of classified documents will soon become public thanks to Executive Order 12958, which came into force Oct. 15 and requires the automatic declassification of most U.S. Government files more than 25 years old."

As the editorial points out: "Uniform standards for classification will apply for the first time to all Federal agencies, and the burden is now on officials to show why a document should be kept secret for 10 years, the new limit for most files. In theory, this should sharply reduce the number of secret files. In practice, it will require continuous oversight by citizens to make sure their public servants abide by the new rules." ("The Struggle Against Secrecy," *The New York Times*, January 3, 1996: A14)

Watt Belatedly Finds Documents in his Garage

Former Secretary of Interior James Watt pleaded guilty to one misdemeanor in exchange for a prosecutor dropping felony charges against him. In 1995, Watt had been indicted on 25 counts of lying to Congress and a grand jury, and obstructing prosecutors. His legal problems resulted from his insistence that he had few documents of "marginal, if any, relevance" to the grand jury investigating political favoritism and mismanagement at the Department of Housing and Urban Development during the Reagan Administration. Watt later found documents in his family garage, including letters he had written to then-HUD Secretary Samuel R. Pierce Jr., to business associates, and a HUD under secretary about certain projects involved in the investigation. When Watt turned them over, prosecutors were angry because he had failed to turn them over sooner. The independent counsel even blamed Watt for dragging out his investigation, and driving up its expense, the cost of which increased $3 million since January 1995. ("When Subpoenaed in 1990, Watt Made the Wrong Call," *Washington Post*, January 5, 1996)

Newly-released Memo Contradicts White House Account of Travel Office Firings

A newly released draft memo by David Watkins, a former top Clinton aide, describes Hillary Rodham Clinton as the principal figure in the 1993 travel office firings. The memo contradicts the White House's official account of Mrs. Clinton as an interested observer of the dismissal of the White House travel staff and their replacement with Clinton associates from Arkansas. Watkins was dismissed in 1994 after using a government helicopter for an excursion to play golf, and White House officials said his description of Mrs. Clinton's role was inaccurate.

In December 1994, Billy Dale, the travel office director, was indicted on charges that he embezzled $68,000 paid by news organizations for presidential trips. In November 1995, he was acquitted by a jury. (Johnston, David, "Memo Places Hillary Clinton at Core of Travel Office Case," *The New York Times*, January 5, 1996: A1)

Missing Whitewater Documents Found at White House

The White House said that it unexpectedly discovered copies of missing documents from the Rose Law Firm, describing the work of Hillary Rodham Clinton for a failing savings and loan association in the 1980s. Federal and Congressional investi- gators have issued subpoenas for the documents since 1994, and the White House said it did not have them. The originals disappeared from the Arkansas law firm, where Mrs. Clinton was a partner, before President Clinton took office. The newly-discovered documents were copies of billing records from the Rose firm, where Mrs. Clinton helped to represent Madison Guaranty, a savings association run by the Clinton's business partner in the Whitewater land venture. The Clinton's personal attorney said the documents show that the work Mrs. Clinton performed was limited both in time and scope, as she has said. (Labaton, Stephen, "Elusive Whitewater Papers Are Found at White House," *The New York Times*, January 6, 1996: A1)

Army Discloses Size of Chemical Arsenal

The Army revealed another Cold War secret. It disclosed that 30,000 tons of nerve and blister agents—stored in eight states—were being destroyed at a cost of $12 billion. Dropping official secrecy, Maj. Gen. Robert Orton, head of the Army's chemical weapons destruction project, told a Pentagon news conference that declassifying the information will hasten efforts by the Army to get the environmental clearances needed to destroy the weapons. "It also may enhance our credibility by confirming that we are not holding back from regulators and the public," Orton said.

According to the article, the overall figure of 30,599 tons is only the amount of "unitary" chemical weapons in the stockpile, or those with one active chemical component. Additionally, the Army keeps 680 tons of "binary" weapons, a newer and safer technology, armed by mixing two active components. The Army also has 13,630 tons of chemical agents not counted in its active inventory, which are used for testing, research, and other purposes. (Associated Press, "U.S. Army Details Extent and Content of Chemical Arsenal," *Washington Post*, January 23, 1996: A12)

Fired Workers Deplore Administration "Lies"

Seven White House travel office employees fired by the Clinton Administration accused their former employer of abusing its power when it dismissed them nearly three years ago. Testifying before the House Government Reform and Oversight Committee, the employees said they continued to suffer White House attacks and that the Administration continuing to spread "lies" about them, especially former director Billy Dale. Dale is waiting for completion of an Internal Revenue Services audit begun during the criminal investigation of the travel office. Each of the former employees has gone into debt—nearly $600,000 total—to pay for the lawyers they had to hire to fight White House charges

that there were gross financial mismanagement in the office. All seven workers denied that they ever did anything wrong. (Locy, Toni, "Ex-Travel Office Workers Condemn Administration 'Lies,'" *Washington Post*, January 25, 1996: A11)

Hillary Clinton Testifies about Recovered Records

On January 26, First Lady Hillary Rodham Clinton testified for four hours before a federal grand jury about matters related to the Whitewater scandal, including the disappearance and sudden recovery of her law firm billing records. (Locy, Toni and Susan Schmidt, "First Lady Testifies for Four Hours," *Washington Post*, January 27, 1996: A1)

Secret Budgets Result in Misplaced Billions

The National Reconnaissance Office, the secret agency that builds spy satellites, misplaced more than $2 billion in 1995, largely because of its own internal secrecy, according to intelligence officials. Critics of the agency said that the money was hidden in several secret accounts. One Senate intelligence committee aide said the accounting problem grew from a lack of accountability, which in turn was created by the extraordinary secrecy under which the reconnaissance office works.

The reconnaissance office operates in the deepest secrecy of any government agency. Financed by the

$28-billion-a-year "black budget" (classified above top secret) for military and intelligence programs, it spends an estimated $5 billion to $6 billion annually. The reconnaissance agency is really a set of secret offices—so secret that they have been shielded from one another. When these offices and programs were consolidated in 1995, top managers found that "no one had a handle on how much money they had," the Senate intelligence committee aide said. Congressional oversight of the reconnaissance office has been sketchy, he said, because few members of Congress understood the highly technical language of spy satellites and some did not know they were approving billions of dollars a year in secret spending. (Weiner, Tim, "A Secret Agency's Secret Budgets Yield 'Lost' Billions, Officials Say," *The New York Times,* January 30, 1996: A1) [Ed. note: In May, it was revealed that the National Reconnaissance Office accumulated about $4 billion in uncounted secret money. (Weiner, Tim, "A Spy Agency Admits Accumulating $4 Billion in Secret Money," *The New York Times,* May 16, 1996: B13)]

Government Shutdown Delays Data Release

The collection and release of community right-to-know information from industry by the Environmental Protection Agency will be delayed due to the recent government shutdown. The reporting delay affected the data which includes for the first time reports on the 286 chemicals EPA Administrator Carol M. Browner added to the list in November 1994. The shutdowns in December 1995 and continued budget cuts also have led to a delay in EPA's ability to process right-to-know data already collected from 1994. The public will receive 1994 community right-to-know information more than two months late this year.

Widespread public access is available from libraries, state and federal environmental offices, CD-ROMs, and a toll-free hotline. Since 1986, reported releases of toxic chemicals under the community right-to-know laws have declined by 43 percent nationwide. (McDermott, Patrice, "Community Right-to-Know Reporting Program Delayed by Government Shutdown," *OMB Watch,* January 30, 1996)

Secret Arms Caches in Austria Revealed

The United States Ambassador to Austria, Swanee Hunt, provided the Austrian Government with the location and contents of 79 arms caches the U. S. set up in Austria in the early 1950s. The weapons were stockpiled in the zone of American occupation after World War II and were meant for use in the event of a Soviet invasion. Hunt apologized to the Austrians for keeping the stockpiles secret for so long. She gave the secret list to Interior Minister Caspar Einem, who said Austria had found five of the weapons depots over the years. Existence of the stockpiles was revealed when the CIA and other U.S. Government agencies reviewed programs from the Cold-War years. ("U.S. Reveals Secret Arms Caches in Austria," *The New York Times*, January 30, 1966: A4)

Gingrich's Office Makes Public Names of Workers' Compensation Task Force

After *Roll Call* reported on January 25 about a task force authorized by House Speaker Newt Gingrich (R-GA) to develop recommendations for states to reform the workers' compensation system, the Speaker's office released the names of the task force members. The membership had not previously been made public, but *Roll Call* revealed that the task force was headed by Richard Scrushy, an Alabama health care executive who is a major fundraiser for Gingrich.

In a letter to *Roll Call*, Tony Blankly, Gingrich's press secretary, disputed the use of the word "secret" to describe the membership of the group, arguing that the list of members was readily available in a report that was "presented last December to the American Legislative Exchange Council (ALEC), a 3,000-member group of state legislators." But ALEC, a conservative, free-market group,

disavowed producing the report Gingrich's office released even though its name appeared on the cover. ALEC said it had "no direct relationship" with the task force and that the proposals "are not a product of ALEC, nor has ALEC adopted them in any fashion." (Chappie, Damon, "Gingrich's Office Releases Task Force Names," *Roll Call*, February 1, 1996)

Justice Department Releases Travel Office Report

On January 31, the Justice Department released a long-sealed report on the White House travel office that criticized White House officials for engaging in "ill-advised and erroneous actions" in abruptly dismissing seven employees of the office in 1993. But the report did not find that Presidential Aides had pressured the FBI to investigate the dismissed employees, as Republicans have suggested. The report, completed in March 1994 by the Justice Department Office of Professional Responsibility, focused primarily on the White House dealings with the FBI. It found that the FBI had engaged in no wrongdoing by investigating the travel office and was released in response to Freedom of Information Act requests by several news organizations. It had been withheld pending the outcome of Dale's prosecution. (Johnston, David, "Justice Department Faults White House in Travel Office Dismissals," *The New York Times*, February 1, 1996: A14)

Cables Show U.S. Deception

A review of classified cables sent by the American Embassy in Haiti to the Defense and State Departments shows that for a year before the United States invaded Haiti in September 1994, the Pentagon knew that the country's most dreaded paramilitary group was not a legitimate opposition political party as the official version maintained. The cables indicate that American intelligence agencies had concluded that the group, the Front for the Advancement and Progress of Haiti, was a gang of "gun-carrying crazies" eager to "use violence against all who oppose it." The documents raise questions about the soldiers' mission, the information given by superiors, and the action taken in the field. It remains uncertain why the Pentagon took a public stance at odds with the classified information it had collected in Haiti. A Pentagon official denied there was any conflict. (Rohter, Larry, "Cables Show U.S. Deception on Haitian Violence," *The New York Times*, February 6, 1996: A8)

Secrets Burden Department of Energy

The Department of Energy and its contractors may have released information they should have kept secret because American makers of nuclear weapons have classified virtually everything for so long that they have more secrets than they can cope with. The department is spending $3 mil-lion to develop a computer program to scan 100 million pages of documents that it wants to review for possible release. The goal is to reduce the secrets to a manageable quantity.

Currently, ideas are "classified at birth," and presumed secret. Hazel R. O'Leary, the Energy Secretary, said that most of what was still secret had "occasional mention of something that was perhaps born classified," but much of that could probably be declassified. Energy Department officials said that some material that is still classified is guarding useless secrets but would be useful in defining the environmental and health damage associated with the production and testing of nuclear weapons. Mrs. O'Leary gave another reason for declassification: the public would be provided with information that could be used in deciding what to do with nuclear wastes that will eventually have to be disposed. (Wald, Matthew L., "Millions of Secrets Burden Energy Agency," *The New York Times*, February 7, 1996: A15)

Workers Allege Secret Air Base Broke Hazardous Waste Act

Two years before he died, Helen Frost says her husband, Robert, returned from his sheet-metal job at a top-secret Air Force base in Nevada with flaming-red skin that soon began peeling off his face. Mrs. Frost is one of two widows, who joined forced with four former civilian workers to sue the

Defense Department, contending that it violated federal hazardous-waste law by repeatedly burning ordinary chemicals and highly toxic, classified materials in open pits at the base. The workers, who say their exposure to toxic fumes throughout the 1980s caused health problems ranging from skin lesions to cancer, are seeking information to facilitate medical treatment and help with medical bills. As employees of government subcontractors, some of the plaintiffs say they have no medical insurance.

So far, the government refuses to confirm or deny their allegations. Instead, it asked a U.S. District Court judge to dismiss the lawsuit, arguing that almost any disclosure about the base could pose a "serious risk" to national security. Apparently, the government has never before cited "national security" in a case in which the effect is to shield itself from criminal liability. The burning alleged by the workers is a serious crime, punishable by up to 15 years in prison and a $1 million fine. Constitutional experts say the case could ultimately go to the Supreme Court because it tests the limits of executive-branch power. In effect, the government argues that the national-security privilege gives the military more leeway than the president has to keep information secret, even if it involves a crime. (Jacobs, Margaret A., "Secret Air Base Broke Hazardous-Waste Act, Workers' Suit Alleges," *Wall Street Journal*, February 8, 1996: A1)

CIA Retains Right to Use Journalists as Cover

CIA Director John M. Deutch said that the agency maintained the right to use U.S. journalists or their organizations as cover for intelligence activities, but only under restrictive regulations published 19 years ago. Disclosure that the CIA's ban on recruiting U.S. journalists or using American news organizations as cover could be waived under a little-publicized regulation surprised many journalists and former government officials. It also undercut a recommendation made recently by an independent blue-ribbon panel sponsored by the Council on Foreign Relations. Leslie H. Gelb, president of the council and a member of the panel, disagreed with the group's recommendation and with current CIA policy. Gelb said, "I was and am flatly opposed to using American journalists as spies and American spies as journalists." (Pincus, Walter, "CIA to Retain Right to Use Journalistic Cover," *Washington Post*, February 17, 1996: A6)

Secrecy Makes Controlling Deadly Weapons Difficult

The secrecy surrounding the small-arms trade is a major reason why controlling these weapons is difficult. Information obtained through the Freedom of Information Act by the Federation of American Scientists, a nonprofit research group, shows that U.S. sales and grants since 1980 include at least 50,000 pistols and revolvers; 170,000 rifles and shotguns; 12,000 grenade launchers as well as anti-personnel land mines; and more than a million hand grenades, demolition charges, and flechette rockets whose warheads discharge clouds of lethal steel darts. Almost 325,000 land mines were sold to El Salvador, Colombia, Ecuador, Lebanon, Niger, Thailand, and Somalia; and 1.4 million hand grenades to Belize, Colombia, El Salvador, Lebanon, Panama, Somalia, Sudan, Trinidad, Bolivia, and Antigua.

Although much of this weaponry was intended for the anti-communist campaigns of the 1980s, currently wars are being fought with U.S.-supplied small arms in Colombia, Liberia, Somalia, and Angola. The weapons are used in continuing political violence in the Philippines, Haiti, and elsewhere. Officially, the Clinton Administration supports increased openness of its own small-arms dealings. But the State Department, which oversees U.S. arms exports, has turned down repeated requests for data on small-arms exports, and State Department officials decline to discuss arms policy or its ramifications. Similarly, the Pentagon routinely withholds information on the weapons it sells or gives away abroad. (Newhouse News Service, "Why Control Is So Difficult," *San Francisco Examiner*, February 18, 1996: A10) [Ed. note: A related article describes a new report by the United Nations Children's Fund that

cites "the proliferation of light weapons" as a major reason for the upsurge in war-related violence against children and the growing practice of using children under the age of 15 as soldiers. UNICEF estimates that about 2 million children have been killed in conflicts during the decade, with 4 million disabled, 12 million homeless, and 10 million traumatized. (Wood, David, "A Small Arms War on Children," *San Francisco Examiner*, February 18, 1996: A10)

CIA Blunders While Spying on France

A report released by the CIA's inspector general concluded that mistakes by the agency as it attempted to gather secret information on French trade negotiations and economic espionage led to an international embarrassment. The classified report is likely to intensify the debate over the risks and rewards of spying on allies for economic intelligence. It found that the United States Ambassador to France, Pamela Harriman, was kept in the dark about important aspects of the CIA station chief's work, who has since retired. Soon after several CIA operatives set out to undercover French positions on world trade talks and to counter French economic espionage against American companies, French officials knew there was a network of CIA officers operating against them. The French, ignoring the traditional protocol in such cases, raised an uproar over the spying instead of letting four accused spies working under diplomatic cover slip out of the country for activities "incompatible with their diplomatic status." (Weiner, Tim, "CIA Confirms Blunders During Economic Spying on France," *The New York Times*, March 13, 1996: A10)

Budget Cuts IRS Publications

Citing budget cuts, officials of the Internal Revenue Service say they may discontinue Publication 17, "Your Federal Income Tax," a summary of tax rules affecting individuals. Publication 334, "Tax Guide for Small Business," might also be dropped. A spokesman said all the information in these free publications is contained in other IRS materials, adding that "budget pressures cause tough decisions." Some members of the House of Representatives are incensed by this idea and by the IRS's move earlier in the year to reduce the number of taxpayer-service walk-in offices. Some IRS tax specialists say eliminating Publication 17 would be a mistake and would antagonize taxpayers. ("The IRS May Eliminate Some Popular Publications Next Year," *Wall Street Journal*, March 20, 1996: A1)

1990 Census Undercount Allowed by Supreme Court

The Supreme Court ruled unanimously that the federal government need not adjust 1990 census figures to compensate for the undercount of Blacks, Hispanics, and other minority groups. The census figures are important because they are used to draw congressional districts and to calculate federal funding to states. New York, other cities, and civil rights groups challenged in a lawsuit the Commerce Department's decision not to increase some cities' 1990 population counts. Parent agency for the Census Bureau, the Department of Commerce acknowledged that Blacks had been undercounted by 4.8 percent, Hispanics by 5.2 percent, Native Americans by 5 percent, and Asian-Pacific Islanders by 3.1 percent, but questioned the value of adjusting the numbers.

Although the 2nd U.S. Circuit Court of Appeals ruled for the cities, the Supreme Court said the Constitution gives Congress virtually unlimited discretion for the census and Congress has delegated authority to the Secretary of Commerce. (Biskupic, Joan, "Census Need Not Adjust for Minority Undercount, Justices Rule," *Washington Post*, March 21, 1996: A18)

U.S. Accused of Withholding Information about Serbian War Crimes

The United States was accused by Bosnia's United Nations representative of failing to turn over information about a notorious Serbian paramilitary leader, known as Arkan, who has been linked to killings of Bosnian Muslims.

The representative, Muhamed Sacirbey, essentially charged that the United States, needing the cooperation of Serbian President Slobodan Milosevic to enforce the Dayton peace accords, was holding back information that might lead to questions about Serbian involvement in the massacres of Bosnians. Sacirbey said Milosevic had been handed an account of the activities of Arkan by Richard Holbrooke, the former Assistant Secretary of State who brought the Balkan parties together at the Dayton conference. "If Mr. Milosevic is entitled to that written information, then I'm not sure why we, the Bosnians, the international community, or The Hague war crimes tribunal is not," Sacirbey said. (Crossette, Barbara, "U.S. Said to Withhold War-Crime Data," *The New York Times*, March 28, 1996: A3)

APRIL

Wartime Native American "Code Talker" Role Revealed

The National Security Agency has declassified more than 1.3 million pages of secret documents, some dating from before World War I. All the declassified material is more than 50 years old, and represents a tiny fragment of the billions of pages of government documents that have been kept secret on the grounds that their release would damage national security.

Among the documents declassified was a January 1919 memorandum from Army Col. A. W. Bloor, a commander of the American Expeditionary Force in France, explaining the origin of the "code talkers," American Indian soldiers who spoke in their native tongues to confuse enemy code breakers in World War I and World War II. These languages were largely unwritten and largely unstudied by foreigners, and so constituted an instant code translatable only by the speakers. Col. Bloor wrote that he had a company of Indians in his regiment who among them spoke 26 languages or dialects, and that "there was hardly a chance in a million" that the Germans could translate them. David Hatch, the National Security Agency's historian, said Choctaws, Navajos, Comanches, Winnebagos, Pawnees, Kiowas, and Cherokees served as code talkers. In World War II, he said, the Marine Corps used more than 400 Navajos as communicators in the Pacific campaign. Hatch could not explain why the documents stayed secret for so long. (Weiner, Tim, "Pentagon Spy Agency Bares Some Dusty Secret Papers," *The New York Times,* April 5, 1996: A22)

Declassification of CIA Documents is Slow

A stack of secret files taller than 50 Washington Monuments awaits the CIA employees who are charged with declassifying agency documents. Yet the agency has committed only three ten-thousandths of its budget and seven full-time employees to the job of making the documents public. In 1993, the CIA publicly promised to release its files on its most important covert actions of the Cold War—coups in Iran and Guatemala and the Bay of Pigs—within a few months. However, according to outside experts, the documents remain secret because of "a clash of cultures" inside the CIA pitting cold warriors against open-minded historians.

The CIA has another explanation. They say that Oliver Stone's 1991 movie, *J.F.K.*, which insinuated that a military-industrial-espionage conspiracy killed President Kennedy in 1963, led Congress to establish a J.F.K. Assassination Records law in 1992. It ordered that the government files on the assassination be made public. President Clinton took nearly a year to name members of a review board to oversee the release of the files. Now the CIA's historians are explaining to the board every one of the thousands of excisions they want to make in its documents. That time-consuming effort has made the promise to release the covert-action records impossible to keep, the agency said. (Weiner, Tim, "CIA is Slow to Tell Early Cold War Secrets," *The New York Times*, April 8, 1996)

Gingrich Accuses Clinton of Misleading Congress

House Speaker Newt Gingrich (R-GA) charged President Clinton with misleading Congress about the United States' true role in Bosnia at a time the Administration was secretly acquiescing to an Iranian arms pipeline to the Bosnian Muslims. Gingrich said that during the past three years, Senate Majority Leader Robert Dole (R-KS), other lawmakers, and himself had many meetings with Clinton about U.S. Bosnia policy—at a time when the U.S. was publicly upholding the international arms embargo against Bosnia. Never, he said, did the President indicate that the United States was condoning Iranian arms smuggling.

In response, White House press secretary Michael McCurry denied that Gingrich had been misled. "Those are truly extraordinary comments by the Speaker, given the high degree of attention that we presume the Congress was paying to Bosnia at the time," McCurry said. "It was clear, from the intelligence information available to the Speaker and his staff at the time, what our understanding was about the nature of arms flows into Bosnia. And at any time there could have been a more thorough discussion of the arms flows into Bosnia, because that information was widely available to Congress." (Risen, James, "Gingrich Charges Clinton With Misleading Congress," *Washington Post*, April 11, 1996)

White House Claims Executive Privilege on Bosnian Report

The White House claimed executive privilege and refused to give Congress a secret internal report on President Clinton's 1994 decision to do nothing about weapons shipments from Iran to Bosnian Muslims. "Consistent with the practice of past administrations," a senior Administration official said, "we will insist on protecting the confidentiality of internal deliberations and communications between the President and his advisers." (Weiner, Tim, "Congress Is Denied Report on Bosnia," *The New York Times*, April 17, 1996: A1)

White House to Seek Budget Total for U.S. Intelligence

The White House announced that beginning this year it would ask Congress to release an overall "bottom line" figure for the budget of American intelligence agencies, a figure now widely estimated at $24 billion to $30 billion a year. It hopes to encourage a sense of openness in the intelligence community by making the figure public, the White House said. (Shenon, Philip, "White House Seeks Release of Intelligence Budget Total," *The New York Times*, April 24, 1996: B7)

MAY

Secrecy Inhibits Efforts to Clean Up River in Washington

A 10-page article, "Nuclear Reactions," details efforts to clean up the area around Hanford, Washington—described as "the biggest environmental disaster in America." The

cleanup is expected to cost about $230 billion over 75 years. The area around Hanford's plutonium factory, built during World War II as part of the U.S. effort to develop an atomic bomb, is home to two-thirds of the country's high-level radioactive waste.

In 1986, when an environmental group in Spokane secured the release of classified documents from Hanford, the public learned that the plutonium factory had poisoned neighbors who were downwind and downstream. Huge releases of radiation into the atmosphere, all them secret and some of them deliberate, occurred throughout the second half of the 1940s and early 1950s. Hanford documents show that biologists secretly discussed closing part of the Columbia River to public fishing and hunting in the late 1950s when plutonium production was at its peak and resident fish and ducks showed dangerously high concentrations of radioactive phosphorus. But no warnings were issued. "Nothing is to be gained by informing the public," Herbert M. Parker, the head of health and safety at Hanford, wrote in 1954. (Harden, Blaine, "Nuclear Reactions," *Washington Post Magazine*, May 5, 1996: 12-19, 26-29)

Nun Seeks Documents from Intelligence Agencies

Columnist Mary McGrory wrote of the struggle of Sister Dianna Ortiz, an Ursuline nun, to pry out of intelligence agencies the documents that could tell her why and with whose help she was kidnaped, tortured, and raped by Guatemalan security forces in 1989. "My crime," she said at one point during her packed news conference at the J. W. Marriott Hotel, "was to teach little Mayan children to read and write." (McGrory, Mary, "CIA's Unlikely Exorcist," *Washington Post*, May 7, 1996: A2)

Congress Cites White House Counsel for Refusing to Release Documents Related to Travel Office Firings

The House Government Reform and Oversight Committee voted to cite the White House counsel, Jack Quinn, for contempt of Congress for refusing to turn over subpoenaed documents related to the firings in the White House travel office. Committee Chair William Clinger (R-PA) has tried to capture the full paper trail on the 1993 firings of seven travel office employees. He has sharply criticized the White House for not being fully forthcoming, while the White House has countered by calling Clinger's demands vague and overly broad. (Melton, R. H., "House Panel Votes for Contempt Citation," *Washington Post*, May 10, 1996)

President Urged to Make Intelligence Budget Public

The *Washington Post* editorialized about the game the Administration and Congress are playing over proposals to make public the aggregate figure for U.S. intelligence spending. Each is waiting for the other to move first to make this information public. "The White House has put out word that the President is 'determined to promote openness in the Intelligence Community' and 'has authorized Congress to make public the total appropriation.' But it is the executive branch that has classified this information in the first place, and the President doesn't need the consent of Congress to declassify it. He may want company in taking this step, but he has the authority to act on his own. If Congress is reluctant to move, he should take the lead." ("The Intelligence Number," *Washington Post*, May 27, 1996: A22)

Less Access to Electronic Foreign Broadcast Data Deplored

Russian military analyst Harriet Scott, and her husband, Bill, are unhappy that they have to use a computer to access the CIA's *Foreign Broadcast Information Service* (FBIS). The service publishes translated transcripts from hundreds of sources per day, including the world's leading news agencies, newspapers, and broadcasts. But the CIA's efforts to keep up with the electronic revolution have provoked a furious reaction from critics who say that instead of making the product more accessible, FBIS is doing the opposite. Before the computer age, FBIS published an indexed pamphlet that readers could easily scan for information. But that simple chore can take nearly two hours, Mrs. Scott said, now that FBIS is on-line.

"It takes me a minute or so to download a piece of e-mail into my computer. That's fine. But the way they've formatted the FBIS material, 100 items are all packaged as separate pieces of e-mail, so it takes me 100 minutes just to download them before I can even think about starting to read them," she said. Mrs. Scott's complaints are being widely echoed. After this summer, FBIS material will only be available electronically on the World News Connection of the National Technical Information Service. A teacher who has used FBIS material for his graduate students noted that key documents once could be easily photocopied and distributed, but now his students have to line up at one or two terminals that have Internet access.

According to CIA officials, ending the published FBIS reports saves significant money. But critics said that people who have used these reports to avoid being dependent on government statements and interpretations of events are not going to have the time or the opportunity to keep up with it once it becomes electronic only. (Sieff, Martin, "Lost in Computer Age," *Washington Times*, May 28, 1996: A9)

Released White House Documents Reveal Request for FBI Check

When the White House relinquished a thousand documents at the end of May to the House Government Reform and Oversight Committee, included was a request for background information on Billy Dale, the ousted head of the White House travel office. This information quickly became one of the biggest stories of the month because it led to the revelation that White House officials obtained FBI background material on Dale and hundreds of other officials, some of whom had worked at the White House in previous administrations. (Schmidt, Susan and Ann Devroy, "White House Obtained FBI Data on Fired Travel Chief," *Washington Post*, June 6, 1996: A4)

Census 2000 Challenged

As it prepares for Census 2000, the Census Bureau is being challenged by minority groups who say the sampling technique planned by the bureau would worsen, not lessen, the problem of undercounting the nation's Black and Hispanic population. Additionally, Republicans say sampling would result in improperly drawn legislative districts. Representative Thomas Petri (R-WI) introduced legislation that would prohibit the Census Bureau from applying sampling techniques of any kind to determine a population count. He said the bureau should do whatever it takes to obtain an accurate count without relying on sampling.

The challenges to Census' plans add to the problems of an agency that is under pressure to increase the accuracy of the census, hold down costs, and respond to the concerns of lawmakers who control its budget. Legislators generally have little understanding of statistical methods, yet their districts are drawn on the basis of the census. (Holmes, Steven A., "Census Plan for 2000 Is Challenged on 2 Fronts," *The New York Times*, June 6, 1996: A21)

FBI Director Says He was "Victimized" by White House Request for Files

Louis Freeh, the Director of the FBI, said that he and the bureau had been "victimized" by improper requests from the Clinton White House for files on more than 400 people, most of them employees of prior Republican Administrations. In a report, Freeh said the White House and the FBI committed "egregious violations of privacy" when the bureau delivered summaries from these files to Presidential aides, beginning in late 1993 and continuing for several weeks. The FBI and the White House, which has described the requests as a result of an innocent bureaucratic mistake, said that new controls have been adopted to prevent future abuses. Freeh blamed himself for a lack of vigilance in safeguarding a longstanding system, vulnerable to political abuse, in which the FBI routinely complied with White House requests for sensitive information.

The Director's choice of words seemed to puzzle the White House. "I do not understand that statement," said President Clinton's press secretary Michael McCurry, who added, "There has been no abuse of the information in the files." (Weiner, Tim, "Request for Files 'Victimized' F. B. I., Its Director Says," *The New York Times*, June 15, 1996: A1)

Senate Whitewater Hearings Conclude

The Senate Whitewater Committee concluded after 13 months, releasing a 768-page report. The final report accused the Clinton White House of stonewalling and obfuscating. The Democrats, in a minority rebuttal, claimed that the President and Mrs. Clinton had been victimized by a modern-day witch hunt. (Maraniss, David, "The Hearings End Much as They Began," *Washington Post*, June 19, 1996: A1)

Independent Counsel Authority Expanded to Include FBI Files

Independent Counsel Kenneth Starr has been given authority to investigate the FBI files controversy, concentrating first on Anthony Marceca, the former White House aide who obtained confidential reports about the Clinton White

House. The order was issued at the request of Attorney General Janet Reno who said she had conducted a preliminary inquiry, enough to convince her that it would be "a political conflict of interest" for the Justice Department to go any further because the matter "necessarily will involve an inquiry into dealings between the White House and the FBI." (Lardner, George, "Starr Gets Authority for FBI Files Probe," *Washington Post*, June 22, 1996)

Has Big Brother Found a Way Around the Constitution?

The *Washington Post Magazine* featured a 10-page article, "Someone to Watch Over Us," by Jim McGee and Brian Duffy, describing the workings of a secret court in the U.S. Department of Justice that authorized a record 697 "national security" wiretaps in 1995 on American soil. These wiretaps were outside normal constitutional procedures. The authors asked: "Is the world growing more dangerous—or has Big Brother found a way around the Fourth Amendment?"

According to Justice Department statistics, in 1994, federal courts authorized more wiretaps for intelligence-gathering and national security purposes than they did to investigate ordinary federal crimes—576 to 554. In 1995, surveillance and search authorizations rose to 697 under the Foreign Intelligence Surveillance Act (FISA).

This 1978 law permits secret buggings and wiretaps of individuals suspected of being agents of a hostile foreign government or international terrorist organization, even when the target is not suspected of committing any crime. Under FISA, requests for such warrants are routed through lawyers in the Office of Intelligence Policy and Review in the Department of Justice. If these lawyers decide a warrant request has merit, they prepare an application and take it before a judge who sits in a restricted area of the courtroom in the Department.

McGee and Duffy assert that the FISA system's courtroom advocacy is monumentally one-sided. In the closed FISA court, when a Justice Department lawyer presents an application for a national security wiretap, no lawyer stands up to argue the other side of the case. Moreover, the target of FISA surveillance normally is never told about it and has no opportunity for formal review or redress later, as would the target of surveillance protected by the Fourth Amendment.

According to the article, the FISA court has never formally rejected an application. The FISA system raises the question of when evidence gathered for national security purposes can be used for regular criminal prosecutions. Yet, the authors acknowledge, sometimes national security wiretaps turn up vital, important evidence of serious domestic crimes. (McGee, Jim and Brian Duffy,

"Someone To Watch Over Us," *Washington Post Magazine,* June 23,1996: 9-13, 21-25)

The Cost of Keeping Secrets Secret Revealed

Representative David Skaggs (D-CO), a member of the House Intelligence Committee, reported that the federal government—not counting the Central Intelligence Agency—spent at least $5.6 billion in 1995 keeping secret documents secret.

The CIA provides no public report on how much it spends to maintain classified documents. Security officials estimate that billions of pages of classified documents exist, although no one knows for sure. Skaggs says that less than 1 percent of the $5.6 billion is being spent on declassifying documents. A billion-page backlog has built up of documents that are more than 25 years old and thus by law are ready for declassification and release to the public.

The Pentagon spent nearly 90 percent of the $5.6 billion. But other agencies spent as well: the Department of Agriculture ($1,153,000), the Federal Reserve Board ($305,000), the Federal Communications Commission ($156,000), and the Marine Mammal Commission ($1,000). Military and intelligence agencies that hold the classified documents maintain that the high cost of declassification is delaying the release of documents older than 25 years that President Clinton has ordered to be made public. (Weiner, Tim, "Lawmaker Tells of High Cost of Keeping Secret Data Secret," *The New York Times,* June 28, 1996: A20)

CIA Knew of Abuses in Guatemala

The Intelligence Oversight Board, a presidential advisory panel, revealed that the Central Intelligence Agency during the past decade employed many informants in the Guatemalan government and military who agency officials knew were involved in assassinations, torture, kidnappings, and murders. The board also concluded that CIA officials kept information about these crimes and other human rights abuses from Congress, violating U.S. law. The board blamed the agency's failure to heed the issue of human rights until 1994. A series of reforms instituted early this year by CIA director John Deutch included "a new directive generally barring the recruitment of unsavory informants except when senior CIA officials decide their assistance is warranted by national interests." ("Panel Confirms CIA Officials Knew of Abuses," *Washington Post,* June 29, 1996: A1)

SEPTEMBER

Report Questions Credibility of Pentagon on Gulf War Illness

Investigators for the Presidential Advisory Committee on Gulf War Veterans' Illnesses, created in 1995 by President Clinton, said that the credibility of the Department of Defense had been "gravely undermined" by its inquiry into the possible exposure of American troops to Iraqi chemical weapons during the 1991 Gulf War. They recommended that an outside body take over the investigation from the Pentagon. Despite reports of mysterious illnesses among thousands of Gulf War veterans, the Pentagon insisted publicly until 1996 that it had no evidence that large numbers of American soldiers were exposed to chemical or biological weapons.

At the same time, a long-classified intelligence report was released showing that officials at the White House, the Pentagon, the Central Intelligence Agency, and the State Department were informed in November 1991 that chemical weapons had been stored at an ammunition depot demolished by American troops in March of that year. (Shenon, Philip, "Report Is Sharply Critical of the Pentagon Inquiry into Troop Exposure to Nerve Gas," *The New York Times*, September 6, 1996: A22) [Ed. Note: This article was one of the earliest on this issue which at press time continues to unfold.]

Scope of Special Counsel's Report Questioned

No findings, analysis, conclusions, or recommendations are included in the document produced by James Cole, the outside counsel hired by the House Committee on Standards of Official Conduct (Ethics), to investigate House Speaker Newt Gingrich (R-GA). One of the former outside counsels who worked for the House ethics committee on prior cases was surprised at the description of Cole's report. "It's very unusual," said Richard Phelan, the Chicago attorney who served as outside counsel in the case that resulted in the resignation of House Speaker Jim Wright (D-TX). "I would say that the committee is minimizing [Cole's] role," Phelan said. "There were no such restrictions placed on my work. I was able to come to conclusions and make recommendations." (Chappie, Damon, "Was the Gingrich Special Counsel Limited in His Probe of Speaker?" *Roll Call*, September 9, 1996)

Documents Show U.S. Knew North Korea Held American P.O.W.s

Recently declassified documents from the Dwight D. Eisenhower Presidential Library and other government depositories show that the United States knew immediately after the Korean War that North Korea kept hundreds of American prisoners known to be alive at the end of the war. The documents deepen the mystery over the fate of Americans still considered missing from the Korean War, adding to growing speculation that American prisoners might still be alive and in custody there.

In June, a Defense Department

intelligence analyst testified before a Congressional subcommittee that on the basis of "very compelling reports," he believed that as many as 15 Americans were still being held prisoner in North Korea. The Defense Department has said it has no clear evidence that any Americans are being held against their will in North Korea, and has pledged to continue to investigate reports of American prisoners there. (Shenon, Philip, "U.S., in 50's, Knew North Korea Held American P.O.W.s." *The New York Times*, September 17, 1996: A1)

House Rejects Release of Preliminary Report on House Speaker

The House voted—without debate—against a Democratic move to force the ethics committee to make public its counsel's preliminary report on charges against Speaker Newt Gingrich. Representative John Lewis (D-GA) accused Republicans of a "systematic, deliberate effort to cover up this report." (Clymer, Adam, "House Rejects Bid to Force Release of Ethics Report on Gingrich," *The New York Times*, September 20, 1996)

U.S. Army Intelligence Manuals Instructed Latins on Coercion

According to a secret Defense Department summary of intelligence manuals compiled during a 1992 investigation, counter-intelligence agents should use "fear, payment of bounties for enemy dead, beatings, false imprisonment, executions, and...truth serum." Pentagon documents show that U.S. Army intelligence manuals used to train Latin American military officers in Army school from 1982 to 1991 advocated executions, torture, blackmail, and other forms of coercion against insurgents, a violation of Army policy and law at the time they were in use. The manuals were used in courses at the U.S. Army's School of the Americas, located at Fort Benning, GA, where nearly 60,000 military and police officers from Latin America and the United States have been trained since 1946.

The Defense Department said the school's curriculum now includes mandatory human rights training. "The problem was discovered in 1992, properly reported, and fixed," said Lt. Col. Arne Owens, a Pentagon spokesman. When reports of the 1992 investigation surfaced this year during a congressional inquiry into the CIA's activities in Guatemala, spokesmen for the school denied the manuals advocated such extreme methods of operation. The Defense Department is trying to collect the manuals but, as the 1992 investigation noted, "due to incomplete records, retrieval of all copies is doubtful." (Priest, Dana, "U.S. Instructed Latins on Executions, Torture," *Washington Post*, September 21, 1996: A1)

Priest Vindicated by Military's Disclosure

In her column, Mary McGrory describes how Father Roy Bourgeois, a Maryknoll priest, was imprisoned for six months in the Atlanta Federal Penitentiary for leading a nonviolent civil disobedience protest at Fort Benning. Now he believes he has been vindicated because the Army has finally admitted the existence of the grisly manuals used in the Army's School of the Americas. The Freedom of Information Act was used to obtain information about the manuals. "They lied," fumed the priest over the prison telephone. "They have kept on lying about it [until] as recently as last month. In an interview with the *Columbus Ledger* the commandant of the school talked about 'the small percentage of graduates who have done some terrible things; we cannot take responsibility for those who have gone astray.' He denied there was a manual." (McGrory, Mary, "Manuals for Murders." *Washington Post*, September 26, 1996: A2)

Six-month Gap Disclosed in White House Logs of Who Read FBI Background Reports

Senate Republicans disclosed there is a six-month gap in White House logs showing who checked out confidential FBI background reports from the Office of Personnel Security. The lapse began in March 1994, after an investigator for the personnel office, Anthony B. Marceca, stopped collecting files on hundreds of Republicans from the Reagan and Bush Administrations. Senator Orrin Hatch (R-UT), chair of the Senate Judiciary Committee, stressed there was still no conclusive evidence to show whether the files were used for a "nefarious purpose." The White House blamed poor record keeping for the gap. (Lardner, George, "GPO Says White House Logs on Readers of FBI Reports Have 6-Month Gap," *Washington Post*, September 26, 1996: A10)

OCTOBER

Gulf War Combat Logs Fail to Report Explosions

An apparent gap in Gulf War combat logs that should have recorded the destruction of an Iraqi ammunition bunker—an incident that may have exposed more than 15,000 American troops to nerve gas and other chemical weapons—is being investigated by the Pentagon. Defense Department officials said that combat logs showed a gap between March 3 and March 12, 1991. The explosions in questions occurred on March 4 and on March 10. The logs may have been lost, destroyed, or there may never have been entries for that period, officials cautioned.

GulfWATCH, a veterans group, got copies of the logs from the Pentagon under the Freedom of Information Act, and detected the gap.

GulfWATCH and other veterans organizations said the gap is evidence that the Defense Department has hidden information about the exposure of American troops to Iraqi chemical weapons in the Gulf War and afterward. A Pentagon spokesman, Captain Michael Doubleday, said, "That absolutely is incorrect," and asked for patience as the Pentagon tried to determine if American troops had been exposed to Iraqi chemicals. (Shenon, Philip, "Records Gap on Gulf War Under Scrutiny," *The New York Times*, October 9, 1996: A14)

Government No Longer Maps Gulf Stream Due to Budget Cuts

After 21 years of charting the position of the Gulf Stream, government oceanographers at the National Oceanic and Atmospheric Administration (NOAA) have been forced by budget cuts to stop mapping the position of the ever-shifting Gulf Stream, a swift current that forms in the Caribbean and flows north to Greenland and Iceland. Thousands of fishermen, researchers, yachtsmen, and freighter captains who navigated by the government's thrice-weekly Gulf Stream charts will be left to find their own way. "People are going to be just a little bit more unsafe than they were before," said oceanographer Stephen Baig. Baig faxed the Gulf Stream charts for free to anyone who asked. David Hendrix of Savannah said, "It helps us to decide in small boats whether to go out or not." Baig's maritime clientele had grown to about 10,000 users a year—including NASA, which used the service to help recover space shuttle boosters.

NOAA, as a matter of government policy, decided to leave the business to several private companies— mostly fishing forecasters—because they provide some limited Gulf Stream charting by fax. While one government agency may be saving money, its action means more expenses for other public agencies that need to know the Gulf Stream's location. The Coast Guard, marine researchers, fishery analysts, and hazardous materials experts must now pay up to $50 apiece for a Gulf Stream chart. "We don't really have the money to buy that service," said Karen Steidinger, a research scientist with the Florida Marine Research Institute in St. Petersburg, who has relied on the Gulf Stream charts to help track red tides before they reach shore. Bradford Benggio, with NOAA's Hazardous Materials Response and Assessment Division, has used the charts to predict the course of oil and chemical spills along the eastern seaboard. "We had so many incidents where that information was really critical," he said. Now his agency must use public money for private Gulf Stream locators. (Nolin, Robert and Maya Bell, "Government No Longer Follows the Gulf Stream," *Washington Post*, October 15, 1996: A13)

U.S. Military Warned by Czechs of Nerve Gas Detected During the Gulf War

Czech solders whose responsibility during the 1991 Persian Gulf War was chemical detection say that American military commanders were repeatedly warned that sensitive detection equipment had identified Iraqi chemical weapons on the battlefield—and that the toxins were spreading over unprotected American troops. Combat logs of officers working for General H. Norman Schwarzkopf show that American commanders ignored Czech warnings that low levels of nerve and mustard gas had been detected in the vicinity of American troops. The Defense Department was informed after the war that Czech soldiers suffered from many of the same health problems that have afflicted the American veterans, according to former Czech military officials. Interviews with Czech officials raise new doubts about public statements from the Pentagon, which has been criticized over its treatment of Gulf War veterans. ("Czechs Told U.S. They Detected Nerve Gas During the Gulf War," *The New York Times*, October 19, 1996: A1)

Declassifying Documents Delayed at the CIA

In 1995, when President Clinton ordered the CIA and other government agencies to release all classified documents more than 25 years old (that would not compromise current national security), the files contained some 40 million pages. Included was the CIA's assessment of the vast military research effort of the former Soviet Union. In their declassification effort, the CIA decided to set up a series of powerful computer workstations, scanners, and printers. Technicians would feed the pages into the scanners, while retired CIA employees, reading each file on screen, would electronically tag information that must remain classified, such as sources whose safety might be endangered if their identity were known. A declassified version of the

THIS MODERN WORLD by TOM TOMORROW

document would then be printed out and made public.

The CIA was supposed to declassify 9 million pages of historical documents this year, but so far not a single document has been released. Embarrassing technical problems have undermined the effort. Apparently, the CIA tried to modify its existing software to censor the sensitive passages, only to discover the software was too inflexible. The agency had to start again from scratch with a newer set of commercial computer programs. Mark Mansfield, a CIA spokesman, refused to tell how much money was spent on the first attempt at the project. The new system is scheduled to go into production by March 1997, but some advisers are not sure it will work. "We appreciate the CIA trying to figure out a way to declassify a lot of records, but we're skeptical as to whether this is going to work," says Page Putnam Miller of the National Coordinating Committee for the Promotion of History, who is a member of a panel that advises the CIA on declassification policy. (Kiernan, Vincent, "Why Cold War Secrets Are Still Under Wraps," *New Scientist*, October 19, 1996)

Editorial Advocates Resumption of Crowd Counts

A *Washington Post* editorial, "When the Park Police Don't Count," encouraged the resumption of crowd counts in major demonstrations by the Park Police. When the Park Police were asked for a crowd estimate for the Latino March in mid-October, spokespersons for the National Park Service said Congress prohibited their crowd estimates. They cited the latest appropriations bill for the Department of the Interior, which stated that if event organizers want crowd counts, they should hire an outside agency. The issue drew attention after the Million Man March. After the Park Police came up with a rough estimate of 400,000, organizers threatened to sue. ("When the Park Police Don't Count," *Washington Post*, October 20, 1996)

Former FBI Aide Pleads Guilty for Role in Ruby Ridge

A senior official of the FBI, E. Michael Kahoe, agreed to plead guilty to obstruction of justice for destroying an internal review of the 1992 siege in Idaho known as Ruby Ridge. The charge against Kahoe involves a review of the FBI's actions at Ruby Ridge that his superiors ordered him to prepare. As Kahoe and his colleagues completed the review in early 1993, federal prosecutors in Idaho asked the FBI to turn over all papers it had about the deadly siege. Kahoe and "certain of his superiors at F.B.I. headquarters," who were not identified, had resisted that request according to the criminal charge. Court papers say that Kahoe then withheld the internal review from the Idaho prosecutors, destroyed his copies of the review, and ordered a subordinate to destroy other copies to make it appear as if the review had never existed. (Labaton, Stephen, "FBI Official to Plead Guilty to Destroying Files on 1992 Siege," *The New York Times*, October 23, 1996: A19)

Publisher Puts Gulf War Data on the Internet

Bruce Kletz, publisher of Insignia Publishing, made public more than 300 government documents about Iraqi chemical weapons removed from a Defense Department Internet site, known as GulfLINK, earlier this year. According to the article, the documents were removed from the Defense site at the request of the CIA. Kletz posted the documents on the Internet because he believes government leaders are "trying to hide the documents only to avoid political and personal embarrassment." The documents concern the release of Iraqi chemical and biological weapons near U.S. troops during the 1991 Persian Gulf War. Kletz declined to tell *The New York Times* how he obtained the documents. ("Civilian Defies Pentagon, Puts Gulf War Data on Internet," *CNN*, October 31, 1996, http://cnn.com/US/9610/31/gulf.war. reports/index.html) [Ed. Note: Soon after this article appeared, the CIA announced that it had restored hundreds of other intelligence reports to the Pentagon's Internet site, known as GulfLINK (http://www. dtic.dla.mil/ gulflink/.) (Shenon, Philip, "CIA Orders Inquiry Into Charges of Chemical Arms Cover-Up," *The New York Times*, November 2, 1996: P9)]

NOVEMBER

Advocates of Less Secrecy Try to Make Government Research Available

Michael Ravnitzky, technical director of the Industrial Fabrics Association International in St. Paul, MN, has been trying to pry information out of the Defense Technical Information Center (DTIC) in Alexandria, VA, for the past nine years. "Decades of work done by the Defense Department and its contractors in the area of safety and protective fabrics would be of enormous use to our industry," Ravnitzky says.

The data could aid the development of protective clothing, helping companies make more fire-resistant tents, sleeping bags, and children's clothing. Even defense contractors who build super-secret weapons systems urge more openness. Jack Gordon is the president of Lockheed Martin's famous Skunk Works, which developed the U-2 spy plane and the F-117 stealth fighter. Last year, he told a government commission that a "culture of secrecy" often leads the military to classify too much and declassify too little. "The consequence of this action directly relates to added cost, affecting the bottom line of industry, and inflating procurement costs to the government," he wrote.

The government is well aware of the potential payoff in declassification and less secrecy. In 1970, the Pentagon produced a study showing that "the U.S. lead in microwave electronics and in computer technology was uniformly and greatly raised after the decision in 1946 to release the results of wartime research in these fields." The same study said an open research policy also benefited nuclear reactor and transistor technology development. (Dupont, Daniel G. and Richard Lardner, "Defense Technology: Needles in a Cold War Haystack," *Scientific American*, November 1996: 41)

U.S. Does Not Participate in Chemical Arms Treaty

Hungary ratified an international treaty banning production or use of nerve gas weapons, becoming the 65th nation to do so, and setting enforcement in motion. With Hungary's deposit of its ratification documents with the United Nations, a six-month clock starts that will bring the Chemical Weapons Convention into force April 29, 1997. Because the Senate has not ratified the treaty, the United States is precluded from participating in enforcement preparations, will have no representatives on the treaty's executive council in The Hague, will not be represented on the teams conducting international challenge inspections, and will not have access to information those inspections develop. "If we don't ratify, we'll be the loser, because we'll have to live under an enforcement regime devised by other countries," said State Department Spokesman Nicholas Burns.

The United States promoted the treaty beginning in the Reagan Administration. The treaty has strong bipartisan support, but the Clinton Administration did little to press for ratification when Democrats controlled the Senate. When control of the Senate shifted, conservative Republicans, including Majority Leader Trent Lott (R-MS) and Foreign Relations Committee Chair Jesse Helms (R-NC) opposed ratification, despite support for the treaty from the Pentagon, the State Department, and the major U.S. chemical manufacturers. (Lippman, Thomas W., "Chemical Arms Treaty Heads for Enactment Without U.S. Participation," *Washington Post*, November 2, 1996: A9)

Bosnian Arms Policy Criticized

The Senate intelligence committee criticized the secrecy of the Clinton Administration's policy of turning a blind eye in 1994 to Iranian weapons shipments to Bosnia's Muslim government. The committee said that the policy caused confusion among high-ranking U.S. policy makers and kept Congress in the dark. "Very, very grave risks are involved here when you violate the protocol and the standard rules," Committee Chairman Senator Arlen Specter (R-PA) told reporters in discussing the White House decision to keep secret from its allies a policy that, he said, "supported a violation of the U.N. arms embargo." He also said, "There are obvious penalties for misleading Congress." At the time Congress was debating whether the United States should unilaterally withdraw from the United Nations embargo without knowing of the Administration's actions. (Pincus, Walter, "Policy on Bosnia Arms Gets Mixed Review," *Washington Post*, November 8, 1996: A26)

EPA Loses Hundreds of Confidential Documents

Confidential documents collected in 1994 and 1995 by the Environmental Protection Agency (EPA) containing sensitive data belonging to chemical companies have been lost by the EPA. The 200 lost documents may contain trade secrets that could be worth millions to the companies. Agency officials have no evidence that the papers were stolen, indicating that they may have been misplaced or destroyed. The EPA is conducting an investigation and has tightened security. An internal memo obtained by the Associated Press said the incident "will be an embarrassment to the agency which could damage our reputation and put into question our ability to handle sensitive information." The agency said the missing documents are not a serious security breach. "More than one-half million of these papers are managed annually by EPA, and about 200 may have been misplaced, most likely within the agency," said Lynn Goldman, assistant administrator for prevention, pesticides, and toxic substances. ("EPA Loses Papers," *Washington Post*, November 14, 1996: A19)

Compensation Awarded to Survivors of Government Radiation Experiments

Energy Secretary Hazel O'Leary said the federal government has agreed to pay $4.8 million as compensation for injecting 12 people with radioactive plutonium or uranium in secret Cold War experiments. The settlement is part of a effort to compensate those subjected to experiments carried out by government doctors, scientists, and military officials from 1944 to 1974. Secretary O'Leary said government officials should make a commitment "that never again will the Government of the United States perform tests on our citizens and do so in secrecy." Soldiers were marched through nuclear explosion sites, without informing them of possible risks, while other experiments involved injecting people with radioactive substances, again without their knowledge. (Hilts, Philip J., "Payments to Make Amends for Secret Tests of Radiation," *The New York Times*, November 20, 1996: A1)

Air Bag Safety Questioned in 1969

It was not until 1991 that the National Highway Traffic Safety Administration warned parents that children in infant safety seats should not be placed in front of an air bag, although federal and auto industry officials had suspected since 1969 that air bags could injure or kill some children and small adults. And it wasn't until late 1995 that the agency publicly stated that air bags could cause injuries and death. According to documents spanning more than 20 years of debate over air bags, the government did not warn the public as it campaigned to win widespread public acceptance of the devices.

Until recently, when news of fatalities caused by air bags became widespread, much of the debate over the safety of the bags was held behind closed doors. Lobbyists, industry representatives, consumer groups, insurers, and the government fought over proposed regulations governing their use. As the government struggled to come up with "passive restraint" regulations, the safety aspects of the proposed rules were stuck in political, economic, and marketing battles waged among these same groups. (Brown, Warren and Cindy Skrzycki, "U.S. Doubts on Air Bags Date to '69," *Washington Post*, November 21, 1996: A1)

Sexual Misconduct Probed at Army's Top Levels

Army Secretary Togo West has ordered an investigation into the responsibility of those in the chain of command at Maryland's Aberdeen Proving Ground concerning the sexual abuse scandal there. In addition, the Pentagon said it does not know how many female service members are victims of sexual violence each year because it does not collect the information, although a 1988 law requires it to do so. Some of the services do not keep centralized statistics on sexual crimes such as rape and indecent assault. Holly Hemphill, a Washington attorney and chairwoman of a defense advisory panel on women in the armed services, said the committee had tried many times to get the services to give it information on sexual violence against female soldiers but "we kept getting the wrong information." She said the services collect statistics on spouse abuse, but not abuse of their female members.

Defense Department spokesman Kenneth Bacon said one problem was that Congress had not given the department any money to create the new database. Congress, he added, still had not come up with any new funds "but basically, after this hadn't been done for a while, somebody decided that it was time to do [it]...." He said the directive was issued October 15. The information in the new Defense Incident Base Reporting System also will be shared with the Justice Department. Other federal agencies are under the same mandate to report crime in their ranks to the Justice Department, but many have not complied either, Pentagon officials noted. (Priest, Dana, "Army Probe to Focus on Top Levels," *Washington Post*, November 22, 1996: A1)

DECEMBER

Public Government Information is Increasingly Privatized

In an op-ed piece, "When Public Business Goes Private," in the December 4 issue of *The New York Times*, Bill Kovach warns that watchdog journalism is facing a new and little-noted challenge. Kovach, curator of the Nieman Foundation at Harvard, describes how for-profit and nonprofit organizations increasingly displace government agencies in running public programs. He points out that as tax-supported public programs become privatized, they may move largely outside the reach of the press. As examples, he gives these:

• The Reporters Committee for Freedom of the Press says that a publisher in Mississippi has exclusive rights to distribute and sell the electronic version of the state's laws.

• The National Technical Information Service grants exclusive rights to private companies to sell once-public data from the National Institutes of Health, the Social Security Administration, and the Federal Communications Commission.

• The Ameritech Corporation wants to acquire the rights to become the sole electronic source of more government information.

In addition to the disappearance of government information into private databases, still another problem will result from the new welfare law: less information about the allocation of public funds will be available. Access to the public and the press to this information will depend on state laws and how each state writes its welfare regulations. Private contractors may take over some state welfare programs. For example, in Texas, Electronic Data Systems, an information technology company, and Lockheed Martin, a military contractor, are bidding to take over the state's $563 million welfare program.

Will corporate rights to privacy be invoked if journalists tried to obtain information about such operations? Kovach warns his colleagues: "If these examples are part of a trend, then the press and the public are being slowly blinded. A press dedicated to the watchdog role is discovering that it lacks the tools to adequately monitor corporate managers of the public weal. Freedom of information laws...do not cover private businesses." (Kovach, Bill, "When Public Business Goes Private," *The New York Times*, December 4, 1996: A29)

We Cannot Afford Not to Know Accurate Numbers

Robert J. Samuelson, writing an op-ed piece, "The Squeeze on Statistics," says that accurate numbers are society's eyes and ears and that we cannot afford *not* to know them. He says that statistics allow us to judge the economy, social conditions, and government policies. Without reliable numbers, we cannot say how well— or poorly—we are doing. And the numbers do not simply materialize; they must be collected, verified, and analyzed. "It's exacting, time-consuming work that Congress is slowly crippling by starving it of money."

Samuelson provides this example: This year, faced with a tight budget,

the Bureau of Economic Analysis (BEA) ended its annual survey of pollution-control spending by business. In 1994 (the survey's last year), companies spent $77 billion to control pollution. But in the future, we won't know exactly how much they're spending. Debates over environmental policy will proceed with less information on costs and benefits.

BEA's experience is typical; not enough money is being spent on statistical agencies to keep up. Between fiscal 1990 and 1997, the BEA requested $36.7 million for statistical improvements. Of the request, Congress approved only $6.5 million. In five of seven years, no money at all was approved. (Samuelson, Robert J., "The Squeeze on Statistics," December 4, 1996)

Security Clearance Revoked for Disclosing Secret to Congress

Departing CIA Director John Deutch revoked the security clearance of a senior State Department official who revealed a CIA secret to Senator-elect Robert Torricelli (D-NJ). The action effectively ends the government career of the official, Richard Nuccio, who was the State Department's envoy on peace talks between the Guatemalan military and Guatemalan guerrillas. Two years ago, Nuccio discovered that a paid informer for the CIA, a Guatemalan colonel, was involved in the killing in Guatemala of an American innkeeper and of a captured Guatemalan guerrilla who was married to an American lawyer. Convinced the CIA was covering up, and that Congress had been misled about what happened, he gave this information to Torricelli. When Torricelli told *The New York Times*, the disclosure led to the dismissal of several CIA officials who had failed to provide Congress and CIA headquarters with clear information about the case. Reportedly, Deutch "felt that the CIA's absolute need to protect the secret identities of its informers outweighed the burden the information had placed on Mr. Nuccio's conscience." (Weiner, Tim, "CIA Chief Disciplines Official for Disclosure," *The New York Times*, December 6, 1996: A20)

FBI Still Does Not Know Who Leaked Jewell Information

FBI Director Louis Freeh acknowledged to the Senate Judiciary Committee that Justice Department investigators have been unable to find the law enforcement official who told reporters that security guard Richard Jewell was a leading suspect in the bombing at the Summer Olympic Games in Atlanta. In late October, the Justice Department said that Jewell was no longer a suspect.

Senator Arlen Specter (R-PA), who chaired the hearing, suggested he might introduce legislation that would make it easier to prosecute government employees who give confidential information to reporters. But Specter stressed, "We've tried to make clear our oversight is over the federal government—not the media." Freeh also disclosed that investigators have been unable to identify the leaker who tipped reporters about the pending arrest of Unabomber suspect Theodore Kaczynski and the planned search of his Montana cabin. (McAllister, Bill, "Probe Has Failed to Detect Leaker in Jewell Episode, Freeh Tells Panel," *Washington Post*, December 20, 1996: A25)

Independent Panel Finds Incomplete Data on Nerve Gas Exposure

An independent panel of scientists from the Institute of Defense Analysis said the Pentagon may never be able to determine with any accuracy the number of troops who were exposed to chemical agents in the one verifiable release known to have occurred during the Persian Gulf War. The group said there is not enough reliable data about the quantity of nerve gas released or about weather conditions at the time to determine how many U.S. troops might have been exposed. Without firm data, the Pentagon has nonetheless estimated that 20,000 troops may have been exposed in the release. The Pentagon is trying to contact the 20,000 troops and is encouraging them to participate in a special medical evaluation program, which 2,000 have joined so far.

(Priest, Dana, "Data Lacking on Nerve Gas Exposure," *Washington Post*, December 21, 1996: A3) [Ed. Note: Two studies of Gulf War veterans' health published in the *New England Journal of Medicine* concluded that the health of veterans of the Persian Gulf War has differed slightly from that of other groups of soldiers, but not in a way that suggests a "mystery illness" is afflicting them. (Brown, David and Bill McAllister, "Two Studies Find No Gulf 'Mystery Illness,'" *Washington Post*, November 14, 1996: A3)]

House Speaker Admits to Ethical Wrongdoing

After more than two years denying wrongdoing, House Speaker Newt Gingrich (R-GA) on December 21 admitted that he broke the rules of the House of Representatives and "brought down on the people's house a controversy which could weaken the faith people have in their government." Responding to allegations of the House Committee on Standards of Official Conduct (Ethics), he said: "In my name and over my signature, inaccurate, incomplete, and unreliable statements were given to the committee, but I did not intend to mislead the committee." Gingrich admitted to the charges in the House ethics committee's 22-page "Statement of Alleged Violations," the House version of an indictment. It said Gingrich failed to ensure that a college course he taught and a tele-vised town hall would not violate federal tax law. Both were financed with tax deductible contributions. Gingrich's admission does not end the committee's investigation of him. (Yang, John E., "Speaker Gingrich Admits House Ethics Violation," *Washington Post*, December 22, 1996: A1) [Ed. Note: The "Statement of Alleged Violation" and the "Respondent's Answer to Statement of Alleged Violation" are available from the House Committee on Standards of Official Conduct; for information, call 202/225-7103).]

Democratic National Committee Will Allow Access to Records

The Democratic National Committee (DNC) said it would allow reporters to have access to some 3,000 documents connected to former political fundraiser John Huang shortly after the White House had cut off media access to the documents. The reversal came after the White House heard the DNC had decided reporters had "ample opportunity" to look at one set of the records during the 10 hours they were available. DNC spokeswoman Amy Weiss Tobe would not comment on how the decision was made to shield the records from further media scrutiny. (Schmidt, Susan and Anne Farris, "In Reversal, DNC Decides Not to Close Records Connected to Huang," *Washington Post*, December 24, 1996: A6)

Panel "Shielded from All Information" about Gingrich Investigation

Representative Jim McDermott (D-WA), senior Democrat on the House Committee on Standards of Official Conduct, said that he and five other committee members were "shielded from all information" while other members of the Committee worked with special counsel James Cole to develop facts on the complex financial transactions and determine that there was reasonable cause to believe Gingrich violated House rules. "At this point, none of the six of us is clear what really occurred. If there are to be public hearings before we set the speaker's punishment, we have to be prepared to ask intelligent questions of Mr. Cole and the speaker's attorney and the speaker himself, if he chooses to appear." McDermott said he had been told by another member of the ethics committee that the files and notebooks they have to review are "voluminous." (Broder, David S. and Helen Dewar, "Swift Vote on Gingrich Faces Hurdle," *Washington Post*, December 30, 1996: A1)

APPENDIX B

The CENSORED Resource Guide

Compiled by Amy S. Cohen with assistance by Ivan Harsløf

One of Project Censored's long-standing goals is to improve the lines of communication between the media and the public. Often people don't know where to begin when seeking new and diverse sources of information, or when they want to offer feedback after becoming enraged or "enlightened" by the media. We have always hoped that putting our work into book form would provide journalists, activists, and the public the tools they need—knowledge and resources—to make a difference. Becoming aware of important issues, seeking out information, and talking back to the media are all means of empowerment. If we have done our job, hopefully you too will be motivated to take the next step.

Contrary to popular belief, letters to the editor, phone calls, faxes, and e-mail can actually make a difference. A small group of well-organized campaigners *can* get the attention of a local, regional, or national media outlet. We can all try to demand a more responsive—and more accountable—media.

With this in mind, Project Censored has assembled a simple, easy-to-use and dependable resource guide for anyone who wants to contact various media to follow-up on our "censored" stories, or to get actively involved in doing something about a significant issue.

Following is a collection of names, addresses, phone and fax numbers, e-mail addresses, and World Wide Web sites, when available, for a variety of organizations, and electronic and print media outlets. You can find a more extensive selection of electronic listings in the On-Line Resource Directory in Appendix C.

Although this information was current as of late 1996, you may want to double-check to ensure the names, addresses, etc., are still accurate. If you are aware of any changes and/or corrections to the list, please send them to: Censored Resource Guide, Project Censored, Sonoma State University, Rohnert Park, CA 94928.

We plan to update the list in the 1998 edition of *Censored*. If you have any additions that should be included, please send them to the same address.

TABLE OF CONTENTS—CENSORED RESOURCE GUIDE

ALTERNATIVE BROADCAST/FILM/ VIDEO PRODUCERS & ORGANIZATIONS

8MM NEWS COLLECTIVE
c/o Squeaky Wheel
175 Elmwood Avenue
Buffalo, NY 14201-1419
Tel: 716/884-7172

ALTERNATIVE RADIO
2129 Mapleton
Boulder, CO 80304
Tel: 303/444-8788
Fax: 303/546-0592

ALTERNATIVE VIEWS
P.O. Box 7295
Austin, TX 78713
Tel: 512/918-3386

AMERICA'S DEFENSE MONITOR
1500 Massachusetts Ave., NW
Washington, DC 20005
Tel: 202/862-0700
Fax: 202/862-0708
E-mail: cdi@igc.apc.org

BLACK PLANET PRODUCTIONS/
NOT CHANNEL ZERO
P.O. Box 435, Cooper Station
New York, NY 10003-0435
Tel: 212/886-3701
Fax: 212/420-8223

CALIFORNIA NEWSREEL
149 9th Street, Suite 420
San Francisco, CA 94103
Tel: 415/612-6196
Fax: 415/621-6522
E-mail: Newsreel@ix.netcom.com
http://www.newsreel.org/

THE CENTER FOR COMMERCIAL-
FREE PUBLIC EDUCATION
Home of the Unplug Campaign
360 Grand Avenue, P.O. Box 385
Oakland, CA 94610
Tel: 510/268-1100
Fax: 510/268-1277
E-mail: unplug@igc.apc.org

COMMON GROUND
Stanley Foundation
216 Sycamore Street, Suite 500
Muscatine, IA 52761
Tel: 319/264-1500

CUBA VA FILM PROJECT
12 Liberty Street
San Francisco, CA 94110
Tel: 415/282-1812
Fax: 415/282-1798

DIVA-TV
(Damned Interfering Video Activists)
12 Wooster Street
New York, NY 10013
E-mail: divatv@aidsnyc.org
http://www.actupny.org/diva/
DIVA-TV.html

EARTH COMMUNICATIONS
(Radio for Peace International)
SJO 577, P.O. Box 025216
Miami, FL 33102-5216
Tel: 506/249-1821 (Costa Rica)
Fax: 506/249-1095 (Costa Rica)
E-mail: rfpicr@sol.racsa.co.cr

EDUCATIONAL VIDEO CENTER
55 East 25th Street, #407
New York, NY 10010-2903
Tel: 212/725-3534

EL SALVADOR MEDIA PROJECT
335 W. 38th Street, 5th Fl.
New York, NY 10018
Tel: 212/714-9118
Fax: 212/594-6417

EMPOWERMENT PROJECT
3403 Highway 54 West
Chapel Hill, NC 27516
Tel: 919/967-1963
Fax: 919/967-1863

FILMFORUM
6522 Hollywood Blvd.
Los Angeles, CA 90028
Tel: 213/466-4143
Fax: 213/466-4144

FREE RADIO BERKELEY/
FREE COMMUNICATIONS
COALITION
1442A Walnut Street, #406
Berkeley, CA 94709
Tel: 510/464-3041
E-mail: frbspd@crl.com
http://www.freeradio.org/

FREE SPEECH TV
P.O. Box 6060
Boulder, CO 80306
Tel: 303/442-8445 or 303/442-5693
Fax: 303/442-6472
E-mail: fstv@fstv.org
http://www:freespeech.org/

GLOBALVISION
1600 Broadway, Suite 700
New York, NY 10019
Tel: 212/246-0202
Fax: 212/246-2677
E-mail: roc@igc.apc.org
http://www.igc.apc.org/globalvision/

INDEPENDENT TELEVISION
SERVICE
190 Fifth Street East, Suite 200
St. Paul, MN 55101
Tel: 612/225-9035
Fax: 612/225-9102

LABOR BEAT
37 S. Ashland Avenue
Chicago, IL 60607
Tel: 312/226-3330
Fax: 773/561-0908
E-mail: lduncan@igc.apc.org
http://www.cs.uchicago.edu/cspr/lb/

MEDIA NETWORK/
ALTERNATIVE MEDIA INFORMA-
TION CENTER
39 W. 14th Street, #403
New York, NY 10011
Tel: 212/929-2663
Fax: 212/929-2732
E-mail: medianetwk@aol.com

MIX: NEW YORK LESBIAN & GAY
EXPERIMENTAL FILM/VIDEO FES-
TIVAL
341 Lafayette Street, #169
New York, NY 10012
Tel: 212/501-2309
Fax: 212/475-1399
E-mail: mix@echonyc.com
http://www.echonyc.com/~mix/

NATIONAL ASIAN AMERICAN
TELECOMMUNICATION
ASSOCIATION
346 9th Street, 2nd Fl.
San Francisco, CA 94103
Tel: 415/863-0814
Fax: 415/863-7428

P.O.V. (Point Of View)
220 W. 19th Street, 11th Fl.
New York, NY 10011-4035
Tel: 212/989-8121
Fax: 212/989-8230

PACIFICA NETWORK NEWS
702 H Street, NW, Suite 3
Washington, DC 20001
Tel: 202/783-1620
Fax: 202/393-1841

PACIFICA RADIO ARCHIVES
3729 Cahuenga Blvd., West
North Hollywood, CA 91604
Tel: 818/506-1077
Fax: 818/506-1085
E-mail: ppspacific@igc.apc.org

PAPER TIGER TV/DEEP DISH
339 Lafayette Street
New York, NY 10012
Tel: 212/420-9045
Fax: 212/420-8223
E-mail: tigertv@bway.net
http://www.papertiger.org/

PEOPLE'S VIDEO NETWORK
2489 Mission Street, #28
San Francisco, CA 94110
Tel: 415/821-6545 or 415/821-7575
Fax: 415/821-5782
E-mail: npcsf@igc.apc.org

RISE AND SHINE PRODUCTIONS
300 West 43rd Street, 4th Fl.
New York, NY 10036
Tel: 212/265-2509

TELEMUNDO NETWORK
2470 West 8th Avenue
Hialea, FL 33010
Fax: 305/888-7610

THIRD WORLD NEWSREEL
Camera News Inc.
335 West 38th Street, 5th Fl.
New York, NY 10018
Tel: 212/947-9277
Fax: 212/594-6417

VIDEO DATABANK
112 S. Michigan Avenue, 3rd Fl.
Chicago, IL 60603
Tel: 312/345-3550
Fax: 312/541-8072

THE VIDEO PROJECT: FILMS
AND VIDEOS FOR A SAFE
AND SUSTAINABLE WORLD
200 Estates Drive
Ben Lomond, CA 95005
Tel: 408/336-0160 or 800/4-PLANET
Fax: 408/336-2168

"VIEWPOINTS" SERIES
c/o PBS
1320 Braddock Place
Alexandria, VA 22314-1698
Tel: 703/739-5000 or
PBS Comment Line: 800/272-2190

ZEITGEIST FILMS, LTD.
247 Centre Street, 2nd Fl.
New York, NY 10013
Tel: 212/274-1989
Fax: 212/274-1644

ALTERNATIVE ELECTRONIC NEWS SOURCES

ACTIVIST NEWS NETWORK
P.O. Box 51170
Palo Alto, CA 94303
Tel: 415/493-4502
Fax: 415/493-4564

ALTERNET
Alternative News Network
77 Federal Street
San Francisco, CA 94107
Tel: 415/284-1420
Fax: 415/284-1414
E-mail: 71362,27@compuserve.com

INSIGHT FEATURES
Networking for Democracy
3411 Diversey, Suite 1
Chicago, IL 60647
Tel: 312/384-8827
Fax: 312/384-3904

INTERPRESS SERVICE
Global Information Network
777 United Nations Plaza
New York, NY 10017
Tel: 212/286-0123 or
BBS: 212/986-3210
Fax: 212/818-9249
E-mail: ipsgin@igc.apc.org

LATIN AMERICA DATABASE
Latin America Institute,
University of New Mexico
801 Yale Blvd., NE
Albuquerque, NM 87131-1016
Tel: 800/472-0888 or 505/277-6839
Fax: 505/277-5989

NEWS INTERNATIONAL PRESS
SERVICE
6161 El Cajon Blvd., #4
San Diego, CA 92115
Tel: 619/536-9218
Fax: 619/563-1514

PACIFIC NEWS SERVICE
450 Mission Street, Room 506
San Francisco, CA 94105
Tel: 415/243-4364

PEACENET; ECONET;
CONFLICTNET; LABORNET
Institute for Global Communications
18 DeBoom Street
San Francisco, CA 94107
Tel: 415/442-0220
Fax: 415/546-1794

PEOPLE'S NEWS AGENCY
7627 16th Street, NW
P.O. Box 56466
Washington, DC 20040
Tel: 202/829-2278
Fax: 202/829-0462
E-mail: proutwdc@prout.org

ALTERNATIVE PERIODICALS & PUBLICATIONS

14850 MAGAZINE
Public Communications, Inc.
104 N. Aurora Street, Suite 3
Ithaca, NY 14850
Tel: 607/277-1021
Fax: 607/277-0801

ABYA YALA NEWS: JOURNAL
OF THE SOUTH AND MESO AMERI-
CAN INDIAN RIGHTS CENTER
P.O. Box 28703
Oakland, CA 94604
Tel: 510/834-4263
Fax: 510/834-4264
E-mail: saiic@igc.apc.org
http://www.igc.apc.org/saiic/saiic.html

ACROSS THE LINE
Seeds of Peace
P.O. Box 12154
Oakland, CA 94604
Tel: 510/420-1799

THE ADVOCATE
6922 Hollywood Blvd., Suite 1000
Los Angeles, CA 90028
Tel: 213/871-1225
Fax: 213/467-6805
E-mail: info@advocate.com

AFRICA NEWS
P.O. Box 3851
Durham, NC 27702
Tel: 919/286-0747
Fax: 919/286-2614

AGAINST THE CURRENT
Center for Changes
7012 Michigan Avenue
Detroit, MI 48210
Tel: 313/841-0161
Fax: 313/841-8884

AKWESASNE NOTES
Mohawk Nation
P.O. Box 196
Rooseveltown, NY 13683-0196
Tel: 518/358-9531
Fax: 613/575-2935

ALTERNATIVE PRESS REVIEW
C.A.L. Press
P.O. Box 1446
Columbia, MO 65205-1446

ALTERNATIVES
Lynne Rienner Publishers
1800 30th Street, Suite 314
Boulder, CO 80301-1032
Tel: 303/444-6684
Fax: 303/444-0824

AMERICAN JOURNALISM REVIEW
8701 Adelphi Road
Adelphi, MD 20783
Tel: 301/431-4771
Fax: 301/431-0097

AMICUS JOURNAL
40 W. 20th Street
New York, NY 10011
Tel: 212/727-2700
Fax: 212/727-1773

THE ANIMAL'S AGENDA
P.O. Box 25881
Baltimore, MD 21224
Tel: 410/675-4566
Fax: 410/675-0066
E-mail: 75543.3331@compuserve.com
http://www.envirolink.org/arrs/aa/

ARMS SALES MONITOR
Federation of American Scientists
307 Massachusetts Ave., NE
Washington, DC 20002
Tel: 202/675-1018
Fax: 202/675-1010
E-mail: llumpe@fas.org
http://www.fas.org/asmp/

THE ATLANTIC MONTHLY
77 N. Washington
Boston, MA 02114
Tel: 617/854-7700

THE BAFFLER
P.O. Box 378293
Chicago, IL 60637

THE BALTIMORE SUN
501 N. Charles Street
Baltimore, MD 21201
Tel: 410/332-0920

BANKCHECK QUARTERLY
1847 Berkeley Way
Berkeley, CA 94703

BILL OF RIGHTS JOURNAL
175 Fifth Avenue, Room 814
New York, NY 10010
Tel: 212/673-2040
Fax: 212/460-8359

BLACK SCHOLAR
P.O. Box 2869
Oakland, CA 94609
Tel: 510/547-6633
Fax: 510/547-6679

BLK
P.O. Box 83912
Los Angeles, CA 90083-0912
Tel: 310/410-0808
Fax: 310/410-9250
E-mail: newsroom@blk.com
http://www.blk.com/blk/

THE BODY POLITIC
P.O. Box 2363
Binghamton, NY 13902
Tel: 607/648-2760
Fax: 607/648-2511
E-mail: annebower@delphi.com

BORDER/LINES
P.O. Box 459
Toronto M5S 29 Ontario
Canada
Tel: 416/921-6446
Fax: 416/921-3984

BOSTON REVIEW
E53-407, MIT
30 Wadsworth Street
Cambridge, MA 02139
Tel: 617/253-3642
Fax: 617/252-1549
E-mail: bostonreview@mit.edu
http://www-polisci.mit.edu/Boston
Review/

THE BOSTON PHOENIX
126 Brookline Avenue
Boston, MA 02215
Tel: 617/536-5390
Fax: 617/859-8201

THE BOYCOTT QUARTERLY
Center for Economic Democracy
P.O. Box 30727
Seattle, WA 98103-0727
E-mail: boycottguy@aol.com

BREAD AND JUSTICE
Southern California Interfaith Hunger
Coalition
2449 Hyperion, Suite 100
Los Angeles, CA 90027
Tel: 213/913-7333
Fax: 213/664-1725

BREAKTHROUGH
P.O. Box 14422
San Francisco, CA 94114

BRIARPATCH: SASKATCHEWAN'S
INDEPENDENT NEWSMAGAZINE
2138 McIntyre Street
Regina SK S4P 2R7
Canada
Tel: 306/525-2949

BROADCASTING & CABLE
1705 DeSales Street, NW, Suite 600
Washington, DC 20036
Tel: 202/659-2340

BULLETIN OF CONCERNED ASIAN
SCHOLARS
3239 9th Street
Boulder, CO 80304-2112

BULLETIN OF THE
ATOMIC SCIENTISTS
Education Foundation for
Nuclear Science
6042 South Kimbark Avenue
Chicago, IL 60637
Tel: 773/702-2555
Fax: 773/702-0725
E-mail: bullatomsci@igc.apc.org
http://neog.com/atomic/

BUSINESS ETHICS
The Magazine of Socially
Responsible Business
P.O. Box 14748
Dayton, OH 45413-9932

THE CALIFORNIA PRISONER
P.O. Box 1019
Sacramento, CA 95812-1019
Tel: 916/441-4214
Fax: 916/441-4297

CANADIAN DIMENSION
91 Albert Street, 2B
Winnipeg, MB, R3B 1G5
Canada
Tel: 204/957-1519
Fax: 204/943-4617
E-mail: INFO@CANADIAN DIMEN-
SION.MB.CA

CAPITAL EYE
Center for Responsive Politics
1320 19th Street, NW, #700
Washington, DC 20036
Tel: 202/857-0044
Fax: 202/857-7809
E-mail: info@crp.org
http://www.crp.org/

CASCADIA TIMES
25-6 NW 23rd Pl., #406
Portland, OR 97210
Tel: 503/223-9036
E-mail: cascadia@desktop.org

CENTER FOR MEDIA LITERACY
4727 Wilshire Blvd., Suite #403
Los Angeles, CA 90010
Tel: 213/931-4177
Fax: 213/931-4474

CHANGING MEN: ISSUES
IN GENDER, SEX
AND POLITICS
P.O. Box 3121
Kansas City, KS 66103

CHICAGO LIFE MAGAZINE
P.O. Box 11311
Chicago, IL 60611-0311
Tel: 312/528-2737

THE CHRONICLE OF HIGHER
EDUCATION
1255 23rd Street, NW
Washington, DC 20037
Tel: 202/466-1000
Fax: 202/296-2691

THE CHRONICLE OF
PHILANTHROPY
1255 23rd St., NW, 7th Floor
Washington, DC 20037
Tel: 202/466-1200
Fax: 202/466-2078

THE CIRCLE
1530 East Franklin Avenue
Minneapolis, MN 55404
Tel: 612/879-1760
Fax: 612/879-1712

CITIZENS CLEARINGHOUSE
FOR HAZARDOUS WASTES
P.O. Box 6806
Falls Church, VA 22040

CITY LIMITS: NEW YORK'S URBAN
AFFAIRS MAGAZINE
40 Prince Street
New York, NY 10012-9801

CITY PAPER
Baltimore's Free Weekly
812 Park Avenue
Baltimore, MD 21201
Tel: 410/523-2300
Fax: 410/523-2222

CO-OP AMERICA QUARTERLY
A Magazine for Building Economic
Alternatives
1612 K Street, Suite 600
Washington, DC 20006

COMMON CAUSE MAGAZINE
1250 Connecticut Ave., NW, 6th Fl.
Washington, DC 20036
Tel: 202/833-1200
Fax: 202/659-3716
E-mail: ccvicki@well.com

COMMUNITIES MAGAZINE
P.O. Box 169
Masonville, CO 80541
Tel: 970/593-5615
Fax: same as above
http://www.ic.org/

COMMUNITY ENDEAVOR NEWS
P.O. Box 2505
Grass Valley, CA 95945
Tel: 916/274-7331
Fax: same as above
E-mail: jaykay@oro.net

COMMUNITY MEDIA REVIEW
The Journal of The Alliance For
Community Media
666 11th Street, NW, Suite 806
Washington, DC 20001

CONGRESSIONAL QUARTERLY
WEEKLY REPORT
1414 22nd Street, NW
Washington, DC 20037
Tel: 202/887-8500
Fax: 202/728-1863

CONSUMER REPORTS
101 Truman Avenue
Yonkers, NY 10703
Tel: 914/378-2000

COUNTER MEDIA
1573 N. Milwaukee Ave., #517
Chicago, IL 60622
Tel: 773/243-8342
E-mail: xmediax@ripco.com
http://www.cs.uchicago.edu/cpsr/
countermedia/

COUNTERPUNCH
P.O. Box 19675
Washington, DC 20036
E-mail: counterpun@aol.com

COUNTERPOISE
1716 Williston Road
Gainesville, FL 32608
Tel: 352/335-2200
Fax: call first
E-mail: willett@afn.org

COVERTACTION QUARTERLY
1500 Massachusetts Ave., NW, #732
Washington, DC 20005
Tel: 202/331-9763
Fax: 202/331-9751

CREATIVE LOAFING
P.O. Box 54223
Atlanta, GA 30308
Fax: 404/420-1402
E-mail: metro@cln.com

CRESTED BUTTE
CHRONICLE & PILOT
P.O. Box 369
Crested Butte, CO 81224
Tel: 303/349-6114

CROSSROADS
Institute for Social and Economic Studies
P.O. Box 2809
Oakland, CA 94609
Tel: 510/843-7495
E-mail: crossroads@igc.apc.org

CUBA ADVOCATE
2635 Mapleton, #143
Boulder, CO 80304
Tel: 303/447-2286
Fax: same as above

CUBA UPDATE
Center for Cuban Studies
124 W. 23rd Street
New York, NY 10011

CULTURAL DEMOCRACY
P.O. Box 545
Tucson, AZ 85702
Tel: 520/791-9359
E-mail: cdemocracy@aol.com

CULTURAL SURVIVAL
QUARTERLY
Cultural Survival, Inc.
46 Brattle Street
Cambridge, MA 02138
Tel: 617/441-5400
Fax: 617/441-5417

THE DAILY CITIZEN
P.O. Box 57365
Washington, DC 20037
Tel: 202/429-6929
Fax: 202/659-1145

THE DAYTON VOICE
1927 N. Main Street
Dayton, OH 45405
Tel: 513/275-8855
Fax: 513/275-6056

DE TODO UN POCO
2830 5th Street
Boulder, CO 80304
Tel: 303/444-8565
Fax: 303/545-2074

DEADLINE
Center for War, Peace and the News
Media
New York University
10 Washington Place, 4th Fl.
New York, NY 10003
Tel: 212/998-7960
Fax: 212/995-4143

DEFENSE MONITOR
1500 Massachusetts Ave., NW
Washington, DC 20005
Tel: 202/862-0700
Fax: 202/862-0708
E-mail: cdi@igc.apc.org

DEMOCRATIC LEFT
Democratic Socialists of America
(DSA)
180 Varick Street, 12th Fl.
New York, NY 10014
Tel: 212/727-8610
Fax: 212/727-8616
E-mail: dsa@dsausa.org

DENVER WESTWORD
P.O. Box 5970
Denver, CO 80217
Tel: 303/296-7744

DETROIT METRO TIMES
743 Beaubien, Suite 301
Detroit, MI 48226
Tel: 313/961-4060
Fax: 313/961-6598

(DIS)CONNECTION
c/o Autonomous Zone
1573 N. Milwaukee Ave., #420
Chicago, IL 60622
Tel: 773/278-0775
E-mail: ugwiller@bgu.edu

DISSENT
521 Fifth Avenue, Suite 1700
New York, NY 10025
Tel: 212/595-3084
Fax: same as above
E-mail: dissent@igc.apc.org

DOLLARS AND SENSE
1 Summer Street
Somerville, MA 02143
Tel: 617/628-8411
Fax: 617/628-2025
E-mail: dollars@igc.apc.org
http://www. igc.apc.org/dollars/

E: THE ENVIRONMENTAL
MAGAZINE
P.O. Box 5098
Westport, CT 06881
Tel: 203/854-5559
Fax: 203/866-0602

THE EARTH FIRST! JOURNAL
P.O. Box 1415
Eugene, OR 97440
Tel: 541/741-9191
Fax: 541/741-9192
E-mail: earthfirst@igc.apc.org

EARTH ISLAND JOURNAL
300 Broadway, Suite 28
San Francisco, CA 94133-3312
Tel: 415/788-3666
Fax: 415/788-7324
E-mail: journal@eii.org
http://www.earthisland.org/ei/

THE ECOLOGIST
c/o MIT Press Journals
55 Hayward Street
Cambridge, MA 02142
Fax: 617/258-6779
E-mail: journals-orders@mit.edu

ECONEWS
879 Ninth Street
Arcata, CA 95521
Tel: 707/822-6918
Fax: 707/822-0827
E-mail: nec@igc.apc.org

THE EL SALVADOR WATCH
c/o CISPES
19 W. 21st Street, Room 502
New York, NY 10010
Tel: 212/229-1290
Fax: 212/645-6657
E-mail: cispesnatl@igc.apc.org

EMERGE: BLACK AMERICA'S
NEWS MAGAZINE
One B.E.T. Plaza, 1900 W Place, NE
Washington, DC 20018-1211
Tel: 202/608-2093
Fax: 202/608-2598

ENVIRONMENTAL ACTION
6930 Carroll Avenue, Suite 600
Takoma Park, MD 20912
Tel: 301/891-1100
Fax: 301/891-2218

ENVIRONMENTAL IMPACT
REPORTER
P.O. Box 1834
Sebastopol, CA 95473
Tel: 707/823-8744

ESSENCE MAGAZINE
1500 Broadway
New York, NY 10036
Tel: 212/642-0600

EXTRA!
Fairness and Accuracy in Reporting
130 W. 25th Street
New York, NY 10001
Tel: 212/633-6700
Fax: 212/727-7668
E-mail: info@fair.org
http://www.fair.org./fair/

EYE MAGAZINE
301 S. Elm Street, Suite 405
Greensboro, NC 27401
Tel: 910/370-1702
Fax: 910/370-1603
E-mail: eye@nr.infi.net
http://www.infi.net/~eye/

FACTSHEET FIVE
c/o Seth Friedman
P.O. Box 170099
San Francisco, CA 94117-0099
Tel: 415/668-1781
E-mail: f5seth@sirius.com

FAT!SO?
P.O. Box 423464
San Francisco, CA 94142-3464
Tel: 800/OHFATSO
E-mail: marilyn@fatso.com
http://www.fatso.com/

FELLOWSHIP OF
RECONCILIATION
Box 271—521 N. Broadway
Nyack, NY 10960
Tel: 914/358-4601
Fax: 914/358-4924
E-mail: fellowship@igc.apc.org
http://www.nonviolence.org/~nvweb/for/

FEMINIST LIBRARY NEWSLETTER
5 Westminster Bridge Road
London SE17XW
U.K.
Tel: 011-44-171-928-7789

FIFTH ESTATE
4632 Second Avenue
Detroit, MI 48201
Tel: 313/831-6800

FOOD & WATER JOURNAL
Food & Water, Inc.
RR1, Box 68D
Walden, VT 05873
Tel: 802/563-3300
Fax: 802/563-3310

FOOD FIRST NEWS
Institute for Food & Development Policy
398 60th Street
Oakland, CA 94618
Tel: 510/654-4400

FOREIGN AFFAIRS
58 E. 68th Street
New York, NY 10021
Tel: 212/734-0400
E-mail: foraff@email.cfr.org
http://www.foreignaffairs.org/

FREETHINKER FORUM
8945 Renken Road
Stauton, IL 62088
Tel: 618/637-2202
Fax: 618/637-2666
E-mail: profreedom@aol.com

FRONT LINES RESEARCH
Public Policy Institute
Planned Parenthood Federation of
America
810 Seventh Avenue
New York, NY 10019
Tel: 212/261-4721
Fax: 212/261-4352

GAO REPORTS & TESTIMONY
U.S. General Accounting Office
Washington, DC 10548-0001
Tel: 202/512-6000

GAY COMMUNITY NEWS
25 West Street
Boston, MA 02111

GENEWATCH
The Council For Responsible Genetics
5 Upland Road, Suite 3
Cambridge, MA 02140
Tel: 617/868-0870
Fax: 617/491-5344

GLOBAL EXCHANGES
2017 Mission Street, Suite 303
San Francisco, CA 94110
Tel: 415/255-7296

GLOBAL PESTICIDE CAMPAIGNER
Pesticide Action Network
116 New Montgomery, #810
San Francisco, CA 94105
Tel: 415/541-9140
Fax: 415/541-9253

GRASSROOTS ECONOMIC
ORGANIZING NEWSLETTER
P.O. Box 5065
New Haven, CT 06525
Tel: 203/389-6194
Fax: 860/486-0387

GRASSROOTS FUNDRAISING
JOURNAL
P.O. Box 11607
Berkeley, CA 94712
Tel: 510/704-8714
Fax: 510/649-1913

GREEN MAGAZINE
P.O. Box 381, Mill Harbour
London E14 9TW
U.K.

GUILD NOTES
National Lawyers Guild
126 University Place, 4th Fl.
New York, NY 10003-4538
Tel: 212/627-2656

HARD TIMES
c/o L.A. Village View
2342 Sawtelle Blvd.
Los Angeles, CA 90064
Tel: 310/477-0403

HEALTH LETTER
1600 20th Street, NW
Washington, DC 20009
Tel: 202/588-1000
Fax: 202/588-7796

HIGH COUNTRY NEWS
P.O. Box 1090
Paonia, CO 81428
Tel: 303/527-4898

THE HUMAN QUEST
Churchman Co., Inc.
1074 23rd Avenue N.
St. Petersburg, FL 33704-3228
Tel: 813/894-0097

HUMAN RIGHTS TRIBUNE
Human Rights Internet
8 York Street, Suite 802
Ottawa, Ontario K1N 5SP
Canada
Tel: 613/789-7407
Fax: 613/789-7414
E-mail: hri@hri.ca
http://www.hri.ca/

HUNGRY MIND REVIEW
1648 Grand Avenue
St. Paul, MN 55105
Tel: 612/699-2610

THE IDLER
15 St. Stephens Gardens
London W2 5NA U.K.
Tel: 011-44-171-792-3501

IN THESE TIMES
2040 N. Milwaukee Avenue, 2nd Fl.
Chicago, IL 60647-4002
Tel: 312/772-0100
Fax: 312/772-4180
E-mail: itt@igc.apc.org

THE INDEPENDENT
540 Mendocino Avenue
Santa Rosa, CA 95401
Tel: 707/527-1200
Fax: 707/527-1288

THE INDEPENDENT FILM
& VIDEO MONTHLY
625 Broadway, 9th Floor
New York, NY 10012
Tel: 212/473-3400
Fax: 212/677-8732

INDEPENDENT POLITICAL
ACTION BULLETIN
c/o NCIPA
P.O. Box 170610
Brooklyn, NY 11217
Tel: 718/624-7807
Fax: 718/643-8265
E-mail: indpol@igc.apc.org

INDEX ON CENSORSHIP
Writers & Scholars Educational Trust
33 Islington High Street
London N1 9LH
U.K.
Tel: 011-44-171-278-2313
Fax: 011-44-171-278-1878
E-mail: index@indexcen.democ.co.uk

INDUSTRIAL WORKER
103 W. Michigan Avenue
Ypsilanti, MI 48197-5438
Tel: 313/483-3548
Fax: 313/483-4050
E-mail: iww@igc.apc.org

INFUSION
Center for Campus Organizing
P.O. Box 748
Cambridge, MA 02142

INSIGHT MAGAZINE
3600 New York Avenue, NE
Washington, DC 20002
Tel: 202/636-8810

INTERNATIONAL JOURNAL OF
HEALTH SERVICES
Baywood Publishing
P.O. Box 337, 26 Austin Avenue
Amityville, NY 11701
Tel: 516/691-1270
Fax: 516/691-1770
E-mail: baywood@baywood.com
http://baywood.com/

IRE JOURNAL: INVESTIGATIVE
REPORTERS & EDITORS
Missouri School of Journalism, 138
Neff Annex
Columbia, MO 65211
Tel: 573/882-2042
Fax: 573/882-5431
http://www.ire.org/

ISSUES IN SCIENCE &
TECHNOLOGY
1636 Hobart Street, NW
Washington, DC 20009
Tel: 202/986-7217
Fax: 202/986-7221

JOURNAL OF COMMUNITY
PRACTICE: ORGANIZING,
PLANNING, DEVELOPMENT &
CHANGE
Haworth Press, 10 Alice Street
Binghamton, NY 13904-1580

JOURNAL OF PRISONERS
ON PRISONS
University of Manitoba
Box 54, University Centre
Winnipeg R3T 2N2
Canada
Tel: 204/783-3707

JUMP CUT: A REVIEW OF
CONTEMPORARY MEDIA
P.O. Box 865
Berkeley, CA 94701

KICK IT OVER
P.O. Box 5811, Station A
Toronto, Ontario M5W 1P2
Canada

KLANWATCH
P.O. Box 548
Montgomery, AL 36104
Tel: 205/264-0286
Fax: 205/264-0629

LA GACETA
P.O. Box 5536
Tampa, FL 33675
Tel: 813/248-3921
Fax: 813/247-5357

L.A. WEEKLY
6715 Sunset Blvd.
Los Angeles, CA 90028
Tel: 213/465-9909

LABOR NEWS FOR WORKING
FAMILIES
I.I.R., 2521 Channing Way
Berkeley, CA 94720
Tel: 510/643-6814
Fax: 510/642-6432
http://violet.berkeley.edu/~iir/
workfam/home.html

LABOR NOTES
7435 Michigan Avenue
Detroit, MI 48210

LAMBDA BOOK REPORT:
A REVIEW OF CONTEMPORARY
GAY AND LESBIAN LITERATURE
1625 Connecticut Avenue, NW
Washington, DC 20009
Tel: 202/462-7924
Fax: 202/462-7257
E-mail: LBREditor@aol.com

LATIN AMERICAN PERSPECTIVES
2455 Teller Road
Newbury Park, CA 91320
Tel: 805/499-0721

LEFT BUSINESS OBSERVER
250 W. 85th Street
New York, NY 10024-3217
Tel: 212/874-4020

LEFT CURVE
P.O. Box 472
Oakland, CA 94604
Tel: 510/763-7193
E-mail: leftcurv@wco.com
http://www.wco.com/~leftcurv/

LEGAL TIMES
1730 M Street, NW, Suite 802
Washington, DC 20036
Tel: 202/457-0686

LIBRARIANS AT LIBERTY
CRISES PRESS, INC.
1716 SW Williston Rd.
Gainesville, FL 32608
Tel: 352/335-2200
Fax: call first
E-mail: willett@afn.org

LONDON INDEPENDENT
40 City Road
London EC1Y 2DB
U.K.

MEDIA AND VALUES
Media Action Research Center
475 Riverside Drive, Suite 1901
New York, NY 10115
Tel: 212/865-6690
Fax: 212/663-2746

MEDIA BYPASS
P.O. Box 5326
Evansville, IL 47716
Tel: 812/477-8670
Fax: 812/477-8677

MEDIA CULTURE REVIEW
77 Federal Street
San Francisco, CA 94107
Tel: 415/284-1420
Fax: 415/284-1414
http://alternet.eline.com/

MEDIA, CULTURE AND SOCIETY
Sage Publications
6 Bonhill Street
London EC24 4PU
U.K.

MEDIAFILE
814 Mission Street, Suite 205
San Francisco, CA 94103
Tel: 415/546-6334
Fax: 415/546-6218
E-mail: ma@igc.org
http://www.media-alliance.org/

MIDDLE EAST REPORT
1500 Massachusettes Ave., NW, Suite 119
Washington, DC 20005
Tel: 202/223-3677
Fax: 202/223-3604
E-mail: merip@igc.apc.org

MIGHT MAGAZINE
150 Fourth Street, Suite 650
San Francisco, CA 94103
Tel: 415/896-1528
E-mail: mightmag@aol.com

MONTHLY REVIEW:
AN INDEPENDENT
SOCIALIST MAGAZINE
122 W. 27th Street
New York, NY 10001

MOTHER JONES
731 Market Street, Suite 600
San Francisco, CA 94103
Tel: 415/665-6637
Fax: 415/665-6696
E-mail: query@motherjones.com
http://www.motherjones.com/

MOTHERING MAGAZINE
P.O. Box 1690
Santa Fe, NM 87504-1690
Tel: 505/984-8112

MOUTH: THE VOICE OF
DISABILITY RIGHTS
61 Brighton Street
Rochester, NY 14607

MS. MAGAZINE
230 Park Avenue
New York, NY 10169
Tel: 212/551-9595

MUCKRAKER
Center for Investigative Reporting
568 Howard Street, 5th Fl.
San Francisco, CA 94105-3008
Tel: 415/543-1200
Fax: 415/543-8311

MULTINATIONAL MONITOR
P.O. Box 19405
Washington, DC 20036
Tel: 202/387-8034
Fax: 202/234-5176
E-mail: monitor@essential.org
http://www.essential.org/

NACLA: REPORT ON
THE AMERICAS
P.O. Box 77
Hopewell, PA 16650-0077

THE NATION
72 Fifth Avenue
New York, NY 10011
Tel: 212/242-8400
Fax: 212/463-9712
E-mail: nation@igc.org
http://www.thenation.com/

NATIONAL CATHOLIC REPORTER
P.O. Box 419281
Kansas City, MO 64141
Tel: 816/531-0538
Fax: 816/968-2280

NATIONAL REVIEW
150 E. 35th Street
New York, NY 10016
Tel: 212/679-7330
Fax: 212/696-0309

THE NEIGHBORHOOD WORKS
Center for Neighborhood Technology
2125 West North Avenue
Chicago, IL 60647
Tel: 312/278-4800

THE NEW INTERNATIONALIST
55 Rectory Road
Oxford OX4 1BW
U.K.
Tel: 011-44-186-572-8181
Fax: 011-44-186-579-3152
E-mail: newint@gn.apc.org

NEW PERSPECTIVES QUARTERLY
10951 W. Pico Blvd., 3rd Fl.
Los Angeles, CA 90064
Tel: 310/474-0011
Fax: 800/336-1007

THE NEW REPUBLIC
1220 19th Street, NW
Washington, DC 20036
Tel: 202/331-7494
Fax: 202/331-0275

NEW STATESMAN & SOCIETY
7th Floor, Victoria Station House
191 Victoria Street
London SWIE SNE
U.K.

NEW TIMES, INC.
P.O. Box 5970
Denver, CO 80217

NEW YORK NATIVE
That New Magazine, Inc.
P.O. Box 1475, Church Street Station
New York, NY 10008

NEWS FROM INDIAN COUNTRY
Rt. 2, Box 2900A
Hayward, WI 54843

NEWSLETTER ON INTELLECTUAL
FREEDOM
American Library Association
50 E. Huron Street
Chicago, IL 60611
Tel: 312/280-4223
Fax: 312/280-4227
E-mail: jkrug@ala.org

NEWT WATCH!
Public Citizen
1600 20th Street, NW
Washington, DC 20009
Tel: 202/588-1000
Fax: 202/588-7798

THE NONVIOLENT ACTIVIST
War Resisters League
339 Lafayette Street
New York, NY 10012

NORTH COAST XPRESS
P.O. Box 1226
Occidental, CA 95465
Tel: 707/874-3104
Fax: 707/874-1453
E-mail: doretk@sonic.net
http://www.north-coast-
xpress.com/~doretk/

NUTRITION ACTION
HEALTH LETTER
Center for Science in the
Public Interest
1875 Connecticut Ave., NW, Suite 300
Washington, DC 20009-5728

OFF OUR BACKS: A WOMEN'S
NEWSJOURNAL
2337-B 18th Street, NW
Washington, DC 20009

ON THE ISSUES
Choices Women's Medical Center
97-77 Queens Blvd., 11th Fl.
Forest Hills, NY 11374
Tel: 718/459-1888

OPEN EYE
BM Open Eye
London WC1N 3XX
U.K.

ORGANIZING
5600 City Avenue
Philadelphia, PA 19131
Tel: 215/878-4253
Fax: 215/879-3148

OUR TIMES:
CANADA'S INDEPENDENT
LABOUR MAGAZINE
390 Dufferin Street
Toronto, Ontario M6K 2A3
Canada

PACIFIC SUN
P.O. Box 5553
Mill Valley, CA 94942
Tel: 415/383-4500
Fax: 415/383-4159

PBI/USA REPORT
Peace Brigades Int'l/USA
2642 College Avenue
Berkeley, CA 94704
Tel: 510/540-0749
Fax: 510/849-1247
E-mail: pbiusa@igc.apc.org
http://www.igc.apc.org/pbi/index.html

PEACE & DEMOCRACY
Campaign for Peace & Democracy
P.O. Box 1640, Cathedral Station
New York, NY 10025

PEACE AND FREEDOM
Women's International League for
Peace & Freedom
1213 Race Street
Philadelphia, PA 19107-1691

PEACE MAGAZINE
736 Bathurst Street
Toronto, Ontario M5S 2R4
Canada
Tel: 416/533-7581
Fax: 416/531-6214
E-mail: mspencer@web.net

PEACE REVIEW: A TRANSNA-
TIONAL QUARTERLY
Peace & Justice Studies
University of San Francisco
2130 Fulton Street
San Francisco, CA 94117
Tel: 415/422-6349 or 415/422-6496
Fax: 415/388-2631 or 415/422-2346
E-mail: eliasr@usfca.edu

PEACEWORK
American Friends Service Committee
2161 Massachusetts Avenue
Cambridge, MA 02140
Tel: 617/661-6130
Fax: 617/354-2832

THE PEOPLE'S WARRIOR
P.O. Box 488
Rockwall, TX 75087
Tel: 800/771-1992 or 214/771-1991

PERCEPTIONS MAGAZINE
10734 Jefferson Blvd., Suite 502
Culver City, CA 90230
Tel: 310/313-5185 or 800/276-4448
Fax: 310/313-5198

THE PERMACULTURE ACTIVIST
P.O. Box 1209
Black Mountain, NC 28711
Tel: 704/298-2812
Fax: 704/298-6441
E-mail: permaheart@aol.com

PITTSBURGH POST-GAZETTE
P.O. Box 957
Pittsburgh, PA 15222
Tel: 412/263-1100

POLITICAL AFFAIRS
235 West 23rd Street
New York, NY 10011

POZ MAGAZINE
1279 Old Chelsea Station
New York, NY 10113-1279
Tel: 212/242-2163
E-mail: pozmag@aol.com

PRACTICE: THE MAGAZINE OF
PSYCHOLOGY AND POLITICAL
ECONOMY
East Side Institute
500 Greenwich Street, Suite 202
New York, NY 10013

PREVAILING WINDS MAGAZINE
Center for the Preservation of Modern
History
P.O. Box 23511
Santa Barbara, CA 93121
Tel: 805/899-3433
Fax: 805/899-4773
E-mail: patrick@silcom.com
http://www.prevailiingwinds.org/

PRISON LEGAL NEWS
2400 N.W. 80th Street, Suite 148
Seattle, WA 98117
Tel: 407/547-9716
http://www.synapse.net/~arrakis/pln/
pln.html

THE PROGRESSIVE
409 E. Main Street
Madison, WI 53703
Tel: 608/257-4626
Fax: 608/257-3373

PROGRESSIVE LIBRARIAN
Progressive Librarians Guild
P.O. Box 2203, Times Square Station
New York, NY 10108
Tel: 212/865-6925

PROPAGANDA REVIEW
Media Alliance
814 Mission Street, Suite 205
San Francisco, CA 94103
Tel: 415/546-6334

PUBLIC CITIZEN
1600 20th Street, NW
Washington, DC 20009
Tel: 202/588-1000
Fax: 202/588-7799
E-mail: pnye@citizen.org

THE PUBLIC EYE
Political Research Associates
120 Beacon Street, 3rd Fl.
Somerville, MA 02143-4304
Tel: 617/661-9313

RACHEL'S ENVIRONMENT &
HEALTH REVIEW
c/o Environmental Research
Foundation
P.O. Box 5036
Annapolis, MD 21403-7036
Tel: 410/263-1584
Fax: 410/263-8944
E-mail: rachel@rachel.clark.net

RADICAL AMERICA
1 Summer Street
Somerville, MA 02143-998

RAISE THE STAKES: THE PLANET
DRUM REVIEW
P.O. Box 31251
San Francisco, CA 94131
Tel: 415/285-6556
Fax: 415/285-6563
E-mail: planetdrum@igc.apc.org

RANDOM LENGTHS
Harbor Independent News
P.O. Box 731
1117 So. Pacific Avenue
San Pedro, CA 90733
Tel: 310/519-1016
Fax: 310/832-1000
E-mail: 71632.210@compuserve.com

REAPPRAISING AIDS
c/o Paul Philpott
7514 Girard Ave., #1-331
La Jolla, CA 92037

REASON
3415 S. Sepulveda Blvd., Suite 400
Los Angeles, CA 90034
Tel: 310/391-2245

RECONSTRUCTION
1563 Massachusetts Avenue
Cambridge, MA 02138
Tel: 617/495-0907

THE RECORDER
625 Polk Street
San Francisco, CA 94102

RED PEPPER
Socialist Newspaper Publications, Ltd.
3 Gunthorpe Street
London E1 7RP
U.K.
Tel: 011-44-171-247-1702
E-mail: redpepper@online.rednet.co.uk

RETHINKING SCHOOLS
1001 E. Keefe Avenue
Milwaukee, WI 53212
Tel: 414/964-9646 or 800/669-4192
Fax: 414/964-7220
E-mail: RS Business@aol.com

REVOLUTIONARY WORKER
P.O. Box 3486
Chicago, IL 60654

RIGHTS
175 5th Avenue
New York, NY 10010

ROC-ROCK OUT CENSORSHIP
P.O. Box 147
Jewett, OH 43986

ROLLING STONE
1290 Ave. of the Americas, 2nd Fl.
New York, NY 10104
Tel: 212/484-1616
Fax: 212/767-8203

S.O.A. WATCH
P.O. Box 3330
Columbus, GA 31903
Tel: 706/682-5369
Fax: same as above
http://www.derechos.org/soaw/

THE SAN FRANCISCO BAY
GUARDIAN
520 Hampshire
San Francisco, CA 94110
Tel: 415/255-3100
Fax: 415/255-8762

SANTA BARBARA NEWS PRESS
715 Anacapa Street
Santa Barbara, CA 93101
Tel: 805/564-5200

SANTA CRUZ SENTINEL
P.O. Box 638
Santa Cruz, CA 95061
Tel: 408/423-4242
Fax: 408/429-9620

SANTA ROSA SUN
1275 Fourth Street, #608
Santa Rosa, CA 95404
Tel: 707/544-3448
Fax: 707/544-4756

SECRECY & GOVERNMENT
BULLETIN
Federation of American Scientists
307 Massachusetts Avenue, NE
Washington, DC 20002
Tel: 202/675-1012
Fax: 202/675-1010
E-mail: saftergood@igc.apc.org
http://www.fas.org/sgp/bulletin/
index.html

SF WEEKLY
425 Brannan Street
San Francisco, CA 94107
Tel: 415/541-0700
Fax: 415/777-1839

SOCIAL POLICY
25 W. 43rd Street, Room 620
New York, NY 10036-7406
Tel: 212/354-8525
Fax: 212/642-1956
E-mail: socpol@socialpolicy.org
http://socialpolicy.org/

SOJOURNERS
2401 15th Street, NW
Washington, DC 20009
Tel: 202/328-8842
Fax: 202/328-8757
E-mail: sojourn@ari.net
http://www.sojourners.com/sojourners/

SOUTH ASIA BULLETIN
Duke University Press
Journal Division
P.O. Box 90660
Durham, NC 27708-0660

SOUTHERN EXPOSURE
P.O. Box 531
Durham, NC 27702
Tel: 919/419-8311, Ext.26
Fax: 919/419-8315
E-mail: Southern@igc.apc.org
http://sunsite.unc.edu/
Southern Exposure/

SPIN
6 West 18th Street
New York, NY 10011
Tel: 212/633-8200
Fax: 212/633-9041

SPIRIT OF CRAZY HORSE
Leonard Peltier Defense Committee
International Office, P.O. Box 583
Lawrence, KS 66044
Tel: 913/842-5774
Fax: 913/842-5796

THE SPOTLIGHT
300 Independence Avenue, SE
Washington, DC 20003
Tel: 202/544-1794

ST. LOUIS JOURNALISM REVIEW
8380 Olive Boulevard
St. Louis, MO 63132
Tel: 314/991-1699
Fax: 314/997-1898

THE STRANGER
1202 E. Pike Street, Suite 1225
Seattle, WA 98122-3934
Tel: 203/323-7002

STRATEGIES
Strategies for Media Literacy
1095 Market Street, Suite 617
San Francisco, CA 94103
Tel: 415/621-2911

THE SUN
107 N. Roberson Street
Chapel Hill, NC 27516
Tel: 919/942-5282

SYNTHESIS/REGENERATION:
A Magazine of Green Social Thought
WD Press, P.O. Box 24115
St. Louis, MO 63130
Tel: 314/727-8554
Fax: call first
E-mail: jsutter@igc.apc.org

TASK FORCE CONNECTIONS
National Task Force on AIDS
Preservation
973 Market St., Suite 600
San Francisco, CA 94103
Tel: 415/356-8110
Fax: 415/356-8138

TERRAIN
Northern California's Environmental
Magazine
2530 San Pablo Avenue
Berkeley, CA 94702
Tel: 510/548-2220
E-mail: ecologycntr@igc.apc.org

TEXAS OBSERVER
307 West 7th Street
Austin, TX 78701-2917
Tel: 512/477-0746
Fax: 512/474-1175
E-mail: observer@eden.com
http://www.hyperweb.com/txobserver/

THIRD FORCE
Center for Third World Organizing
1218 East 21st Street
Oakland, CA 94606-9950
Tel: 510/533-7583

THIS MAGAZINE
35 Rivera Drive, #17
Markham, Ontario L3R 8N4
Canada

THRESHOLD
Student Environmental Action
Coalition (SEAC)
P.O. Box 1168
Chapel Hill, NC 27514-1168
Tel: 919/967-4600
Fax: 919/967-4648
E-mail: seac@igc.apc.org

TIBET PRESS WATCH
International Campaign for Tibet
1825 K Street, NW, Suite 520
Washington, DC 20006
Tel: 202/785-1515
Fax: 202/785-4343
E-mail: ict@peacenet.org
http://www.peacenet.org/ict/

TIKKUN
251 W. 100th Street, 5th Fl.
New York, NY 10025
Tel: 212/864-4110
Fax: 212/864-4137

TOWARD FREEDOM
209 College Street
Burlington, VT 05401
Tel: 802/658-2523
Fax: 802/658-3738

TRADESWOMEN:
A Magazine for
Women in Blue Collar Work
P.O. Box 2622
Berkeley, CA 94702
Tel: 510/433-1378
E-mail: Tradeswmn@aol.com

TRANSITION
1430 Massachusetts Ave., 4th Fl.
Cambridge, MA 02138
Tel: 617/496-2847
Fax: 617/496-2877
E-mail: transit@fas.harvard.edu

TRANSPORTATION
ALTERNATIVES
92 St. Mark's Place
New York, NY 10009
Tel: 212/475-4600

TURNING THE TIDE: JOURNAL OF
ANTI-RACIST ACTIVISM,
RESEARCH & EDUCATION
People Against Racist Terror
P.O. Box 1055
Culver City, CA 90232
Tel: 310/288-5003
E-mail: mnovicktt@igc.org

U. THE NATIONAL COLLEGE
MAGAZINE
1800 Century Park East, #820
Los Angeles, CA 90067-1503
Tel: 310/551-1381
Fax: 310/551-1659
E-mail: editor@umagazine.com

UNCLASSIFIED
Association of National Security
Alumni
2001 S Street, NW, Suite 740
Washington, DC 20009
Tel: 202/483-9325

THE URBAN ECOLOGIST
Urban Ecology
405 14th Street, Suite 701
Oakland, CA 94612
Tel: 510/251-6330
E-mail: urbanecology@igc.apc.org

URGENT ACTION BULLETIN
Survival International
11-15 Emerald Street
London WC1N 3QL
U.K.
Tel: 011-44-171-242-1441
Fax: 011-44-171-242-1771

URGENT ACTION NEWSLETTER
Urgent Action Program Office
Amnesty International USA
P.O. Box 1270
Nederland, CO 80466-1270
Tel: 303/440-0913
Fax: 303/258-7881
E-mail: sharris@igc.apc.org

UTNE READER
1624 Harmon Place, Suite 330
Minneapolis, MN 55403
Tel: 612/338-5040
Fax: 612/338-6043
E-mail: editor@utne.com
http://www.utne.com

VEGETARIAN VOICE
Perspectives on Healthy,
Ecological & Compassionate Living
P.O. Box 72
Dolgeville, NY 13329

VIBE
205 Lexington Avenue, 3rd Fl.
New York, NY 10016
Tel: 212/522-7092
Fax: 212/522-4578

VILLAGE VOICE
36 Cooper Square
New York, NY 10003
Tel: 212/475-3300
Fax: 212/475-8944

THE VVA VETERAN
1224 M Street, NW
Washington, DC 20005
Tel: 202/628-2700

WAR AND PEACE DIGEST
War and Peace Foundation
32 Union Square East
New York, NY 10003-3295
Tel: 212/777-6626
Fax: 212/995-9652

WASHINGTON FREE PRESS
1463 E. Republican Street, #178
Seattle, WA 98112
Tel: 206/233-1780
E-mail: freepres@scn.org
http://freepres@scn.org/wfp/

THE WASHINGTON SPECTATOR
London Terrace Station
P.O. Box 20065
New York, NY 10011

WELFARE MOTHER'S VOICE
Welfare Warriors
2711 W. Michigan Street
Milwaukee, WI 53208-4044

WHO CARES: A JOURNAL OF SER-
VICE AND ACTION
511 K Street, NW, Suite 1042
Washington, DC 20005
Tel: 202/628-1691
Fax: 202/628-2063
E-mail: info@whocares.mag

WHOLE EARTH REVIEW
27 Gate Five Road
Sausalito, CA 94965
Tel: 415/332-1716
Fax: 415/332-3110

WILD FOREST REVIEW
P.O. Box 86373
Portland, OR 97286
Tel: 503/788-1998

WILLAMETTE WEEK
Portland's Newsweekly
822 SW 10th Avenue
Portland, OR 97205
Tel: 503/243-2122
Fax: 503/243-1115

WIRED MAGAZINE
520 Third Street, 4th Fl.
San Francisco, CA 94107
Tel: 415/222-6205
Fax: 415/222-6209
http://www.hotwired.com/

WOMEN AND ENVIRONMENTS
Centre for Urban and Community
Studies
736 Bathurst Street
Toronto, Ontario M5S 2R4
Canada
Tel: 416/516-2600
Fax: 416/531-6214
E-mail: weed@web.net
http://www.web.net/~weed/

WOMEN'S HEALTH LETTER
2245 E. Colorado Blvd., Suite 104
Pasadena, CA 91107-3651
Tel: 818/798-0638
Fax: 818/798-0639

WOMEN'S REVIEW OF BOOKS
Center for Research on Women
Wellesley College
Wellesley, MA 02181
Tel: 617/283-2087
Fax: 617/283-3845

THE WORKBOOK
Southwest Research and Information
Center
P.O. Box 4524, 105 Stanford, SE
Albuquerque, NM 87106
Tel: 505/262-1862
Fax: 505/262-1864

WORKING MOTHERS MAGAZINE
230 Park Avenue
New York, NY 10069
Tel: 212/551-9500
Fax: 212/551-9757

WORLD POLICY JOURNAL
65 Fifth Avenue, Suite 413
New York, NY 10003
Tel: 212/229-5808
Fax: 212/229-5579
E-mail: pera@newschool.edu
http://worldpolicy.org/

WORLD PRESS REVIEW
200 Madison Avenue, Suite 2104
New York, NY 10016
Tel: 212/889-5155
Fax: 212/889-5634

WORLD WATCH
Worldwatch Institute
1776 Massachusetts Avenue, NW
Washington, DC 20036
Tel: 202/452-1999
Fax: 202/296-7365

WRITER'S GUIDELINES
P.O. Box 608
Pittsburg, MO 65724
Fax: 417/993-5544

YES! POSITIVE FUTURES
NETWORK
P.O. Box 10818
Bainbridge Island, WA 98110
Tel: 206/842-0216
Fax: 206/842-5208
E-mail: yes@futurenet.org
http://www.futurenet.org/

YO!-YOUTH OUTLOOK
Pacific News Service
450 Mission Street, Room 204
San Francisco, CA 94105
Tel: 415/243-4364
E-mail: yo@pacificnews.org
http://www.pacificnews.org/yo/

YOUTH ACTION FORUM
Youth Action Network
67 Richmond St., West, Suite 410
Toronto, Ontario, MS4 125
Canada
Tel: 800/718-LINK or 416/368-2277
Fax: 416/368-8354
E-mail: ak027@torfres.net

Z MAGAZINE
18 Millfield Street
Woods Hole, MA 02543
Tel: 617/251-0755
Fax: 617/251-0756

FREEDOM OF INFORMATION/MEDIA ANALYSIS ORGANIZATIONS & PUBLICATIONS

ACCURACY IN MEDIA (AIM)
4455 Connecticut Avenue, NW
Suite 330
Washington, DC 20005
Tel: 202/364-4401
Fax: 202/364-4098
E-mail: ar@aim.org
http://www.aim.org/aim.html

ADBUSTERS: A Magazine of Media and Environmental Strategies
The Media Foundation
1243 W. Seventh Avenue
Vancouver, British Columbia
Canada V6H 1B7
Tel: 604/736-9401
Fax: 604/737-6021

THE ADVOCACY INSTITUTE
1730 Rhode Island Ave., NW, Suite 600
Washington, DC 20036-3118
Tel: 202/659-8475

ADVOCATES FOR YOUTH'S MEDIA PROJECT
3733 Motor Ave., Suite 204
Los Angeles, CA 90034
Tel: 310/559-5700
Fax: 310/599-5784

ALLIANCE FOR COMMUNITY MEDIA
666 11th Street, NW, Suite 806
Washington, DC 20001-4542
Tel: 202/393-2650
Fax: 202/393-2653
E-mail: acm@alliancecm.org

ALLIANCE FOR CULTURAL DEMOCRACY
P.O. Box 192244
San Francisco, CA 94119
Tel: 415/437-2721 or 212/533-3032
Fax: 718/488-8296
E-mail: CDemocracy@aol.com
http://www.f8.com/ACD/

ALTERNATIVE PRESS CENTER
P.O. Box 33109
Baltimore, MD 21218-0401
Tel: 410/243-2471
Fax: 410/235-5325
E-mail: altpress@igc.apc.org
http://www.igc.apc.org/altpress/

AMERICAN CIVIL LIBERTIES UNION
132 W. 43rd Street
New York, NY 10036
Tel: 212/944-9800
Fax: 212/944-9065
E-mail: aclu@aclu.org
http://www.aclu.org/

THE AMERICAN EDITOR
ASNE
11690 B Sunrise Valley Drive
Reston, VA 20191
Tel: 703/453-1122
Fax: 703/453-1133
E-mail: asne@asne.com
http://www.asne.org/

AMERICAN LIBRARY ASSOCIATION OFFICE FOR INTELLECTUAL FREEDOM
50 E. Huron Street
Chicago, IL 60611
Tel: 312/280-4223 or 800/545-2433
Fax: 312/280-4227

AMERICAN SOCIETY OF
JOURNALISTS AND AUTHORS
1501 Broadway, Suite 302
New York, NY 10036
Tel: 212/997-0947
Fax: 212/768-7414
E-mail: 75227.1650@compuserve.com
http://www.asja.org/

ANTI-CENSORSHIP AND
DECEPTION UNION
Porter Square, P.O. Box 297
Cambridge, MA 02140
Tel: 617/499-7965

ARTICLE 19: INTERNATIONAL
CENTRE AGAINST
CENSORSHIP
33 Islington High Street
London N1 9LH
U.K.
Tel: 011-44-171-278-9292
Fax: 011-44-171-713-1356

ASIAN AMERICAN JOURNALISTS
ASSOCIATION
1765 Sutter Street, Suite 1000
San Francisco, CA 94115
Tel: 415/346-2051
Fax: 415/931-4671
E-mail: aaja1@aol.com

THE ASPEN INSTITUTE
Communications and Society Program
1333 New Hampshire Avenue, NW
Suite 1070
Washington, DC 20036
Tel: 202/736-5818
Fax: 202/467-0790

ASSOCIATION FOR EDUCATION IN
JOURNALISM AND MASS COMMU-
NICATION
1621 College Street, University of
South Carolina
Columbia, SC 29208
Tel: 803/777-2005

ASSOCIATION FOR PROGRESSIVE
COMMUNICATIONS
Institute for Global Communications
Presidio 1012, 1st Floor, Torney Ave.
P.O. Box 29904
San Francisco, CA 94129-0904
Tel: 415/561-6100
Fax: 415/561-6101
E-mail: apcadmin@apc.org

ASSOCIATION OF ALTERNATIVE
NEWSWEEKLIES (AAN)
1001 Connecticut Ave., NW, Suite 822
Washington, DC 20036-4104
Tel: 202/822-1955
Fax: 202/822-0929
http://aan.org

ASSOCIATION OF AMERICAN
PUBLISHERS
71 Fifth Avenue
New York, NY 10003
Tel: 212/255-0200
Fax: 212/255-7007

ASSOCIATION OF HOUSE
DEMOCRATIC PRESS ASSISTANTS
House of Representatives
2459 Rayburn Bldg.
Washington, DC 20515
Tel: 202/224-9154
Fax: 202/225-4951

BLACK AWARENESS IN
TELEVISION
13217 Livernois
Detroit, MI 48238-3162
Tel: 313/931-3427

BLACK PRESS INSTITUTE
2711 E. 75th Place
Chicago, IL 60649
Tel: 312/375-8200
Fax: 312/375-8262

BLACK WOMEN IN PUBLISHING
P.O. Box 6275, FDR Station
New York, NY 10150
Tel: 212/772-5951

CALIFORNIA FIRST AMENDMENT
COALITION
926 J Street, Suite 1406
Sacramento, CA 95814-2708
Tel: 916/447-2322
Fax: 916/447-2328

CALIFORNIANS AGAINST
CENSORSHIP TOGETHER
(ACT)
1800 Market Street, Suite 1000
San Francisco, CA 94103
Tel: 510/548-3695

THE CENTER FOR DEMOCRACY
AND TECHNOLOGY
1001 G Street, NW, 500 East
Washington, DC 20001
Tel: 202/637-9800
Fax: 202/637-0968
E-mail: info@cdt.org
http://www.cdt.org/

CENTER FOR INVESTIGATIVE
REPORTING
500 Howard Street, Suite 206
San Francisco, CA 94105-3000
Tel: 415/543-1200
Fax: 415/543-8311
E-mail: CIR@igc.org

CENTER FOR MEDIA AND PUBLIC
AFFAIRS
2100 L Street, NW, Suite 300
Washington, DC 20037-1526
Tel: 202/223-2942
Fax: 202/872-4014

CENTER FOR MEDIA EDUCATION
1511 K Street, NW, Suite 518
Washington, DC 20005
Tel: 202/628-2620
Fax: 202/628-2554

CENTER FOR MEDIA LITERACY
1962 South Shenandoah Street
Los Angeles, CA 90034
Tel: 310/559-2944
Fax: 310/559-9396

CENTER FOR THIRD WORLD
ORGANIZING
1218 East 21st Street
Oakland, CA 94606-9950
Tel: 510/533-7583

CENTER FOR WAR, PEACE AND
THE NEWS MEDIA
New York University
10 Washington Place, 4th Fl.
New York, NY 10003
Tel: 212/998-7960
Fax: 212/995-4143
E-mail: manoff@is2.nyu.edu

CHRISTIC INSTITUTE
5276 Hollister Avenue
Santa Barbara, CA 93111
Tel: 805/967-8232
Fax: 805/967-5060

CITIZENS FOR MEDIA LITERACY
34 Wall Street, Suite 407
Asheville, NC 28801
Tel: 704/255-0182
Fax: 704/254-2286
E-mail: cml@unca.edu

CIVIL LIBERTIES
American Civil Liberties Union
132 W. 43rd Street
New York, NY 10036
Tel: 212/944-9800
Fax: 212/869-9065

COALITION VS. PBS CENSORSHIP
3000 W. Olympic Blvd.
Santa Monica, CA 90404-5073
Tel: 310/315-4779
Fax: 310/315-4773
E-mail: 72607,2610@compuserve.com

COLUMBIA JOURNALISM REVIEW
Columbia University
700 Journalism Building
New York, NY 10027
Tel: 212/854-1881
Fax: 212/854-8580

COMMITTEE ON INTERNATIONAL
FREEDOM TO PUBLISH
c/o Association of American Publishers
71 5th Avenue
New York, NY 10003
Tel: 212/255-0200
Fax: 212/255-7007

COMMITTEE TO PROTECT
JOURNALISTS
330 Seventh Avenue, 12th Fl.
New York, NY 10001
Tel: 212/465-1004
Fax: 212/465-9568
E-mail: info@cpj.org
http://www.cpj.org/

COMMUNICATIONS CONSORTIUM
AND MEDIA CENTER
1333 H Street, NW, Suite 700
Washington, DC 20005
Tel: 202/682-1270
Fax: 202/682-2154

COMMUNICATION WORKS
2017 Mission Street, #303
San Francisco, CA 94110
Tel: 415/255-1946
Fax: 415/255-1947
E-mail: works@igc.org

COMMUNITY MEDIA WORKSHOP
c/o Columbia College
600 S. Michigan Avenue
Chicago, IL 60605-1996
Tel: 312/663-1600, ext. 5498
Fax: 312/663-3227
E-mail: commnews@mcs.net
http://www.mcs.net/~commnews/

CONSUMER PROJECT ON
TECHNOLOGY
P.O. Box 19367
Washington, DC 20036
Tel: 202/387-8030
Fax: 202/234-5176
E-mail: love@tap.org
http://www.essential.org/cpt/

CONTEXT INSTITUTE
P.O. Box 946
Langley, WA 98260
Tel: 360/221-6044
Fax: 360/221-6045
http://www.context.org/

CULTURAL ENVIRONMENT
MOVEMENT
University City Science Center
3508 Market Street, One East
Philadelphia, PA 19104
Tel: 215/387-8034
Fax: same as above
E-mail: cem@libertynet.org
http://ccwf.cc.utexas.edu/~cmbg/
cem.html

CULTURE WATCH
Data Center
464 19th Street
Oakland, CA 94612
Tel: 510/835-4692
Fax: 510/835-3017
E-mail: datactr@tmn.com
http://www.igc.org/culturewatch/

DATA CENTER
Right-to-know Project
464 19th Street
Oakland, CA 94612
Tel: 510/835-4692
Fax: 510/835-3017
E-mail: datacenter@datacenter.org
http://www.igc.org/datacenter/

EDITOR AND PUBLISHER
11 West 19th Street
New York, NY 10011
Tel: 212/675-4380
Fax: 212/691-7287

ELECTRONIC FRONTIER
FOUNDATION
1550 Bryant Street, Suite 725
San Francisco, CA 94103
Tel: 415/436-9333
Fax: 415/436-9993
E-mail: eff@eff.org
http://www.eff.org/

ENVIRONMENTAL RESEARCH
FOUNDATION
P.O. Box 5036
Annapolis, MD 21403-7036
Tel: 410/263-1584
Fax: 410/263-8944

ESSENTIAL INFORMATION
P.O. Box 19405
Washington, DC 20036
Tel: 202/387-8030
Fax: 202/234-5176

FAIRNESS AND ACCURACY IN
REPORTING
(FAIR)
130 W. 25th Street
New York, NY 10001
Tel: 212/633-6700
Fax: 212/727-7668
E-mail: info@fair.org
http://www.fair.org./fair/

FEMINISTS FOR FREE
EXPRESSION
2525 Times Square Station
New York, NY 10108
Tel: 212/702-6292
Fax: 212/702-6277
E-mail: freedom@well.com
http://www.well.com/user/freedom/

FIRST AMENDMENT CONGRESS
2200 S. Josephine Street
Denver, CO 80208
Tel: 303/871-3430
Fax: 303/871-4514

FOUNDATION FOR AMERICAN
COMMUNICATIONS
3800 Barham Blvd, Suite 409
Los Angeles, CA 90068
Tel: 213/851-7372
Fax: 213/851-9186

FREE PRESS ASSOCIATION
P.O. Box 63
Port Hadlock, WA 98339
Tel: 360/385-5097
Fax: 360/385-3704

FREE RADIO BERKELEY/ FREE
COMMUNICATIONS COALITION
1442-A Walnut Street, #406
Berkeley, CA 94709
Tel: 510/464-3041
E-mail: frbspd@crl.com

FREE THINKER FORUM
Project Freedom
P.O. Box 14447
St. Louis, MO 63178
Tel: 618/637-2202
E-mail: profreedom@aol.com

FREEDOM FORUM
First Amendment Center
1207 18th Avenue South
Nashville, TN 37212
Tel: 615/321-9588

FREEDOM FORUM
1101 Wilson Blvd.
Arlington, VA 22209
Tel: 703/528-0800

FREEDOM OF EXPRESSION
FOUNDATION
5220 S. Marina Pacifica
Long Beach, CA 90803
Tel: 310/985-4301
Fax: 310/985-2369

FREEDOM OF INFORMATION
CENTER
University of Missouri at Columbia
127 Neff Annex
Columbia, MO 65211
Tel: 573/882-4856
Fax: 573/884-4856
E-mail: jourke@muccmail.missouri.edu
http://www.missouri.edu/foiwww/

FREEDOM OF INFORMATION
CLEARINGHOUSE
P.O. Box 19367
Washington, DC 20036
Tel: 202/588-7790

FREEDOM WRITER
Institute for First Amendment Studies
P.O. Box 589
Great Barrington, MA 01230
Tel: 413/274-3786

FUND FOR INVESTIGATIVE
JOURNALISM
5120 Kenwood Drive
Annandale, VA 22003
Tel: 202/462-1844 or 703/750-3849

FUND FOR OBJECTIVE NEWS
REPORTING
422 1st Street, SE
Washington, DC 20003
Tel: 202/546-0856

GENDER & MASS MEDIA
Stockholm University-JMK
P.O. Box 27861
Stockholm 11593
Sweden

THE GIRAFFE PROJECT
P.O. Box 759
Langley, WA 98260
Tel: 206/221-7989

GLAAD
Gay & Lesbian Alliance Against
Defamation
150 W. 26th Street, Suite 503
New York, NY 10001
Tel: 212/807-1700
Fax: 212/807-1806
E-mail: glaad@glaad.org
http://www.glaad.org/

GLAAD MEDIA WATCH
San Francisco Bay Area
1360 Mission Street, Suite 200
San Francisco, CA 94103
Tel: 415/861-2244
Fax: 415/861-4893
E-mail: glaad.sfba@aol.com

GLOBAL INFORMATION NETWORK
777 United Nations Plaza
New York, NY 10017
Tel: 212/286-0123
Fax: 212/818-9249
E-mail: ipsgin@igc.apc.org

GOVERNMENT ACCOUNTABILITY
PROJECT
810 First Street, NE, Suite 630
Washington, DC 20002-3633
Tel: 202/408-0034
Fax: 202/408-9855
http://www.halcyon.com/tomgap/

THE GUSTAVUS MYERS CENTER
FOR THE STUDY OF HUMAN
RIGHTS IN NORTH AMERICA
2582 Jimmie
Fayetteville, AR 72703-3420
Tel: 501/442-4600 or 501/575-4301
E-mail: jbennet@comp.uark.edu

HEAL
Hanford Education Action League
1720 North Ash Street
Spokane, WA 99205
Tel: 509/326-3370

HISPANIC EDUCATION AND
MEDIA GROUP, INC.
P.O. Box 221
Sausalito, CA 94966
Tel: 415/331-8560
Fax: 415/331-2636

THE HUCK BOYD NATIONAL
CENTER FOR COMMUNITY MEDIA
Kansas State University
105 Kedzie Hall, School of Journalism
Manhattan, KS 66506-1501
Tel: 913/532-6890
Fax: 913/532-7309

HUMAN RIGHTS WATCH
485 Fifth Avenue
New York, NY 10017
Tel: 212/972-8400
Fax: 212/972-0905
E-mail: hrwnyc@hrw.org
http://www.hrw.org/

INFACT
256 Hanover Street
Boston, MA 02113
Tel: 617/742-4583
Fax: 617/367-0191
E-mail: infact@igc.apc.org
http://www.boutell.com/infact/

INSTITUTE FOR ALTERNATIVE
JOURNALISM
77 Federal Street
San Francisco, CA 94107
Tel: 415/284-1420
Fax: 415/284-1414
E-mail: alternet@alternet.org
http://www.alternet.org/an/

INSTITUTE FOR FIRST
AMENDMENT STUDIES
P.O. Box 589
Great Barrington, MA 01230
Tel: 413/528-3800
E-mail: ifas@crocker.com

INSTITUTE FOR MEDIA ANALYSIS
145 W. 4th Street
New York, NY 10012
Tel: 212/254-1061
Fax: 212/254-9598

INTER AMERICAN PRESS
ASSOCIATION
2911 N.W. 39th Street
Miami, FL 33142
Tel: 305/634-2465
Fax: 305/635-2272

INTERNATIONAL FEDERATION OF
NEWSPAPER PUBLISHERS
25, rue d'Astorg
Paris F-75008
France
Tel: 1 47428500

INTERNATIONAL FEDERATION OF
PERIODICAL PRESS (FIPP)
Queen's House, 55/56 Lincoln's Inn
Fields
London WC2A 3LJ U.K.
Tel: 011-44-171-404-4169
Fax: 011-44-171-404-4170
E-mail: fipp.nemo@nemo.geis.com

INTERNATIONAL FEDERATION
OF SOCIALIST AND
DEMOCRATIC PRESS
Casella Postale 737
Milan I-20101
Italy
Tel: 2 6690555
Fax: 2 6706139

INVESTIGATIVE JOURNALISM
PROJECT
Fund for Constitutional Government
122 Maryland Avenue, NE, Suite 300
Washington, DC 20002
Tel: 202/546-3732
Fax: 202/543-3156

INVESTIGATIVE REPORTERS &
EDITORS
Missouri School of Journalism
138 Neff Annex
Columbia, MO 65211
Tel: 573/882-2042
Fax: 573/882-5431
E-mail:
jourire@muccmail.missouri.edu
http://www.ire.org/

THE INVESTIGATIVE REPORTING
FUND
2 Wall Street, #3203
Asheville, NC 28801-2710
Tel: 704/259-9179
Fax: 704/251-1311

JOURNALISM QUARTERLY
George Washington University
Journalism Program
Washington, DC 20052
Tel: 202/994-6226

JUST THINK FOUNDATION
221 Caledonia Street
Sausalito, CA 94965
Tel: 415/289-0122
Fax: 415/289-0123
E-mail: think@justthink.org

LEONARD PELTIER DEFENSE
COMMITTEE
P.O. Box 583
Lawrence, KS 66044
Tel: 913/842-5774
Fax: 913/842-5796
E-mail: lpdc@idir.net
http://www.unicom.net/Peltier/
index.html

LEONARD PELTIER FREEDOM
CAMPAIGN
c/o International Action Center
39 West 14th Street, Room 206
New York, NY 10011
Tel: 212/633-6646
Fax: 212/633-2889

MEDIA ACCESS PROJECT
2000 M Street, NW, Suite 400
Washington, DC 20036
Tel: 202/232-4300
Fax: 202/223-5302

MEDIA ACTION RESEARCH
CENTER
475 Riverside Drive, #1948
New York, NY 10115
Tel: 212/870-3802
Fax: 212/870-2171

MEDIA ALLIANCE
814 Mission Street, Suite 205
San Francisco, CA 94103
Tel: 415/546-MEDIA
Fax: 415/546-6218

MEDIA COALITION/AMERICANS
FOR CONSTITUTIONAL FREEDOM
139 Fulton Street, Suite 302
New York, NY 10038
Tel: 212/587-4026
Fax: 212/587-2436
E-mail: 73770.3472@compuserve.com

THE MEDIA EDUCATION
FOUNDATION
26 Center Street
Northampton, MA 01060
Tel: 800/897-0089 or 413/584-8500
Fax: 800/659-6882 or 413/586-8398
E-mail: mediated@igc.apc.org
http://www.igc.apc.org/mef/

THE MEDIA INSTITUTE
1000 Potomac Street, NW, Suite 301
Washington, DC 20007
Tel: 202/298-7512
Fax: 202/337-7092
E-mail: tmi@clark.net

MEDIA REPORT TO WOMEN
10606 Mantz Road
Silver Spring, MD 20903-1247
Tel: 301/445-3231
E-mail: sheilagib@aol.com

MEDIA WATCH
P.O. Box 618
Santa Cruz, CA 95061-0618
Tel: 408/423-6355
Fax: 408/423-6355
E-mail: mwatch@cruzio.com

MEIKLEJOHN CIVIL LIBERTIES
INSTITUTE
P.O. Box 673
Berkeley, CA 94701
Tel: 510/848-0599
Fax: 510/848-6008

MSRRT NEWSLETTER
"Library Alternatives"
Chris Dodge/Jan DeSirey
4645 Columbus Ave. S.
Minneapolis, MN 55407
Tel: 612/541-8572
E-mail: cdodge@sun.hennepin.lib.mn.us
http://www.cs.unca.edu/~davidson/
msrrt/

NATIONAL ASSOCIATION OF
BLACK JOURNALISTS
11600 Sunrise Valley Drive
Reston, VA 22091
Tel: 703/648-1270
Fax: 703/476-6245

NATIONAL ASSOCIATION OF HIS-
PANIC
JOURNALISTS
National Press Building, Suite 1193
Washington, DC 20045
Tel: 202/662-7145
Fax: 202/662-7144

NATIONAL ASSOCIATION OF
INDEPENDENT PUBLISHERS
c/o Ralph Woodward
111 E. 14th Street, Suite 157
New York, NY 10003

NATIONAL ASSOCIATION OF
MINORITY MEDIA EXECUTIVES
P.O. Box 9806
Arlington, VA 22219
Tel: 703/556-4119
Fax: same as above
http://www.namme.com/

NATIONAL ASSOCIATION OF
RADIO TALK SHOW HOSTS
134 Saint Botolph Street
Boston, MA 02115-4819
Tel: 617/437-9757
Fax: 617/437-0797

NATIONAL BLACK MEDIA
COALITION
38 New York Avenue, NE
Washington, DC 20002
Tel: 202/387-8155
Fax: 202/462-4469

NATIONAL CAMPAIGN FOR
FREEDOM OF EXPRESSION
1402 3rd Avenue, #421
Seattle, WA 98101
Tel: 206/340-9301
Fax: 206/340-4303
E-mail: ncfe@nwlink.com
http://www.artswire.org/~ncfe/

NATIONAL COALITION AGAINST
CENSORSHIP
275 7th Avenue, 20th Fl.
New York, NY 10001
Tel: 212/807-6222
Fax: 212/807-6245
E-mail: ncac@netcom.com
http://ncac.org/

NATIONAL COMMITTEE AGAINST
REPRESSIVE LEGISLATION
3321 12th Street, NE
Washington, DC 20017
Tel: 202/529-4225
Fax: 202/526-4611
E-mail: kgage@igc.apc.org

NATIONAL CONFERENCE OF
EDITORIAL WRITERS
6223 Executive Boulevard
Rockville, MD 20852
Tel: 301/984-3015

NATIONAL EDUCATIONAL MEDIA
NETWORK
655 13th Street, Suite 1
Oakland, CA 94612
Tel: 510/465-6885
Fax: 510/465-2835
E-mail: NEMN@aol.com

NATIONAL INSTITUTE FOR
COMPUTER ASSISTED
REPORTING, IRE
Missouri School of Journalism
138 Neff Annex
Columbia, MO 65211
Tel: 573/882-2042
Fax: 573/882-5431
E-mail:
jourire@muccmail.missouri.edu
http://www.nicar.org/

NATIONAL LESBIAN & GAY
JOURNALISTS ASSOCIATION
1718 M Street, NW, #245
Washington, DC 20036
Tel: 202/588-9888
Fax: 202/588-1818
E-mail: nlgja@aol.com

NATIONAL NEWSPAPER
ASSOCIATION
525 Wilson Blvd., Suite 550
Arlington, VA 22209
Tel: 703/907-7900
Fax: 703/907-7901

NATIONAL TELEMEDIA COUNCIL
120 East Wilson Street
Madison, WI 53703
Tel: 608/257-7712
Fax: 608/257-7714
E-mail: ntelemedia@aol.com
http://danenet.wicip.org./ntc/

NATIONAL WRITERS UNION
113 University Place
New York, NY 10003
Tel: 212/254-0279

THE NEW CITIZEN
Citizens for Media Literacy
34 Wall Street, #407
Asheville, NC 28801
Tel: 704/255-0182
Fax: 704/254-2286
E-mail: cml@unca.edu

NEWSPAPER ASSOCIATION OF
AMERICA
11600 Sunrise Valley Drive
Reston, VA 22091
Tel: 703/648-1000
Fax: 703/620-4557

THE NEWSPAPER GUILD
8611 Second Avenue
Silver Spring, MD 20910
Tel: 301/585-2990
Fax: 301/585-0668
E-mail: http://www.newsguild.org/

NEWSPAPER RESEARCH JOURNAL
Scripps Hall School of Journalism
Ohio University
Athens, OH 45701
Tel: 614/593-2590
Fax: 614/593-2592

NEWSPRINTS
Essential Information
P.O. Box 19405
Washington, DC 20036
Tel: 202/387-8030
Fax: 202/234-5176
E-mail: newsprints@essential.org
http://www.essential.org/

NEWSWORTHY
Minnesota News Council
12 S. 6th Street, Suite 1122
Minneapolis, MN 55402-1515
Tel: 612/341-9357

OMB WATCH
1742 Connecticut Avenue, NW
Washington, DC 20009-1171
Tel: 202/234-8494
Fax: 202/234-8584

ORGANIZATION OF NEWS
OMBUDSMEN
c/o Art Nauman, Sacramento Bee
P.O. Box 15779
Sacramento, CA 95852
Tel: 916/442-8050
http://www.infi.net/ono/

PEOPLE FOR THE AMERICAN WAY
2000 M Street, NW, Suite 400
Washington, DC 20036
Tel: 202/467-4999
Fax: 202/293-2672

POLITICAL RESEARCH
ASSOCIATES
120 Beacon Street, Suite 202
Somerville, MA 02143-4304
Tel: 617/661-9313
Fax: 617/661-0059
E-mail: publiceye@igc.apc.org
http://www.publiceye.org/pra/

PR WATCH
Center for Media and Democracy, Inc.
3318 Gregory Street
Madison, WI 53711
Tel: 608/233-3346
Fax: 608/238-2236
E-mail: 74250.735@compuserve.com
http://users.aol.com/srampton/
center.html

PROGRESSIVE MEDIA PROJECT
409 East Main Street
Madison, WI 53703
Tel: 608/257-4626
Fax: 608/257-3373
E-mail: pmproj@itis.com

PROJECT CENSORED
Sociology Department,
Sonoma State University
1801 E. Cotati Avenue
Rohnert Park, CA 94928-3609
Tel: 707/664-2500
Fax: 707/664-2108
E-mail: project.censored@sonoma.edu
http://censored.sonoma.edu/
ProjectCensored/

PROJECT CENSORED CANADA
School of Communication
Simon Fraser University
8888 University Drive
Burnaby BC V5A 1S6
Canada
Tel: 604/291-4905
Fax: 604/291-4024
E-mail: censored@sfu.ca
http://cc6140mac.comm.sfu.ca/
index.html

PROJECT ON GOVERNMENT
OVERSIGHT
2025 Eye Street, NW, Suite 1117
Washington, DC 20006-1903
Tel: 202/466-5539
Fax: 202/466-5596
E-mail: pogo@mnsinc.com
or pogodef@mnsinc.com
http://www.mnsinc.com/pogo/

PUBLIC MEDIA CENTER
446 Green Street
San Francisco, CA 94133
Tel: 415/434-1403
Fax: 415/986-6779

QUILL
Society of Professional Journalists
16 S. Jackson Street, P.O. Box 77
Greencastle, IN 46135-0077
Tel: 317/653-3333
Fax: 317/653-4631
E-mail: spj@internetmci.com

REPORTER'S COMMITTEE FOR
FREEDOM OF THE PRESS
1101 Wilson Blvd., Suite 1910
Arlington, VA 22209
Tel: 703/807-2100
Fax: 703/807-2109

ROCKY MOUNTAIN MEDIA WATCH
P.O. Box 18858
Denver, CO 80218
Tel: 303/832-7558
Fax: same as above

SMALL PUBLISHERS ASSOCIATION
OF NORTH AMERICA
P.O. Box 1306
Buena Vista, CO 81211-1306
Tel: 719/395-4790
Fax: 719/395-8374
E-mail: span@span-assn.org

SOCIETY OF ENVIRONMENTAL
JOURNALISTS
P.O. Box 27280
Philadelphia, PA 19118-0280
Tel: 215/836-9970
Fax: 215/836-9972
E-mail: SEJoffice@aol.com
http://www.sej.org

SOUTHWEST ALTERNATE MEDIA
PROJECT
1519 West Main Street
Houston, TX 77006
Tel: 713/522-8592
Fax: 713/522-0953

STRATEGIES FOR MEDIA
LITERACY
1095 Market Street, Suite 617
San Francisco, CA 94103
Tel: 415/621-2911
Fax: 415/255-9392

STUDENT PRESS LAW CENTER
1101 Wilson Blvd., Suite 1910
Arlington, VA 22901
Tel: 703/807-1904
Fax: 703/807-2109
E-mail: splc@splc.org
http://www.splc.org/

THE THOMAS JEFFERSON CENTER
FOR THE PROTECTION OF FREE
EXPRESSION
400 Peter Jefferson Place
Charlottesville, VA 22901-8691
Tel: 804/295-4784
Fax: 804/296-3621

TIMES MIRROR CENTER FOR THE
PEOPLE & THE PRESS
1875 Eye Street, NW, Suite 1110
Washington, DC 20006
Tel: 202/293-3126

TREATMENT REVIEW
AIDS Treatment Data Network
611 Broadway, Suite 613
New York, NY 10012-2809
Tel: 800/734-7104
Fax: 212/260-8869
E-mail: atdn@aidnyc.org
http://www.aidsnyc.org/network/

TYNDALL REPORT
135 Rivington Street
New York, NY 10002
Tel: 212/674-8913
Fax: 212/979-7304

UNDERGROUND PRESS
CONFERENCE
Mary Kuntz Press
P.O. Box 476617
Chicago, IL 60647
Tel: 312/486-0685
Fax: 312/226-1168

WOMEN IN COMMUNICATIONS
10605 Judicial Drive, Suite A-4
Fairfax, VA 22030
Tel: 703/359-9000
Fax: 703/359-0603

WOMEN'S INSTITUTE FOR
FREEDOM OF THE PRESS
3306 Ross Place, NW
Washington, DC 20008-3332
Tel: 202/966-7783
Fax: same as above
E-mail: wifponline@igc.apc.org
http://www.igc.org/wifp/

WORLD PRESS FREEDOM
COMMITTEE
c/o The Newspaper Center
11600 Sunrise Valley Drive
Reston, VA 22091
Tel: 703/648-1000
Fax: 703/620-4557

LIBRARY & REFERENCE
SOURCES

ABC NEWS TRANSCRIPTS
Capital Cities / ABC, Inc.
77 W. 66th Street
New York, NY 10023
Tel: 800/ALL-NEWS

THE ACTIVIST'S ALMANAC:
The Concerned Citizen's Guide to
the Leading Advocacy Organizations
in America
By David Walls, 1993
Simon & Schuster Fireside Books
New York

ALTERNATIVE PRESS INDEX
Alternative Press Center, Inc.
P.O. Box 33109
Baltimore, MD 21218
Tel: 410/243-2471
Fax: 410/235-5325

AP DATASTREAM
The Associated Press (AP)
50 Rockefeller Plaza
New York, NY 10020
Tel: 212/621-1585

BBC SUMMARY OF WORLD
BROADCASTS
British Broadcasting Corporation, BBC
Monitoring
Caversham Park
Reading RG4 8TZ
U.K.
Tel: 011-44-0734-472742
Fax: 011-44-0734-461105

THE CAPITAL SOURCE
National Journal, Inc.
1501 M Street, NW, Suite 300
Washington, DC 20005
Tel: 202/739-8400
Fax: 202/833-8069

CENTER FOR DEFENSE
INFORMATION
Library for Press and Public
1500 Massachusetts Avenue, NW
Washington, DC 20005
Tel: 202/862-0700
Fax: 202/862-0708
E-mail: cdi@igc.apc.org

CNN NEWS TRANSCRIPTS
Cable News Network (CNN)
One CNN Center
Atlanta, GA 30303-2705
Tel: 404/827-2491

DIRECTORY OF ELECTRONIC
JOURNALS,NEWSLETTERS AND
ACADEMIC DISCUSSION LISTS
by Kovacs and Strangelove
Association of Scientific and
Academic Publishing
1527 New Hampshire Avenue, NW
Washington, DC 20036

ECOLINKING: EVERYONE'S GUIDE
TO ONLINE ENVIRONMENTAL
INFORMATION
by Don Rittner, 1992
Peachpit Press
2414 6th Street
Berkeley, CA 94710

ENCYCLOPEDIA OF
ASSOCIATIONS
1995 ed., 4 vols.
Gale Research, Inc., Detroit and
London

ERIC
Clearinghouse on Information &
Technology
Syracuse University
Schools of Information
Studies/Education
4-194 CST
Syracuse, NY 13244-4100
Tel: 315/443-3640

ETHNIC NEWSWATCH
SoftLine Information, Inv.
65 Broad Street
Stamford, CT 06901
Tel: 203/975-8292
or 800/524-7922
Fax: 203/975-8347

THE FEDERAL INTERNET SOURCE
Published by National Journal, Inc.
and The Internet Letter
1501 M Street, NW
Washington, DC 20036
Tel: 800/424-2921
E-mail: njcirc@clark.net

FORBES MEDIA GUIDE
1400 Route 206 N., P.O. Box 89
Bedminster, NJ 07921
Tel: 908/781-2078
Fax: 908/781-6635

FROM RADICAL
TO EXTREME RIGHT
A bibliography of current periodicals
of protest, controversy, advocacy,
or dissent
by Gail Skidmore and Theodore Jurgen
Spahn, 1987, 3rd ed.
Scarecrow Press, Inc.
Metuchen, NJ, and London

GALE DIRECTORY OF
PUBLICATIONS & BROADCAST
MEDIA
1995 ed., 3 vols., plus supplement
Gale Research, Inc., Detroit and London

HOW TO ACCESS THE FEDERAL
GOVERNMENT ON THE INTERNET,
1995:
WASHINGTON ONLINE
by Bruce Maxwell
Congressional Quarterly, Inc.

THE INTERNATIONAL DIRECTORY
OF LITTLE MAGAZINES OF
SMALL PRESSES
Len Fulton, ed., 30th ed., 1994/95
Dustbooks
P.O. Box 100
Paradise, CA 95967

INTER PRESS SERVICE
INTERNATIONAL DATABASE,
Global Information Network, Ltd.
777 United Nations Plaza, Concourse
Level
New York, NY 10017
Tel: 212/286-0123
Fax: 212/818-9249
E-mail: ipsny@igc.apc.org

INTERNATIONAL HERALD-TRIBUNE
181 Ave., Charles de Gaulle
Neuilly, F-92200
France
Fax: 46 372133

LEXIS/NEXIS GUIDE LIBRARY
Mead Data Central, Inc.
9443 Springboro Pike, P.O. Box 933
Dayton, OH 45401-0933
Tel: 513/865-6800
or 800/227-4908
Fax: 513/865-6909

LIBRARIES FOR THE FUTURE
521 Fifth Avenue, Suite 1612
New York, NY 10175-1699
Tel: 1-800/542-1918
http://www.inch.com/~lff/lffhome.html

LIBRARY JOURNAL
249 W.17th Street
New York, NY 10011
Tel: 212/463-6819

MACROCOSM USA: POSSIBILITIES
FOR A NEW PROGRESSIVE ERA
Sandi Brockway, ed., 1993
Macrocosm USA, Inc.
P.O. Box 185
Cambria, CA 93428-8030
Tel: 805/927-8030
Fax: 805/927-1713
BBS (MacroNet): 805/927-1987

MEDIAWATCH
The Arbitron Company
142 W. 57th Street
New York, NY 10019
Tel: 212/887-1300

NATIONAL FORUM ON
INFORMATION LITERACY
c/o American Library Association
50 East Huron Street
Chicago, IL 60611

NET ACTIVISM: HOW CITIZENS
USE THE INTERNET
O'Reilly & Associates, 1996
101 Morris Street
Sebastopol, CA 95472
Tel: 707/829-0515
Fax: 707/829-0104
E-mail: info@ora.com
http://www.ora.com/

THE NEW YORK TIMES
New York Times On-Line Services
1719A Route 10
Parsippany, NJ 07054
Tel: 201/267-2268
Fax: 201/267-3464

NEWS/RETRIEVAL WORLD
REPORT
Dow Jones & Company, Inc.
P.O. Box 300
Princeton, NJ 08543-0300
Tel: 609/520-4000
Fax: 609/520-4660

NEWSLETTER DATABASE
Information Access Company (IAC)
362 Lakeside Drive
Foster City, CA 94404
Tel: 415/358-4643
or 800/321-6388
Fax: 415/358-4759

NEWSPAPER & PERIODICALS
ABSTRACTS
UMI
620 S. Third Street
Louisville, KY 40202-2475
Tel: 502/583-4111
or 800/626-2823
Fax: 502/589-5572

OCLC ONLINE COMPUTER
LIBRARY CENTER, INC. - OCLC
FIRSTSEARCH SERVICE
6565 Frantz Road
Dublin, OH 43017
Tel: 614/764-6000
or 800/848-5878
Fax: 614/764-6096
http://www.oclc.org

THE PEOPLE'S RIGHT TO KNOW:
MEDIA, DEMOCRACY AND THE
INFORMATION HIGHWAY
by Frederick Williams and John V.
Paulik, eds.
Lawrence Erlbaum Associates, 1994

PROGRESSIVE PERIODICALS
DIRECTORY
by Craig T. Canan
2nd ed., 1989
Progressive Education
P.O. Box 120574
Nashville, TN 37212

REUTERS NEWSLINE®
Reuters Ltd.
85 Fleet Street
London EC4P 4AJ
U.K.
Tel: 011-44- 071-250 1122
Fax: 011-44-071-696 8761

RIGHT-TO-KNOW NETWORK
(RTK NET)
OMB Watch
1742 Connecticut Avenue, NW
Washington, DC 20009-1171
Tel: 202/234-8494
Fax: 202/234-8584

ULRICH'S INTERNATIONAL
PERIODICALS DIRECTORY
34th ed., 1996, 5 vols.
R.R. Bowker, Reed Reference
Publishing
121 Chanlon Road
New Providence, NJ 07974
Tel: 800/521-8110
Fax: 908/665-2867

WESTLAW®
First Amendment Library
West Publishing Corporation
620 Opperman Drive
Eagan, MN 55123
Tel: 612/687-7000
or 800/328-9352
Fax: 612/687-7302

THE WORKING PRESS
OF THE NATION
1996 ed., Reed Reference Publishing
121 Chanlon Road
New Providence, NJ 07974
Tel: 800/521-8110
Fax: 908/665-2867

WORLDPAPER
World Times Incorporated
210 World Trade Center
Boston, MA 02210
Tel: 617/439-5400

NATIONAL BROADCAST AND CABLE MEDIA

20/20
ABC News
147 Columbus Avenue
New York, NY 10023
Tel: 212/456-2020
Fax: 212/456-2969

48 HOURS
CBS News
524 W. 57th Street
New York, NY 10019
Tel: 212/975-4848

60 MINUTES
CBS News
524 W. 57th Street
New York, NY 10019
Tel: 212/975-2006

ABC WORLD NEWS TONIGHT
47 W. 66th Street
New York, NY 10023
Tel: 212/456-4040

AMERICAN JOURNAL
CBS-TV
402 E. 76th Street
New York, NY 10021

ASSOCIATED PRESS RADIO
NETWORK
1825 K Street, NW, Suite 710
Washington, DC 20006
Tel: 202/736-9500
Fax: 202/736-1199

BILL MOYERS
Public Affairs Television
356 W. 58th Street
New York, NY 10019
Tel: 212/560-6960

C-SPAN
400 N. Capitol Street, NW, Suite 650
Washington, DC 20001
Tel: 202/737-3220
Fax: 202/737-3323

CBS EVENING NEWS
524 W. 57th Street
New York, NY 10019
Tel: 212/975-3693

CBS THIS MORNING
524 W. 57th Street
New York, NY 10019
Tel: 212/975-2824

CHRISTIAN BROADCASTING
NETWORK
700 CBN Center
Virginia Beach, VA 23463-0001
Tel: 804/523-7111

CNN
One CNN Center
Box 105366
Atlanta, GA 30348
Tel: 404/827-1500
http://www.cnn.com/

CNN
Washington Bureau
820 First Street, NE
Washington, DC 20002
Tel: 202/898-7900
http://www.cnn.com/

CONUS COMMUNICATIONS
3415 University Avenue
Minneapolis, MN 55414
Tel: 612/642-4646

CROSSFIRE
CNN
820 First Street, NE
Washington, DC 20002
Tel: 202/898-7951

DATELINE
NBC News
30 Rockefeller Plaza, Room 510
New York, NY 10112
Tel: 212/664-6170

DAY & DATE
CBS-TV
514 West 57th Street, 6th Fl.
New York, NY 10019
Tel: 800/884-1136

DAY ONE
ABC NEWS
147 Columbus Avenue, 8th Fl.
New York, NY 10023
Tel: 212/456-6100

ESPN
ESPN Plaza
Bristol, CT 06010
Tel: 203/585-2000

FACE THE NATION
CBS News
2020 M Street, NW
Washington, DC 20036
Tel: 202/457-4481

FOOD NOT BOMBS RADIO
NETWORK
3145 Geary Blvd., #12
San Francisco, CA 94118
Tel: 415/386-9209

FRONT PAGE
FOX-TV
5746 W. Sunset Blvd., #F-158
Los Angeles, CA 90028-8588

FRONTLINE
125 Western Avenue
Boston, MA 02134
Tel: 617/783-3500
Fax: 617/254-0243

THE GERALDO RIVERA SHOW
555 West 57th Street
New York, NY 10019
Tel: 212/265-8520

GOOD MORNING AMERICA
ABC News
147 Columbus Avenue
New York, NY 10019
Tel: 212/456-5900
Fax: 212/456-7290

HIGHTOWER RADIO
P.O. Box 13516
Austin, TX 78711
Tel: 512/477-5588
Fax: 512/478-8536
E-mail: hightower@essential.org
http://www.essential.org/hightower/

HOME BOX OFFICE
1100 Avenue of the Americas
New York, NY 10036
Tel: 212/512-1329

INSIGHT (Radio Program)
The Progressive
409 E. Main Street
Madison, WI
Tel: 608/257-4626
Fax: 608/257-3373
http://www.progressive.org/

INVESTIGATIVE REPORTS
Arts & Entertainment Network
235 E. 45th Street
New York, NY 10017
Tel: 212/661-4500

JULIANNE MALVEAUX SHOW
Pacifica Radio
702 H Street, NW
Washington, DC 20001
Tel: 202/783-3100
Fax: 202/462-6612
E-mail: jmnia@aol.com

LARRY KING LIVE TV
CNN
820 First Street, NE
Washington, DC 20002
Tel: 212/898-7900

MEET THE PRESS
NBC News
4001 Nebraska Avenue, NW
Washington, DC 20016
Tel: 202/885-4200
Fax: 202/362/2009

MORNING EDITION / ALL THINGS
CONSIDERED
National Public Radio
635 Massachusetts Avenue, NW
Washington, DC 20001-3753
Tel: 202/414-2000
Fax: 202/414-3329

MTV NEWS
1515 Broadway, 24th Fl.
New York, NY 10036
Tel: 212/258-8000

NATIONAL PUBLIC RADIO
635 Massachusetts Ave., NW
Washington, DC 20001-3753
Tel: 202/414-2000
Fax: 202/414-3329

NBC NIGHTLY NEWS
30 Rockefeller Plaza
New York, NY 10112
Tel: 212/664-4971

NEWSHOUR
New York Office, WNET-TV
356 W. 58th Street
New York, NY 10019
Tel: 212/560-3113
http://www.pbs.org/newshour/

NEWSHOUR
Washington Office
Arlington, VA 22206
Tel: 703/998-2870
http://www.pbs.org/newshour/

NIGHTLINE (New York)
ABC News
47 W. 66th Street
New York, NY 10023
Tel: 212/456-7777

NIGHTLINE (Washington DC)
ABC News
1717 DeSales Street, NW
Washington, DC 20036
Tel: 202/887-7360

NOW
NBC News
30 Rockefeller Plaza
New York, NY 10112
Tel: 212/664-7501

OUT ACROSS AMERICA
Network Q
884 Monroe Avenue
Atlanta, GA 30308
Tel: 800/368-0638
E-mail: networkQ@aol.com

PBS
1320 Braddock Place
Alexandria, VA 22314-1698
Tel: 703/739-5000
Fax: 703/739-5295
E-mail: PBS Comment Line:
800/272-2190
http://www.pbs.org/

PERSPECTIVES-ABC RADIO
125 West End Avenue
New York, NY 10023
Tel: 212/456-5554

POLITICALLY INCORRECT
c/o CBS-TV
7800 Beverly Blvd., Suite D
Los Angeles, CA 90036
Tel: 213/852-4524
E-mail: pi@cis.compuserve.com

PRI-PUBLIC RADIO
INTERNATIONAL
100 North Sixth Street, Suite 900 A
Minneapolis, MN 55403
Tel: 612/338-5000
Fax: 612/330-9222

PRIMETIME LIVE
ABC News
147 Columbus Avenue
New York, NY 10023
Tel: 212/456-1600

RADIO FREE EUROPE/
RADIO LIBERTY
1201 Connecticut Avenue, NW
Suite 1100
Washington, DC 20036
Tel: 202/457-6900
Fax: 202/457-6997

RELIABLE SOURCES
CNN
820 First Street, NE
Washington, DC 20002
Tel: 202/898-7900

RUSH LIMBAUGH
WABC Radio
2 Penn Plaza, 17th Fl.
New York, NY 10121
Tel: 212/613-3800 or 800/282-2882
Fax: 212/563-9166

SCRIPPS/HOWARD NEWS SERVICE
1090 Vermont Avenue, NW, Suite 1000
Washington, DC 20005
Tel: 202/408-1484

STATES NEWS SERVICE
1333 F Street, NW
Washington, DC 20004
Tel: 202/628-3100

STREET STORIES
CBS News
555 W. 57th Street
New York, NY 10019
Tel: 212/975-8282

TIME MAGAZINE
Time Warner, Inc.
Time & Life Building
Rockefeller Center
New York, NY 10020-1393
Tel: 212/522-1212

TODAY SHOW
NBC News
30 Rockefeller Plaza
New York, NY 10112
Tel: 212/664-4249

TURNER BROADCASTING SYSTEM
1 CNN Center
Atlanta, GA 30348-5366
Tel: 404/827-1792

TV NATION
E-mail: tvnatfans@aol.com

WE THE PEOPLE
Jerry Brown-Radio
200 Harrison Street
Oakland, CA 94607
Tel: 510/836-DARE or 800/426-1112

NATIONAL PUBLICATIONS & NEWS SERVICES

ASSOCIATED PRESS
National Desk
50 Rockefeller Plaza
New York, NY 10020
Tel: 212/621-1600

BRITISH MEDICAL JOURNAL
B.M.A. House
Tavistock Square
London WC1H 9JR
U.K.
Tel: 011-44-171-383-6123
Fax: 011-44-171-383-6403

CHICAGO TRIBUNE
435 N. Michigan Avenue
Chicago, IL 60611
Tel: 312/222-3232

CHIRISTIAN SCIENCE MONITOR
One Norway Street
Boston, MA 02115
Tel: 617/450-2000

COPLEY NEWS SERVICE
1100 National Press Building
Washington, DC 20045
Tel: 202/737-6960

COX ENTERPRISES, INC.
P.O. Box 105357
Atlanta, GA 30348
Tel: 404/843-5123

DOW JONES NEWS SERVICE
P.O. Box 300
Princeton, NJ 08543
Tel: 609/520-4638

FORTUNE
Time Warner, Inc.
Time & Life Building
Rockefeller Center
New York, NY 10020
Tel: 212/586-1212

HARPER'S MAGAZINE
666 Broadway
New York, NY 10012-2317
Tel: 212/614-6500
Fax: 212/228-5889

KNIGHT-RIDDER NEWS SERVICE
790 National Press Building
Washington, DC 20045
Tel: 202/383-6080

LOS ANGELES TIMES
Times-Mirror Square
Los Angeles, CA 90053
Tel: 800/528-4637

MCCLATCHY NEWS SERVICE
P.O. Box 15779
Sacramento, CA 95852
Tel: 916/321-1895

NATIONAL JOURNAL
1501 M Street, NW, Suite 300
Washington, DC 20005
Tel: 202/739-8400

NATIONAL NEWSPAPER
ASSOCIATION
1525 Wilson Boulevard, Suite 550
Arlington, VA 22209-2434
Tel: 703/907-7900
Fax: 703/907-7901

NEW YORK TIMES
229 W. 43rd Street
New York, NY 10036
Tel: 212/556-1234

NEW YORK TIMES
Washington Bureau
1627 Eye Street, NW, 7th Fl.
Washington, DC 20006
Tel: 202/862-0300
Fax: 202/862-0340

NEWSDAY
235 Pinelawn Road
Melville, NY 11747-4250
Tel: 516/843-2020

NEWSNET, INC.
945 Haverford Road
Bryn Mawr, PA 19010
Tel: 610/527-8030
Fax: 610/527-0338
E-mail: info@newsnet.com
http://www.newsnet.com/

NEWSWEEK
Newsweek, Inc.
251 West 57th Street
New York, NY 10019
Tel: 212/445-4000

PR NEWSWIRE
810 7th Avenue
New York, NY 10019
Tel: 800/832-5522
Fax: 212/596-1566
http://www.prnewswire.com/

REUTERS INFORMATION
SERVICES
1700 Broadway
New York, NY 10019
Tel: 212/603-3300
Fax: 212/603-3446

SAN FRANCISCO CHRONICLE
901 Mission Street
San Francisco, CA 94103
Tel: 415/777-1111
Fax: 415/512-8196

SAN FRANCISCO EXAMINER
110 Fifth Street
San Francisco, CA 94103
Tel: 415/777-2424
Fax: 415/512-1264

SUBURBAN NEWSPAPERS OF
AMERICA
401 North Michigan Avenue
Chicago, IL 60611
Tel: 312/644-6610

TRIBUNE MEDIA SERVICES
435 N. Michigan Avenue, Suite 1500
Chicago, IL 60611
Tel: 800/245-6536
Fax: 800/424-4747

U.S. NEWS & WORLD REPORT
2400 N Street, NW
Washington, DC 20037
Tel: 202/955-2000
Fax: 202/955-2049

UNITED PRESS INTERNATIONAL
1400 Eye Street, NW
Washington, DC 20005
Tel: 202/898-8000

USA TODAY
1000 Wilson Boulevard
Arlington, VA 22229
Tel: 703/276-3400

WALL STREET JOURNAL
200 Liberty Street
New York, NY 10281
Tel: 212/416-2000

WASHINGTON POST
1150 15th Street, NW
Washington, DC 20071
Tel: 202/334-6000

THE WASHINGTON TIMES
3600 New York Avenue, NE
Washington, DC 20002
Tel: 202/636-3008
Fax: 202/529-4074

APPENDIX C

The Project Censored Guide to On-line Resources

Compiled by Jeffrey A. Fillmore, Project Censored net.geek

The World Wide Web sites listed here highlight other media and journalism-related sites or groups whose emphases reflect the issues presented in past censored stories.

All of the following sites are conveniently linked at:

> THE PROJECT CENSORED WEB SITE
> http://censored.sonoma.edu/ProjectCensored/
> E-mail: censored@censored.sonoma.edu
> Project Censored net.geek: fillmore@sonoma.edu

For inclusion in next year's Guide to On-line Resources or to be linked from the Project Censored Web site, send E-mail to the Project Censored net.geek at: Censored@censored.sonoma.edu. Thanks.

MEDIA WATCH AND RESEARCH ORGANIZATIONS

ARMS SALES MONITORING PROJECT OF THE FEDERATION OF AMERICAN SCIENTISTS
http://www.fas.org/asmp/
E-mail: llumpe@fas.org

This site includes extensive information on U.S. conventional (non-nuclear, non-chemical) weapons exports and export policy. The project works for increased transparency, oversight, and restraint in the global weapons trade.

CENTER FOR RESPONSIVE POLITICS (FOLLOW THE MONEY)
http://www.crp.org
E-mail: info@crp.org

The Follow the Money Web site offers a broad view of the world of money in politics. The Center's site deciphers campaign finance data and helps users to understand the role that money plays in elections and in policy deliberations at both the legislative and executive levels of government.

DEATH PENALTY INFORMATION CENTER
http://www.essential.org/dpic
E-mail: dpic@essential.org

DPIC provides analysis and information on issues concerning capital punishment. Included are statistics, in-depth reports, and information regarding other resources to those working on this issue.

ELECTRONIC FRONTIER FOUNDATION
(See listing under 'Internet and Technology-Related Sites')

FAIR (FAIRNESS & ACCURACY IN REPORTING)
http://www.fair.org/fair
E-mail: fair@fair.org

FAIR (Fairness & Accuracy in Reporting) is the progressive national media watch group. It publishes the magazine *EXTRA!* and produces the syndicated radio program *CounterSpin*.

GLAAD (GAY & LESBIAN ALLIANCE AGAINST DEFAMATION)
URL: http://www.glaad.org
E-mail: glaad@glaad.org

The on-line resource for promoting fair, accurate, and inclusive representation as a means of challenging discrimination based on sexual orientation or identity.

LABOR PROJECT FOR WORKING FAMILIES
http://violet.berkeley.edu/~iir/
     workfam/home.html
E-mail: netsy@violet.berkeley.edu

Labor Project for Working Families Web site has information on unions and work/family issues. It includes excerpts from their quarterly newsletter, sample contract language, and special projects with unions on work/family issues.

MEDIA WATCHDOG
http://theory.lcs.mit.edu/~mernst/media/
E-mail: mernst@theory.lcs.mit.edu

Media Watchdog is a collection of on-line media watch resources, including specific media criticism articles and information about media watch groups. The emphasis is on critiquing the accuracy and exposing the biases of the mainstream media.

ALTERNATIVE AND INDEPENDENT MEDIA

ALLIANCE FOR CULTURAL DEMOCRACY (ACD)
http://www.f8.com/ACD/
E-mail: acdemocracy@f8.com

The Alliance for Cultural Democracy (ACD) is an international network of community artists and activists that has been in existence for 20 years. Its goal is to defend and develop cultural rights and community arts in neighborhoods and communities throughout the U.S. and the world. The Web site contains general information on the organization, our Draft for a Cultural Bill of Rights (which we are soliciting and inviting comment and feedback on), membership information, excerpts from its 'zine *Cultural Democracy*, and will eventually have specific information on member organizations and individuals.

THE BULLETIN OF THE ATOMIC SCIENTISTS ON-LINE
http://neog.com/atomic/
E-mail: bullatomsci@igc.apc.org

The Bulletin of the Atomic Scientists is not a technical publication—it's the world's premier magazine on nuclear weapons and international affairs. Their Web site features a "Nuclear FAQ," five years' worth of articles on topics like weapons, the former Soviet republics, military spending and the global arms trade, a history of our famous "Doomsday Clock," and much more.

COMMUNITY MEDIA WORKSHOP
(See listing under "Journalism-Related Sites and Resources")

GLOBALVISION/ *RIGHTS & WRONGS*: HUMAN RIGHTS TELEVISION
http://www.globalvision.org/globalvision/
E-mail: rights@globalvision.org

Globalvision is a leading progressive television company which produces the human rights televisions series: *Rights & Wrongs*. The site contains information on Globalvision programming, a human rights resource list, and an interactive human rights map of the world.

MULTINATIONAL MONITOR ON-LINE
http://www.essential.org/monitor/monitor.html
E-mail: monitor@essential.org

The Internet's most extensive database on the activities of multinational corporations, *Multinational Monitor* On-line contains a full set of back issues of *Multinational Monitor*, as well as links to other sources of information on corporation and international issues. The monthly *Multinational Monitor* is the leading critical source on the activities of multinational corporations.

PACIFICA RADIO
http://www.pacifica.org
E-mail: pos@pacifica.org

The Web site of the Pacifica Radio Network, an alternative, community-based broadcaster.

THE TEXAS OBSERVER
(THE TEXAS OBSERVER
DOWN HOME PAGE)
http://www.hyperweb.com/txobserver
E-mail: observer@eden.com
webmaster: mandabob@bga.com

Since 1954, *The Texas Observer* has been hounding corrupt politicians, poking fat cats in the belly, and printing stories that Texas dailies won't touch. *The Texas Observer* Down Home Page continues that tradition by bringing you the best in Texas news, politics, and culture. (And don't miss their clearinghouse of progressive Web sites.)

ON-LINE PUBLICATIONS AND E-'ZINES

BANNED BOOKS ON-LINE
http://www.cs.cmu.edu/People/spok/
   banned-books.html

Banned Books On-Line is an on-line exhibit of books that have been banned by government authorities or removed from schools. The text of all the books in the exhibit can be read on-line, so readers can see what the censors considered too dangerous to publish. (Because newer books tend to be copyrighted the exhibit mostly concentrates on older books that are now in the public domain. Also note that the definition of "banning"is rather tight; the sorts of media downplaying that Project Censored focuses on wouldn't qualify, but actual government suppression would.)

FAT!SO?
http://www.fatso.com/
E-mail: marilyn@fatso.com

FAT!SO? is the 'zine for people who don't apologize for their size! It's for people who believe that life is too short for self-hatred and celery sticks.

FOCALPOINT F/8
http://www.f8.com
E-mail: focalpt@f8.com

FocalPoint f/8 is about trying to develop a new type of interactive and multimedia journalism for the World Wide Web that combines digital technology with truly interactive components of the Web. Their goal is nothing short of trying to break down the traditional roles and barriers between journalists, subjects, and site visitors or users, engaging all three in the process of creation, interpretation, and discussion of the topics and issues raised and covered.

FREE SPEECH TV
http://www.freespeech.org/
Web Editor: jmanley@tesser.com
FStv Communications Manager:
fstv@fstv.org

Free Speech TV is a 24-hour "netcasting station," running at least one new audio/video work and one new standard HTML work daily. Regular "programs" include *Dyke TV, Political Playhouse, Activism 101*, and *AIDS Community Television.*

FIRST AMENDMENT AND FREE SPEECH ORGANIZATIONS

AMERICAN CIVIL LIBERTIES UNION

http://www.aclu.org
E-mail: aclu@aclu.org

All that you would expect from the nation's premier civil liberties organization, and more. Fax and e-mail your members of Congress, read ACLU briefs in key cases, and get resources for local activism.

AMERICAN LIBRARY ASSOCIATION

http://www.ala.org
E-mail: ala@ala.org

The mission of the American Library Association is to provide leadership for the development, promotion, and improvement of library and information services and the profession of librarianship in order to enhance learning and ensure access to information for all.

AMERICAN SOCIETY OF NEWS EDITORS

(See listing under 'Journalism-Related Sites and Resources')

BLACKLISTED

http://www.crocker.com/~blklist
E-mail: blklist@crocker.com

Blacklisted, a three-hour public radio dramatic documentary starring Stockard Channing, Ron Leibman, and Carroll O'Connor, is the story of the Hollywood blacklist and one of its principal figures, screenwriter Gordon Kahn, who was blacklisted from 1947 until his death in 1962. The Web site provides background information about the show, and resources for people interested in learning more about this dark period in our country's history. The show was broadcast nationally during fall 1995 by National Public Radio, and will be broadcast nationally again in fall 1997 (the 50th anniversary of the House Un-American Activities Committee hearings) by Public Radio International (http://www.pri.org).

ELECTRONIC FRONTIER FOUNDATION

(See listing under 'Internet and Technology-Related Sites')

FEDERATION OF AMERICAN SCIENTISTS' PROJECT ON GOVERNMENT SECRECY

http://www.fas.org/sgp/
E-mail: saftergood@igc.apc.org

This site provides news and resources concerning national security classification and intelligence policy, with proposals for reform.

FEMINISTS FOR FREE EXPRESSION

http://www.well.com/user/freedom
E-mail: ffe@aol.com or freedom@well.com

FFE is a group of diverse feminists working to preserve the individual's right to read, hear, view, and produce material of her choice without the intervention of the state "for her own good." It is the only feminist anti-censorship organization in America. Its Web site provides substantive information about censorship issues, their speakers bureau, membership information, a list of networking links with other free speech organizations, essays, bibliographies, and a list of books by FFE members.

INDEX ON CENSORSHIP
http://www.oneworld.org/index_oc/
E-mail: indexoncenso@gn.apc.org

An electronic edition of the international magazine for free speech, complete with extracts from the current issue, frequent news updates on censorship around the world, a gallery of banned cartoons, and a whole host of useful and informative links to other groups and publications interested in freedom of expression.

NATIONAL COALITION AGAINST CENSORSHIP
http://www.ncac.org

What's up in the obscene world of censorship, and what you can do about it, including excerpts from their quarterly newsletter *Censorship News*.

JOURNALISM-RELATED SITES AND RESOURCES

AJR NEWSLINK
http://www.newslink.org

The Web's most extensive news resource, with 4,000 links to on-line newspapers, magazines, broadcasters, and news services; original columns about on-line news; and the on-line contents of *American Journalism Review* magazine.

AMERICAN SOCIETY OF NEWS EDITORS
http://www.asne.org
E-mail: asne@asne.org

Founded in 1922, ASNE is an organization of the main editors of daily newspapers in the United States and Canada. There are currently 850 members. ASNE's Web site contains resources of use to students, journalists, and people interested in the profession; it includes links to on-line newspapers, journalism associations and organizations and the text of *The American Editor* magazine, and much more.

COMMUNITY MEDIA WORKSHOP
http://www.mcs.net/~commnews
E-mail: commnews@mcs.net

Community Media Workshop provides Chicago-community news tips, grass-roots story ideas, briefing papers, and names of sources of organizations and people working to improve and re-energize Chicago from the bottom up. Their aim is to help get grass-roots stories in mainstream media and beyond.

CENTER FOR RESPONSIVE POLITICS (FOLLOW THE MONEY)
(See listing under 'Media Watch and Research Organizations')

INTERNET AND TECHNOLOGY-RELATED SITES

ELECTRONIC FRONTIER FOUNDATION
http://www.eff.org
E-mail: webmaster@eff.org

The Electronic Frontier Foundation's mega-archive of political, legal, social, and economic information on on-line civil liberties, commerce, regulation, social responsibility, and culture. EFF is a non-profit public interest organization.

ELECTRONIC PRIVACY
INFORMATION CENTER (EPIC)
http://www.epic.org/

EPIC is a public interest organization established in 1994 to focus public attention on civil liberties issues relating to the National Information Infrastructure, such as the Clipper Chip, the Digital Telephony proposal, medical record privacy, national ID systems, and the sale of consumer data. EPIC is sponsored by the Fund for Constitutional Government. EPIC publishes the *EPIC Alert* and *EPIC Reports*, pursues Freedom of Information Act litigation, and conducts policy research on emerging privacy issues. EPIC also acts as the Washington Office of Privacy International.

FREE THE PLANET!
(See listing under 'Activist Organizations')

PAULA DAVIDSON—
MESOELECTRONIC
HUNTER/GATHERER
http://www.cs.unca.edu/~davidson/
E-mail: davidson@cs.unca.edu

Specializing in exploration and tool use on the matrix of the 'net.

ACTIVIST ORGANIZATIONS

AMERICANS AGAINST
POLITICAL CORRUPTION
http://www.essential.org/aapc
E-mail: cressman@essential.org

This site outlines five policy proposals for tough campaign reform, including a constitutional amendment, and lists members of the 105th Congress who have pledged support for these reforms.

COMPUTER PROFESSIONALS FOR
SOCIAL RESPONSIBILITY (CPSR)
http://www.cpsr.org/dox/home.html
E-mail: cpsr@cpsr.org

ELECTRONIC FRONTIER
FOUNDATION
(See listing under 'Internet
and Technology-Related Sites')

FREE THE PLANET!
http://www.essential.org/freetheplanet/
home.html

Free The Planet!'s Web site provides information about critical environmental issues, opportunities to network regionally with other student environmental activists, and the opportunity to take action right over the Internet. Send free pro-environmental faxes to polluters and politicians over the Web!

THE NAUTILUS INSTITUTE FOR
SECURITY AND SUSTAINABLE
DEVELOPMENT
http://www.nautilus.org/
Email: nautilus@nautilus.org

Extensive resources on international environmental protection and cooperation in the Asia-Pacific region, including daily news updates, a sizable library of policy reports and documents to download, an energy/environment curriculum under development, a "green boat" environmentally conscious boating demonstration project, and much more.

NUCLEAR INFORMATION AND RESOURCE SERVICE
http://www.nirs.org
E-mail: nirsnet@igc.apc.org

Alerts, news and information on nuclear power, radioactive waste, grass-roots environmental activism. Fully-indexed and searchable database of more than 5,000 government and other documents. WebBoard conversation center. Site updated 3-5 times weekly.

PHYSICIANS FOR A NATIONAL HEALTH PROGRAM (PNHP)
http://www.pnhp.org
E-mail: pnhp@aol.com

PNHP recognizes the need for universal, national health insurance. Its Web site contains articles and research on issues such as access to insurance and health care, "corporatization" and administrative waste in health care, and the impact of for-profit managed care.

THE VOTERS TELECOMMUNICATIONS WATCH
http://www.vtw.org/
E-mail: vtw@vtw.org

The nexus of the on-line fight for free speech in America.

APPENDIX D

Alternative Writer's Market

Edited by Amy S. Cohen

Throughout its 21-year history, Project Censored has received numerous queries from journalists and authors seeking publishers for exposés that challenge the conventional wisdom of the establishment press. We have also received many queries from interested citizens wondering how they can get their own "story" told. One of our goals has always been to empower people with information. With this in mind, we developed the following guide. Whether you are an experienced journalist, an aspiring writer, or a concerned citizen, we hope the "Alternative Writer's Market" (AWM) is a useful resource when you seek media outlets for your work.

In the fourth edition of the AWM, we have added 27 publications, bringing the total number of listings to 102. We hope this will serve as a valuable tool for writers who are seeking markets beyond the bounds of the traditional resource book, *Writer's Market: Where & How To Sell What You Write*, published annually by Writer's Digest Books. This edition of the AWM includes a number of new publications and features some of the most promising markets open to investigative journalists.

All AWM listings have been updated whenever possible. You may, however, want to verify relevant information with individual publications.

If you know of any additional listings that should be included in the 1998 AWM, please write the "Alternative Writer's Market," Project Censored, Sonoma State University, Rohnert Park, CA 94928, for a listing application.

Also, if you are aware of any changes and/or corrections for the current list, please send them to the same address.

14850 MAGAZINE
104 N. Aurora Street
Ithaca, NY 14850
Tel: 607/277-1021 Fax: 607/277-0801
Editor-in-Chief: Corey Shane

14850 Magazine (named after its zip code) is published monthly. About 95 percent of its articles are provided by freelance writers. It is interested in interviews, reviews, opinion, and think pieces, ranging from 800 to 1,600 words.

RATES: $30 in credit

QUERIES are not required; send SASE for Writer's Guidelines; response time is two weeks.

TIPS: "We like local stuff, but we're wide open; we've done pieces on JFK, Leonard Peltier, health care, censorship, and other political issues. We really publish a pretty broad array of material."
—Editor-in-Chief Corey Shane

ABYA YALA NEWS,
NOTICIAS DE ABYA YALA
P.O. Box 28703
Oakland, CA 94604
Tel: 510/834-4263 Fax: 510/834-4264
E-mail: saiic@igc.apc.org

Abya Yala News is a quarterly journal, published by the South and Meso American Indian Rights Center. About 30 percent of its articles are provided by freelance writers. It is interested in feature articles, profiles, interviews, and

book reviews of about 2,500 words; and news pieces, or urgent actions of 800 words.

RATES: None offered

QUERIES are not required; send SASE for Writer's Guidelines; response time is one to two weeks.

TIPS: "Try to let the voices of Indigenous peoples come through and not take on a representative tone. Indigenous writers are strongly encouraged to submit articles."

THE ADVOCATE
6922 Hollywood Boulevard, Suite 1000
Los Angeles, CA 90028
Tel: 213/871-1225 Fax: 213/467-6805
E-mail: info@advocate.com

The Advocate is a biweekly publication with about 80 percent of its articles provided by freelance writers. It is interested in articles, profiles, and interviews with an average length of 1,500 words.

RATES: Negotiable

QUERIES with published clips required; send SASE for Writer's Guidelines; response time is two weeks.

AKWESASNE NOTES
P.O. Box 196
Mohawk Nation
Rooseveltown, NY 13683-0196
Tel: 518/358-9531 Fax: 613/575-2935
Editor: Salli Benedict

Akwesasne Notes is a quarterly publication with about 75 percent of its articles provided by freelance writers. It is interested in articles, profiles, book reviews, music reviews, interviews, letters-to-the-editor, poetry.

RATES: Yes, though very minimal

QUERIES with published clips required; response time is two to four weeks.

TIPS: "Environmental, Native issues across the U.S. and Canada, Native/natural issues of aboriginal people."—Jann Day/ Mark Neursisian

ALTERNATIVE PRESS REVIEW
P.O. Box 1446
Columbia, MO 65205-1446
Tel: 573/442-4352
Editor: Jason McQuinn

Alternative Press Review is a quarterly publication that monitors and reports on the activities and performance of America's alternative media. About 10 percent of its articles are provided by freelance writers. It is interested in articles, profiles, and book reviews covering alternative media and their relationship to society, radical movements, and mainstream media.

RATES: 2 cents per word for reprints or reviews; 5 cents per word for original articles

QUERIES with published clips required; send SASE for Writer's Guidelines; response time is one to two months.

TIPS: "We're looking for critical, perceptive assessments of alternative media organizations, conferences, publications, genres, movements; no puff pieces."—Editor Jason McQuinn

AMERICAN JOURNALISM REVIEW
8701 Adelphi Road
Adelphi, MD 20783
Tel: 301/431-4771 Fax: 301/431-0097
Editor: Rem Rieder

The American Journalism Review, formerly the *Washington Journalism Review*, is published ten times a year. About 80 percent of its articles are provided by freelance writers. It is interested in articles, analysis, book reviews, interviews, exposés, upwards of 2,000 words; short pieces of 500-700 words.

RATES: Features—20 cents a word; short features—$100

QUERIES with published clips required; response time three to four weeks.

TIPS: "Read the magazine before submitting queries; know what we've done, what we do, what we're looking for. We're always looking for good ideas, especially investigations of media coverage."—Associate Editor Chip Rowe

BACKGROUNDERS
(See FOOD FIRST NEWS & VIEWS)

THE BAFFLER
P.O. Box 378293
Chicago, IL 60637
Editor: Thomas Frank

The Baffler is a quarterly publication with about 80 percent of its articles provided by freelance writers. It is interested in articles, profiles, book reviews, interviews, opinion pieces, essays, and exposés ranging from 500 to 10,000 words.

RATES: Offered

QUERIES are not required; response time is six months.

TIPS: "Read the magazine first."

BORDER/LINES MAGAZINE
P.O. Box 459, Stn. P.
Toronto, Ontario
Canada M58 2S9
Fax: 416/921-3984
Managing Editor: Julie Jenkinson

Border/Lines is published February, June, September/October with 100 percent of its articles provided by freelance writers. It is interested in articles, profiles, book reviews, interviews, opinion pieces, essays, and exposés, with a maximum length of 4,000 words.
RATES: $75 to $250
QUERIES with published clips required; send SASE for Writer's Guidelines; response time is three months.
TIPS: "Please write in for formal guidelines. Be sure to include an SASE with all requests and your articles."
—Managing Editor Julie Jenkinson

BOSTON REVIEW
E53-407, MIT
30 Wadsworth Street
Cambridge, MA 02139
Tel: 617/253-3642 Fax: 617/252-1549
E-mail: bostonreview@mit.edu
Editor: Joshua Cohen;
Managing Editor: Matthew Howard

Boston Review is published six times a year, with about 90 percent of its material provided by freelance writers. It is interested in articles, book reviews, opinion pieces, and essays, as well as poetry and fiction; material must not be longer than 5,000 words. No unsolicited reviews or electronic submissions accepted.
RATES: $40 to $125
QUERIES with published clips required; send SASE for Writer's Guide-lines; response time is six to eight weeks.
TIPS: "*Boston Review* is a magazine of ideas, combining commitments to public reason and literary imagination."
—Managing Editor Matthew Howard

BOYCOTT QUARTERLY
P.O. Box 30727
Seattle, WA 98103-0727
E-mail: BoycottGuy@aol.com
Editor: Zachary D. Lyons

Boycott Quarterly, as it name suggests, is published quarterly; please contact publisher for dates. Currently a low percentage of its articles are provided by freelance writers. It is interested in articles, opinion pieces, and exposés, ranging from 1,500 to 2,000 words.
RATES: Free subscription only
QUERIES with published clips required; response time varies.
TIPS: "Boycotts, corporate injustice and irresponsibility, related topics, reports on economic democracy topics (co-ops, barter, farmers markets, etc.). We solicit or produce in-house almost all articles but like to reprint well-written articles on related topics published elsewhere."—Editor Zachary D. Lyons

BRIARPATCH
Saskatchewan's Independent
News Magazine
2138 McIntyre Street
Regina, SK
Canada S4P 2R7
Tel: 306/525-2949
Editor: George Manz

Briarpatch is an independent news magazine written by and for political activists. It is published 10 times a year, with about 75 percent of its material provided by freelance writers. It is interested in news articles ranging from 600 to 1,200 words.

RATES: Free magazines only; "...no money!"

QUERIES are not required, but are encouraged along with published clips; response time is one month.

TIPS: "Most of our readers are Canadians so articles must be of interest to them. Articles must be broadly pro-leftwing (pro-labour, feminist, environmental, etc."—Editor George Manz

THE BULLETIN OF THE ATOMIC SCIENTISTS
6042 S. Kimbark Avenue
Chicago, IL 60637
Fax: 312/702-0725

The Bulletin of the Atomic Scientists publishes both solicited and unsolicited manuscripts dealing with nuclear issues. While the Bulletin is a serious magazine, it is not a scholarly journal. Articles should be written in a lively style and should be suitable for the non-technical reader. In most cases, articles should be no longer than 3,000 words.

QUERIES with published clips are suggested; send SASE for Writer's Guidelines.

CALIFORNIA ALTERNATIVE NEWS BUREAU
1015 20th Street
Sacramento, CA 95616
Tel: 916/498-1234 Fax: 916/498-7920
Editor: Tom Johnson

The California Alternative News Bureau is a monthly news service which includes

15 California alternative papers among its subscribers. About 50 percent of its articles are provided by freelance writers. It is interested in hard news, features, and profiles of statewide California interest. Articles range from 500 to 2,000 words.

RATES: $100 to $400 depending on quality and work involved

QUERIES with published clips required; response time normally within a week.

TIPS: "Take a story the mainstream papers have missed or downplayed, and, with lively writing, tell Californians about it. No polemics, editorials. If you want your audience outraged, reflect it in your writing, not your lead."
—Editor Tom Johnson

THE CALIFORNIA PRISONER
P.O. Box 1019
Sacramento, CA 95812-1019
Tel: 916/441-4214 Fax: 916/441-4297
Editors: CAP Editorial Committee

The California Prisoner is a quarterly publication available to members of the Prisoners' Rights Union. About 60 percent of its material is provided by freelance writers. It is interested in articles, profiles, interviews, essays, exposés, surveys, and statistics, as well as artwork, related to jail, prison, or prisoners.

RATES: Annual membership to Prisoners' Rights Union, which includes a subscription to the publication

QUERIES are not required; send SASE for Writer's Guidelines; CAP will respond upon receipt.

TIPS: "Jail/prison/prisoner-related articles in medical or legal areas; confinement conditions, wrongful convictions, brutality, jail or prison programs;

visiting a prisoner, rights of prisoners, visitors, and prison staff; advocacy and petitions."—Editorial Committee Member Cynthia Edmonton

CANADIAN DIMENSION (CD)
228 Notre Dame Ave., Room 401
Winnipeg, Manitoba, R3B1N7
Canada
Tel: 204/957-1519 Fax: 204/943-4617
Office Manager: Michelle Torres

Canadian Dimension (CD) relies on freelance writers for about 25 percent of its material. It is primarily interested in articles (2,000 words maximum) and book reviews (750 words maximum).

RATES: 10 cents per published word; maximum of $300 per article

QUERIES preferred; send SASE for Writer's Guidelines; response time is two months.

TIPS: "We're looking for articles on issues affecting women, gays/lesbians, aboriginals, the environment, and labour."

CAPITAL EYE
Center for Responsive Politics
1320 19th Street, NW, #700
Washington, DC 20036
Tel: 202/857-0044 Fax: 202/857-7809
E-mail: info@crp.org
Editor: Paul Hendrie

Captial Eye is published every other month by the Center for Responsive Politics. About 30 percent of its material is provided by freelance writers. It is looking for relatively short reporting pieces—from 400 to 700 words—about campaign finance issues and particularly about money in politics. It is also interested in

state and local government issues.

RATES: Fifty cents a word

QUERIES with published clips required; response time is two weeks.

TIPS: "Looking for news, not opinion pieces, generally. Reporting on unique or original issues about campaign finance. Also, movements for reform as well as coverage of abuses or scandals. Stories that connect influence of money to other issues concerning people."—Editor Paul Hendrie

CASCADIA TIMES
25-6 Northwest 23rd Place, #406
Portland, OR 97201
Tel: 503/223-9036
E-mail: cascadia@desktop.org
Editor: Paul Koberstein

Cascadia Times, a regional publication with a focus ranging from San Francisco to Alaska, is published monthly. About 75 percent of its articles are provided by freelance writers. It is interested in investigative journalism on the environment and health, and book reviews on the same subjects. It publishes six to eight articles monthly, ranging from 500 to 3,000 words.

RATES: 20 cents per word

QUERIES not required; send SASE for Writer's Guidelines; response time is up to two weeks.

TIPS: "No opinion pieces, please." —Editor Paul Koberstein

CITY PAPER
Baltimore's Free Weekly
812 Park Avenue
Baltimore, MD 21201
Tel: 410/523-2300 Fax: 410/523-8437
Managing Editor: Heather Joslyn

The City Paper is a free weekly newspaper distributed in the Baltimore area. About 50 percent of its articles are provided by freelance writers. It is interested in articles, profiles, book reviews, interviews, essays, and exposés, all of which should have a strong Baltimore connection.

RATES: $25 to $400 depending on length

QUERIES with published clips required; response time normally two weeks; send SASE for Writer's Guidelines.

TIPS: "We are particularly interested in the issues, people, and character of Baltimore City."

COMMUNITIES MAGAZINE

P.O. Box 169
Masonville, CO 80541-0169
Tel: 970/593-5615 Fax: same
Editor: Diana Christian

Communities Magazine is a thematic quarterly publication that covers "intentional communities" in North America. One hundred percent of its material is written by freelancers. It is interested in articles, profiles, and interviews (800-2,500 words); opinion pieces (800-1,700 words); and book reviews (400-500 words).

RATES: Free subscription or four copies of issue

QUERIES and published clips are sometimes required; send SASE for Writer's Guidelines; response time is four weeks.

TIPS: "We seek articles on our quarterly themes, written by, for, or about people living in intentional communities. Our readers already know what intentional communities are; they want to know how various communities function, what the members have learned, what works, what doesn't work, etc."
—Editor Diana Christian

COMMUNITY ENDEAVOR NEWS

P.O. Box 2505
Grass Valley, CA 95945
Tel: 916/274-7331
Fax: 916/274-7357
E-mail: jaykay@oro.net
Publisher: Susan Lukasha

Community Endeavor News is a monthly publication with 80 percent of its material provided by freelance writers. It is interested in political, social, and environmental issues. It will consider articles, interviews, profiles, opinion pieces, events and exposés, and some short book reviews with a maximum of 500 words.

RATES: Not usually offered, with some exceptions

QUERIES are not required; normal response time is two weeks; contact for submission requirements.

TIPS: "Timely articles concerning political, social, and environmental issues with emphasis on 'personal involvement' for readers. Contact and further information requested at end of articles. If longer than 1,500-2,000 words, it may be published in two parts."
—Publisher Susan Lukasha

COMMON CAUSE MAGAZINE

2030 M Street, NW
Washington, DC 20036
Tel: 202/833-1200
Fax: 202/659-3716
E-mail: ccvicki@well.com
Editor: Vicki Kemper

Common Cause Magazine, longtime scourge of Washington's political high-rollers, is published quarterly. About 30 percent of its articles are provided by freelance writers. It is primarily interested in investigative political pieces.
RATES: Vary
QUERIES are not required.
TIPS: "We're interested in articles about money in politics, political corruption, real-life impacts of government policy, and social issues."—Editor Vicki Kemper

COUNTERPOISE
1716 SW Williston Road
Gainesville, FL 32608
Tel: 352/335-2200 Fax: Call first
E-mail: willett@afn.org
Editor: Charles Willett

Counterpoise is the alternative library review journal, published quarterly. It will be sponsored by the American Library Association. It is interested in articles, profiles, book reviews, opinion pieces, essays, and exposés. Write for details.
QUERIES: Send for requirements.
TIPS: "Interested in reviews by librarians and other qualified persons of noteworthy new titles ignored or dismissed by the mainstream review media. Volunteers should write the editor, enclosing samples of their work."—Editor Charles Willett

COUNTERPUNCH
P.O. Box 18675
Washington, DC 20036
Tel: 202/986-3665 Fax: 202/986-3665
Editors: Ken Silverstein and
Alexander Cockburn

CounterPunch is published twice monthly. About five percent of its articles are provided by freelance writers. It is specifically interested in politics with a Washington, D.C. angle.
RATES: Very low, negotiable
QUERIES not required; response time is a week.

COVERTACTION QUARTERLY
1500 Massachusetts Ave., NW
Room 732
Washington, DC 20005
Tel: 202/331-9763 Fax: 202/331-9751
Editors: Terry Allen and Phil Smith

CovertAction Quarterly, a publication that lives up to its name, is naturally published quarterly. Fifty to eighty percent of its articles are provided by freelance writers. It is interested in substantive articles, well-researched (with footnotes), exposés, interviews, etc. Average article length is 4,000-5,000 words, sometimes longer.
RATES: Negotiable
QUERIES with published clips required; send SASE for Writer's Guidelines; response time is 10 days.
TIPS: "We're interested in stories about U.S. and allied intelligence operations (foreign and domestic), non-intelligence related topics demonstrating U.S. intervention or involvement, right-wing and/or racist activities, environmental issues, private (non-governmental) activities of a secret and/or detrimental nature."—Director of Research Louis Wolf

CULTURAL DEMOCRACY
P.O. Box 545
Tucson, AZ 85702
Tel: 602/791-9359

Cultural Democracy is a quarterly publication of the Alliance for Cultural Democracy, an 18-year-old national network of community and neighborhood-based cultural workers.

RATES: None

QUERIES not required; response time is two weeks to two months; send SASE for Writer's Guidelines.

TIPS: "We are looking for writings that express the interconnection between cultural rights, community, arts, and ecology and ongoing, or historical, examples of projects or programs reflecting these concerns."

THE DAYTON VOICE
1927 N. Main Street
Dayton, OH 45405
Tel: 513/275-8855 Fax: 513/275-6056
E-mail: thevoice@dayton.net
Editor: Marrianne McMullen

The Dayton Voice is an alternative weekly that focuses primarily on local, state, or regional news and entertainment features surrounding the Dayton, Ohio area. About 80 percent of its articles are provided by freelance writers. It is interested in investigative reporting, profiles, and popular culture features. Article length ranges from 500 to 2,500 words.

RATES: $30 to $200

QUERIES not required but preferred; send SASE for Writer's Guidelines; response time is two weeks.

DE TODO UN POCO
2830 5th Street
Boulder, CO 80304
Tel: 303/444-8565 Fax: 303/545-2074
E-mail: tmoore@igc.apc.org
Editors: Nancy Sullo and Tom Moore

De Todo Un Poco is specifically interested in "first-hand" news and analysis about Central America and the Caribbean. About 10 percent of its articles are provided by freelance writers. It is interested in articles, profiles, and opinion pieces ranging up to 500 words.

RATES: None

QUERIES required; response time is two weeks.

TIPS: "Particularly interested in 'first-hand experience' pieces. News and analysis pertaining to Central America and the Caribbean. In general, should be 500 words or less. We have a different 'focus' (nation or theme) each month and only have space for material pertaining to this focus. Inquire first; we're happy to hear your ideas."—Editor Nancy Sullo

THE DETROIT METRO TIMES
743 Beaubien, Suite 301
Detroit, MI 48226
Tel: 313/961-4060

The Detroit Metro Times is a weekly newspaper; about 70 percent of its material is provided by freelance writers. It is interested in articles, profiles, reviews, and opinion pieces of 600 to 3,500 words on cutting edge culture and progressive political and social change. It is not interested in consumer news or mainstream religion, medicine, or sports.

RATES: None cited

QUERIES with published clips required; response time two weeks.

TIPS: "We are interested in feminism, progressive politics, analysis of U.S. government and corporate abuse, environmentalism, race relations, danger of the right-wing, media monopoly and manipulation, etc."—Jim Dulzo

(DIS)CONNECTION
1573 N. Milwaukee, #420
Chicago, IL 60622
E-mail: ugwiller@bgu.edu

(DIS)CONNECTION is a collectively produced journal of the network of Anarchist Collectives. Published four to six times a year, 100 percent of its material is provided by freelance writers. It is interested in articles, book reviews, exposés, opinion pieces, and essays related to anarchism, radical movements, collectives, cooperatives, alternative economics, community organizing, and building revolutionary movements.

RATES: None cited

QUERIES are not required.

TIPS: "This is an advertisement-free publication. The distribution is approximately 3,000 and thus far has been very much a 'zine. That may change."

DISSENT
521 Fifth Avenue, Suite 1700
New York, NY 10025
Tel: 212/595-3084 Fax: same
E-mail: dissent@igc.apc.org
Editors: Mitchell Cohen
and Michael Walzer

Dissent is a quarterly publication looking for articles and opinion pieces on "political, economic, social, and cultural issues from a democratic left perspective." Ninety percent of its material is provided by freelance writers.

RATES: Nominal

QUERIES are not required; order a sample issue for submission guidelines; response time is three weeks.

DOLLARS AND SENSE
1 Summer Street
Somerville, MA 02143
Tel: 617/628-8411 Fax: 617/628-2025
Editors: Abby Scher and Marc Breslow

Dollars and Sense is a bimonthly magazine that focuses on economic issues and perspectives not normally found in *Forbes Magazine* or the *Wall Street Journal*. About 20 percent of its articles are provided by freelance writers. It will consider full-length features, interviews, and book reviews (200-600 words each) for publication.

RATES: Regrets that it cannot compensate authors at this time

QUERIES required; response time is a month; send SASE for Writer's Guidelines.

TIPS: "Articles on progressive economics and political economy will be of interest."

E: THE ENVIRONMENTAL
MAGAZINE
P.O. Box 5098
Westport, CT 06881
Tel: 203/854-5559 Fax: 203/866-0602
Managing Editor: Jim Motavalli

E: The Environmental Magazine is a bimonthly magazine that focuses on the environment as its name suggests. About 75 percent of its articles are provided by freelance writers. It is interested in environment-oriented articles, interviews, exposés, news briefs, and feature stories, as well as health-related articles, eco-home, and eco-tourism.

RATES: Twenty cents a word

QUERIES with published clips required; send SASE for Writer's Guidelines; response time is 4 to 6 months with an acknowledgment in one week.

TIPS: "Investigative exposé pieces are good; anything that takes the corporate superstructure to task."

EARTH ISLAND JOURNAL
300 Broadway, Suite 28
San Francisco, CA 94133-3312
Tel: 415/788-3666
Fax: 415/788-7324
Editor: Gar Smith

Earth Island Journal is a quarterly international environmental news magazine. About 25 percent of its articles are provided by freelance writers. However, half-page (500 words) and full page (1,000 words) stories are most likely to win consideration; feature-length reports (1,500-3,000 words) occasionally come from outside writers.

RATES: Year's free subscription in exchange

QUERIES required; response time normally ten days to three months; send SASE for Writer's Guidelines.

TIPS: "Our beat: 'Local News From Around the World.' First-person reports on under-reported environmental stories from abroad—particularly with a U.S. hook. Is some U.S. corporation causing harm overseas? Are there solutions from abroad that we can apply in the U.S.?" —Editor Gar Smith

THE ECOLOGIST
Agricultural House
Bath Road, Sturminster Newton
Dorset DT10 1DU, U.K.
Tel: 011-44-1258-473476
Fax: 011-44-1258-473748

The Ecologist is published every two months, with 100 percent of its material provided by freelance writers. It is interested in articles of 5,000 words, and book reviews of 750 words.

RATES: £20 per 1,000 printed words

QUERIES required, preferably with published clips; send SASE for Writer's Guidelines; response time is two months.

TIPS: *The Ecologist* publishes "a wide range of topics, so it's best to look at back copies."—Co-editor S. Sexton

ECONEWS
879 Ninth Street
Arcata, CA 95521
Tel: 707/822-6918 Fax: 707/822-0827
E-mail: nec@igc.apc.org
Editor: Sid Dominitz

ECONEWS is a northern California monthly publication with "a bioregional outlook." About 30 percent of its material is provided by freelance writers; copy deadline is the 20th of each month. It is interested in hard news or features (no opinion pieces). It will consider book reviews on environmental subjects only, preferably focused on northwestern California and southwestern Oregon.

RATES: "Alas, we don't pay anyone."

QUERIES are required; response time is a week.

TIPS: "Forest issues (on public or private lands), toxics, nuclear and alternative energy, recycling, land-use planning, endangered species, water and air pollution. Emphasis on northern California and the Pacific Northwest." —Editor Sid Dominitz

ENVIRONMENTAL ACTION MAGAZINE

6930 Carroll Avenue, Suite 600
Takoma Park, MD 20912
Tel: 301/891-1100 Fax: 301/891-2218

Environmental Action Magazine (EA) is a quarterly magazine that primarily explores the human environment. About 10 percent of its articles are provided by freelance writers. While it is mainly interested in book reviews and essays by established experts/leaders in particular fields, it does publish a few investigative pieces.

RATES: Up to $300 but most authors are unpaid

QUERIES with published clips and résumé required; response time four to eight weeks.

TIPS: "We stopped taking most freelance work in 1992 due to budget cuts and reduced frequency of the magazine. *EA* focuses primarily on the human environment (as opposed to wilderness issues) and on issues relating to the environmental movement itself. Issues in 1996 will focus on big money in politics and its effects on the environment; transportation; and strategies to target corporate power."—Magazine Associate Francis Wilkins

EXTRA!

130 W. 25th Street
New York, NY 10001
Tel: 212/633-6700 Fax: 212/727-7668
Editor: Jim Naureckas

EXTRA! is a bimonthly news media review journal published by Fairness and Accuracy In Reporting, a national media watchdog organization. It is interested in well-documented articles related to issues of media bias.

RATES: Ten cents a word

QUERIES not required; send SASE for Writer's Guidelines.

TIPS: "Stories should focus more on the media than on the information not reported by the media. We look at media coverage of specific issues relating to government control of the media, corporate interference, racial and gender bias, etc."—Editor Jim Naureckas

FAT!SO?

P.O. Box 423464
San Francisco, CA 94142-3464
Tel: 1-800/OH-FATSO
E-mail: marilyn@fatso.com
Editor: Marilyn Wann

FAT!SO? is a 'zine published three times a year with 90 percent of its material written by freelancers. It is interested in rants, humor essays, personal tales of wit and woe of one paragraph, or 1,200 words.

RATES: Free copies of 'zine

QUERIES not required; send SASE for Writer's Guidelines; response time is three months.

TIPS: "Fat- or body-size-related, and fat-positive. No fat-bashing, diet advice, or cruel anti-fat humor need apply."
—Editor Marilyn Wann

FACTSHEET FIVE

P.O. Box 170099
San Francisco, CA 94117
Tel: 415/668-1781 Fax: 415/668-1781
E-mail: f5seth@sirius.com
Editor: R. Seth Friedman

Factsheet Five, a publication that focuses

exclusively on 'zines, is published four times a year. About 30 percent of its articles are provided by freelance writers. It primarily prints reviews but also publishes a number of freelance articles covering 'zines, publishing, and the alternative/underground culture.

RATES: Range from $50 to $100

QUERIES not required but published clips are welcome; send SASE for Writer's Guidelines; response time is one month.

TIPS: "*Factsheet Five* is exclusively devoted to the world of 'zines. While we do print an occasional political piece, we only accept them from writers who have written for us before. We only accept articles about 'zine culture from new writers."—Editor R. Seth Friedman

FOOD FIRST NEWS & VIEWS/ BACKGROUNDERS
398 60th Street
Oakland, CA 94618
Tel: 510/654-4400 Fax: 510/654-4551
Managing Editor: Kathleen McClung

Food First News & Views, and its companion publication, *Backgrounders*, are quarterly publications of the Food First Institute. Both publications explore the causes of hunger, poverty, and environmental deterioration. Fewer than 10 percent of their articles are provided by freelance writers. They are interested in short articles or interviews with a 2,000-word maximum.

RATES: Negotiable; small stipend only

QUERIES with published clips required; response time is one to two months.

TIPS: "Food First is a non-profit research and education center focusing on the root causes of hunger, poverty, and environmental deterioration. Most of our writers are on staff or closely associated with the institute."—Managing Editor Kathleen McClung

FREETHINKER FORUM
8945 Renken Road
Staunton, IL 62088
or P.O. Box 14447
St. Louis, MO 63178
Tel: 618/637-2202 Fax: 618/637-2666
E-mail: profreedom@aol.com
Editor/Publisher: Susan Duncan

Freethinker Forum is a monthly publication focusing on liberal issues and individuals. About 50 percent of its articles are provided by freelance writers. It is interested in political (liberal) articles, interviews with liberal activists, politicians, etc., opinion pieces, and essays, with a liberal bent only. Length usually ranges from a minimum of 500 words to a maximum of 3,000 words.

RATES: $50 for 500 words; $100 for 1,000 to 2,000 words; longer articles negotiable; all paid on publication

QUERIES are not required; send SASE for Writer's Guidelines; response time is 21 days.

TIPS: "Commentary on the state of the country under conservative rule, liberal activism, feminist issues, animal rights, anti-religion or exposés involving religious zealots, etc., environmental issues, single mothers, welfare, the penal system."—Editor Susan Duncan

FRONT LINES RESEARCH
Public Policy Institute
Planned Parenthood Federation
of America
810 7th Avenue
New York, NY 10019
Tel: 212/261-4721 Fax: 212/261-4352
Editor: Frederick Clarkson

Front Lines Research features "journalism with footnotes" in defense of reproductive health, education, and democracy. It is published bimonthly. About 20 percent of its articles are provided by freelance writers. It is interested in investigative, analytical, rigorous, footnoted, documentary features on the radical right. Maximum length is 2,000 words plus footnotes.

RATES: 10 cents per word plus expenses

QUERIES with published clips required; send SASE for Writer's Guidelines; response time is two weeks.

TIPS: "Considerable expertise on the far-right is a pre-requisite. We are generally publishing definitive work in this field. The style is a mix of investigative journalism and academic journalism. I call it journalism with footnotes. Stories in this journal should be compelling reading and have a long shelf life."
—Editor Frederick Clarkson

GLOBAL EXCHANGES
2017 Mission Street
Suite 303
San Francisco, CA 94110
Tel: 415/255-7296
Editor: Kevin Danaher

Global Exchanges is a quarterly publication which focuses on international affairs and citizen diplomacy. Only about two percent of its articles are provided by freelance writers. It publishes in February, May, August, and October.

RATES: None

QUERIES with published clips required; send SASE for Writer's Guidelines; response time is one to two weeks.

GRASSROOTS FUNDRAISING JOURNAL
P.O. Box 11607
Berkeley, CA 94712
Tel: 510/704-8714 Fax: 510/649-7913
E-mail: chardn@aol.com
Publisher: Kim Klein

Grassroots Fundraising Journal is published six times a year using 100 percent freelance material. It will consider 2,000 to 2,500 word articles regarding grassroots fundraising.

RATES: $75 per article

QUERIES are not required; send SASE for Writer's Guidelines; response time is four months.

TIPS: "All aspects of grass-roots fundraising; i.e., how-to and true stories, philosophy."—Publisher Kim Klein

HARD TIMES
c/o L.A. View
2342 Sawtelle Boulevard
Los Angeles, CA 90064
Tel: 310/477-0403
Founder/Editor/Publisher: Len Doucette

Hard Times, an aptly named publication about homelessness, is published bimonthly. One hundred percent of its articles are provided by freelance writers. One hundred percent of its funds are from street sales of the paper.

RATES: Can't afford to pay writers
QUERIES are not required.

TIPS: "We are dedicated to educating the general public about all issues regarding homelessness. We welcome all submissions but are unable to guarantee publication."—Editor Len Doucette

HIGH COUNTRY NEWS
P.O. Box 1090
Paonia, CO 81428
Tel: 303/527-4898

High Country News is a regional Colorado publication with a national impact. Published biweekly, 90 percent of its articles are provided by freelance writers. It is interested in magazine-style leads, essays on environmental issues, planning, shorter roundups on local issues with regional resonance.

RATES: Twenty cents a word and up

QUERIES with published clips required; send SASE for Writer's Guidelines; response time varies.

TIPS: "Read the paper first, know what we cover, and where we are in that coverage."

THE HUMAN QUEST
1074 23rd Avenue N.
St. Petersburg, FL 33704-3228
Tel: 813/894-0097
Editor: Edna Ruth Johnson

The Human Quest is a bimonthly national magazine that is "in the mail on the 25th of the month." One hundred percent of its material is provided by freelance writers. Emphasis of *The Human Quest* is world peace; its religious conviction is spiritual humanism. It welcomes thoughtful articles ranging from 150 to 500 to 1,000 words in length.

RATES: None

QUERIES are not required; response time normally within a week; in lieu of formal guidelines, editor will "happily furnish a copy of the publication" on request.

TIPS: "*The Human Quest* is an independent journal of religious humanism, under the sponsorship of The Churchman Associates, Inc. It is edited in the conviction that religious journalism must provide a platform for the free exchange of ideas and opinions; that religion is consonant with the most advanced revelations in every department of knowledge; that we are in a fraternal world community; and that the moral and spiritual evolution of man is only at the beginning."—Editor Edna Ruth Johnson

THE INDEPENDENT FILM & VIDEO MONTHLY
625 Broadway, 9th Floor
New York, NY 10012
Tel: 212/473-3400 Fax: 212/677-8732
Editor: Patricia Thomson

The Independent Film & Video Monthly is a national magazine with about 90 percent of its articles provided by freelance writers. It is interested in news articles, 500-800 words; profiles of film/video makers, distributors, festival directors, 700-1,000 words; business, legal, technical articles, 700-1,200 words; features 1,500-3,000 words.

RATES: News articles, $50; profiles, $100; features, 10 cents a word

QUERIES with published clips required; response time from two weeks to two months.

TIPS: "Interested in film/video-related

articles that are not too theoretical or too mainstream. Recent features include 'The Money Game: Foundation Insiders Explain the Rules,' and 'Made in Japan: Current Trends in Japanese Independent Filmmaking.'"—Michele Shapiro.

INDEX ON CENSORSHIP
33 Islington High Street
London, England N1 9LH
Tel: 171-278-2313 Fax: 171-278-1878
E-mail: index@indexcen.demon.co.uk
    indexoncenso@gn.apc.org
Editor: Ursula Owen

Index on Censorship is an international bimonthly review and analysis of censorship issues. It is interested in articles, profiles, book reviews, interviews, opinion pieces, essays, exposés, etc. Also interested in factual news and analytic articles on censorship and freedom of expression issues. Articles range from 800 to 4,000 words.

RATES: £60 per 1,000 words for original pieces

QUERIES are not required.

TIPS: Special interests include "All areas concerned with freedom of expression and censorship, worldwide (including Britain)."—Editor Ursula Owen.

INDUSTRIAL WORKER
103 W. Michigan Avenue
Ypsilanti, MI 48197-5438
Tel: 313/483-3548
Fax: 313/483-4050
E-mail: iww@igc.apc.org
Editor: Jon Bekken

Industrial Worker, a labor-oriented publication, is published monthly. About 10 percent of its articles are provided by freelance writers. It is interested in labor-related articles, profiles, book reviews, interviews, opinion pieces, essays, and exposés, up to about 500 words maximum.

RATES: Free subscriptions

QUERIES are not required; response time is one month.

TIPS: "Labor and social issues from a progressive perspective."—General Secretary/Treasurer Fred Chase

IN THESE TIMES
2040 N. Milwaukee
Chicago, IL 60647-4002
Tel: 312/772-0100
Fax: 312/772-4180
E-mail: itt@igc.apc.org
Editor: James Weinstein;
Managing Editor: Deidre McFayden

In These Times (ITT) is a biweekly news and views magazine. About 50 percent of its articles are provided by freelance writers. It is interested in articles, book reviews, interviews, opinion pieces, essays, and exposés.

RATES: None cited

QUERIES with published clips required; response time normally two to three weeks; send SASE for Writer's Guidelines.

TIPS: "Writers should be familiar with the magazine before sending submissions. Many of our rejections are pieces that are submitted by writers who obviously haven't read ITT."

KICK IT OVER
P.O. Box 5811, Station A
Toronto, Ontario M5W 1P2
Canada
Editor: Bob Melcombe

Kick It Over is an irregularly published anarchist magazine with 90 percent of its material provided by freelancers. It will consider articles, essays, interviews, and opinion pieces ranging from 1,500 to 3,500 words; book reviews of 800 words; photos and artwork are welcome, as well.

RATES: Payment in copies of magazine only

QUERIES are not required; response time is about two months.

TIPS: *"Kick It Over* is an anarchist magazine, concerned with all aspects of anarchist theory and practice. Special interests are ecology, feminism, strategies for change. Influences include Colin Ward, Murray Bookchin."—Editor Bob Melcombe

LAMBDA BOOK REPORT
1625 Connecticut Avenue, NW
Washington, DC 20009
Tel: 202/462-7924 Fax: 202/462-7257
E-mail: LBREditor@aol.com
Managing Editor: Jim Marks

Lambda Book Report, a gay and lesbian book review magazine, is published monthly. Ninety-five percent of its material is provided by freelance writers. It will consider book reviews ranging from 150 to 750 words; interviews of approximately 1,000 words; and essays of 750 words.

RATES: $10 to $100

QUERIES with published clips required; send SASE for Writer's Guidelines; response time is two to three weeks.

TIPS: "Send query letter: outline areas of interest and background (fiction, poetry, gender studies, history, etc.)."
—Managing Editor Jim Marks

LEFT BUSINESS OBSERVER
250 W. 85th Street
New York, NY 10024
Tel: 212/874-4020 Fax: 212/874-3137
E-mail: dhenwood@panix.com
Editor: Doug Henwood

Left Business Observer is published monthly and features all the business news you won't find in the *Wall Street Journal.* Ten to twenty percent of its articles are provided by freelance writers. It is interested in articles and reviews on economics and politics—all genres okay.

RATES: Twelve cents a word

QUERIES with published clips required; response time is one week.

TIPS: "Know the publication—be smart, witty, interesting, and radical."
—Editor Doug Henwood

LEFT CURVE
P.O. Box 472
Oakland, CA 94604
Tel: 510/763-7193
E-mail: leftcurv@wco.com
Editor/Publisher: Csaba Polony

Left Curve, published irregularly, is a critical journal concerned with cultural, social, aesthetic, and philosophic essays and reviews (books, literature, arts), and interviews. All forms will be considered. Length can be up to 5,000 words, but most are about 2,500 words.

RATES: Payment in copies only

QUERIES are not required; send SASE for Writer's Guidelines; response time is three months.

TIPS: *"Left Curve* publishes work concerning the problems of cultural forms, emerging from the crises of modernity, that strive to be independent from the control of dominant institutions, and free from the shackles of instrumental rationality."—Editor/Publisher Csaba Polony

LIBRARIANS AT LIBERTY
1716 SW Williston Road
Gainesville, FL 32608
Tel: 352/335-2200 Fax: call first
E-mail: willett@afn.org
Editor: Charles Willett

Librarians at Liberty (L@L) provides an unrestrained opportunity for critics to sound off about censorship regarding libraries and the book trade. It is published semi-annually. About 50 percent of its articles are provided by freelance writers. It is interested in non-fiction articles, profiles, book reviews, interviews, opinion pieces, essays, and exposés, ranging from 250 to 2,000 words. L@L is anti-copyright. The editor reserves the right to edit all material submitted.
RATES: $30 to $50
QUERIES are not required; there is no response unless published.
TIPS: "Non-fiction only. Censorship, self-censorship of/by libraries and the book trade. All aspects of the alternative press related to libraries. Material which deals frankly and honestly with issues of independent, non-corporate writing and libraries. Gives library workers, publishers, booksellers, and users an unconstrained opportunity to express their concerns."—Editor Charles Willett

MEDIAFILE
814 Mission Street, Suite 205
San Francisco, CA 94103
Tel: 415/546-6334 Fax: 415/546-6218
Editor: Andrea Buffa

MediaFile is a bimonthly newspaper published by the Media Alliance, an organization of more than 3,000 San Francisco Bay Area media professionals. About 80 percent of its articles are provided by freelance writers. It is interested in articles and analyses relating to the media, with a specific interest in the San Francisco Bay Area; book reviews on books about media; profiles of interesting media workers; and investigative media exposés encouraged.
RATES: Depends on experience; frequently free copies of newspaper.
QUERIES are not required but helpful, along with published clips; response time normally in two weeks; send SASE for Writer's Guidelines.
TIPS: "Media, First Amendment, censorship issues are our bag."

MIGHT
150 4th Street, #650
San Francisco, CA 94103-3048
Tel: 415/896-1528 Fax: 415/974-1216
E-mail: mightmag@aol.com
Editors: David Eggers, David Moodie, Paul Tullis

Might, published bimonthly, does not want to see anything about Generation X! Its freelance articles range from 10 to 80 percent depending on the issue. It is interested in well-researched hard journalism up to 5,000 words; profiles and interviews up to 2,500 words; pranks up to 2,000 words; satire up to 2,000 words, book reviews up to 1,000 words. No personal essays.
RATES: "Nobody here gets paid, including the editors. We hope that will change in '96."
QUERIES with published clips

required ("unless you're somebody we've heard of"; for Writer's Guidelines, read the magazine; response time ranges from one day to four months.

TIPS: "No first person, nothing about Generation X."—Editor Paul Tullis

MOTHER JONES
731 Market Street, Suite 600
San Francisco, CA 94103
Tel: 415/665-6637 Fax: 415/665-6696
Editor: Jeffrey Klein; Managing Editor: Katharine Fong

Mother Jones is a bimonthly magazine known for its investigative journalism and exposés, and its coverage of social issues, public affairs, and popular culture. Most of its articles are written by freelancers. It is interested in hard-hitting investigative reports exposing government, corporate, scientific, institutional cover-ups, etc.; thoughtful articles that challenge conventional wisdom on national issues; and people-oriented stories on issues such as the environment, labor, the media, health care, consumer protection, and cultural trends. "Outfront" stories run 250-500 words; short features run 1,200-3,000 words, and longer features run 3,000-5,000 words.

RATES: 80 cents per word for commissioned stories

QUERIES with published clips required; send SASE for Writer's Guidelines; please do not query by phone or fax.

TIPS: "Keep in mind that our lead time is three months and submissions should not be so time-bound that they will appear dated. We are not a news magazine."

MS.
230 Park Avenue
New York, NY 10169
Tel: 212/551-9595

Ms. is a bimonthly magazine that focuses primarily on women's issues and news. About 80 percent of its articles are provided by freelance writers. It is interested in articles, profiles, book reviews, opinion pieces, essays, and exposés. Article lengths: most departments, 1,200 words; features, 3,000-4,000 words; U.S. news, 1,000-2,000 words.

RATES: Between 70 cents and $1 per word, approximately

QUERIES with published clips required; address queries to Manuscripts Editor; response time about 12 weeks; send SASE for Writer's Guidelines.

MULTINATIONAL MONITOR
P.O. Box 19405
Washington, DC 20036
Tel: 202/387-8030
Fax: 202/234-5176
E-mail: monitor@essential.org
Editor: Robert Weissman

The Multinational Monitor is a monthly news magazine that focuses on the activities and escapades of multinational corporations. About 50 percent of its articles are provided by freelance writers. It is interested in articles, profiles, book reviews, interviews, essays, exposés, features, and news items relating to multinational corporate issues. No fiction.

RATES: Ten cents a word

QUERIES required; send SASE for Writer's Guidelines.

TIPS: "Issues include all topics related to the activities of multinational corporations and their impact on labor, health, consumer issues, and environment, especially in the Third World." —A. Freeman

THE NATION
72 Fifth Avenue
New York, NY 10011
Tel: 212/242-8400
Fax: 212/463-9712
Editor-in-Chief: Katrina Vanden Heuvel

The Nation is a weekly magazine (biweekly through the summer) dedicated to reporting on issues dealing with labor, national politics, business, consumer affairs, environmental politics, civil liberties, and foreign affairs. About 75 percent of its articles are provided by freelance writers. It is interested in articles, book reviews, opinion pieces, essays, and exposés.

RATES: $75 per Nation page
QUERIES with published clips required; normal response time is four weeks; send SASE for Writer's Guidelines.
TIPS: "Leftist politics."—Dennis Selby

NATIONAL CATHOLIC REPORTER
P.O. Box 419281
Kansas City, MO 64141
Tel: 816/531-0538
Fax: 816/968-2280
Editor: Tom Fox

The National Catholic Reporter is published weekly from September through May with the exception of Thanksgiving week and the first week in January. It publishes articles, profiles, book reviews, interviews, opinion pieces, essays, exposés, features, and news items. About 50 percent of its articles are

provided by freelance writers. Average length is from 750 to 1,500 words.
RATES: Fifteen cents a word
QUERIES are required.

NEWSLETTER ON
INTELLECTUAL FREEDOM
50 E. Huron Street
Chicago, IL 60611
Tel: 312/280-4223 Fax: 312/280-4227
Editor: Judith F. Krug

The Newsletter On Intellectual Freedom is a bimonthly magazine published by the American Library Association (ALA). Book reviews are published in every issue of the *Newsletter*. Interested reviewers should contact the ALA Office for Intellectual Freedom for guidelines. Articles focusing on intellectual freedom, freedom of the press, censorship, and the First Amendment will be considered for publication.
RATES: Pro bono
QUERIES required; send SASE for Writer's Guidelines.
TIPS: "Authors should contact the Office for Intellectual Freedom for information and guidelines."—Editor Judith Krug

NORTH COAST XPRESS
P.O. Box 1226
Occidental, CA 95465
Tel: 707/874-3104
Fax: 707/874-1453
E-mail:doretk@sonic.net
Senior Editor: Doret Kollerer

North Coast Xpress is a bimonthly publication dedicated to justice issues. Eighty percent of its material is provided by freelancers. It is "reluctant to print interviews, but does occasionally. Otherwise, anything goes." Prefers articles under 2,400 words on Macintosh compatible disk.

RATES: Operates at a loss; no funds available now

QUERIES are not required; response time is two weeks.

TIPS: "Open to any topic related to justice (economic, political, social, or environmental). We are a voice for the voiceless, particularly prisoners and minorities, and/or poor populations in the U.S."—Senior Editor Doret Kollerer

OPEN EYE
BM Open Eye
London, WC1N 3XX, U.K.
Tel: 0441-956-250654
Editors: Matthew Kalman
and John Murray

Open Eye is a British publication which is dedicated to "challenging media censorship." It cites its publication schedule as yearly/biyearly. About 50 percent of its articles are provided by freelance writers. It is particularly interested in exposés, which are its specialty, particularly investigation of military and security services and of "New-Age Nazism." Other subject areas include Green and Transpersonal issues, radical politics, and book reviews on these topics. Maximum length is 4,000-5,000 words.

RATES: Costs only

QUERIES are required; response time is one month.

TIPS: "Open Eye uncovers the issues the media conceals."

PACIFIC SUN
P.O. Box 5553
Mill Valley, CA 94942
Tel: 415/383-4500
Fax: 415/383-4159
E-mail: PSun@aol.com
Publisher/Editor: Steve McNamara;
Managing Editor: Linda Xiques

Pacific Sun is a weekly newspaper published on Wednesdays, circulated primarily in Marin and Sonoma counties in northern California. About 75 percent of its articles are provided by freelance writers. It is interested in articles, profiles, book reviews, interviews, and exposés. In-depth articles are 2,500-3,000 words; short newsy articles are 800 words; short features range from 1,200 to 1,500 words; and reviews are 500-800 words.

RATES: $75 to $150 to $400

QUERIES with published clips required; send SASE for Writer's Guidelines; response time is one month.

TIPS: "We are a local interest paper. No national or international news unless there is a strong Marin/Sonoma hook." —Managing Editor Linda Xiques

PEACE MAGAZINE
736 Bathurst Street
Toronto, Ontario M5S 2R4
Canada
Tel: 416/533-7581
E-mail: mspencer@web.net
Editor: Metta Spencer

Peace Magazine is a bimonthly publication dedicated to peace, social justice, and non-violence. One hundred percent of its material is from freelance writers. It will consider articles, profiles, interviews, and features ranging from 500 to

2,500 words; and book reviews from 500 to 1,200 words.

RATES: Copies of magazine only

QUERIES are required; normal response time is between two and four weeks.

PEACE REVIEW:
A TRANSNATIONAL QUARTERLY
Peace & Justice Studies
University of San Francisco
2130 Fulton Street
San Francisco, CA 94117
Tel: 415/422-6349/6496
Fax: 415/422-2346 or 415/388-2631
E-mail: eliasr@usfca.edu
Editor: Robert Elias

Peace Review is a quarterly, multidisciplinary journal of essays addressing broad issues of peace, human rights, and development. It publishes relatively short essays, ranging from 3,000 to 3,500 words, short reviews of not more than 800 words, and brief biographies of distinguished peace activists. A transnational journal with distribution to more than 40 countries, it is edited for a wide readership.

RATES: Fifty offprints of each essay accepted for publication and a copy of the relevant journal issue

QUERIES are not required; send SASE for Writer's Guidelines (each issue is organized around a particular theme).

TIPS: "We are most interested in the cultural and political issues surrounding conflicts occurring between nations and peoples. Relevant topics include war, violence, human rights, political economy, development, culture and consciousness, the environment, and related issues."

THE PEOPLE'S WARRIOR
P.O. Box 488
Rockwall, TX 75087
Tel: 214/771-1991
Publisher: David Parker

The People's Warrior is a monthly publication which seeks to explore and profile legal or political corruption. About 90 percent of its articles are provided by freelance writers. All articles, profiles, book reviews, interviews, opinion pieces, essays, and exposés that deal with legal or political corruption will be given serious consideration. Manuscript length varies from two through ten typewritten, single-spaced pages.

RATES: $45 credit for 12-month subscription

QUERIES are not required; response time is two weeks.

TIPS: "We're particularly interested in well-documented articles which profile legal or political corruption."
—Publisher David Parker

PERCEPTIONS MAGAZINE
c/o 10734 Jefferson Boulevard
Suite 502
Culver City, California 90230
Tel: 310/313-5185 or 800/276-4448
Fax: 310/313-5198
E-mail: Perceptions@Primenet.Com
Editor: Judi V. Brewer

Perceptions Magazine is a bimonthly publication with 100 percent of its articles written by freelance writers. It is interested in articles, profiles, book reviews, interviews, essays, and exposés up to 2,500 words.

RATES: Gratitude, $5, and three magazines

QUERIES required; send SASE for Writer's Guidelines; response time is less than six weeks.

TIPS: "Must read magazine first before enquiry."

PREVAILING WINDS MAGAZINE
P.O. Box 23511
Santa Barbara, CA 93121
Tel: 805/899-3433 Fax: 805/899-4773
E-mail: patrick@silcom.com
Director: Patrick Fourmy

Prevailing Winds Magazine, published semi-annually, uses 100 percent freelance material. It will consider articles, interviews, book reviews, exposés, and editorials, from one to twenty pages, though most are ususally two to four pages.

RATES: Does not monetarily commission pieces

QUERIES with published clips required; response time is six weeks.

TIPS: "Progressive yet inclusive attempt to illustrate specific issues (environment, health, corporate, military, government, intelligence, media, socio-economic, etc.) as part of a larger picture. We examine a wide range of issues as though they are interrelated."

PRISON LEGAL NEWS
2400 N.W. 80th Street, Suite 148
Seattle, WA 98117
Tel: 407/547-9716
Editors: Paul Wright and Dan Pens

Prison Legal News, a monthly publication, focuses on prison-related issues. About 30 percent of its articles are provided by freelance writers. It is interested in articles, book and video reviews, com-mentary, and exposés, ranging from 500 to 3,000 words.

RATES: Complimentary subscriptions
QUERIES are not required; send SASE for Writer's Guidelines; response time is two weeks.

TIPS: "Prison struggle, prison-related issues, legal analysis relating to prison civil rights."—Editor Paul Wright

THE PROGRESSIVE
409 E. Main Street
Madison, WI 53703
Tel: 608/257-4626 Fax: 608/257-3373
Editor: Matt Rothschild

The Progressive is a politically-oriented monthly magazine. About 80 percent of its articles are provided by freelance writers. It is interested in features, 2,500 words; activist profiles, 750 words; Q&A, 2,500 words; book reviews, 300-1,500 words; and exposés, 2,500-3,500 words.

RATES: Features, $300; book reviews, $150; interviews, $300; exposés, $300; and activist profiles, $100

QUERIES preferred with published clips; normal response time is ten days; send SASE for Writer's Guidelines.

PROGRESSIVE LIBRARIAN
P.O. Box 2203
New York, NY 10108
Tel: 212/865-6925
E-mail: librfmcr@vaxa.hofstra.edu
Editor: Mark Rosenzweig

Progressive Librarian is published twice a year by the Progressive Librarians Guild. One hundred percent of its material is provided by freelance writers. Length of submissions should be between one and thirty pages.

RATES: None cited

QUERIES are not required.

TIPS: "Librarianship, information technology and industry, academic freedom, self-censorship in education, the politics of information production and distribution, labor issues in librarianship; book reviews relating to librarianship; documents from library organizations."
—Managing Editor Elaine Harger

PUBLIC CITIZEN MAGAZINE
1600 20th Street, NW
Washington, DC 20009
Tel: 202/588-1000 Fax: 202/588-7799
E-mail: pnye@citizen.org
Editor: Peter Nye

Public Citizen Magazine is published six times a year and focuses on national policy issues and their impact on the public. About 15 percent of its articles are provided by freelance writers. It is interested in book reviews, 400 words (two reviews per magazine page); features up to 4,500 words; profiles of extraordinary individuals who work for improving their local community up to three pages.

RATES: Negotiable, $400 tops; buys one-time rights only

QUERIES required; normal response time is two weeks.

TIPS: "Our articles deal with national policy involving accountability of corporations and the government. It's best to read our magazine and be familiar with how our stories are published, their slant. We also rely heavily on facts, quotes, specific information."—Editor Peter Nye

RANDOM LENGTHS NEWS
P.O. Box 731
San Pedro, CA 90733

Tel: 310/519-1016 Fax: 310/832-1000
E-mail: 71632.201@compuserve.com
Editor: James Elmendorf

Random Lengths News is an independent biweekly publication out of the harbor area of Long Beach, California. While only 5 to 10 percent of its material is from freelance writers, it will consider investigative pieces and issue-based articles, ranging from 500 to 2,000 words. Reviews are rare, unless local.

RATES: 5 cents a word

QUERIES with published clips required; send SASE for Writer's Guidelines; response time is two to four weeks.

TIPS: "Labor issues, particularly as they relate to shipping and world trade, and poverty-related stuff appears regularly in our pages. Progressive, lefty economics is our main balliwick. We do need more civil rights coverage, and particularly welcome submissions from people of color."—Editor James Elmendorf

RETHINKING SCHOOLS
1001 E. Keefe Avenue
Milwaukee, WI 53212-1710
Tel: 414/964-9646 Fax: 414/964-7220
Managing Editor: Barbara Miner

Rethinking Schools is a publication that focuses on analysis or critique of current educational policy, theory, or practice. From 5 to 10 percent of its articles are provided by unsolicited freelance writers. Its essays range from 600 to 2,000 words; how-to-articles (first-person reflections, tips on classroom materials, curriculum, and practices) are 200 to 1,500 words; poetry, student work, bibliography, and photos/graphics also considered.

RATES: From none to small

QUERIES not required; published clips preferred; send SASE for Writer's Guidelines; response time is six to eight weeks.

SOJOURNERS
2401 15th Street, NW
Washington, DC 20009
Tel: 202/328-8842
Fax: 202/328-8757
Editor: Jim Wallis

Sojourners is published bimonthly (6 times a year) and about 25 percent of its articles are provided by freelance writers. It is interested in features on issues of faith, politics, and culture (1,800-3,200 words); book, film, and music reviews (600-1,000 words).

RATES: Features, $100-$200; reviews, $40

QUERIES are not required; submit published clips; normal response time is six to eight weeks; send SASE for Writer's Guidelines.

SONOMA COUNTY INDEPENDENT
540 Mendocino Avenue
Santa Rosa, CA 95401
Tel: 707/527-1200
Fax: 707/527-1288
E-mail: Indy@livewire.com
Editor: Greg Cahill

Sonoma County Independent is an alternative weekly newspaper in Sonoma County in northern California. From 60 to 75 percent of its articles are provided by freelance writers. It is interested in 2,000 to 3,000 word news features, usually in-depth local stories, but always looking for well-written people-oriented features identifying social or cultural

trends. Also interested in 600-750 words on books, music, film, and theater, as well as opinion pieces.

RATES: Ten cents a word for news and features (more when appropriate); $35-$60 for columns

QUERIES with published clips required; send SASE for Writer's Guidelines; response time is two weeks.

TIPS: "We are less interested in 'topics' than interesting people who can tell the 'story' within the topic. Writing style is always important, and our publication is always on the look-out for good writers who are good story-tellers."
—Editor Greg Cahill

SOUTHERN EXPOSURE
P.O. Box 531
Durham, NC 27702
Tel: 919/419-8311, Ext. 26
Editor: Pat Arnow

Southern Exposure is a quarterly magazine that focuses on Southern politics and culture. About 50 percent of its articles are provided by freelance writers. It is interested in investigative journalism, essays, profiles, book reviews, oral histories, and features on Southern politics and culture.

RATES: $50-$250

QUERIES are not required; submit published clips; normal response time is four to six weeks; send SASE for Writer's Guidelines. Send $5.00 for a sample copy.

THE SPOTLIGHT
300 Independence Avenue, SE
Washington, DC 20003
Tel: 202/544-1794
Managing Editor: Fred Blahut

The Spotlight is a Washington, DC-based weekly newspaper which focuses on political/economic issues. About 20 percent of its articles are provided by freelance writers. It is interested in articles, opinion pieces, and profiles ranging from 700 to 1,000 words.

RATES: Negotiable

QUERIES required; response time is three weeks.

TIPS: "Economic-Nationalism, American-First Politics, Constitutional Rights."

ST. LOUIS JOURNALISM REVIEW
8380 Olive Boulevard
St. Louis, MO 63132
Tel: 314/991-1699 Fax: 314/997-1898
Editor/Publisher: Ed Bishop
Emeritus: Charles L. Klotzer

The St. Louis Journalism Review is a regionally based but nationally oriented journalism review magazine published monthly except for combined issues in July/August and December/January. About 80 percent of its articles are provided by freelance writers. It is interested in articles, profiles, interviews, opinion pieces, essays, and exposés dealing with the news media.

RATES: $20 to $100

QUERIES not required; normal response time is three to four weeks.

TIPS: "While the St. Louis region is of primary interest, national and international pieces dealing with media criticism are considered."

THE SUN
107 N. Roberson Street
Chapel Hill, NC 27516
Tel: 919/942-5282
Editor: Sy Safransky

The Sun is published monthly. About 90 percent of its articles are provided by freelance writers. It is interested in interviews and essays.

RATES: $300 to $750

QUERIES not required; send SASE for Writer's Guidelines; response time is three months.

TIPS: "Send $3.50 for a sample copy before submitting."

SYNTHESIS/REGENERATION
A Magazine of Green Social Thought
WD Press / P.O. Box 24115
St. Louis, MO 63130
Tel: 314/727-8554 Fax: call first
E-mail: jsutter@igc.apc.org
Editor: Don Fitz

Synthesis/Regeneration is a publication dedicated to environmental, labor, and social justice issues. It is interested in articles, profiles, essays, interviews, exposés, and opinion pieces with this emphasis.

RATES: "Authors donate time. We are not restrained by financial obligations."

QUERIES are required; response time is three months.

TIPS: "Environmental issues (toxics, dioxins, lead, mercury, nuclear); labor, especially as it relates to environmental issues; social justice; progressive electoral efforts."—Editor Don Fitz

TEXAS OBSERVER
307 W. 7th Street
Austin, TX 78701
Tel: 512/477-0746
Fax: 512/474-1175
E-mail: observer@eden.com
Editor: Lou Dubose

Texas Observer, a publication that focuses on Texas but creates national waves, is published every two weeks. About 50 percent of its articles are provided by freelance writers. It is interested in articles, profiles, book reviews, interviews, essays, and exposés.

RATES: $50 to $300

QUERIES requested first; send SASE for Writer's Guidelines.

TIPS: "Texas-oriented politics and culture."—Associate Editor Michael King

THIRD FORCE MAGAZINE
1218 E. 21st Street
Oakland, CA 94606
Tel: 510/533-7583 Fax: 510/533-0923
Managing Editor: John Anner; Senior Editor: Andrea Lewis

Third Force Magazine, a bimonthly, is interested in "Issues and actions in communities of color." It will consider virtually any article that offers a fresh and interesting look at issues that relate to communities of color—especially political analysis, grass-roots organizing, low-income communities, etc. It is not interested in pop-psychology, self-help, fashion and beauty, business success stories, etc. About 70 percent of its articles are provided by freelance writers.

RATES: Negotiable

QUERIES with published clips, or writing sample, preferred; send SASE for Writer's Guidelines; response time is from four to six weeks.

TIPS: "We're interested in grass-roots organizing, gender and sexuality issues, low-income communities and class issues, political and cultural analysis relating to communities of color, multi-

racial coalition efforts, police and community safety issues, etc. All issues must relate to, or be of interest to, communities of color."—Senior Editor Andrea Lewis

TIKKUN MAGAZINE
251 W. 100th Street, 5th Floor
New York, NY 10025
Tel: 212/864-4110 Fax: 212/864-4137
Editor & Publisher: Michael Lerner

Tikkun is a bimonthly magazine that focuses on political and cultural issues. It is interested in articles, profiles, book reviews, interviews, opinion pieces, essays, exposés, features, and news items; all types of material of varying lengths.

RATES: Varies

QUERIES are not required; normal response time is four months.

TIPS: "Political/cultural critiques— magazine has a liberal/progressive slant but does publish all sorts of viewpoints. A non-profit magazine."

TOWARD FREEDOM
209 College Street
Burlington, VT 05401
Tel: 802/658-2523 Fax: 802/658-3738
E-mail: mavmedia@aol.com
Editor: Greg Guma

Toward Freedom, an international journal of news, analysis, and advocacy, is published eight times a year. About 75 percent of its articles are provided by freelance writers. It is interested in international perspectives: features from 2,000 to 3,000 words; international news reports from 800 to 1,200 words; reviews, essays. Focus on human rights, politics and culture, environment, women, global media, post-nationalist movements, and creative solutions to world problems.

RATES: 10 cents per printed word

QUERIES required; send SASE for Writer's Guidelines; response time is 30 days.

TIPS: "Query with one to three ideas; we look for writers who combine research with direct experience and a passionate approach. Special issues each year, e.g. environment and native peoples, global media and women. We cover the world with special emphasis on revealing relationships between cultures and political trends. Profiles also welcome."
—Editor Greg Guma

TRADESWOMEN MAGAZINE
A Magazine for Women
in Blue Collar Work
P.O. Box 2622
Berkeley, CA 94702
Tel: 510/433-1378
E-mail: Tradeswmn@aol.com
Editor: Molly Martin

Tradeswomen Magazine is, as its subtitle suggests, dedicated to women in blue collar work. It is published quarterly, with 50 percent of its material provided by freelance writers.

RATES: None offered

QUERIES are not required.

TRANSITION MAGAZINE
1430 Massachusetts Avenue, 4th Fl.
Cambridge, MA 02138
Tel: 617/496-2847
Fax: 617/496-2877
E-mail: Transit@fas.harvard.edu
Editor: Henry Louis Gates, Jr.

Transition Magazine, published quarterly, uses only 10 percent freelance material. It will consider articles, reviews, essays, and interviews for publication.

RATES: None offered

QUERIES are not required; response time is from one to six weeks.

TIPS: "Topics in politics and culture, focused on race and ethnicity, but broadly interested in issues around the globe. Interviews with musicians, writers, politicians, especially from the developing world."—Executive Editor M. Vazquez

TURNING THE TIDE:
JOURNAL OF ANTI-RACIST
ACTIVISM, RESEARCH
& EDUCATION
P.O. Box 1055
Culver City, CA 90232
Tel: 310/288-5003
E-mail: mnovickttt@igc.apc.org
Editor: Michael Novick

Turning the Tide: Journal of Anti-Racist Activism, Research & Education is published quarterly in March, June, September, and December. From 30 to 40 percent of its articles are provided by freelance writers. It is interested in articles, profiles, book reviews, interviews, opinion pieces, essays, exposés, and poetry.

RATES: In contributor's copies

QUERIES preferred but not required; send 9x12 envelope and 78-cents postage for sample copy; response time is one to two months.

TIPS: "We would like to see material that looks at far-reaching solutions, as well as thorough analyses of the problems

related to issues of racism, sexism, and colonialism. We prefer material at no higher than a low high school reading level, light on rhetoric."
—Editor Michael Novick

U. THE NATIONAL
COLLEGE MAGAZINE
1800 Century Park East, #820
Los Angeles, CA 90067
Tel: 310/551-1381 Fax: 310/551-1659
E-mail: umagazine@aol.com
editor@umagazine.com
Editor: Frances Huffman

U. The National College Magazine focuses on collegiate subjects and publishes 9 issues a year. About 90 percent of its articles are provided by freelance writers. It is looking for college news briefs: 300 words; feature articles: 1,000 words; profiles and interviews of celebrities, authors, athletes, politicians, etc.: 1,000 words; opinion pieces: 500 words; mini-features: 400 words; movie previews and music reviews: 100 words.

RATES: Range from $25 to $100

QUERIES with published clips required (by phone, fax, or mail); send SASE for Writer's Guidelines; response time is one to two months.

TIPS: "Our articles are written by college students and must have a college focus."—Editor Frances Huffman

UTNE READER
1624 Harmon Place
Minneapolis, MN 55403
Tel: 612/338-5040
Managing Editor: Lynette Lamb

The Utne Reader is an eclectic bimonthly magazine that has earned the reputation of being the *Reader's Digest* of the alternative media. About 20 percent of its articles are provided by freelance writers. It is interested in short essays, articles, and opinion pieces.

RATES: $100-$500

QUERIES are not required; submit published clips; normal response time is two to three months; send SASE for Writer's Guidelines.

TIPS: "We use unsolicited material most often in our 'Gleanings' section. Most of our other freelance articles are assigned. The majority of *Utne Reader* articles are reprinted from other publications."—Managing Editor Lynette Lamb

THE WASHINGTON FREE PRESS
1463 E. Republican, #178
Seattle, WA 98112
Tel: 206/233-1780
E-mail: freepres@scn.org

The Washington Free Press emphasizes investigative reporting with a focus on Seattle or the Northwest. It is published six times a year. About 35 percent of its articles are provided by freelance writers. It is interested in feature stories, from 700 to 4,000 words, on labor, environmental, political, cultural, or media-critical topics; book reviews (chiefly of Northwest authors) 700 words or less; interviews at 1,200 words.

RATES: "All of our writing is volunteer."

QUERIES with published clips required; send SASE for Writer's Guidelines; response time is two weeks.

TIPS: "Please contact us first with story idea before you write the whole shebang! Address queries to Submissions Editor."

WASHINGTON SPECTATOR
541 E. 12th Street
New York, NY 10009
Tel: 212/995-8527
Fax: 212/979-2055
Editor: Ben Franklin
Publisher: Phillip Frazer

The Washington Spectator is a small, but influential, political watchdog newsletter published 22 times a year. About 10 percent of its articles are provided by freelance writers. It is primarily interested in articles and exposés.

RATES: Varies: 50 cents a word and up

QUERIES with published clips required; normal response time is one week.

TIPS: "Write a very brief (one page maximum) note as a first proposal."
—Publisher Phillip Frazer

WHO CARES: A JOURNAL
OF SERVICE AND ACTION
1511 K Street, NW, Suite 1042
Washington, DC 20005
Tel: 202/628-1691
Fax: 202/628-2063
E-mail: info@whocares.org
Editors: Heather McLeod,
Cheryl Cole-Dodwell,
Leslie Crutchfield

Who Cares Magazine, the only national publication covering the cutting edge of community service and activism, is published quarterly. It is interested in "Partners in Change" articles on service programs throughout the country (1,000 to 1,300 words); features (1,500 to 2,500 words); entrepreneurial programs (1,500 to 2,500 words); and department items ranging from 100 to 1,500 words.

RATES: Small stipends or minimal fees-per-word for commissioned articles; solicited features negotiable

QUERIES with published clips required; send SASE for Writer's Guidelines.

TIPS: "*Who Cares* informs its readers through incisive, nonpartisan coverage of new service initiatives; inspires them with profiles of volunteers making a difference; and challenges them to consider new solutions to old problems."

WILLAMETTE WEEK
822 SW 10th Avenue
Portland, OR 97205
Tel: 503/243-2122 Fax: 503/243-1115
Editor: Mark Zusman

Willamette Week is an alternative weekly newspaper published and distributed in the Portland, Oregon area. About 50 percent of its articles are provided by freelance writers. It is interested in articles (if regional in perspective), interviews, book reviews, music reviews, profiles—again with a regional focus.

RATES: Ten cents a word

QUERIES with published clips required; normal response time is about three weeks; send SASE for Writer's Guidelines.

THE WOMEN'S REVIEW OF BOOKS
Center for Research on Women
Wellesley College
Wellesley, MA 02182
Tel: 617/283-2087 Fax: 617/283-3645
Editor: Linda Gardiner

The Women's Review of Books, published monthly, is interested in book reviews ranging from 1,500 to 2,000 words. One hundred percent of its material provided by freelance writers.

RATES: 12 cents a word

QUERIES with published clips required; response time is four to eight weeks.

TIPS: "Only experienced book reviewers, with expertise in specific fields."
—Editor Linda Gardiner

WORLD POLICY JOURNAL
65 Fifth Avenue, #413
New York, NY 10003
Tel: 212/229-9808 Fax: 212/229-5579
E-mail: pera@newschool.edu
Editor: James Chase

World Policy Journal, published quarterly, uses only 5 percent freelance material. It will consider historical and cultural essays, reportage, profiles, policy pieces, and book reviews for publication.

RATES: $500

QUERIES are not required; send SASE for Writer's Guidelines; response time is one month.

TIPS: "*World Policy Journal* focuses on the political, economic, and cultural issues that are shaping our world today. We prefer articles written in a journalistic, rather than academic, style."

WRITER'S GUIDELINES
P.O. Box 608
Pittsburg, MO 65724
Fax: 417/993-5544
Publisher & Editor: Susan Salaki

Writer's Guidelines is a bimonthly magazine designed to help writers get published. About 99 percent of its articles are provided by freelance writers. It is interested in articles, book reviews, interviews, opinion pieces, and essays that will help writers.

RATES: Depends on quality of material

QUERIES are not required; normal response time is two weeks; send SASE for Writer's Guidelines.

TIPS: "Use a friendly relaxed style in your material but not chummy. Our objective is to help writers get published. If your article or essay contains information that will make that happen, we want to see it. We look for material the other writer publications usually overlook."
—Editor Susan Salaki

YES! A JOURNAL OF
POSITIVE FUTURES
P.O. Box 10818
Bainbridge Island, WA 98110
Tel: 206/842-0216 Fax: 206/842-5208
E-mail: yes@futurenet.org
Editor: Sarah van Gelder

Yes! A Journal of Positive Futures, a successor to *In Context*, is published quarterly by the Positive Futures Network. Ten to twenty percent of its material is provided by freelance writers. It is interested in positive articles, essays, and opinion pieces.

RATES: Honorariums

QUERIES with clips required; send SASE for Writer's Guidelines; response time is one to two months.

TIPS: "Articles should be positive and include examples of projects and programs that are working to make the world more sustainable."
—Assistant Editor Jane Engel

Top 5 Censored Reprints

1 CENSORED

Risking the World: Nuclear Proliferation in Space

**"RISKING THE WORLD:
NUCLEAR PROLIFERATION
IN SPACE"**
By Karl Grossman; *CovertAction
Quarterly*; Summer 1996

Despite enormous danger, huge expense, and a clear alternative—solar power—the U.S. government is pushing ahead with the deployment of nuclear technology in space. In October 1997, NASA plans to launch the Cassini probe to Sat-

urn. Carrying 72.3 pounds of plutonium-238 fuel—the largest amount of plutonium ever used in space, the probe will sit atop a Lockheed Martin-built Titan IV rocket. This same kind of rocket has undergone a series of mishaps including a 1993 explosion in California soon after take-off which destroyed a $1 billion spy satellite system and sent its fragments falling into the Pacific Ocean.

Space News, the space industry trade newspaper, reported that "the high risk and cost of the Cassini mission to Saturn troubled NASA Administrator Daniel Goldin so much that he would cancel the program if it were not so important to planetary science."

But it is not science alone that is driving the project or causing scientists, politicians, and the military to discount the risks. NASA Chief Scientist Frances Cordova acknowledges that the Titan IV "does not have a 100 percent success rate" and admits that using it for Cassini "is truly putting all your eggs in one basket—your 18 instruments on one firecracker." She says, "We can't fail with that mission. It would be very, very, damaging for the agency."

To say nothing of the Earth and the life on it if something goes wrong. Plutonium has long been described by scientists as the most toxic substance known. It is "so toxic," says Dr. Helen Caldicott, founder of Physicians for Social Responsibility, "that less than one-millionth of a gram is a carcinogenic dose. One pound, if uniformly distributed, could hypothetically induce lung cancer in every person on Earth."

In addition to the specter of radioactivity spread by an accident on launch, another, potentially more lethal, scenario is causing concern. Because Cassini does not have the propulsion power to get directly from Earth to Saturn, NASA plans a "slingshot maneuver" in which the probe will circle Venus twice and hurtle back at Earth. It will then buzz the Earth in August 1999 at 42,300 miles per hour just 312 miles above the surface. After whipping around Earth and using its gravity, Cassini would then have the velocity, says NASA, to reach Saturn. But during that Earth flyby, if Cassini comes in too close, it could burn up in the 75-mile-high atmosphere and disperse plutonium across the planet.

Dr. Michio Kaku, professor of nuclear physics at the City University of New York, explains the catastrophic consequence of such a fly-by accident:

"[I]f there is a small misfire [of Cassini's] rocket system, it will mean that [it] will penetrate into the Earth's atmosphere and the sheer friction will begin to wipe out the heat shield and it will, like a meteor, flame into the Earth's atmosphere. This thing, coming into the Earth's atmosphere, will vaporize, release the payload and then particles of plutonium dioxide will begin to rain down on populated areas, if that is where the system is going to be hitting. [Pulverized plutonium dust] will rain down on people's hair, people's clothing, get into people's bodies. And because it is not water soluble, there is a very good chance that it could be inhaled and stay within the body causing cancer over a number of decades."

Indeed, NASA says in its *Final Environmental Impact Statement for the Cassini Mission*, that if an "inadvertent reentry occurred" during the flyby, approximately five billion of the seven to eight billion people on Earth, "could receive 99 percent or more of the radiation exposure." As for the death toll, which NASA labels "health effects," the agency says that only 2,300 deaths "could occur over a 50-year period to this exposed population" and these "latent cancer fatalities" would likely be "statistically indistinguishable from normally occurring cancer fatalities among the world population."

However, after reviewing the data in the NASA report, Dr. Ernest Sternglass, professor emeritus of radiological physics at the University of Pittsburgh School of Medicine, concluded that NASA "underestimate[s] the cancer alone by about 2,000 to 4,000 times. Which means that not counting all the other causes of death—infant mortality, heart disease, immune deficiency diseases, and all that—we're talking in the order of ten to twenty million extra deaths." The actual death toll, then, the physicist warned, may be as high as 30 to 40 million people.

Dr. Horst Poehler, for 22 years a scientist for NASA contractors at the Kennedy Space Center, commented on the Cassini mission: "Remember the old Hollywood movies when a mad scientist would risk the world to carry out his particular project? Well, those mad scientists have moved to NASA."

IGNORED OPTIONS

Madder yet is that the deadly plutonium on Cassini is unnecessary. It will be used not for propulsion—that will be done by a chemically-fueled rocket—but to power three radioisotope thermal generators (RTGs) to generate a modest 745 watts of electricity to run instruments— a task that could be accomplished with solar energy. In 1994, the European Space Agency (ESA) announced a "technology milestone"—development of new high-performance silicon solar cells with 25 percent efficiency. According to ESA, the cells have "the highest efficiency ever reached worldwide,... [and] could profitably be used in deep space missions."

"If given the money to do the work, within five years [ESA] could have solar cells ready to power a space mission to Saturn," said ESA physicist Carla Signorini.

But NASA, the Department of Energy's (DOE) national nuclear laboratories, and the corporations that have been involved in producing nuclear hardware for the space mission insist on sticking with nuclear on Cassini.

RUSSIAN ROULETTE

While refusing to embrace European technology for Cassini, with the end of the Cold War, the U.S. chose Russian-made reactors for other space activities. The Air Force is currently ground-testing six Russian Topaz II nuclear reactors—originally purchased for use in the Strategic Defense Initiative or Star Wars—at its Phillips Laboratory in New Mexico. A flight test scheduled for December 1995 was postponed after complaints from U.S. astronomers.

The members of the governing council of the American Astronomical Society "emphasized they were not opposing the mission or the use of nuclear reactors in space.... Instead, they wanted to put pressure on the government to use a "more powerful rocket" that would put the reactor into a higher orbit "to avoid any interference with current or planned astronomy missions." Astronomical interference could occur because Topaz II "would leave a trail of nuclear particles."

IN THE UNLIKELY EVENT OF A WATER LANDING...

In fact, the Topaz II reactor could leave more than that. According to a Sandia National Laboratories safety report, if an accident occurs on launch and the reactor falls into the water, it could undergo a runaway nuclear reaction; if it falls from orbit it "may break up on reentry." Physicist Ned S. Rasor, who has worked on U.S. space reactor development, argues that because Topaz II "will go critical— meaning an uncontrolled nuclear reaction—if immersed in water, [it] is therefore unsafe for launch according to both U.S. and Russian safety standards." Also, he points out that "no Topaz II system has been operated in space."

While the lack of actual experience in space worries Rasor, those interested in the military potential of space are eager to start testing in the field. Proponents of orbiting battle platforms for Star Wars look to reactors like Topaz II as a future power source for hyper-velocity guns, particle beams, and laser weapons on battle platforms. As Lt. Gen. James Abrahamson, head of the Strategic Defense Initiative Organization, warned the Fifth Annual Symposium on Space Nuclear Power and Propulsion in 1988, "Without reactors in orbit [there is] going to be a long, long light cord that goes down to the surface of the Earth" bringing up power. Abrahamson said: "Failure to develop nuclear power in space could cripple efforts to deploy anti-missile sensors and weapons in orbit."

Indeed, Star Wars as conceived by the U.S. national nuclear laboratories and military has had a large nuclear component. Work proceeded secretly through the 1980s, at a cost of $800 million, on development of rockets propelled by nuclear power to loft "giant weapons and other military payloads into space." From the start, scientists calculated the risk in lives and took the gamble. A flight-test of a nuclear rocket, codenamed Timberwind, was planned, mostly across Antarctica to avoid areas of human population, but the route also took the rocket over New Zealand. Sandia National Laboratories projected the likelihood of the atomic rocket crashing there at 1 in 2,325.

CLINTON CARRIES ON

Despite some expectations that the Clinton administration would put an end to the Reagan/Bush Administrations' vision of Star Wars, it has continued to budget $3 billion annually for the endeavor. And a 1993 White House policy statement asserted that "space nuclear power and propulsion systems can contribute to scientific, commercial, and national security space missions." Later that year, the Department of Energy placed a notice in the Federal Register announcing that it sought to "fund research and development studies directed at...identifying innovative approaches using nuclear reactor power and propulsion systems for potential future NASA, DOD, and commercial space activities." Not to be outdone, the Republican congressional majority under Newt Gingrich has been seeking a major Star Wars revival as promised in its "Contract With America." And former Senate Majority Leader Bob Dole is demanding a revived "missile defense." In fact, since the end of the Cold War, the biggest change in the program has been in name: from the Strategic Defense Initiative to Ballistic Missile Defense.

The commitment to nuclearize space continues. Last year, Terry Lash, director of the Energy Department's Office of Nuclear Energy, told the subcommittee of the House Committee on Appropriations that the "purpose" of his agency's "Space and Defense Power Systems program is to produce radioisotope power systems for U.S. civilian space missions and national security terrestrial missions. Radioisotope power systems have been used for three decades and are proven, reliable, and maintenance-free power supplies that are capable of producing up to several kilowatts of electricity for tens of years.... Radioisotope power systems are the cornerstone of the nation's space nuclear energy program.... In addition, the program provides support for terrestrial Radioisotope Thermoelectric Generator applications for national security missions."

Nuclear technology is being incorporated into a wide variety of scientific and military space projects. Among them:

• Sandia National Laboratories is embarking on a project to develop nuclear-powered satellites to transmit "high-definition, multichannel television" signals. It is intended to be a pathway to make the U.S. a global telecommunications superpower, and would pair controversial space nuclear power with entertainment and communications on demand. Sandia's Roger X. Leonard, who unveiled the project at the 11th Annual Symposium on Space Nuclear Power and Propulsion in Albuquerque in 1994, said a "constellation of five such satellites, powered by high-energy reactors and strategically located in orbit around the Earth" could be in place by 2000. He dismissed concerns about using nuclear technology in space, exclaiming: "Look, space already is highly radioactive."

• NASA is planning to launch a pair of plutonium-fueled space probes for a mission to Pluto in 1999.

• NASA intends to have a plutonium-powered heating system on board the Mars Pathfinder which is scheduled for launch this December.

• The U.S. Air Force has been studying the use of nuclear reactors to "provide power and propulsion for military satellites." The "bi-modal" nuclear spacecraft would serve both as a "propulsion system and for electric power."

• What *Space News* described as "an aerospace industry alliance" of seven companies, including Lockheed Martin and a Russian firm, has come up with a scheme to build a "high-powered" nuclear communications satellite.

Meanwhile, NASA is moving ahead with plans for a nuclear-powered colony on the moon.

NOT OVER MY PLANET

As the number and variety of programs increases, so does the potential for disaster. A worldwide coalition is challenging the use of nuclear power in space: The Global Network Against Weapons and Nuclear Power in Space was formed at a meeting in Washington, D.C., in 1992. Bruce Gagnon, one of the coalition's co-coordinators, declared:

"Our concern is that the United States military and major weapons corporations view space as a new market, ultimately to profit from. They are using taxpayers' dollars to put a new round of the arms race in space. At the same time the nuclear power industry views space as its new market, a place where they can put plutonium and other radioactive sources, whether it's military missions or civilian inter-planetary missions....What is needed now is for the American public to speak out."

Local groups around the world have. On the island of Kauai in Hawaii, for example, a series of test launches—now dubbed "Stars" launches—has been met with protests that have included civil disobedience resulting in arrests. Polaris missiles are being fired along a range that ends at the Kwajalein Atoll 2,200 miles to the west. Ancient Hawaiian burial grounds and important natural habitats on the island are in the "evacuation zone" set up by the military in case launches go bad. Suzanne Marinelli of the Sierra Club of Hawaii, one of those arrested in the protests, warns that an accident on launch could be "catastrophic, raining burning debris and hazardous waste.

"We are enslaving our own people for the empowerment of particular individuals and programs, and it's a sin."

Meanwhile, the Global Network and others are digging in and insisting that the policy-making process be "opened up" to "re-examine basic fundamental assumptions," declared Network co-coordinator Bill Sulzman. One of those core assumptions—that the development of U.S. nuclear superiority in technology and weaponry is essential to national security—began with the Manhattan Project. That crash program to build the atomic bombs dropped on Japan also created the base for spreading nuclear power to space. But, declared Sulzman, "The Manhattan Project needed to end [with] World War II. We don't need it still alive and controlling our national security apparatus."

Instead, with an impressive half-life of its own, the nuclear establishment easily survived the end of the war. The military men and scientists, the government officials, and corporate contractors of the Manhattan Project sought to do more with nuclear technology in order to perpetuate the vast enterprise that had been created—to hold their jobs and contracts. More nuclear weapons could be built, and tens of thousands were. But what else could be done to keep the new nuclear establishment going?

In 1946, the Manhattan Project became the Atomic Energy Commission (AEC) which "hastened to build a number of new atomic toys," according to

Nukespeak. "The commission had an early interest in nuclear-powered planes, and the Nuclear Energy Propulsion for Aircraft project was begun in 1948. Atomic-powered airplanes would make long-distance bombing easier, since the planes were expected to be able to circle the globe without refueling." More than $1 billion (in 1950s dollars) was spent on this scheme before it was canceled by the Kennedy Administration in 1961. Washington was concerned about an atomic plane crashing and—as then Secretary of Defense Robert S. McNamara told Congress—because nuclear aircraft would "expel some small fraction of radioactive fission products into the atmosphere, creating an important public relations problem if not an actual physical hazard."

SNAP, CRACKLE, BOOM

An early program to develop nuclear rockets began in the 1950s at Los Alamos, *Nukespeak* relates, "with the development of the Kiwi reactors, inauspiciously named after the flightless New Zealand bird." In fact, even after the expenditure of $2 billion for such programs as NERVA, and Projects Pluto, Rover, and Poodle, no nuclear rocket ever got off the ground. There were government concerns about a nuclear rocket crashing. And there were no military orders then for nuclear rockets.

A 1961 editorial in a special edition of the trade magazine *Nucleonics* heralded "The Nuclear Space Age—the joining in inevitable matrimony of two of contemporary man's most exciting frontiers, nuclear energy and outer space." The nuclear rocket, it continued, "gives this country its only chance to catch up with—indeed to surpass—the USSR."

However, neither the Air Force nor Navy had requested nuclear rockets, a situation which *Nucleonics* deplored because there would be an "easier flow of development dollars" if there was "a clear-cut military requirement."

Meanwhile, starting in 1961, General Electric's RTGs were put into use for space satellites—until a 1964 accident in which a SNAP-9A (Systems for Nuclear Auxiliary Power) fell to earth, burning up in the atmosphere. According to a 1989 report by European nuclear agencies, the satellite's 2.1 pounds of plutonium-238 "vaporized" and "dispersed widely." After conducting a worldwide sampling, scientists found "SNAP-9A debris to be present at all continents and all latitudes." Dr. John Gofman, professor emeritus of medical physics at the University of California at Berkeley, an M.D. and Ph.D. and a co-discoverer of isotopes of plutonium and uranium as a member of the Manhattan Project, has long attributed an increased rate of lung cancer to the SNAP-9A incident.

Although the SNAP-9A accident spurred NASA to develop and use solar photovoltaic technology for the satellites, the agency continued to employ nuclear power for space probes and also as a power source on the Apollo moon missions. Indeed, noticeably absent from the blockbuster 1995 movie *Apollo 13* was mention of a nuclear device aboard the mission—a SNAP-27 carrying 8.3 pounds of plutonium.

While omitted from the film, concern over the SNAP-27 breaking up and spreading plutonium as it came down along with the astronauts took up three pages in the book on which *Apollo 13* was based. In *Lost Moon: The Perilous Voyage of Apollo 13*, mission commander Jim Lovell and his co-author write: "On the surface of the moon, the tiny generator posed no danger to anybody. But what, some people worried...would happen if the little rod of nuclear fuel never made it to the moon?...Now [SNAP-27] was on its way home, heading for just the fiery reentry the doomsayers had feared."

As Apollo 13 struggled to regain control, NASA jettisoned the plutonium-laden reactor. According to a 1980 NASA document, SNAP-27 "was successfully targeted to deposit intact in the Tonga Trench in the South Pacific [off New Zealand], where it is effectively isolated from man's environment."

RISKY BUSINESS

There have been three accidents out of the 24 known U.S. space missions involving nuclear power. The Soviet failure rate is even higher: six of their 39 nuclear missions failed. In 1978, a Cosmos 954 satellite disintegrated as it crashed to Earth over northwest Canada leaving a 124,000-square kilometer swath of nuclear debris.

The most recent U.S. missions involving RTGs lofted many times the plutonium of the earlier flights. The Galileo, launched in 1989, carried 49.25 pounds of plutonium fuel on a mission to Jupiter; the 1990 Ulysses took 25 pounds on its orbit around the sun. Those missions had been postponed after the January 28, 1986 Challenger explosion. The Florida Coalition for Peace and Justice and other parties brought lawsuits to block the nuclear launches and organized protests at the Kennedy Space Center. Even so, "[t]he American people don't realize that on the very next mission after the Challenger accident, the Ulysses spacecraft, was supposed to be sent into outer space with 25 pounds of plutonium," notes Dr. Kaku. "Now imagine that very same Challenger with the Ulysses spacecraft exploding on our television screens." Had that rocket blown up instead of the Challenger, far more people than seven astronauts could have perished.

Despite the enormous danger, NASA is committed to nuclear technology in space. And despite advances in solar power, it continues to insist—in fact, its witnesses swore in court that Galileo could only be completed with plutonium RTGs. Yet, two weeks after the 1989 launch, in response to a Freedom of Information Act request I had filed two years earlier with NASA and DOE, I received reports from the Jet Propulsion Laboratory acknowledging that solar energy could substitute for nuclear power. "Based on the current study, it appears that a Galileo Jupiter orbiting mission could be performed with a concentrated photovoltaic solar array power source without changing the mission sequence or impacting science objectives," one report began. A year later when Ulysses was launched, NASA actually admitted in its pre-launch *Final Environmental Impact Statement* that solar could substitute for nuclear power but would require a "redesign."

NUCLEAR MADNESS

Driving this seemingly mad policy is a combination of corporate, bureaucratic, and military interests. By the early 1980s, with the advent of the Reagan Star Wars program, the military was no longer resisting ordering nuclear rockets, as *Nucleonics* had complained about two

decades earlier. And NASA, with the end of its Apollo man-on-the-moon flights and fearful of decreased funding, jumped into bed with the Pentagon: the shuttle was developed in large part to fulfill military missions. NASA, DOD, and DOE in 1991 set up a joint Office for Nuclear Propulsion.

Also, NASA and DOE moved to limit the U.S. government's financial exposure in the event of the inevitable: further accidents involving nuclear space hardware. In 1991, the agencies signed a "Space Nuclear Power Agreement" restricting death or damage benefits from an accident caused by a US space nuclear device to the limits of the Price-Anderson Act. That law, passed in 1957, supposedly on a temporary basis, now caps U.S. payouts at $7.3 billion and assigned a mere $100 million for all damage to other countries and their people.

"Nuclear energy in outer space," says Dr. Kaku, is the linchpin of the U.S. space program and the key to the militarization of space. "We have nuclear weapons on the land. We have nuclear weapons in the ocean. We have nuclear weapons in the air." And now, Kaku warns:

"What we are headed for is a nuclear-propelled rocket with nuclear-propelled lasers in outer space. That's what the military and that's what NASA would really like to do. With a Timberwind rocket, a booster rocket to hoist large payloads in outer space, we are talking about the ultimate goal of all of this madness. First, we have small little reactors called the SNAP reactors. Then, we have the RTGs and Galileo and Cassini. Then we have the big Timberwind projects. And ultimately what they would like to do is have nuclear-powered battle stations in outer space. That's what all of this is leading up to."

Kaku went on to say that it is up to environmentalists, activists, and concerned citizens, "to stop this now before it reaches the point of militarization of outer space.

"We have to stop these Cassinis. We have to stop these Ulysses now before we have full-blown Timberwinds, before we have Alpha lasers, before we have genuine nuclear booster rockets and nuclear power plants in outer space. That's why we have to send a signal to Congress. We have to send a signal to NASA, and a signal to the United States Pentagon that we're not going to tolerate the nuclearization of outer space, and it stops now."

The Global Network Against Weapons and Nuclear Power in Space intends through a variety of planned actions—from organizing protests to circulating petitions to political activities to press on sending that signal, to "continue the resistance," says Gagnon, "to this sheer and utter madness."

This article was reprinted from *Covert-Action Quarterly*, 1500 Massachusetts Ave., #732, Washington DC 20005, phone (202) 331-9763. The issue of *CovertAction* containing the full text of the article with footnotes is available from *CAQ* for $8 in the U.S. and $12 other.

2 CENSORED

Shell's Oil, Africa's Blood

"SHELL'S OIL, AFRICA'S BLOOD: THE EXECUTION OF KEN SARO-WIWA HIGHLIGHTS A MULTI-NATIONAL'S POLICY OF EXPLOITATION"
By Ron Nixon and Michael King, *The Texas Observer*, January 12, 1996

"SHELL GAME"
By Vince Bielski, *San Francisco Bay Guardian*, February 7, 1996

Shell's Oil, Africa's Blood: The Execution of Ken Saro-Wiwa Highlights a Multi-National's Policy of Exploitation

Shortly before the Nigerian government executed activist-writer Ken Saro-Wiwa and eight other Ogoni activists last November 10 for the alleged murders of members of a rival activist group, Saro-Wiwa's supporters from around the world called on Shell Oil to intervene. The Royal Dutch/Shell Group, the multi-national oil company whose U.S. subsidiary, Shell Oil Company, is headquartered in Houston, had been the object of protest by Saro-Wiwa and the Movement for the Survival of Ogoni People (MOSOP) for its drilling activities in the Niger Delta region, home of the Ogoni people. Supporters of Saro-Wiwa and his allies believed that intervention from the oil company would help to win a stay of execution.

Despite the international pleas, however, Shell declined to act. In a written statement prior to the executions, Shell explained its position: "We made it clear...that the trials of Saro-Wiwa and the others were for murder, which is a criminal matter," Shell said. "They were not in court for their protest against Shell. Our position has always been that a private company has no right to involve itself in the criminal proceedings of a court." According to *The New York Times*, only when the hangings were imminent did Shell's chairman write to Nigeria's rulers, asking for clemency.

Yet despite Shell's insistence that it does not intervene "in the legal processes of a sovereign state," internal documents uncovered by journalists and human rights groups show that Shell was more than a passive player in the political affairs of Nigeria and in the death of Saro-Wiwa. According to David Wheeler in the November issue of the British magazine the *New Statesman and Society*, in a March 1995 meeting between Shell and the Nigeria High Commission, Shell's director of public affairs reportedly gave the Nigerians advice on how to counter the "vicious campaign...to discredit Shell and Nigeria." And according to a report by Andy Rowell in the *Village Voice* (November 21), there is evidence that Shell has been bankrolling Nigerian military action against protesters for some time, and that two key prosecution witnesses were offered bribes by Shell to testify against Saro-Wiwa in his trial by a military tribunal. Shell has denied the charges.

"Shell has very, very intimate links with the Nigerian government, particularly in the areas in which they operate," said Mike Fleshman, of the New York-based human rights group The Africa Fund.

Further evidence linking Shell to the Nigerian military and human rights abuses is a July 1995 report by Human Rights Watch, titled "The Ogoni Crisis: A Case-study of Military Repression in Southeastern Nigeria," based on Shell internal documents and interviews with Shell officials and former Nigerian security force members.

A letter cited in the report, from a division manager of Shell in the Ogoni region, illustrates the close relationship between the Nigerian security forces and the oil company. On October 29, 1990, following the first major demonstration against Shell by Ogoni activists, Shell's division manager, J.R. Udofia, wrote to the local Commissioner of Police, requesting "security protection" in anticipation of an attack on Shell's facilities. A day later, following a peaceful protest by Ogoni youth at the Shell plant, Udofia made an additional request to the military governor of the region. The next day, a mobile police force attacked demonstrators with tear gas and gunfire, and a day afterwards, the police returned again. This time eighty people were killed, and four hundred ninety-five houses were destroyed or badly damaged. A judicial commission established by the government later found no evidence of a threat from villagers. Yet Shell maintained its relationship with the security forces.

On April 28, 1993, Willbros, a contractor for Shell working on the construction preparation for a pipeline, bulldozed freshly planted crops on farmland in the Ogoni village of Biara. When the Ogonis staged a protest, government troops were called in to quell the disturbance. Eleven people were injured when troops opened fire; afterward, a representative from Willbros praised the troops' actions. After the incident, Udofia wrote to the military governor, requesting "the usual assistance" so the work on the pipeline could proceed.

Shell defended its position, stating that the company is required by law to contact the Nigerian authorities in the event of a disturbance, and that otherwise contact with the Nigerian military is limited. But a 1994 article in the *Multinational Monitor*, by Greenpeace campaigner Steve Kretzman, suggested that a revolving door exists between the management of Shell and the Nigerian government. For example, two prominent Nigerian officials, Chief Rufus Ada George, the former governor of the River State Region where Ogoniland is located, and Ernest Shonenkan, former President of Nigeria (preceding current dictator General Sani Abacha), are both Shell alumni. Human Rights Watch says Shell representatives meet regularly with the director of the local security service, and with Lt. Colonel Paul Okuntimo, commander of the Internal Security Task Force. Okuntimo reportedly admitted to detained Ogoni activists that he had been "risking his life" to protect Shell Oil installations.

A spokeswoman for Shell Oil Company in Houston declined to comment directly on the "highly complex" Nigerian situation, saying only that the American subsidiary has no operations or employees in Nigeria. She directed all inquiries to the London offices of Shell's Nigerian subsidiary. But she also called attention to a two-page advertisement published in *The New York Times* (December 6). The ad purports to represent the viewpoint of a Nigerian citizen defending the executions of Saro-Wiwa and the other activists. But, critics of the Nigerian military regime have pointed out that the ad parrots the military's version of events, and its cost (more than one hundred thousand dollars) was almost certainly supplied by the Nigerian government.

Julius Ihonvbere is a professor of government at the University of Texas, and president of the Organization of Nigerians in America, which took part in protests of the executions at the state capitol in Austin and at Shell's offices in Houston. He argued that while Shell Oil Company does not have direct operations in Nigeria, they are part of the same multi-national corporate body, and that while claiming no involvement, they have been quietly sustaining and disseminating Royal Dutch/Shell's position. Ihonvbere described the *Times* ad as a notorious instance of Nigerian government propaganda: "So [for Shell Oil Company] to point to that advertisement [in] defense of their position, to me is a clear demonstration that they know what is going on there, they are involved in what is going on there, and they are as responsible as any other branch of Shell."

Other observers have noted that Shell's current embarrassments in Nigeria are not without precedent. "Shell activities in Nigeria are not isolated incidents," says John Stauber, editor of the newsletter *PR Watch*. According to Stauber, Shell has engaged in similar activities in other parts of Africa. For example, during the height of the anti-apartheid movement in the 1980s, U.S. activists were pressuring companies to divest their holdings in South Africa. Shell responded to a boycott by hiring the PR firm Pagan International and developing what they called the "Neptune Strategy"—recruiting a front group of black clergy, the "Coalition of Southern Africa." The ostensible purpose of COSA was to develop black-black business links between South Africa and the United States, to promote education and training for South African blacks, and to pressure the South African government to end apartheid. But according to Donna Katzin, one of the leaders of the boycott against Shell, the COSA was in fact a front group created to "divide and weaken the position of the religious community with regard to South Africa." Other companies with South African operations began pointing to the COSA as proof that not all blacks supported divestment in South Africa. Finally, after someone at Pagan leaked the Neptune Strategy, public embarrassment forced Shell to end its contract with Pagan, and company revenues plunged.

In the aftermath of the Saro-Wiwa execution, Shell again finds itself the object of international scorn. The U.S. Congress is considering a bill that would impose sanctions against Nigeria. Human rights groups are calling for a boycott of Shell gas stations worldwide. And on the day of the Nigerian executions, the International Finance Corporation (the investment arm of the World Bank), pulled out of a project with Shell in the Ogoni region, where the company intends to resume operations. The IFC cited "macroeconomic considerations," and also hinted that it would ask its members to veto a one-hundred-million-dollar loan planned for the project.

"Their [the activists'] bodies weren't even cold before Shell started plans to resume operations in the region," said Mike Fleshman of the Africa Fund. "Even the World Bank was uncomfortable doing business in the Ogoni region after the deaths of Saro-Wiwa and the others." Greenpeace's Kretzman doubts that the loss of one hundred million dollars will hurt Shell, but he believes that the action of the IFC has added fuel to a growing coalition of groups pushing for an oil embargo against Nigeria and Shell. "This is by far the largest growing coalition of groups that I have seen," Kretzman said. "The groups include environmentalists, labor, human rights groups, and civil rights organizations. This has the potential to be even larger than the coalition that helped to end apartheid in South Africa."

Shell remains defiant and says it plans to go ahead with the Ogoniland project before the end of the year. Speaking to the industry publication *Oil and Gas Journal*, a spokesman for Shell said that it's too early to judge the effects of any embargo, and suggested that protesters are using the issue to raise their public profile rather than debate the issue of Nigeria. "You have to be clear who would be hurt," Dick van der Broek, Shell's International Director, told *Oil and Gas Journal*. "The people of the Niger Delta would certainly suffer—the thousands who will work on the project and the thousands more who will benefit in the local economy."

But Professor Ihonvbere suggests that the Ogoni people might be better judges of who is "hurt" by Shell's operations in Nigeria. He described the government and industry activities in Ogoniland as "basically the invasion of a defenseless community, the destruction of land and marine life, the very brutal exploitation of a defenseless people, the hanging of their leaders, the suffocation of the civil society, and the destruction of the democratic process by the Nigerian government, aided by Shell."

Shell Game

Following the execution of nine environmental activists by Nigeria last November, the Royal Dutch/Shell Group faced a public relations disaster: how to convince the world that there was no blood on its hands. The victims, including acclaimed writer Ken Saro-Wiwa, had led massive protests against the oil giant's ecological devastation in southern Nigeria's Ogoniland, damaging the company's reputation and even causing a partial shutdown of some of its facilities.

After the activists' deaths, Shell mounted an international media campaign to combat the negative publicity. Company officials said over and over that there was nothing they could have done to stop the hanging executions, which they described as a political matter between the government and environmentalists belonging to the country's Movement of the Survival of the Ogoni People (MOSOP) organization.

But Dr. Owens Wiwa, Ken Saro-Wiwa's brother, has now presented evidence that debunks Shell's claims of innocence. Wiwa, a Nigerian physician living in exile in London, said that Brian

Anderson, the managing director of Shell Petroleum Development Company in Nigeria, offered to make a quid pro quo deal on three separate occasions during secret negotiations with Wiwa: Shell would try to save the activists from the gallows if the environmentalists would call off their protests.

"Anderson told me, 'Write a press release on MOSOP letterhead and get it published in a Nigerian paper saying there is no environmental devastation in Ogoniland.' And if MOSOP called off the international protest campaign against Shell, he would see if he could get my brother and the others freed," Wiwa said during a Feb. 5 visit to San Francisco as part of a U.S. speaking tour.

With the lives of MOSOP leaders on the line, the offer was tempting. But because the air, land, and water in Ogoniland had been so devastated by Shell, MOSOP chose not to back away from its protests, which had captured the interest of influential international environmental groups such as Greenpeace. Wiwa told Anderson such a deal wasn't possible.

"Even if I had wanted to, I didn't have the power to control the international environmental protests," Wiwa said.

A Royal Dutch/Shell Group spokesperson in New York who requested anonymity confirmed to the *Bay Guardian* that the meetings between Wiwa and Anderson took place. But he said Anderson never made the offer alleged by Wiwa. The executions have prompted a broad coalition of environmental, human rights, and labor groups (including the Sierra Club and Human Rights Watch) to call for a boycott of Shell petroleum and an embargo of Nigeria's oil exports.

"I've never seen this level of outrage on an international issue," said Stephen Mills, human rights and environmental campaign director for the Sierra Club. "People now see the insidious relationship between Shell and a murderous regime, and the extreme measures a multinational corporation will use to protect the bottom line."

The dictatorship of General Sani Abacha, considered one of the most corrupt and brutal governments on the globe, lives almost entirely off oil revenues.

"No other government since Nigerian independence has been so blatantly corrupt," said Paul Lewis, a visiting fellow at Stanford University's Hoover Institution and an expert on Nigeria. "The military has been diverting $2 billion annually to nonbudget accounts. Abacha has probably amassed a fortune for himself."

Nigeria derives 90 percent of its foreign revenue from oil exports. The United States imports almost 50 percent of Nigeria's annual oil production. The oil from the Niger Delta in southern Nigeria is also very important to Shell, which draws nearly 14 percent of its total oil production from the African country. As these numbers make clear, an effective boycott and embargo could certainly hurt Nigeria's ability to repress MOSOP.

"Exports provide the money to buy the weapons of violence. Two thousand people have been killed in the last three years," Dr. Wiwa said.

The crackdown against Nigerian protesters began when a division manager at Shell Petroleum Development Company called the military for help in October 1990. The Shell official feared that the company's operations in southern Nige-ria would come under attack by protesters from Umuechem, a village near Ogoniland.

The villagers had occupied part of a Shell facility and demanded compensation for farm lands taken over by Shell. Under Nigerian law, Shell had to pay villagers only for the crops that were destroyed, not for the land itself.

"Farmers said: 'This is my ancestors' land. Now where am I supposed to farm?'" explains Barika Idamkue, a spokesperson for MOSOP who is living in exile in Los Angeles.

Although a Nigerian judicial inquiry later concluded that the protest was peaceful, the military fired on the villagers. Some 80 people were killed and 495 homes were either destroyed or badly damaged, according to Amnesty International.

The massacre led to the creation of MOSOP, which by 1993 had rallied 300,000 Ogonis—more than half of the population of Ogoniland—under the banner of environmental justice. Threatened by the rapid growth of MOSOP, Nigeria's military dictatorship waged a campaign of terror on behalf of Shell. After MOSOP protests forced Shell to shut down some of its oil-pumping facilities in 1993, a revealing memo written by Major Paul Okuntimo said: "Shell operations still impossible unless ruthless military operations are undertaken for smooth economic activities to commence." By 1995, Human Rights Watch–Africa in Washington, D.C., had documented hundreds of incidents of rape, torture, and murder of civilians by marauding soldiers. Entire villages were burnt to the ground.

FERTILE GROUND

Since Shell began operations in the Niger Delta region in 1958, countless acres of fertile farm land have been destroyed by oil spills. In only an eight-year period, from 1985 to 1993, there were 87 spills, the Shell spokesperson said. He added, however, that 60 percent of them were the result of sabotage. "We try to get the land back to the way it was to the best of our ability, but we haven't been able to get into Ogoniland since '93 due to violence. So there may be spills that haven't been cleaned up," he said.

Professor Claude Ake, a Nigerian environmental expert living in exile in London, said that Shell's clean-up work has been superficial at best.

"Shell hasn't cleaned up any of its spills. They use cosmetics," Ake said. "In all of the Niger Delta there is a thin film of oil in the streams and rivers everywhere you go. And the groundwater is polluted."

Even more pernicious is the burning of gas, a byproduct of the oil production process, that turns the night sky an eerie orange color.

"This action has destroyed wildlife, plant life, and has made the residents half-deaf and prone to respiratory diseases," Saro-Wiwa wrote in 1992. "Whenever it rains in Ogoni, all we have is acid rain, which further poisons watercourses, streams, creeks, and agricultural land."

Few observers outside Nigeria paid much attention to the growing ecological and human-rights crisis until Saro-Wiwa and eight others were executed on trumped-up murder charges.

"I and my colleagues are not the only ones on trial," Saro-Wiwa said in his closing statement before the military tribunal. "Shell is here on trial and...there is no doubt in my mind that the ecological war that the company has waged in the delta will be called into question sooner rather than later and the crimes of that war will be duly punished."

Now, with the launching of the boycott, Saro-Wiwa's prediction is coming to pass.

Vince Bielski is a San Francisco–based freelance writer. For information about the boycott, contact Stephen Mills at the Sierra Club, 408 C St. NE, Washington, DC 20002; (202) 675-6691; or send E-mail to stephen.mills@sierraclub.org.

3 CENSORED

Big Perks for the Wealthy Hidden in Minimum Wage Bill

"BARE MINIMUM: GOODIES FOR THE RICH HIDDEN IN WAGE BILL"
By John Judis, *The New Republic*, October 28, 1996

"This is a cause for celebration for all Americans of all parties, all walks of life, all faiths. By coming together across lines that have too often divided us and finding common ground, we have made this a real season of achievement for the people of America," Bill Clinton said, as he signed the minimum wage bill on August 20.

The close of the 104th Congress occasioned many such moments of self-congratulation, as Congress passed a flurry of legislation with bipartisan support. Even liberals were impressed.

But beneath the carapace of constructive reform lies a legislative record filled with outrages.

And the minimum wage bill, supposedly the great progressive achievement of this year, is no exception. It may be the best example of all.

The bill that raised the minimum wage from $4.25 to $5.15 an hour is called the Small Business Job Protection Act of 1996. It contains several measures that Republicans sought for their allies in the National Federation of Independent Business and the U.S. Chamber of Commerce.

Most of these—like an increase in the amount the self-employed can deduct for health insurance—were either innocuous or commendable.

But the bill also includes at least 10 other significant provisions aimed at neither small business owners nor their employees. And they more than negate whatever good the bill may do. Here are the lowlights:

• Leveraged buyouts: In a moment of temporary sanity, Congress put into the 1986 tax reform bill a measure preventing firms that engage in leveraged buyouts (LBOs) from claiming a tax deduction for the exorbitant fees they pay investment banks and advisors. The measure removed the incentive for such buyouts, which, during their height in the 1980s, had distorted investment priorities, bankrupted firms, and led to laid-off workers.

This year's minimum wage bill once again makes these fees deductible and does so retroactively, producing a billion-dollar windfall for companies that contested the 1986 ruling.

And Congress didn't stop there. In the past, one kind of LBO was generally worthwhile—employee buyouts of companies that would otherwise have closed.

Congress even provided a special incentive for these buyouts by allowing banks to exclude half the interest payments they receive on loans for employee buyouts. But Congress stuck into the minimum wage bill a provision eliminating that incentive.

In short, the bill rewards managers that engage in high-stakes LBOs intended merely to enrich themselves and their investment advisors but penalizes employees trying to save their own ailing companies.

• Multinational corporations: During the Cold War, Congress, eager to prop up our allies' economies in Europe and Asia, provided incentives for American firms to invest overseas.

American multinationals didn't have to pay U.S. taxes on their foreign income unless or until they repatriated it, and they could deduct whatever payments they had made to foreign governments. By the Cold War's end, these incentives had outlived their usefulness.

In the 1992 campaign, candidate Clinton promised to eliminate them, but in 1993 his Administration predictably backed down, merely requiring overseas firms to reinvest their unrepatriated profits in foreign plants and equipment rather than banking them.

This year's Congress, in a minimum wage bill supposedly aimed at helping low income workers, rescinded even that caveat. So the Treasury still won't be able to tax the profits, and now multinational corporations won't even have to do anything useful with them.

• Pensions: Most workers and companies assume the Employee Retirement Income Security Act of 1974 protects their pensions from insurance company abuse and incompetence. According to ERISA, when a company gives insurance companies its pension fund to manage and invest, the company must do so "solely in the interest of workers and retirees."

If the insurance companies take enormous fees for themselves or invest the funds in risky ventures, they can be sued. But for two decades insurance companies have tried to convince the courts that they shouldn't be subject to ERISA.

In 1993 the Supreme Court ruled clearly in John Hancock vs. Harris Trust that they were. The 104th Congress came to the rescue.

In the minimum wage bill, Senate Republican and Democratic leaders inserted a last-minute rider effectively reversing the Supreme Court decision and making insurance companies subject to a lesser standard of conduct. The measure, dubbed the ERISA clarification Act, was even applied retroactively to what companies did prior to this year.

There's more. The minimum wage bill eliminated a requirement that companies extend to lower-wage employees the same pension benefits they grant higher-paid workers; and it ended a surtax on one-year pension withdrawals over $150,000, a boon to the ultra-rich.

The bill removed a surtax on luxury car purchases and on diesel fuel for yachts. And it allowed newspaper publishers to treat their distributors and carriers as independent carriers rather than employees, so they won't have to pay their Social Security and unemployment compensation.

As often happens, Congress used a bill touted as poor relief as cover for its pandering to some of the most powerful lobbies in Washington—investment banks, multinationals like Microsoft and Johnson & Johnson, life insurance firms, and newspaper publishers.

Republicans took the lead. Oklahoma Sen. Don Nickles pressed for change in LBO tax laws. House Ways and Means Chairman Bill Archer, as always, championed tax breaks for the wealthy. But all these measures enjoyed bipartisan support.

Life insurance companies got both Kansas Sen. Nancy Kassebaum and Connecticut Sen. Chris Dodd to press their case. Secretary of Labor Robert Reich wrote a letter endorsing the changes in ERISA. And, of the 16 members of the Senate Labor and Human Resources Committee, only two, Paul Simon and Paul Wellstone, dissented.

What about the 104th Congress's other great achievements? Senators Kassebaum and Ted Kennedy claimed their health reform bill required insurers to cover people with pre-existing conditions, and both President Clinton and Bob Dole have crowed about it on the stump.

But the bill doesn't limit what the insurers charge and allows them to shunt these undesirables off to Medicaid-like high-risk pools. Welfare reform expands the supply of low-wage job applicants without expanding the supply of jobs, holding down the wages that the minimum wage bill was supposed to raise.

A "cause for celebration for all Americans"? I don't think so.

4 CENSORED

Deforming Consent: The PR Industry's Secret War on Activists

"DEFORMING CONSENT: THE PUBLIC RELATIONS INDUSTRY'S SECRET WAR ON ACTIVISTS"
by John Stauber and Sheldon Rampton,
CovertAction Quarterly, Winter 1995/96

"The 20th century has been characterized by three developments of great political importance: the growth of democracy, the growth of corporate power, and the growth of corporate propaganda as a means of protecting corporate power against democracy." —Alex Carey

All Lynn Tylczak wanted to do was keep a few kids from being poisoned.

A housewife in Oregon, her imagination was captured by a PBS documentary about a technique used in Europe to prevent children from accidentally swallowing household poisons. Common antifreeze, for example, is made of ethylene glycol, whose sweet taste and smell belies its highly poisonous nature. As little as two teaspoons can cause death or blindness. About 700 children under the age of six are exposed to antifreeze each year, and it is the leading cause of accidental animal poisoning affecting both pets and wild animals.

European antifreeze makers poison-proof their products by adding the "bitterant" denatonium benzoate. Two cents worth makes a gallon of antifreeze taste so vile that kids spit it out the instant it touches their mouth.

Tylczak launched a one-woman crusade, the "Poison Proof Project," to persuade antifreeze makers to add bitterant. Her story made *The New York Times* and *Oprah Winfrey*, prompting a swift backlash from antifreeze makers.

She remembers one company's PR representative threatening that he could pay someone $2,000 to have her shot if she didn't back off.

When Tylczak began pushing for legislation to require bitterant, another PR firm was sent into the breach: National Grassroots and Communications, which specializes in "passing and defeating legislation at the federal and state level." Tylczak had never even heard of the firm until its CEO, Pamela Whitney, made the mistake of bragging about her exploits at a PR trade seminar. "The key to winning anything is opposition research," she said. "We set up an operation where we posed as representatives of the estate of an older lady who had died and wanted to leave quite a bit of money to an organization that helped both children and animals. We went in and met with [Tylczak] and said, 'We want to bequeath $100,000 to an organization; you're one of three that we are targeting to look at. Give us all of your financial records..., all of your game plan for the following year, and the states you want to target and how you expect to win. We'll get back to you.'"

Whitney claimed that the records she received contained two bombshells: The Poison Proof Project's tax-exempt status had lapsed, and it had taken funding from bitterant manufacturers. "Without leaving any fingerprints or any traces," Whitney boasted, "we then got word through the local media and killed the bill in all the states."

When the story got back to Tylczak, she noted that only $100 of the $50,000 in family savings spent on the campaign came from bitterant makers. "She's got a very foolish client," Tylczak said. "Her story has got more bullshit than a cattle ranch." In fact, she noted, her bill requiring bitterant did pass in Oregon.

What did the PR industry accomplish in its battle against Lynn Tylczak? Were news stories or legislation killed because of Whitney's intervention? In this and other cases, the degree of success PR firms have in manipulating public opinion and policy is almost impossible to determine. By design, the PR industry carefully conceals many of its activities. "Persuasion, by its definition, is subtle," says one PR executive. "The best PR ends up looking like news. You never know when a PR agency is being effective; you'll just find your views slowly shifting."

Using money provided by its special interest clients—usually large corporations, business associations, and governments—the PR industry has vast power to direct and control thought and policy. It can mobilize private detectives, lawyers, and spies; influence editorial and news decisions; broadcast faxes; generate letters; launch phony "grass-roots" campaigns; and use high-tech information systems such as satellite feeds and Internet sites.

Activist groups and concerned individuals often fail to recognize the tech-

niques and assess the impact of PR campaigns. And indeed, with its $10 billion-a-year bankroll and its array of complex, sophisticated persuasive weaponry, the PR industry can often outmaneuver, overpower, and outlast true citizen reformers. Identifying the techniques of the industry and understanding how they work are the first steps in fighting back.

SPIES FOR HIRE

In 1990, David Steinman's book, *Diet for a Poisoned Planet*, was scheduled for publication. Based on five years of research, it detailed evidence that hundreds of carcinogens, pesticides, and other toxins contaminate the U.S. food chain. It documented, for example, that "raisins had 110 industrial chemical and pesticide residues in 16 samples," and recommended buying only organically-grown varieties.

Diet for a Poisoned Planet enabled readers to make safer food choices. But before they could use the information, they had to know about the book so that they could buy and read it. In the weeks after it came out, Steinman's publisher scheduled the usual round of media reviews and interviews, not suspecting that the California Raisin Advisory Board (CALRAB) had already launched a campaign to ensure that Steinman's book would be dead on arrival.

The stakes were high. In 1986, CALRAB had scored big with a series of clever TV commercials using the "California Dancing Raisins" that pushed up raisin sales by 17 percent. Steinman's book threatened to trip up the careful PR choreography.

To kill the Steinman book, CALRAB

hired Ketchum PR Worldwide, whose $50 million a year in net fees made it the country's sixth largest public relations company. Months before the publication of *Diet for a Poisoned Planet*, Ketchum sought to "obtain [a] copy of [the] book galleys or manuscript and publisher's tour schedule," wrote senior vice-president Betsy Gullickson in a secret September 7, 1990 memo outlining the PR firm's plan to "manage the crisis."

"All documents...are confidential. Make sure that everything even notes to yourself are so stamped.... Remember that we have a shredder; give documents to Lynette for shredding. All conversations are confidential, too. Please be careful talking in the halls, in elevators, in restaurants, etc. All suppliers must sign confidentiality agreements. If you are faxing documents to the client, another office or to anyone else, call them to let them know that a fax is coming. If you are expecting a fax, you or your Account Coordinator should stand by the machine and wait for it."

Gullickson's memo outlined a plan to assign "broad areas of responsibility," such as "intelligence/information gathering," to specific Ketchum employees and to Gary Obenauf of CALRAB. She recommended that spokespeople "conduct one-on-one briefings/interviews with the trade and general consumer media in the markets most acutely interested in the issue.... [Ketchum] is currently attempting to get a tour schedule so that we can 'shadow' Steinman's appearances; best scenario: we will have our spokesman in town prior to or in conjunction with Steinman's appearances."

After an informant involved with the book's marketing campaign passed Ketchum a list of Steinman's talk show bookings, Ketchum employees called each show. The PR firm then made a list of key media to receive low-key phone inquiries. They tried to depict Steinman as an off-the-wall extremist without credibility, or argued that it was only fair that the other side be presented. A number of programs canceled or failed to air interviews. In the end, an important contribution to the public debate over health, the environment, and food safety fell victim to a PR campaign designed to prevent it from ever reaching the marketplace of ideas.

DIVIDE AND CONQUER

Ronald Duchin, senior vice-president of another PR spy firm Mongoven, Biscoe, and Duchin would probably have labeled Steinman and Tylczak radicals. A graduate of the U.S. Army War College, Duchin worked as a special assistant to the secretary of defense and director of public affairs for the Veterans of Foreign Wars before becoming a flack. Activists, he explained, fall into four categories: radicals, opportunists, idealists, and realists. He follows a three-step strategy to neutralize them: 1) isolate the radicals; 2) "cultivate" the idealists and "educate" them into becoming realists; then 3) co-opt the realists into agreeing with industry.

According to Duchin, radical activists "want to change the system; have underlying socio/political motives [and] see multinational corporations as inherently evil....These organizations do not trust the...federal, state, and local governments to protect them and to safeguard the environment. They believe, rather, that individuals and local groups should have direct power over industry.... I would categorize their principal aims right now as social justice and political empowerment."

Idealists are also "hard to deal with." They "want a perfect world and find it easy to brand any product or practice which can be shown to mar that perfection as evil. Because of their intrinsic altruism, however, and because they have nothing perceptible to be gained by holding their position, they are easily believed by both the media and the public, and sometimes even politicians." However, idealists "have a vulnerable point. If they can be shown that their position in opposition to an industry or its products causes harm to others and cannot be ethically justified, they are forced to change their position.... Thus, while a realist must be negotiated with, an idealist must be educated. Generally this education process requires great sensitivity and understanding on the part of the educator."

Opportunists and realists, says Duchin, are easier to manipulate. Opportunists engage in activism seeking "visibility, power, followers and, perhaps, even employment.... The key to dealing with [them] is to provide them with at least the perception of a partial victory." And realists are able to "live with trade-offs; willing to work within the system; not interested in radical change; pragmatic. [They] should always receive the highest priority in any strategy dealing with a public policy issue.... If your industry can successfully bring about these relationships, the credibility of the radicals will be lost and opportunists can be counted on to share in the final policy solution."

BEST FRIENDS MONEY CAN BUY

Another crude but effective way to derail potentially meddlesome activists is simply to hire them. In early 1993, Carol Tucker Foreman, former executive director of the Consumer Federation of America, took a job for what is rumored to be an exceptionally large fee as a personal lobbyist for bovine growth hormone (rBGH), the controversial milk hormone produced by chemical giant Monsanto. With Foreman's help, Monsanto has successfully prevented Congress or the FDA from requiring labeling of milk from cows injected with rBGH. In fact, the company used threats of lawsuits to intimidate dairy retailers and legislators who wanted to label their milk "rBGH-free."

While she is helping Monsanto wage its all-out campaign for rBGH, Foreman is also the coordinator and lobbyist for the Safe Food Coalition, "an alliance of consumer advocacy, senior citizen, whistle-blower protection, and labor organizations." Formed by Foreman in 1987, the Coalition's members include such public interest heavyweights as Michael Jacobson's Center for Science in the Public Interest (CSPI), Ralph Nader's Public Citizen, and Public Voice for Food and Health Policy.

Foreman said she saw no conflict of interest in simultaneously representing rBGH and the Safe Food Coalition. "The FDA has said rBGH is safe," she explained, adding "Why don't you call CSPI; they say rBGH is safe too." Asked how much money she has received from Monsanto to lobby for rBGH, she angrily retorted, "What in the world business is that of yours?" Her D.C. consulting firm,

Foreman & Heidepriem, refused to provide further information and referred journalists to Monsanto's PR department.

BOTH SIDES OF THE STREET

William Novelli, a founder of the New York-based Porter/Novelli PR firm, cheerfully uses the term "cross-pollination" to describe his company's technique of orchestrating collusion between clients with seemingly conflicting interests. By "donating" free work to health-related charities, for example, Porter/Novelli gains leverage to pressure the charities into supporting the interests of the firm's paying corporate clients. In 1993, this strategy paid off when produce growers and pesticide manufacturers represented by Porter/Novelli learned that PBS was about to air a documentary by Bill Moyers on pesticide-related cancer risks to children. The PR firm turned to the American Cancer Society (ACS), to which it had provided decades of free services. The national office of ACS dutifully issued a memo charging that the Moyers program "makes unfounded suggestions...that pesticide residues in food may be at hazardous levels." The industry then cited the memo as "evidence" that Moyers' documentary overstated dangers to children from pesticides.

Hill & Knowlton executive Nina Oligino used a similar "cross-pollination" technique in 1994 to line up national environmental groups behind "Partners for Sun Protection Awareness," a front group for Hill & Knowlton's client, Schering-Plough. Best known for Coppertone sun lotion, the drug transnational uses the Partners to "educate" the public to the dangers of skin cancer, cataracts, and damaged immune systems caused by a thinning ozone layer and an increase in ultraviolet radiation.

In the past, Hill & Knowlton has also worked for corporate clients who hired them to "disprove" or belittle the environmental warnings of global climate change. Seamlessly shifting gears into "environmentalist mode," Hill & Knowlton convinced leaders of the Natural Resources Defense Council and the Sierra Club to add their names to the "Partners for Sun Protection" letterhead.

A representative (who asked not to be named) of one of the environmental groups said he was ignorant of the Schering-Plough funding and its hidden agenda to sell sun lotion. Had he examined the Partners campaign, however, he might have noticed that it offered no proposals for preventing further ozone depletion and failed to mention that covering up completely was the best sun screen of all. Instead, the primary action the drug company-funded coalition recommended was to "liberally apply a sunscreen...to all exposed parts of the body before going outdoors." One of the campaign's clever "video news releases" shows scores of sexy, scantily-clad sun worshippers overexposing themselves to UV rays, while slathering on suntan oil.

SYNTHETIC GRASSROOTS

PR firms often bypass activist organizations and custom design their own "grass-roots citizen movements" using rapidly evolving high-tech data and communications systems. Known in the trade as "Astroturf," this tactic is defined by *Campaigns & Elections* magazine as a "grass-roots program that involves the instant manufacturing of public support for a point of view in which either uninformed activists are recruited or means of deception are used to recruit them."

Astroturf is particularly useful in countering NIMBY or "Not in my back yard" movements community groups organizing to stop their neighborhood from hosting a toxic waste dump, porno bookstore, or other unwanted invaders.

John Davies, who helps neutralize these groups on behalf of corporate clients such as Mobil Oil, Hyatt Hotels, Exxon, and American Express, describes himself as "one of America's premier grassroots consultants." His ad in *Campaigns & Elections* is designed to strike terror into the heart of even the bravest CEO. It features a photo of the enemy: a "little old white-haired lady" holding a hand-lettered sign, "Not In My Backyard!" The caption warns, "Don't leave your future in her hands. Traditional lobbying is no longer enough....To outnumber your opponents, call Davies Communications."

Davies promises to "make a strategically-planned program look like a spontaneous explosion of community support for needy corporate clients by using mailing lists and computer databases to identify potential supporters." He claims his telemarketers will make passive supporters appear to be concerned advocates. "We want to assist them with letter writing. We get them on the phone [and say], 'Will you write a letter?' 'Sure.' 'Do you have time to write it?' 'Not really.' 'Could we write it for you?...Just hold, we have a writer standing by.'"

Another Davies employee then helps create what appears to be a personal letter. If the appropriate public official is "close by, we hand-deliver it. We handwrite it out on 'little kitty cat stationery'

if it's a little old lady. If it's a business we take it over to be photocopied on someone's letterhead. [We] use different stamps, different envelopes.... Getting a pile of personalized letters that have a different look to them is what you want to strive for."

BLENDING IN

"Grass-roots" PR is the specialty of Pamela Whitney at National Grassroots & Communications, the firm that spied on Lynn Tylczak.

"My company basically works for major corporations and we do new market entries," she says. "Wal-Mart is one of our clients. We take on the NIMBYs and environmentalists." They also work for "companies who want to do a better job of communicating to their employees because they want to remain union-free. They aren't quite sure how to do it, so we go in and set that up."

One of National Grassroots' first tasks, after information gathering/spying, is to set up its own local organizations by hiring "local ambassadors who know the community inside and out to be our advocates, and then we work with them," explains Whitney. "They report to us. They are on our payroll, but it's for a very small amount of money. [O]ur best community ambassadors are women who have possibly been head of their local PTA; they are very active in their local community or women who are retired and who have a lot of time on their hands." They are supervised by professionals with "field organizing experience" on electoral campaigns who "can drop in the middle of nowhere and in two weeks they have an organization set up and ready to go."

These professional grass-roots organizers dress carefully to avoid looking like the high-priced, out-of-town hired guns they really are. "When I go to a zoning board meeting," Whitney explained, "I wear absolutely no make-up, I comb my hair straight back in a ponytail, and I wear my kids' old clothes. You don't want to look like you're someone from Washington, or someone from a corporation.... People hate outsiders; it's just human nature."

With enough money, the same techniques can be applied on a national scale. As the health care debate heated up in the early days of the Clinton Administration, Blair G. Childs masterminded the Coalition for Health Insurance Choices (CHIC). An insurance industry front group, CHIC received major funding from the National Federation of Independent Businesses and the Health Insurance Association of America (HIAA), a trade group of insurance companies. According to *Consumer Reports*, "The HIAA doesn't just support the coalition; it created it from scratch."

Health reform opponents used opinion polling to develop a point-by-point list of vulnerabilities in the Clinton Administration proposal and organized over 20 separate coalitions to hammer away at each point. Each group chose a name with "a general positive reaction....That's where focus group and survey work can be very beneficial," explained Childs. "'Fairness,' 'balance,' 'choice,' 'coalition,' and 'alliance' are all words that resonate very positively." Childs, who has been organizing grass-roots support for the insurance industry for a decade, wasn't the only PR genius behind the anti-health care campaign, but his coalition can honestly claim the kill.

CHIC's multi-coalition strategy assured numbers and cover, and took advantage of different strengths. "Some have lobby strength, some have grassroots strength, and some have good spokespersons," Childs said. In its campaign against "mandatory health alliances," CHIC drew in "everyone from the homeless Vietnam veterans...to some very conservative groups." It also sponsored the legendary "Harry and Louise" TV spot which, according to *The New York Times*, "symbolized everything that went wrong with the great health care struggle of 1994: A powerful advertising campaign, financed by the insurance industry, that played on people's fears and helped derail the process."

CHIC and the other coalitions also used direct mail and phoning, coordinated with daily doses of misinformation from radio blowtorch Rush Limbaugh, to spread fears that government health care would bankrupt the country, reduce the quality of care, and lead to jail terms for people who wanted to stick with their family doctor. Childs explained how his coalition used paid ads on the Limbaugh show to generate thousands of citizen phone calls from the show's 20 million listeners. First, Limbaugh would whip up his fans with a calculated rant against the Clinton plan. Then, during a commercial break, listeners would hear an anti-health care ad and an 800 number to call for more information. The call would ring a telemarketer who would ask a few questions, then "patch them through" electronically to their congressmembers' offices. Staffers fielding the resulting barrage of phone calls typically had no idea that the constituents had been primed, loaded, aimed, and fired at them by radio ads paid for by the insurance industry, with the goal of orchestrating the appearance of overwhelming grass-roots opposition to health reform.

When the health care debate began in 1993, Childs said, popular demand for change was so strong that the insurance industry was "looking down the barrel of a gun." By 1994, industry's hired PR guns had shot down every proposal for reform.

MANAGING THE MEDIA

Many PR pros think that the media, both national and local, are easier to handle than the public. To begin with, the media itself is a huge, profitable business, the domain of fewer and fewer giant transnational corporations. Not surprisingly, these transnationals often find that their corporate agenda and interest are compatible with, or even identical to, the goals of the PR industry's biggest clients. While this environment may be demoralizing to responsible journalists, it offers a veritable hog heaven to the public relations industry.

In their 1985 book, Jeff and Marie Blyskal write that "PR people know how the press thinks. Thus, they are able to tailor their publicity so that journalists will listen and cover it. As a result much of the news you read in newspapers and magazines or watch on television and hear on radio is heavily influenced and slanted by public relations people. Whole sections of the news are virtually owned by PR....Newspaper food pages are a PR man's paradise, as are the entertainment, automotive, real estate, home improvement and living sections.... Unfortunately, 'news' hatched by a PR

person and journalist working together looks much like real news dug up by enterprising journalists working independently. The public thus does not know which news stories and journalists are playing servant to PR."

As a result, notes a senior vice-president with Gray & Company public relations, "Most of what you see on TV is, in effect, a canned PR product. Most of what you read in the paper and see on television is not news."

The blurring of news and ads accelerated in the 1980s, when PR firms discovered that they could film, edit, and produce their own news segments even entire programs and that broadcasters would play them as "news," often with no editing. Video news releases (VNRs) typically come packaged with two versions: The first is fully edited, with voiceovers pre-recorded or scripted for a local anchor to read. The second, a "B-roll," is raw footage that the station can edit and combine with tape from other sources.

"There are two economics at work here on the television side," explains a Gray & Company executive. "The big stations don't want prepackaged, pretaped. They have the money, the budget, and the manpower to put their own together. But the smaller stations across the country lap up stuff like this."

With few exceptions, broadcasters as a group have refused to consider standards for VNRs, in part because they rarely admit to airing them. But when MediaLink, the PR firm that distributed about half of the 4,000 VNRs made available to newscasters in 1991, surveyed 92 newsrooms, it found that all had used VNRs supplied free by PR firms. *CBS*

Evening News, for example, ran a segment on the hazards of automatic safety belts created by a lobby group largely supported by lawyers.

CYBERJUNK MAIL

The PR industry is innovating rapidly and expanding into cyberspace. Hyped as the ultimate in "electronic democracy," the information superhighway will supposedly offer "a global cornucopia of programming" offering instant, inexpensive access to nearly infinite libraries of data, educational material, and entertainment. But as computer technology brings a user-friendlier version of the internet to a wider spectrum of users, it has attracted intense corporate interest.

Given that a handful of corporations now control most media, media historian Robert McChesney finds it is "no surprise that the private sector, with its immense resources, has seized the initiative and is commercializing cyberspace at a spectacular rate effectively transforming it into a giant shopping mall." Thirty PR firms are jumping on the on-line bandwagon, establishing "World Wide Web" sites and using surveys and games to gather marketing and opinion information about the users of cyberspace, and developing new techniques to target and reach reporters and other on-line users.

"Today, with many more options available, PR professionals are much less dependent upon mass media for publicity," writes industry pro Kirk Hallahan in *Public Relations Quarterly*. "In the decade ahead, the largest American corporations could underwrite entire, sponsored channels...[which] will be able to reach coveted super-heavy users...with a highly tailored message over which [corporations could] exert complete control."

FIGHTING BACK AT FLACKS

The groups that most scare the PR industry are the local grass-roots groups they derisively label "NIMBYs." Unlike national environmental groups and other "professional" reformers, the local groups are hard to manipulate precisely because they aren't wired in to the systems that PR firms like to manipulate. Most "Not in My Backyard" activists commit to a cause after some personal experience drives them to get involved. Typically, they act as individuals or with small groups of citizens who come together to address a local, immediate threat to their lives, cities, and neighborhoods. They are often treated with contempt by the professional environmentalists, health advocates, and other public interest organizations headquartered in Washington, D.C. Many times, they lack organizing expertise and money. They don't have budgets or polished grant proposals needed to obtain funding from foundations and major donors. But corporations and the U.S. government are spending tens of millions of dollars on PR and lobbying to fight these local community activists.

The most visible manifestations of NIMBYism, and its biggest success stories, have been in stopping toxic waste sites and toxin-belching incinerators from invading communities. Author Mark Dowie sees this new wave of grass-roots democracy as the best hope for realizing the public's well-documented desire for a clean and healthy environment in sustainable balance with nature.

"Today, grass-roots anti-toxic environmentalism is a far more serious threat to polluting industries than the mainstream environmental movement," Dowie writes. "Not only do local activists network, share tactics, and successfully block many dump sites and industrial developments, they also stubbornly refuse to surrender or compromise. They simply cannot afford to. Their activities and success are gradually changing the acronym NIMBY to NIABY—Not In Anybody's Backyard."

But before that can happen, local groups need to develop a strategy for confronting the powers-that-be in their backyard, and that means learning to recognize and fight the techniques of PR. Until they learn this lesson, local activists may continue to win local battles, while finding themselves outmaneuvered and outgunned at the national level.

This article was reprinted from *Covert-Action Quarterly*, 1500 Massachusetts Ave., #732, Washington, DC 20005, phone (202) 331-9763. The issue of *CovertAction* containing the full text of the article with footnotes is available from *CAQ* for $8 in the U.S. and $12 other.

5 CENSORED

White-Collar Crime: Whitewash at the Justice Department

"WHITE-COLLAR CRIME: WHITEWASH AT THE JUSTICE DEPARTMENT"
By David Burnham, *CovertAction Quarterly*, Summer 1996

For many years, business organizations such as the Chamber of Commerce and the National Association of Manufacturers have waged sophisticated propaganda campaigns to convince the American people that the federal government restricts business with unnecessary and heavy-handed regulations.

A central purpose of this crusade, of course, is to persuade Congress to cut back on the series of broad government programs put in place to clean up the environment and improve health and safety. Ronald Reagan—at the time a middle-aged and mediocre actor on the corporate payroll of General Electric—began his amazing political career as one of the earliest and most successful promoters of business' anti-government theme. While GE, a major defense contractor, was delighted to get the massive contracts from the Air Force, it was a good deal less enthusiastic about being accused of endangering the lives of its employees and violating safety and health standards.

More recently, the anti-regulation message of the business organizations and their corporate backers has become a favorite mantra of the Republican Congress, conservative Democrats and, to some extent, the pro-business Clinton Administration. The current drive, pumped up by high-priced lobbying and hyped-up public relations efforts, has been aimed mostly at three federal agencies: the Environmental Protection Agency (EPA), the Food and Drug Administration (FDA), and the Occupational Safety and Health Administration (OSHA).

Armed with a few anecdotal horror stories, the propagandists and lobbyists try to persuade media, politicians, and the public that regulations are crippling free enterprise and costing jobs. But even if business wished to present a more comprehensive picture of how the hated government agencies work, it would be hampered by the fact that EPA, FDA, OSHA, and other agencies all have separate record-keeping systems that do not easily yield a good overview.

THE ULTIMATE GATEKEEPER

One critical aspect of government regulation, however, the criminal prosecution of corporate malefactors, produces a wealth of data which is subject to systematic analysis. Based on the centralized records maintained by the Department of Justice, the data show that when it comes to business—contrary to the sad stories told by Ronnie Reagan and the National Association of Manufacturers—the federal government may occasionally growl but rarely bites.

Here's how the process works: When federal agencies find that their regulations have been violated, they are authorized by law to impose administrative penalties. In this kind of situation, the penalties paid by the miscreants—say, a nuclear utility that has not fully complied with a rule of the Nuclear Regulatory Commission are usually negligible.

When there is evidence that a business or individual corporate manager has violated the criminal law, however, the agencies are almost always required to refer the matter to the Justice Department. The DOJ and its 90-plus independent United States attorneys around the country then become the ultimate gatekeepers. They have sole authority to decide if a crime has been committed; who, if anyone, will be charged; and what specific law will be cited in the indictment. That last element is important because the statute chosen by the prosecutor largely determines the sentence that the judge must impose.

Under Justice Department procedures, the U.S. attorneys are required to submit to Washington detailed information about every matter that has been referred to them for prosecution by each of the investigating agencies: the FBI, FDA, EPA, or OSHA. The records include information on: What was the leading charge of each referral? Did the assistant U.S. attorney handling the referral decide not to prosecute? Why? If the referral resulted in formal charges, was the individual found guilty? What was the sentence?

These tens of thousands of individual records, obtained each year under the FOIA and analyzed by the Transactional Records Access Clearinghouse (TRAC), provide a unique window on the actual enforcement priorities of the federal government. The TRAC analysis proves that—despite all the heavy breathing of the National Association of Manufacturers and its political allies—the federal government almost never brings criminal charges against business.

In fiscal year 1994, for example, the government indicted more than 51,000 people. It will shock few Americans that more than a third of the cases—20,000—involved drugs. Given the commitment by Attorney General Janet Reno and her recent predecessors to fight a federal war against white-collar crime, however, it may come as a surprise how little the DOJ actually does in this area. Of the more than 51,000 federal criminal indictments in 1994, only 250, less than half of one percent, involved criminal violations of the nation's environmental, occupational safety and health, and consumer product safety laws.

Given the huge number of corporations, the private admission by business lawyers that their organizations often break the law, and a well-documented record of repeated violations, the minuscule number of federal allegations of crime that involve pollution and the safety and health of workers and consumers hardly squares with the corporate view of business as the victim of a federal government run amok. And while the nation has a total of more than 3,000 criminal statutes and scores of heavily publicized enforcement programs for cleaning up the environment and protecting workers, the data show that individual federal prosecutors are looking elsewhere. They are concentrating their heaviest fire power on small-time drug dealers and immigrants rather than on corporate America.

The tiny number of people charged with criminal violation of environmental, occupational health and consumer product safety laws is only one indication of the pro-business bias of the federal establishment revealed in the DOJ's own data. The difference in penalties for boardroom vs. street crime also showed a system-wide bias. Several years ago, Susan Long, my colleague at the TRAC, looked at data on the outcomes of all the criminal matters and cases disposed of by the Justice Department during a single sample week in 1993. Of the 18 disposals that touched upon the environment and public health that week, not one resulted in a prison sentence. Of the 695 disposals during the same period that were drug-related, almost half the defendants went to prison.

SOME CRIME PAYS

Violations of workplace health and safety standards are similarly downplayed. The 1970 legislation that created OSHA gave it the authority to impose fines on employers who failed to provide safe working conditions. But the DOJ alone was given authority to institute criminal proceedings, and then, only if a worker died because an employer willfully violated federal safety standards. In the years since, the fines have typically been trivial, the criminal prosecutions exceedingly rare, and the human cost incalculable. With an acceptable and largely predictable risk, corporations can build in the cost of violating health and safety standards—all the while decrying overregulation. Under five separate administrations—beginning with Nixon and extending to Clinton—the DOJ and the 90-plus U.S. attorneys have been lead players in an unstated government policy that abets that calculation. In direct violation of the 1970 law, they have almost always protected from the unpleasant mess of criminal charges even those corporate executives who knowingly exposed workers to conditions that caused death.

Since 1970, ten million workers have suffered non-fatal on-the-job injuries. In 1987 alone, 50-70,000 workers died prematurely from on-the-job exposure to benzene, arsenic, asbestos, coal dust, vinyl chloride, dioxin, and other toxins roughly three times the 21,500 people murdered that same year.

Here is another perspective. Between 1970, when OSHA was created, and 1992, 200,000 Americans died at work. While some of these deaths were the consequence of worker carelessness or unavoidable mishaps, a significant number resulted from knowing negligence or greed by the employer.

Nonetheless, according to a 1992 study by OSHA, during those 22 years, the agency referred a grand total of 88 criminal cases to the Justice Department. On the basis of those referrals, federal prosecutors brought 25 criminal cases, and only one business executive was sent to prison. He served 45 days. The final toll: 200,000 dead, one executive in prison.

CAUTION: CLASS BIAS AT WORK

Seen in this context, the propaganda campaign by business against over-regulation is a red herring. It matters less how many unheeded regulations Congress passes than whom and what the law protects. Considered together, the data provide hard evidence of a powerful class bias in the U.S. that works in favor of the rich and powerful and against the interests of workers. Congress covered its butt by passing the Occupational Safety and Health Act of 1970. But the actual impact of the law is greatly reduced by the insertion of a hard-to-enforce criminal section. Operating funds are voted for OSHA, but are insufficient to provide an effective force of well-trained and well-managed investigators. The Reagan and Bush Administrations doubled the number of federal prosecutors, but ignored regulatory white-collar crimes to focus on the nonsensical "war on drugs."

At work is a complex and subtle systemic bias that almost no one wants to acknowledge. Every once in a while, however, probably by accident, one of the troops in America's class warfare blurts out the truth. A few years ago, Barry Hartman was first deputy, and then acting, assistant attorney general for the DOJ's Environmental and Natural Resources Division. The hot issue of the day was why the Department of Justice had stepped in to prevent a federal grand jury in Colorado from bringing criminal charges against the Rockwell Corporation, which had managed Rocky Flats, a government-owned weapons facility near Denver that had spilled massive quantities of dangerous pollutants into local rivers.

The decision to let Rockwell off the hook, Hartman told a reporter, was totally justified. "Environmental crimes are not like organized crimes or drugs," he declared. "There, you have bad people doing bad things. With environmental crimes you have decent people doing bad things. You have to look at it this way."

David Burnham is an investigative writer and co-director of the Transactional Records Access Clearinghouse, 202-544-8722; e-mail: burnam@epic.org. Material for this article is referenced in his new book on the Justice Department, Above the Law *(New York: Scribner, 1996).*

This article was reprinted from *Covert-Action Quarterly*, 1500 Massachusetts Ave., #732, Washington DC 20005, phone (202) 331-9763. The issue of *CovertAction* containing the full text of the article with footnotes is available from *CAQ* for $8 in the U.S. and $12 other.

About the Author

Peter Phillips came to Sonoma State University in 1994 as an Assistant Professor of Sociology. He teaches classes in Media Censorship, Power, Class Stratification, and Social Welfare. He assumed the directorship of Project Censored in the spring of 1996.

Phillips had a long career in human service administration. His experiences include two and half decades of community service and social activism, including serving both as a CETA administrator and a Head Start director.

Phillips earned a B.A. degree in social science in 1970 from Santa Clara University, and an M.A. degree in social science from California State University at Sacramento in 1974. Several years of adjunct college teaching led him to the University of California at Davis, where he earned an M.A. in Sociology in 1991 and a Ph.D. in sociology in 1994. His doctoral dissertation was entitled *A Relative Advantage: Sociology of the San Francisco Bohemian Club.*

Phillips is a fifth generation Californian, who grew up on a family-owned farm west of the Central Valley town of Lodi. He has a 25-year-old son named Jeff, who is also a U.C. Davis graduate. Phillips lives today in rural Sonoma County with his cat and two pet chickens.

PROJECT CENSORED MISSION STATEMENT Project Censored, founded in 1976, is a non-profit project within the Sonoma State University Foundation, a 501(c)3 organization. Its principle objective is the advocacy for and protection of First Amendment rights and freedom of information in the United States. Through a faculty, student, community partnership, Project Censored serves as a national press/media ombudsman by identifying important national news stories that are under-reported, ignored, misrepresented, or censored by media corporations in the United States. It also encourages and supports journalists, faculty, and student investigations into First Amendment issues through its annual Project Censored Yearbook and nationwide free press advocacy.

Index

Belize, 222
Bell Atlantic, 100-101
Bentsen, Lloyd, 37
Bernay, Edward, 184
Big Brother, 45, 106, 230
"binary" weapons, 217
birth defects, 60, 118
black sexuality, 167
Blockbuster, 105
Board of Education v. Pico, 176-178
Boeing, 75-76
book censorship, 178
book publishers, 105
booksellers, 105, 113, 190, 324
bookstore chains, 105
Border/Lines, 254, 310
Bosnia, 47, 51, 92, 223, 225-226, 240
Boston Globe, 44
Boston Phoenix, 129, 254
Boston Review, 254, 310
bovine growth hormone, 57-58, 359 *See also* rBGH.
Boycott Quarterly, 254, 310
breast cancer, 58, 98
Briarpatch, 254, 310
Britain, 45, 48, 121, 322 *See also* United Kingdom.
British Atomic Energy Authority, 49
British Royals, 133-134, 136
British Telecommunications, 103
Brokaw, Tom, 187
Brown & Williamson, 104, 189
Buchanan, Pat, 123, 191
budget of American intelligence agencies, 226
Bulletin of the Atomic Scientists, The, 254, 301, 311
Bureau of Economic Analysis, 243 *See also* BEA.
Bush Administration, 182
Business Week, 36, 70, 72, 105
butyric acid, 63
By Invitation Only, 157, 180-183
C.A.A., 190-191 *See also* Creative Artists Agency.
Cable Rate Reduction Act, 100
California Alternative News Bureau, 311
California Prisoner, The, 254, 311
California Raisin Advisory Board, 357 *See also* CALRAB.
CALRAB, 357-358 *See also* California Raisin Advisory Board.
Calvin Klein, 112
Canada, 48, 65, 73, 254-255, 261-262, 266, 270, 272-274, 285, 304, 309-310, 312, 322, 327, 345
Canadian Dimension (CD), 255, 312
cancer, 30, 57-58, 60, 74, 85, 98, 118, 184, 221, 340, 345, 360
Cancer Prevention Coalition, 58

Capital Eye, 255, 312
Capital Cities, 162-163, 287
Caribbean, 79, 235, 315
Cascadia Times, 255, 312
Cash America, 43
Cassini Mission, 28-30,131, 339-347
Castro, 175
Catholic Church, 65
CBS, 60, 62, 78, 103-104, 148, 169, 187, 189, 291-292, 295, 363
    Westinghouse's ownership of, 103
celebrity pregnancies, 133, 135-136
"Censored Déjà Vu of 1996," 107-129
"Censored Resource Guide," 247-297
censorship, 9-11, 14-15, 18, 91, 93, 114, 139-147, 149, 151, 153, 155, 157-159, 162, 172, 178, 191, 193, 204, 261, 268, 275-277, 283, 304, 308, 322, 324, 326-327, 383
    and education, 176-178
    in modern democracies, 140
    latent-defensive field, 140
    latent-offensive field, 144
    manifest-defensive field, 143
    manifest-offensive, 144
    offensive traits, 140
    role of the media audience, 144
Census Bureau, 223, 228
census figures, 223
Census 2000, 228
Center for Living Democracy, 17, 93
Center for Science in the Public Interest, 61, 265, 359
Center for Study of Responsive Law, 41, 110
Centers for Disease Control, 128
Central Intelligence Agency, 231-232 *See also* CIA.
cesium-137, 118
    half-life of, 118
CFCs, 82-84, 120 *See also* chlorofluorocarbons.
CFTC, 70
chain stores, 105
Challenger explosion, 345
Chase Manhattan, 40
Chamber of Commerce, 38, 79, 354, 365
check-cashing outlets, 42-43, 95
Chemical, 40
chemical and biological warfare (CBW) agents, 126-127
chemical arms treaty, 239-240
Chemical Weapons Convention, 239
chemicals, 37, 49, 60, 73-74, 82-91, 95, 120-121, 126-128, 184, 216-218, 221, 232, 234-236, 238-240, 244, 357, 359
Chernobyl, 117
Chevron, 125
CHIC, 37, 362 *See also* Coalition for Health Insurance Choices.

Department of Corrections, 205-206, 212
Department of Defense, 47, 232 *See also*
    DOD; Defense Department.
Department of Energy, 29-30, 48, 114, 116,
    118, 220, 341-342 *See also* DOE; Energy
    Department.
Department of Interior, 125-126, 237 *See also*
    DOI.
Department of Justice, 38, 80, 92, 366, 368
    See also DOJ; Justice Department.
depleted uranium, 47-51, 92, 128
    exposure, 48-49, 51 *See also* DU.
derivatives, 68-70, 95
Desert Storm, 49, 192
detention centers, 80, 82
Detroit Metro Times, The, 315
Detroit News, 129
dioxins, 73, 85, 332
(DIS)CONNECTION, 257, 316
Disney, 24, 148, 162, 187, 189
Disneyland, 162
disparagement laws, 60-62, 93
Dissent, 258, 316
DOD, 342, 346 *See also* Department of
    Defense; Defense Department.
DOE, 341, 346 *See also* Department of
    Energy; Energy Department.
Department of Housing and Urban Develop-
    ment, 215
DOI, 125-126 *See also* Department of Interior.
DOJ, 38-39, 366-368 *See also* Department of
    Justice; Justice Department.
Dole, Bob, 66, 191-192, 225, 342, 355
Dollars and Sense, 258, 316
downsizing, 11, 71
Drug Abuse and Warning Network, 66 *See
    also* DAWN.
drug abuse, 66-68
drug crisis, 65-67, 95
Drug Enforcement Agency, 87 *See also* DEA.
drugs, 39, 45, 66-68, 91-92, 116, 123-125,
    209, 367-368
drug smuggling, 88, 123-124, 140
drug war, 67-68
DTIC, 238 *See also* Defense Technical Infor-
    mation Center.
DU, 47-51
    half-life, 49 *See also* depleted uranium.
DU Citizens' Network, 49-50
E: The Environmental Magazine, 258, 316
Earth Island Journal, 36, 87-88, 91, 121, 258,
    317
Ecologist, The, 258, 317
Econews, 258, 317
Economist, The, 46
Ecuador, 222
education, 53, 56, 74, 110, 176-178, 202,
    249, 254-255, 271, 275-276, 280, 282,
    319-320, 330, 334, 350

and censorship, 176-178
Electronic Privacy Information Center, 113,
    305
El Salvador, 125, 222, 249, 258
Employee Retirement Income Security Act,
    36, 355 *See also* ERISA.
Energy Department, 115, 220, 342 *See also*
    Department of Energy; DOE.
entertainment-oriented news coverage, 149
Environmental Action Magazine, 318
environmental crimes, 39, 368
environmental, health, and safety laws, 38,
    367
Environmental Protection Agency, 73, 89,
    218, 240, 366 *See also* EPA.
Environmental Working Group, 61-62
EPA, 39, 73-75, 86, 89-91, 218, 240, 366 *See
    also* Environmental Protection Agency.
ERISA, 36, 355 *See also* Employee Retire-
    ment Income Security Act.
ESA, 29, 341 *See also* European Space
    Agency.
European Space Agency, 29, 341 *See also*
    ESA.
Executive Order 12958, 215
Extra!, 30, 65, 110, 123-124, 259, 300, 318
Exxon, 125, 361
Factsheet Five, 259, 318-319
FAIR, 174, 278, 300 *See also* Fairness and
    Accuracy in Reporting.
Fair Labor Standards Act (FLSA), 112
Fairness and Accuracy in Reporting, 174,
    190, 278, 300, 318 *See also* FAIR.
Fairness Doctrine, 173
Faludi, Susan, 16, 93
Family Channel, 192
FAO, 52-54 *See also* Food and Agriculture
    Organization.
Farrakhan, Louis, 129
FAT!SO?, 302, 318
FBI, 45, 163, 170, 205, 219, 228-230, 234,
    238, 244, 366 *See also* Federal Bureau of
    Investigations.
FBIS, 227-228 *See also* Foreign Broadcast
    Information Service.
FCC, 17, 108, 113, 147, 163, 173, 189, 192
    See also Federal Communications Commis-
    sion.
FDA, 57-58, 116-117, 359, 366 *See also* Food
    and Drug Administration.
Federal Bureau of Investigations, *See* FBI.
Federal Bureau of Prisons, 201
Federal Communications Commission, 103,
    147, 189, 231, 242 *See also* FCC.
Federal Insecticide, Fungicide, and Rodenti-
    cide Act (FIFRA), 88
Federal News Service, 115
Federal Oil and Gas Royalty Simplification
    and Fairness Act, 126

How to Nominate a Censored Story

Some of the most interesting stories Project Censored evaluates are sent to us as nominations from people all over the world. These stories are clipped from small-circulation magazines or the back pages of local newspapers. If you see a story and wonder why it hasn't been covered in the mainstream media, we encourage you to send it to us as a Project Censored nomination. To nominate a *Censored* story send us a copy of the article and include the name of the source publication, the date that the article appeared and page number.

CRITERIA FOR PROJECT CENSORED
NEWS STORIES NOMINATIONS

1. A censored news story is one containing information that the general United States population has a right and need to know, but to which it has had limited access. 2. The news story is timely, ongoing, and has implications for a significant number of residents in the United States. 3. The story has clearly defined concepts and is backed up with solid, verifiable documentation. 4. The news story has been published, either electronically or in print, in a circulated newspaper, journal, magazine, newsletter, or similar publication from either a foreign or domestic source. 5. The news story has direct connections to and implications for people in the United States, which can include activities that U.S. citizens are engaged in abroad.

We evaluate stories year-round and post important under-published stories on our World Wide Web site every month. However, the final deadline for nominating a most censored story of the year is October 15. Please send regular mail nominations to the address below and e-mail nominations to: project.censored@sonoma.edu. Our phone number for more information on Project Censored is 707-664-2500.

Project Censored Nominations
Sociology Department
Sonoma State University
1801 East Cotati Avenue
Rohnert Park, CA 94928

Thank you for your support.

Peter Phillips
Director, Project Censored

Project Censored

needs your support for our work to protect the First Amendment. Please help us by becoming a national sponsor. National sponsors receive our newsletter "Censored Alert," and regular notices of important under published news stories.

YES, I would like to become a national sponsor of Project Censored and support the continuing effort to protect our First Amendment rights.

ENCLOSED IS MY TAX-DEDUCTIBLE DONATION OF

_____\$25 _____\$50 _____\$100 _____\$1000

other_____ Monthly Pledge_____

NAME _____

E-MAIL _____

ADDRESS _____

_____

TELEPHONE _____

PLEASE CHARGE MY DONATION TO: _____VISA _____Mastercard

NAME _____
AS IT APPEARRS ON CREDIT CARD

_____
CREDIT CARD NUMBER   EXPIRATION DATE   SIGNATURE

Please Return to:
PROJECT CENSORED
Sonoma State University
1801 East Cotati Ave.
Rohnert Park, CA 94928